RACHAEL

A REMARKABLE CHILD EXPLORER

RACHAEL
A REMARKABLE CHILD EXPLORER

JOYCE BUXTON

Published in 2017 by Buxton and Moseley.
Old Water View, Patterdale, Penrith, Cumbria CA11 0NW

All photographs by Ian Moseley unless otherwise credited.

Front cover: Rachael in traditional Nepalese costume, Nepal 2016.

This book is a work of non-fiction based on the life, experiences and recollections of Ian and Rachael Moseley.
In some limited cases the names of people, places, dates and sequences or the detail of events have been
changed solely to protect the privacy of others. The author states that, except in such minor respects not
affecting the substantial accuracy of the work, the contents of the book are true.

A CIP catalogue record for this book is available from the British Library.

ISBN: 978-1-909461-54-3

Printed and bound in China on behalf of Latitude Press Ltd.

DEDICATION

This book is dedicated to Rotary International and to all similar inspiring and dedicated
organisations and individuals throughout the world who care for vulnerable people
and those less fortunate than themselves. A shining example is our dear friend, Indira Ranamagar:
an amazing lady who founded Prisoners Assistance Nepal. She has devoted her life to
improving conditions for prisoners and their families and has built many children's homes
and orphanages where poor children are lovingly nurtured,
educated and prepared for life.

Service Above Self

CONTENTS

FOREWORD BY IAN MOSELEY

As Rachael's dad, I am truly honoured to have been asked to write this foreword.

This dad and his daughter have had a magical journey that most can never imagine nor will ever experience. I'm sure this story of a twelve-year-old girl will astound, delight and inspire readers, young and old.

I am writing my foreword directly to you, Rachael because I am so proud of you. Sometimes, you know, dads are allowed to be proud. ☺

Dear Rachael,
Namaste!

It is my honour to have been your walking buddy, mentor, friend, safety advisor, annoying dad and teller of dreadful jokes, travel guide, bill payer and expert at being proud of your achievements.

As you know, I have walked every step with you along this journey and each one of those steps has been taken in admiration and wonder at the way you achieved all this in such a spirit of fun. It has been an amazing experience to watch you grow, understand and enjoy the world around you.

I remember the humpback whale off the coast of Iceland, the yeti in Florida, paragliding in the Himalaya, flying over Everest, riding an elephant in a Nepalese river and you standing on top of the highest mountain in the UK – Ben Nevis, and all with equal joy.

I also remember the sheep that saw your pink knickers on the way to Black Sail and the dog that peed right down your leg on Hadrian's Wall – embarrassing Dad, ha ha! I remember your tenacity in adversity when completing the Coast to Coast walk in England, in spite of you being really ill on one stage: I learned a lot from you that day.

Your achievements in this book are incredible and it was my privilege to be your companion throughout your adventures.

You are a wonderful daughter and I am very proud of you.

Dad xx

PREFACE

This is the continuing story of the adventures of that intrepid child explorer – my 'granddaughter', Rachael Moseley.

Readers of *Rachael: A Remarkable Record Breaker* will be well aware of the achievements of this inspiring, joyful, courageous and determined girl who completed the last of her three Coast to Coast Walks (St. Bees to Robin Hood's Bay – 192 miles x 3) on her 9th birthday.

Of course, Rachael has never stopped adventuring but continues with the same infectious enthusiasm to explore the many different landscapes and cultures in the UK and abroad with her dedicated and proud dad, Ian. He has always given her the freedom to pursue her thirst for adventure and encouraged her various exploits whilst ensuring her safety and helping to increase her skills, understanding and knowledge.

Not only is Rachael a scintillating and eager companion, she has a true traveller's soul which delights in the wonders of the surrounding landscape, whether it be spectacular mountain scenery, verdant valleys, sparkling glaciers and pristine snow or the dirty, noisy, hectic streets and alleys of Kathmandu, Nepal. All enthral her, as do the different ethnic cultures she experiences. She is always ready for a new challenge.

This book mainly records her adventures since her remarkable Coast to Coast endeavours. However the first chapter is in many ways the story of a caring and dauntless family.[1] It includes a condensed version of how Rachael, incredibly, became the youngest Triple Coast to Coaster and into this I have woven my own experiences of my three C2Cs. Throughout, this part is in grey text and typeset in a smaller font.

You can read Rachael's tales about the West Highland Way, Hadrian's Wall, the South Coast and Golden Circle Drive and Hike tour in Iceland and three explorations in the Nepal Himalaya and Kathmandu Valley, as well as following her progress as she develops many new and exciting skills.

---

1 Some years ago, Rachael, her sister Catherine and their Dad, Ian 'adopted' me as Grandma Joyce; it is an honour that I treasure.

CHAPTER

THREE COAST TO COAST
WALKS IN ENGLAND

Training with an ice cream.

WHAT IS THE COAST TO COAST WALK?

For readers who are unfamiliar with the C2C and those who are planning to walk it for the first time, the Coast to Coast Walk is a long distance walk – around 192 miles – across England from one coast to another as originally written and illustrated by Alfred Wainwright. It has a definite beginning, usually St. Bees in Cumbria, and an ending at Robin Hood's Bay in Yorkshire. Traditionally at the start you dip your boots in the Irish Sea and pick up a pebble from the beach. You carry this pebble across the breadth of England and throw it into the North Sea, where you dip your boots again. You can, of course, walk the route in reverse starting at Robin Hood's Bay.

Although the traditional route passes through fabulous and varied scenery and is generally waymarked, as Wainwright always pointed out, the route taken is up to the individual: there are no specific rules. However, many people, especially those walking the C2C for the first time, faithfully follow Wainwright's route; it gives them confidence. More adventurous walkers plan their own route. The choice is yours. Just make sure that you can read a map and use a compass efficiently – relying solely on a GPS or Sat-Nav may not be a good idea …

Rachael's route mainly followed the traditional one but, necessarily at times, Ian chose a different route according to the weather and the condition of the terrain. Safety was paramount, especially as his daughter Rachael was only seven years old on her first C2C and only eight years old when she started her third C2C! She celebrated her 9th birthday at Robin Hood's Bay at the end of her C2C3.

HOW IT ALL BEGAN FOR RACHAEL

It all started in 2007 when Rachael was around three years old. She was sitting with her daddy, Ian, by Goldrill Beck in the lovely garden of her home, Old Water View, Patterdale – a well-known inn owned and run by Ian. Some guests, as they frequently do, asked Ian about the direction of the C2C path from Patterdale to Shap. Ian pointed out the path up the side of Place Fell towards the Hause and explained.

'You just cross the bridge over Goldrill Beck then follow that path up to the Hause, turn to the right and you'll soon reach lovely Angle Tarn, then up to The Knott, over Kidsty Pike and down to Haweswater. Then it's just a gentle walk up to Shap. You'll love it!'

Rachael was listening intently and studying where Ian's hand was pointing.

'Daddy, what's on the other side of that mountain?' she asked.

It was a beautiful day and all of Ian's guests had departed so he put Rachael in his backpack and carried her up to the summit of Place Fell. She ran about, laughing and clapping her hands in happiness and was absolutely fascinated when Ian pointed out the dolls-house-like image of Old Water View and Patterdale village far below.

'It's magic, Daddy!' she cried. 'I don't need a carry. Can I walk down, please?'

Bless her – she managed to walk about a third of the way down before Ian put her in his backpack again. She was so happy; she sang and chatted all the way back home. From that moment, Rachael's love of walking and her enthusiasm and ambition to be a Coast to Coaster began. A wonderful walker was born; a spark was ignited which was to grow into a massive passion for adventure.

When she was aged five she began to ask questions about the Coast to Coast – quite understandable as most Coast to Coasters stay at Old Water View, including the famous Alfred Wainwright and, more recently, Julia Bradbury.

Rachael asked, 'Daddy, is the Coast to Coast that van that brings the bags to our house and takes them away next day?'

She was, of course, referring to the Packhorse and Sherpa vans which transfer walkers' luggage along the C2C.

Ian explained that the C2C was a very long walk right across England – you started at St. Bees, got your feet wet in the sea and picked up a pebble. Then you carried that pebble nearly 200 miles all the way to Robin Hood's Bay so you could throw it into the sea and get your feet wet again. You know what came next …

'Wow!' shouted Rachael, 'Can I do it? Please Daddy! Can I do it with you, please?'

Ian, of course, has walked the C2C many times and led walking parties.

'Yes, darling, we can,' promised Ian, 'but you will have to wait until you are fifteen. It is such a long walk and very hard in places.'

The discussion ended there but Rachael did not forget because a year or so later when she and Ian were out on the fells and had just climbed Sheffield Pike, Rachael, quite out of the blue, suddenly said, 'Daddy, you know that I could do the C2C now, don't you?'

Initially Ian replied that she was too young but then had to admit that what she said was true. Rachael had become a fantastic, eager little walker and a wonderful companion, who was never happier than when she was out on the fells with her dad – whatever the weather. He realised that they could do the walk together using his special C2C knowledge and with a solid, back-up safety plan.

And so the idea of their first C2C was born. Obviously because of Rachael's age, a great deal of planning had to be done including allowing a slightly longer time than most adult Coast to Coasters aim for. A target of seventeen days was set. Also Ian, naturally concerned for Rachael's safety, arranged support vehicles all the way. Neither of them could wait to start.

HOW THE FAMILY STORY BEGAN FOR GRANDMA JOYCE – 'THE BIG RUCKSACK WITH THE LITTLE ARMS AND LEGS'.

Towards the end of my long career as a junior school teacher, I became increasingly unwell. I was exhausted all the time with a raised temperature, aching limbs and swollen joints; it was just like having permanent flu. Hospital tests revealed that I had a serious infection but not what or indeed where it was. I felt like an old lady.

Until this happened, I had always been very active, playing racketball at national level and walking long distances in my native Peak District, the Lake District and tackling many of the national trails such as Offa's Dyke and the Pennine Way. My ultimate ambition was that, when I retired, I would trek to Everest Base Camp. (Unfortunately in teaching, the summer holidays coincide with the monsoon period in Nepal and the Himalaya, so not a practical time for trekking.)

After innumerable tests including ones for leukaemia and cancer, it was decided (erroneously with hindsight) that I had polymyalgia rheumatica and I was treated with huge doses of steroids. These alleviated the symptoms for a while but by 2001, I was spending most of my life on the loo.

I had the most dreadful abdominal cramps, swelling, faintness and nausea. Eating and drinking even very small amounts resulted in a swift 'chain reaction'. Inevitably I lost lots of weight and many times I was in such severe pain and so anaemic that I was too weak to walk. I had to crawl to the toilet, terrified of having an embarrassing accident. In the end it was safer just to stay there so I wrapped myself in a duvet and dozed on a pillow on the bathroom floor.

Eventually, after what amounted by then to ten years of investigations and tests, PCR analysis of biopsies ordered by Chesterfield Hospital revealed that I had Whipple's Disease a very rare condition that can affect one in ten million women (the rate for men is four times higher).

It is caused by a soil-based bacterium that finally settles in the gut destroying the tissue, causing haemorrhages and preventing the body from absorbing nutrients by destroying the villae: you literally starve to death. Of more concern was the fact that the bacteria could affect all major organs of the body and cross the blood/brain barrier producing conditions like dementia and there was no known effective treatment.

I was treated with a variety and combination of antibiotics: some appeared to work for a while – others not at all. Frequent blood transfusions failed to combat the anaemia and I began to deteriorate rapidly. I had massive weight loss; I was housebound and crippled with pain; I had no quality of life. Even I, a great optimist, began to despair.

My dedicated consultant at the Hallamshire Hospital, Dr. Mark McAlindon, contacted all his colleagues nationally and internationally but no one had any solution. My daughter, Maddie, refused to give up and put an appeal out over the Internet. Miraculously, she was contacted by Dr. Axel von Herbay, a pathologist at Heidelberg University, who with his London colleague Dr. Annette Fritscher-Ravens, was researching Whipple's Disease. They were optimistic that they could treat me but needed my consultant Mark to work with them – by then, I was too ill to travel to Germany. Luckily, Mark agreed – a very brave decision because at that time Axel was not registered with the NHS.

Analysis of a Capsule Endoscopy and a whole batch of biopsies revealed that my condition was extremely severe – as Axel put it:

'The worst case I have seen in anyone still alive.'

Remember he was a pathologist. Great!

They planned a regime of treatment for me – a cocktail of very high doses of a specific combination of antibiotics to be given intravenously for fourteen days (chemotherapy). I was warned that as I was so weak, this could be fatal – but what choice did I have? I had been thrown a lifeline and I grabbed it.

Mark supervised my chemotherapy and many tests to see if the disease had spread: unbelievably it hadn't. Fantastic! We were overjoyed and Mark became a true friend and wonderful support.

Gradually I began to put on weight as the severe diarrhoea and other symptoms reduced. Tests in August 2003 showed I was in partial remission but some bacteria were still present in the lining of my intestines so I underwent another fourteen days of chemotherapy.

With Mark's blessing, I began training again and before I saw Mark again in 2004 for further tests, I had walked over 500 miles in the Peak and Lake District and completed my first C2C.

This is when I first met Ian Moseley. Just like Rachael on her first C2C, I was blown off my feet as I tried to find my way around Grisedale Tarn, which was shrouded in mist. The wind, rain and hailstones were driving into my face and the rocks were very slippery so I decided it would be mad to try the St. Sunday Crag route.

As I descended Grisedale Valley, I met a lovely man with a yellow Labrador. He introduced himself as Ian and asked me what I was doing. He was curious as to who was enveloped in the big blue rucksack. He joked that all he had been able to see from behind was 'a big rucksack with little arms and legs'!

I explained about my 'pilgrimage' and he told me that he owned a B&B – Old Water View – next to my destination for the day, the Youth Hostel at Patterdale. He wished me good luck and said that I was an inspiration. I made my mind up then that, at some point, I would return to the Lakes and stay at his B&B.

Finally, in August 2004 tests confirmed that I was (and still am) in full clinical remission, so I booked my long-awaited trek to Everest Base Camp. During one of my darkest nights in hospital, I had dreamt that I was actually at Everest Base Camp so, when I found out I was in full remission, I was determined to achieve my dream. As a test of my ability, I decided that if I could walk the C2C on my own carrying a full pack, then perhaps I could tackle Everest Base Camp. So you see, my first C2C was indeed a true pilgrimage.

My eldest daughter, Steph, and I stayed at Old Water View with Ian when we went back to climb St. Sunday Crag and after that I was a frequent visitor. I grew to love Ian's two fabulous daughters, Catherine and Rachael, and Ian and I became firm friends. We had lots of similar interests and a profound love of the countryside, walking and adventure; that casual meeting coming down Grisedale Valley was a meeting of minds and ambitions.

Gradually I became part of their loving, caring family and eventually, to my absolute joy, they decided to 'adopt' me as Grandma Joyce. So you see my first C2C brought so much happiness and fulfilment into my life.

RACHAEL'S FIRST COAST TO COAST – 2011

FROM ST. BEES TO KIRKBY STEPHEN VIA ENNERDALE, ROSTHWAITE, GRASMERE AND PATTERDALE

The first part of the C2C was done by using Old Water View as a base; walking each day to the next stop and returning home to Old Water View each evening. However, Rachael and Ian did stay overnight at our favourite hostel – Black Sail Hut in Ennerdale.

The start was not auspicious! They set off by bus and called in at Keswick on their way to St. Bees because Ian wanted to buy Rachael a new waterproof jacket. Somehow they managed to lose each other for twenty minutes in Booths supermarket. (Incidentally, Ian teaches navigation. Whoops!) Luckily they found each other and, somewhat shamefaced, (especially Ian) they eventually reached St. Bees.

The weather that first morning was glorious – bright sunshine with a gentle breeze. Rachael was incredibly excited as she duly picked up two pebbles – one for herself and one for her sister, Catherine. Then after the obligatory dip of her boots in the Irish Sea, she set off at a run up the beach and over the cliffs towards the lighthouse. Ian had a job to keep up with her.

I must admit on my first C2C, at this point, I was really apprehensive; my tummy was full of butterflies and my throat was dry. That morning, before I started, I had written in my diary these words, which reveal the dark cloud of Whipple's Disease was still hovering over me:

'I feel excited and grateful that I am in clinical remission but apprehensive as to how my body will cope with the strain of walking day after long day over tough terrain for nearly 200 miles carrying a full pack. I have trained hard and planned well so God willing, I should succeed. Then I will have earned the right to go to Everest Base Camp. This is my pilgrimage!'

Rachael had no worries whatsoever: she was just so exuberant; she radiated joy and eagerness.

'What an absolute delight she is to have as a companion,' thought Ian. 'I am so lucky!'

From the lighthouse they set off inland facing east towards Robin Hood's Bay some 190 miles away: an awesome challenge for a seven-year-old girl. Blissfully unaware of this and just completely happy to be walking with Daddy, Rachael could hardly wait to reach their target in two days' time – the Black Sail Hut in the wild but lovely Ennerdale Valley. She had heard so much about this wonderful remote bothy set in magnificent scenery from her daddy and me. We just knew that this would be Rachael's special place and we were right.

Over the years I had spent many happy days at Black Sail escaping from the pressures of teaching,

especially when my friend Brian Wilkinson was warden there. It was always a haven of peace, solitude and warm companionship.

About halfway up the very long valley path in Ennerdale, Rachael was desperate for a wee. Ian suggested that she just popped behind a nearby bush as no one was around; no one, that is, except an inquisitive sheep who watched her intently.

'I think that sheep liked my pink knickers – cheeky thing!' giggled Rachael. 'Perhaps it's never seen pink knickers before.'

And she skipped on happily.

She was absolutely captivated when she finally reached Black Sail Hut and so full of joy and happiness that she ran around jumping, skipping and singing with arms outstretched like Maria in *The Sound of Music* – she was ecstatic. From the hut, Ian watched her bouncing along in the evening sunshine, with tears of pride and joy in his eyes.

GRANDMA JOYCE EXPERIENCED FAR MORE HAZARDS IN HER EFFORTS TO REACH BLACK SAIL ...

Although it was raining, I took the alternative path to the right of Ennerdale Water. I tried in vain to find the path over Anglers Crag and ended up sliding down two vertical cracks in the rock face and got my rucksack jammed: it was wider than me! Eventually with a lot of hazardous wriggling while overhanging the deepest part of the lake, I managed to struggle up the other side of the crag and join the correct path, which, as always, was clear from that side. However it was full of tree roots and uneven stones and was crossed by many small streams so not easy walking at all. Also the ford in the River Liza, which you have to cross, was deeper than usual so I ended up at Black Sail with very wet boots! Thank goodness for the hot stove.

Back to our lucky 'sunshine' pair – Rachael and her dad, Ian.

After Black Sail, Rachael and Ian continued their C2C journey via Grasmere and up to Grisedale Tarn. It was a beautiful day – bright sunshine again with a clear blue sky. As usual Rachael was dashing ahead of Ian, leaping like a mountain goat up the steep, rocky path on the right-hand side of the beck. When the tarn unexpectedly appeared she stood there open-mouthed, completely entranced.

'Wow, Daddy!' she exclaimed in wonderment. 'Look at this amazing tarn – isn't it fantastic?'

Ian had been so happy that they were walking on that particular day in the relative peace and solitude of this lovely part of the C2C because it was the day of the Royal Wedding between William and Catherine – April 29th 2011. He thought he had managed to avoid all the fuss and celebrations – poor man!

As they walked around the tarn, they became increasingly aware of considerable noise and laughter just ahead. They soon found the cause: a group of ladies were sitting on some rocks boisterously celebrating the Royal Wedding helped by several libations each from a shared bottle of port. They were all wearing Union Jack hats and waving flags while they listened to the whole of the wedding ceremony on their radio.

Of course, Ian and Rachael stopped to chat and discovered that these ladies were also walking the C2C. Eventually they had to say goodbye and carried on their way cheered by many fervent and hearty congratulations from the ladies.

As walkers who have descended the valley towards Patterdale from Grisedale Tarn will know very well, the weather is unpredictable. The wind suddenly began to blow

very hard and Rachael had to shelter behind her daddy, holding on to his rucksack most of the way down because sudden gusts threatened to blow her off her feet!

Where the path is more level and runs above the stream there is a wood and, incredibly, Rachael spotted and identified a tawny owl. She is so observant – Ian had walked straight past it.

Around 4 p.m. as she was running ahead, inevitably she missed her footing on the stony path and fell quite heavily injuring her knee. Did she cry? Of course not! A quick clean-up from Daddy and she soldiered on, limping but still happy, towards home at Old Water View.

Rachael had a nice surprise when she and Ian reached the Post Office because the celebrating ladies were outside and they bought Rachael an ice cream of her choice to show just how impressed they were by her courage and determination.

From home, Rachael and Ian walked via Bampton Grange, a little village just before Shap, to Orton where there is a quite a famous chocolate factory. Rachael treated herself to a thoroughly deserved chocolate mobile phone before they returned home.

By this stage in their walk Old Water View was becoming too remote to use as a base so they continued their magical C2C journey staying at a variety of hotels and B&Bs on the way.

I delivered their luggage to Old Croft House in Kirkby Stephen, having dropped them off back at Orton from where they planned to walk to Kirkby Stephen that day. From here, completely free of charge, The Packhorse Company would transport their heavy luggage every day as far as Robin Hood's Bay.

On my first C2C I actually managed to walk the high route over to Shap as the weather was sunny with a slight, very welcome breeze. It was hard work climbing up to the Knott and the steep descent from Kidsty Pike really tested my knees. My feet were very painful due to the extensive blisters on both of them.

I was really looking forward to walking along Haweswater as I anticipated seeing some wonderful views over the lake. This wasn't to be! I am only five feet tall and unfortunately the bracken was so high that I could not even see the water. Instead, I trudged along in a hot green tunnel!

As many walkers will confirm, the undulating path along the lake seems endless so I was delighted when eventually I reached the end. I managed to get lost when crossing the farmer's fields leading up to Shap – I could find the stiles to enter but not the gates to exit! It was well after 6 p.m. when I finally reached my destination – The Hermitage – where I was given a huge hug by Jean and then reprimanded sternly for walking on my own!

On their approach to Kirkby Stephen, Rachael and Ian had to cross a huge field full of cows, horses and sheep. Unfortunately the farmer suddenly appeared on a noisy quad bike panicking all the animals. They scattered everywhere and for a while it was quite scary.

Rachael sensibly managed to dash to safety in a sheep tunnel within a stone wall and her dad was saved by the farmer's young son who herded the animals to the other side of the field. Undeterred, Rachael marched merrily on until they reached their destination, where she was delighted to be greeted by a flock of red and green parrots – magic!

She had a fit of giggles when she spotted a toilet abandoned in the middle of a garden, obviously the result of renovation work. Laughingly she said to Ian, 'It must be very windy and cold using that Daddy – I hope ours isn't like that!'

That evening this extraordinary little girl who had coped so maturely with every adverse condition so far on her C2C walk was happily building sandcastles in the pub sandpit: an ordinary child just having fun.

She phoned me that evening full of news and utterly elated and eager to continue her great adventure with her dad.

PART TWO OF RACHAEL'S FIRST COAST TO COAST: KIRKBY STEPHEN VIA KELD TO RICHMOND AND ON TO DANBY WISKE

Unfortunately next morning as they left for Keld, the rain just poured down and very low clouds scudded across a dull grey sky. In these conditions, Nine Standards Rigg, a high, exposed, boggy moorland ridge, can be very dangerous with deep, soggy peat – just one quagmire after another – and in such poor visibility even experienced walkers can have great difficulty locating the vague path. Knowing this, and obviously concerned for Rachael's safety, Ian decided that the country road route was the most sensible option.

As Rachael skipped happily along the quiet road to Keld, she was intrigued by a loud, croaking sound very close to them.

'What's that funny noise, Daddy?' she enquired.

Ian explained it was a grouse and right on cue several appeared just ahead of them in the heather.

'Daddy, Daddy!' begged Rachael, 'Can I catch one, please?'

'Of course, you can, darling,' replied Ian, knowing full well that it was impossible. 'If you can catch one, you can keep it. Good luck!'

Undeterred Rachael kept trying different methods, all unsuccessful, at intervals all the way into Keld. In fact all she managed to catch was a single discarded feather, which she proudly put in her daypack and still has to this day. These attempts at capture were interspersed by Rachael measuring herself against every tall foxglove that she spotted on the verges. Most of them were far taller than Rachael but eventually, to her joy, she found one that was slightly smaller and thought that one with its beautiful pink trumpet-shaped flowers, was by far the best. Her antics kept both of them amused and the miles sped by.

They both kept hearing sounds of shooting and Ian had to explain that this was what game hunters did – they shot the grouse for sport. Rachael was genuinely incensed by this and thought it very unjust so at the end of the day, they both agreed that they were going to adopt a grouse and from that day onwards, it would be their favourite bird.

In one place, the mist was so thick that Ian could scarcely see the road ahead. He turned round to check on Rachael, who for once was behind him, and discovered her standing completely still staring upwards, utterly mesmerised.

'What kind of bird is that, Daddy?' she whispered, 'It's not moving.'

Ian peered upwards too and eventually could make out the vague outline of a kestrel hovering silently above them.

'It's a kestrel, darling,' he answered, marvelling at her acute sight – how had she seen it?

'Wow!' said Rachael awed, 'I wish I could just float in the air like that.'

She loved sitting quietly by several of the wonderful waterfalls of the River Swale – she was completely entranced, gazing at the sparkling water tumbling down, marvelling at the spray 'shining like diamonds' and listening, as she said to Ian, 'to the music of the water'. She truly does have the gift of seeing magic in everything and she has never lost this.

Shortly after they had crossed the border into Yorkshire, they overtook two young men who were also doing the C2C and had stopped for a picnic. Determined not to let a mere girl (and a small one at that) beat them, they packed up quickly and sprinted past Rachael, disappearing into the distance. This episode was repeated later, when they stopped to eat their lunch, not realising just how near to Keld they actually were. So as they rounded a bend, Rachael and Ian were surprised to see these two young men again, one of which had obviously stopped to answer a call of nature. Ever the opportunist, Rachael took full advantage of this pause and sprinted ahead to Keld Lodge where she triumphantly touched the wall.

'I've beaten them, Daddy – hurray!'

'You only got here first because we were ill and had to stop!' grumbled one of the youths.

'What a shame!' Rachael smiled triumphantly, understanding completely that they were telling lies because they didn't want to admit that she had beaten them. 'Sorry, no excuses – I really did get here first!'

What a competitor!

That evening as they ate their meal, a man who was sitting at a nearby table got up and confronted Rachael and Ian.

'Excuse me, but are you trying to convince people that this little girl has walked all the way from St. Bees? I don't believe it – she must have had a carry!'

He rudely turned round and walked away so Ian had no chance to reply and Rachael just ignored him. Revenge is sweet though because in a few days' time, this man was to get his comeuppance …

Later that evening Ian explained to Rachael that Keld was where the C2C and the first ever long distance walk, the Pennine Way crossed each other. Rachael's response was perhaps to be expected.

'Really, Daddy? Can we walk that one too, please?'

On my first C2C, I chose a different route to Keld because when I left Kirkby Stephen, the weather was sunny so I decided to climb to and cross the infamous watershed of Nine Standards Rigg. Wow! Was it soggy! Fortunately I wasn't very heavy so I didn't sink too far in the morass of wet peat and evil-smelling bog; however many walkers did – up to and over their knees in some cases accompanied by very colourful language!

On the way up to the top, I met a charming and handsome Canadian called Scott Harradine so we talked and walked together for a while. He too wished me good luck and called me his inspiration. He still calls me this now for we have stayed friends over the years. In fact he returned ten years later to walk part of my C2C3 with me and we celebrated at Robin Hood's Bay with a wee dram!

KELD VIA REETH TO RICHMOND

Two memorable ladies enlivened the walk into Reeth the following day: the first was an American lady who was walking the C2C the same time as Rachael and Ian. She always seemed to set off before them but Rachael and Ian frequently overtook her. Then, surprisingly, she would pop up in front of them again. As there were several helicopters flying that day, Rachael decided that the American lady was somehow getting a lift and christened her 'The Helicopter Lady'. They solved the mystery later on.

The second lady was me – Grandma Joyce. At every stream Rachael saw on the way from Keld to Reeth, she asked Ian if that was the one that Grandma Joyce had fallen into three times and got a crinkly bottom!

LET ME EXPLAIN ...

On my first C2C I took the high moors' route to Reeth climbing up past Crackpot Hall (aptly named!) and explored all the interesting buildings and relics left from the once prosperous lead mining industry; a fascinating glimpse into the past. After descending to Surrender Bridge (again aptly named for this is a strenuous route) I followed Wainwright's narrow twisting path up and down a bank towards a stream in Cringley Bottom. Wainwright does warn his Coast to Coasters that care must be taken when crossing the stream as it is deeper than it seems and the bed is a mass of very slippery mossy stones and boulders. Yes! I did slip on that greasy moss and fell with a great thump and splash into the freezing water – not once but three times – desperately trying to climb out.

As I had sat in that cold water for a considerable time, my nether regions were somewhat wrinkled so I renamed that stream 'Crinkly Bottom' for obvious reasons.

This had really amused Rachael. Not knowing the location exactly, Ian eventually just chose a stream. Needless to say, sensible Rachael did not fall into it; she arrived in Reeth happy and dry.

In view of the competitive remarks and rank disbelief of the previous evening, Ian decided to have a bit of fun with Rachael. He picked her up and carried her all of twelve inches and put her down again.

'Now, Rachael,' he said smiling down at her, 'you haven't walked all the way after all!'

'Oh yes I have!' shouted Rachael and promptly walked back to the spot she had been picked up from and very deliberately walked forward again.

'I've walked this bit twice!'

You just cannot beat that little girl – she was absolutely determined to walk every step and nothing and no one was going to stop her!

REETH ONWARDS

When they reached the pub in Reeth, they met Ian's friend, Alan, who was to be their support driver for the next few days. Rachael gave him a big hug – she was one happy, happy girl.

Later as they were sitting outside on The Buck Hotel patio enjoying a well-earned drink, Rachael, still full of energy and bounce, asked Ian if she could go and play on the village green just opposite them.

'Yes, of course you can, darling,' answered Ian. 'But be careful. Remember you are wearing your Crocs.'

Rachael had changed from her boots to her pink Crocs to give her feet a deserved rest. Crocs, for readers unfamiliar with this type of footwear, are like rubber open-backed sandals and sometimes, like flip-flops, are difficult to keep on your feet on uneven ground or when you are running.

They were just marvelling at Rachael's antics – she was absolutely full of beans – laughing and singing, skipping, jumping and running when there was a terrifying scream and a sickening thud.

Everyone shuddered and looked up in horror. Disaster! Rachael had tried to hurdle the low retaining wall that runs around the green but had caught the front of both of her Crocs on the top. She was violently pitched headfirst onto the hard, unforgiving concrete below.

Ian and Alan truly thought that she would have some horrifying head injuries and that this was going to be the end of Rachael's C2C. Ian sprang up and rushed to pick her up, dreading what he would find. She clung to him, sobbing with pain and in shock. Miraculously when he cleaned her up and examined her, Ian was amazed to discover that although she had quite a few nasty grazes and would obviously be bruised the next day, this was the extent of her injuries.

As soon as Rachael realised she wasn't too badly hurt, she bravely stopped crying, wiped her tears and in a tearful voice, admitted her fears to Ian:

'Daddy, I was so scared that I wouldn't be able to carry on walking with you. That's why I was heartbroken and cried so much but I'm okay now and we can carry on tomorrow, can't we?'

'Of course, we can,' responded Ian, amazed at her courage and determination, 'but you are going to be very sore in the morning.'

'I don't care!' said Rachael emphatically. 'I'm going to finish this C2C – you see!'

Ian looked at her in pride – he had absolutely no doubt that his wonderful little daughter would do just that!

Rachael's next goal was the historic town of Richmond and the day was absolutely baking hot – really too hot to be able to walk comfortably. For once Ian underestimated the amount of water they would need and they ran out long before Richmond. However Alan, their support driver, came to the rescue with

several bottles of welcome cold water. He certainly earned his Brownie points that day!

Just before Richmond, when they were crossing a large beautiful lush green field, Rachael, eyes sparkling, suddenly asked, 'Daddy, please can I do cartwheels on this lovely grass, please?'

Ian replied that it was very hot and she really ought to conserve her strength but Rachael was determined.

'I'll be okay, Daddy – just watch me!'

And off she went; doing awesome cartwheels across the whole length of the field corner to corner, at least 200 yards, grazes and bruises completely forgotten. Ian watched her in admiration. 'Where does she get all that vitality, especially after her accident yesterday?' he wondered.

Then she noticed some strangely shaped white clouds gathering overhead and spent quite some time trying to decide which animal they looked like – eventually she decided that they were most like an elephant. She is just so interested in everything around her, she inspires you to see the world anew through her eyes and you are often challenged to answer her wide-ranging questions.

On reaching Richmond, they had to do some necessary shopping for Daddy. Before they started, Ian was so engrossed in ensuring that he packed everything he thought Rachael would need (plus some spares) he had completely forgotten to pack enough shirts for himself. He only had two shirts – the shirt he was wearing and one spare. Rachael pointed out that he was going to become very smelly soon so new shirts were essential!

'You are a silly, funny Daddy forgetting your shirts!' she giggled, wrinkling her nose as she helped him to choose. 'I do love you!' and she gave him a huge hug.

Then they solved the helicopter lady mystery – Rachael spotted her getting out of a taxi!

'That's cheating!' she protested, triumphantly adding, 'I am going to walk all the way – every single step!'

What about Grandma Joyce? Well I must confess that I really felt a taxi ride would have been wonderful, except, just like Rachael, I was determined not to cheat and to walk every inch of the way so I reluctantly resisted the temptation.

My first quest when I hobbled into Richmond was to find a chemist for some very necessary plasters and anti-septic lotion as I had the most horrendous blisters that had first begun to really hurt on the way down from Honister Pass to Borrowdale. By now both toes were swollen with blood underneath the nails. My right toe-nail was badly infected – all squashy and the nail was loose and sort of 'floating' on blood and pus. The kind pharmacist took pity on me, removed the nail and dressed my toes – what a blessed relief! (Although my boots were the correct size, my feet are very narrow so they were roll-ing from side to side in the boots, which were obviously too wide. I have since replaced them with Asolo boots and have never had another blister or even a sore spot.)

DANBY WISKE TO INGLEBY CROSS

It was another very hot day as Ian and Rachael set off for Danby Wiske. When they reached Bolton-on-Swale, Rachael was fascinated to see a table at the side of the road full of essentials for hungry and thirsty Coast to Coasters – energy drinks and chocolate bars, fruit and crisps with an honesty box for payments. Actually they thought this was such a good idea that

they decided to adopt it and put one outside Old Water View: all the money raised would to be donated to the Patterdale Mountain Rescue Team.

Thankfully, when they reached The White Swan at Danby Wiske it was open and they were made very welcome. (Years before, as readers will know, Wainwright had complained that it was always shut when he passed.) Rachael treated herself to a large Aero bar and a cup of hot chocolate – a double chocolate hit! This remarkable seven-year-old had certainly earned it – many times over.

The White Swan was not closed when I stayed at Danby Wiske, in fact Scott and several Coast to Coasters stayed there and we all had a lovely meal and a few drinks to celebrate.

The next day started quite dramatically for Ian and Rachael. Just beyond Danby Wiske is a train line, which you have to cross. Rachael looked horrified.

'You aren't supposed to cross railway lines, Daddy!' she protested.

Rachael had been thoroughly schooled about the danger of railways.

Ian explained that on this occasion, it was quite safe

to cross as it was on the official C2C path and you could see clearly in both directions and hear too. Rachael was not convinced so Ian crossed the line and, after looking very carefully, he beckoned her over. Looking unusually apprehensive, Rachael crossed the line very gingerly. Unfortunately Ian's photo of her did not come out properly so she had to go back and do it all again! She was not impressed!

She soon regained her high spirits thanks to the antics of a farmer who obviously did not like Coast to Coasters. To deter walkers, he had fastened a plastic rat and a skull on the next stile just where you had to put your hands to pull yourself over. He failed miserably because Rachael thought that it was a huge joke and deliberately posed on the stile for several photos. Humour restored, she decided to try to catch some of his chickens – they were of a similar disposition to their owner and looked at her in a supercilious way before flying off! Fortunately the farmer did not see her.

Outside the Blue Bell Inn at Ingleby Cross, Rachael was fascinated by a very unusual sculpture of a woman made completely from chains. Of course this was a good excuse for lots of posing and photos. She is very photogenic and loves having her photo taken.

That evening they were invited for dinner by some

friends, Ruth and Gerry, who had stayed with Ian at Old Water View. Rachael had an absolute ball in the garden frolicking with their three Labradors, Pip, Jet and Leader, who was old and blind. Rachael hugged him especially tenderly. Then Gerry took her to the allotment part of the garden where she was able to choose her own vegetables for the evening meal. Magic! (Rachael and Ian are both vegetarians so this was a special treat.)

They all had a fabulous relaxed evening with a wonderful dinner in the garden in beautiful sunshine – a perfect end to a dramatic day.

TO CHOP GATE, THE LION INN AND FRYUP HEAD

The next part of their amazing walk was along the Cleveland Way over Carlton Bank on a partially paved track. As often happens on this stretch, the clouds were low so it was rather misty and drizzling quite hard. However the mist kept drifting and swirling and at times it lifted briefly to give entrancing glimpses of wonderful views below. Rachael thought this was awesome – like a series of photos of different scenes, each equally magical. She was walking on air.

They stopped for a drink and snack at the unusual

Lord's Stone Café – a really welcoming place that is built into the bank so that at a distance it looks like a huge green mound. Here they met their friends, Trish and Kevin, who took over driving the support vehicle from Alan. Rachael loves Trish: she is the only lady who can brush Rachael's hair and put it in a French plait without any complaints from Rachael!

Their climb up the steep path to the panoramic viewpoint of Cringle End was in hazy sunshine but the sun shone brightly on them as they climbed up again to the high and spectacular Wainstones. As always, Rachael posed for photos on every interesting rock formation (and there are many) and in front of every breathtaking view.

However the session was cut short by a sudden cloudburst – the rain absolutely poured down – it was torrential and the lightning quite scary for Ian, being concerned about his beloved seven-year-old. However

Rachael thought it was great. Enthusiastically she scrambled down over the rocks and down the now squelchy path, completely oblivious to the fact she was soaked and her boots, like Daddy's, were full of water. Did she complain? Of course not! She loved it.

They were picked up at Clay Bank Top by Trish and Kevin and taken down to their overnight stay at the picturesque Forge House, a smallholding run by a lovely couple, Robin and Jenny. Rachael was thrilled to be able to sit on their cow, Nelly – she really does have an affinity with animals of all kinds.

That evening they all went to the local pub where they met again that disgruntled and unbelieving man from Keld Lodge.

'Bet you didn't walk today, Rachael,' he crowed. 'Not in all that dreadful rain and lightning.'

Rachael smiled and borrowed Ian's camera.

'Oh yes I did!' she exclaimed smugly. 'Look at our

photos – they prove that I walked over the Wainstones with Daddy and he will tell you I climbed down in all that dreadful rain!'

Shamefaced the man retreated, his tail between his legs. (I told you he would get his comeuppance!) Shortly afterwards, his wife came over to Rachael and Ian and apologised.

'We really didn't believe you. Sorry,' she said. 'May we give you a donation for Mountain Rescue please?'

She offered five pounds which Rachael and Ian accepted graciously – another triumph!

GRANDMA JOYCE'S EXPERIENCE ON THIS SECTION:

Although I didn't have to walk the extra miles to Great Broughton and back on my first C2C, I did find this day a long tiring one as I had stayed at Osmotherly Youth Hostel instead of Ingleby Cross and so had a lengthy walk up the road before the steep climb to Carlton Moor. It was raining heavily and the mist was down so I was quite apprehensive about crossing the moors on my own. Thankfully the footpath was made of flagstones so finding the way was comparatively easy.

I stopped to dry out and have some welcome hot soup in the Lord's Stone Café and was delighted to find that all my clothes underneath my waterproofs were completely dry. (Thank you, Gore-Tex). Most walkers there were very wet and the whole café was so full of steam from the piles of drying clothes, it was more like a huge sauna!

The rain stopped as I climbed Cringle End so I was able to stop and admire the beautiful panoramic views from there and all the following ridges and summits. The Wainstones were magnificent; nature is a far better architect than any human.

George, a former farmer, picked me up from Clay Bank Top and took me to meet his wife, Nancy at their home, Forrester's Cottage, below Hasty Bank. George and Nancy were a lovely, old couple who had been married for fifty-four years. The welcome was fantastic: Nancy hugged me and fussed over me but couldn't help grumbling at me for walking on my own. They fed me so well that I didn't need to go to the pub but had a long, welcome soak in their bath.

With Kevin and Trish.

ON TO THE LION INN FOR OUR INTREPID PAIR AND THEIR HELPERS

From Forge House, next day, Trish drove the support vehicle so that Kevin could walk with Rachael and Ian. It was an uneventful day as the path is a flat cinder track that was once the Ironstone Railway going past Bloworth Crossing to the famous Lion Inn at Blakey Ridge. However the panoramic views over the moors from the path are fabulous: an undulating patchwork of myriad colours.

They reached Blakey Ridge quite early as this section is only about seven miles long, so after chatting to Trish, they agreed to walk on to the strangely named Fryup Dale where Trish would pick them up.

Of course she arrived before them and fell asleep in the car. With a mischievous grin Rachael crept up to the car and poor Trish was rudely awakened with a loud **boo**! Bless her; she still drove them back to the Lion Inn – what a lovely lady!

FRYUP DALE HEAD TO GROSMONT

Kevin volunteered to drive the support vehicle next morning so Trish could walk with Rachael and Ian. He dropped them off at the head of Fryup Dale where they had finished the previous day, very near to the aptly named huge, white boundary stone – Fat Betty. (She must have been a lady of generous proportions!)

The track here over the heather moor is wide and gravelly but the excellent easy walking is enhanced by the wide-reaching views of Eskdale and the Matterhorn-like peak of Roseberry Topping some ten miles distant to the north. Rachael skipped happily ahead in the sunshine as they walked down to Glaisdale and over the much photographed 17th century Beggar's Bridge – another chance for Rachael to pose for the obligatory photo!

Beggar's Bridge (171 miles of the C2C) was the target for the day but as they were all full of walking, they decided to carry to Egton Bridge and through the welcoming shade of Arncliffe Wood to Grosmont – home of the fantastically restored station of The North York Railway.

Now they were faced by the endless steep climb out of Grosmont. This hill (1 in 3 and over a mile long) puts a sinking feeling into the stomachs of many C2C walkers whether it is tackled at the end of a day or the beginning of the next (as I had to do on my first C2C because I was staying at a B&B just over the summit). Did that infamous hill deter our intrepid walkers? Of course not! Rachael and Trish marched up steadily, hand in hand and singing *The Grand Old Duke of York* almost to the top. Then they turned right and climbed the moor road, stopping at the cattle grid before the open moorland stretch. Here they had reached the marker of 176 miles of the C2C – only fifteen miles to go for our brilliant little walker, Rachael.

Kevin picked them up and took them back to their B&B in Glaisdale before they all went to the local pub for a pizza and chips. While they were waiting and enjoying a well-earned drink, pizzas were served to some diners on a nearby table – they were enormous. Concerned that the size would outface Rachael, Ian reassured his daughter.

'Just look at the size of those pizzas – you really don't have to try to eat all of yours, Rachael, it's quite alright to leave some – just eat as much as you can, darling.'

He need not have worried; Rachael demolished all of her pizza and chips and ate Daddy's chips too! They all looked at her with astonishment, admiration and disbelief. Where did she put all that food?

THE FINAL DAY – DESTINATION: ROBIN HOOD'S BAY

Beautiful sunshine greeted them for their final day. Magic! This would be Rachael and Ian's longest day of the entire C2C – fifteen miles! Trish walked with them again down to the picturesque Littlebeck, where the shallow sparkling stream is the home of some very noisy ducks. They crossed the road and followed the woodland path gently upwards to a massive boulder, out of which a remarkable cave-like shelter with seats has been carved. In beautiful lettering on the outside of the boulder is inscribed, 'The Hermitage – 1790' with the initials GC. More posing and memorable photos. From here they followed the trail to the spectacular Falling Foss waterfall.

Rachael however was more interested in her reward of a big ice cream from the tranquil tearooms just beyond Falling Foss. As they were sitting down enjoying their well-deserved treat, Rachael noticed a man going past them. He was around thirty years old and obviously a fellow Coast to Coaster. That was not to be allowed! Rachael sprang up and rapidly followed him with Ian and Trish trailing behind. At the entrance to the strangely named Bottoms Lane, they overtook the unfortunate man who had stopped to have a sandwich.

'Hello, again!' said Rachael in a friendly way, but ever the competitor, she whispered to Ian, 'He is not going to beat me to Robin Hood's Bay – no way!'

Kevin joined them just beyond High Hawsker where, together, they followed the picturesque cliff path to their destination. The views out to sea are absolutely stunning but for once Rachael didn't really look. She was completely engrossed in watching that man, ensuring that he was some distance behind them and couldn't overtake.

When Robin Hood's Bay came into view for the very first time, Ian pointed out the beach just over a mile away.

'See that beach down there, Rachael – that is the beach at Robin Hood's Bay. You have been walking towards that beach all the way from the beach at St. Bees – 192 miles – isn't that awesome?'

Rachael was quiet for a while and looked very thoughtful and a little sad.

'I don't want to stop, Daddy! Can we go home for two days, see Mummy and then do this all over again?' she pleaded.

'No darling,' responded Ian firmly. 'Once you have done the Coast to Coast that's it – you've done it. There are lots more challenges in the world.'

''That's not fair!' Rachael cried, downhearted and sat down on a nearby rock, 'I'm tired.'

(This was the very first time she had ever said this, and readers will no doubt realise, she wasn't really tired, just upset.)

'That's okay, darling,' replied Ian sympathetically. 'Just have a little rest, a drink and a chocolate bar and you'll be fine.'

When I reached this point and glimpsed that wonderful beach for the first time, I just burst into tears of joy and relief and experienced an overwhelming humbling feeling of gratitude to all those who had helped and supported me. The struggle to regain my life was over: I had emerged triumphant from the long dark nightmare that was Whipple's Disease, and the promise of Everest Base Camp shone like the sunshine over Robin Hood's Bay.

Rachael did actually rest for a brief moment but then she spotted her adversary – that man – he was catching them up! Tiredness completely forgotten, Rachael sprang up and set off with renewed vigour along the grassy path towards her goal. She actually ran down the hill towards the beach at Robin Hood's Bay, with Ian, Trish and Kevin in hot pursuit. Alan joined them. He had walked along the cliffs from Whitby so he could greet this marvellous little walker and congratulate her.

Rachael ran on to the beach – the tide was right in.

'I've done it! Hurray!' she exclaimed, adding, 'And I've beaten him!'

And so she had, as that man, her adversary, appeared a few minutes later. She was absolutely ecstatic, exploding with excitement and triumph. Rachael threw her pebble along with the one she had carried 192 miles for her sister Catherine into the North Sea and then jumped into the sea herself, trying very hard to pull Dad in too. She was so incandescent with joy – she just glowed!

Ian watched proudly, trying hard but unsuccessfully to hold back his tears. What an incredible achievement for his amazing daughter and, importantly, not one single blister.

Rachael was seven years, three months and twenty-three days when she finished her first C2C. What a star!

They duly went into Wainwright's Bar to sign the register and have a celebratory drink. Then they visited

The Plaque Shop at the bottom of the hill to order a special plaque for Rachael. The owner was full of admiration – he told them that Rachael was the youngest person for whom he had ever made a plaque and it was a real honour to make one for her.

On her way home to Old Water View, Rachael again pleaded with Ian:

'Are you really sure, Daddy, that we can't do it again? I really, really want to.'

'No,' replied Ian emphatically, 'there are too many other fun things we can do together. You will definitely not be doing the C2C again.'

How wrong he was!

THE ENDING TO GRANDMA JOYCE'S FIRST C2C

I had a lovely surprise when I went into Wainwright's Bar to sign the register. My lovely Canadian friend Scott had left £10 in an envelope behind the bar with the message:

'Congratulations, Joyce! My inspiration! Have a couple of wee drams on me to celebrate finishing the C2C!'

I had also celebrated on the beach where my friends Derek and Margaret met me, (they had finished the day before me) along with my daughter Steph, who had brought a bottle of champagne but forgot the glasses so we all had to drink out of the bottle. It was a good job we had a hearty meal afterwards!

MONEY RAISED BY RACHAEL

On her first C2C, Rachael was sponsored by innumerable people: guests at Old Water View, family, friends, neighbours and even passers-by. Few of them had really expected her to complete that astonishing challenge at only seven years old, but they were full of admiration and very happy to sponsor such an inspirational little girl. All proceeds were divided between the local primary school and the Patterdale Mountain Rescue Team.

COAST TO COAST 2 – 2012

Although Ian was adamant that they were not going to do the C2C again, he had to review his decision because of Catherine. Not surprisingly, as both she and Rachael attended the same local primary school, Catherine became sick and tired of all the attention centred on Rachael – her younger sister. Bravely she admitted this to Ian and asked if she could walk the C2C with him. Ian readily agreed; he was delighted that Catherine was prepared to tackle this challenging walk but added that she must be prepared to train hard. Catherine promised, bless her, which was really courageous as, unlike Rachael, she is not a natural walker. It is just not her thing; to Rachael long distance walking is a delight, to Catherine it is a penance.

Catherine is a lovely girl, very academic and a talented actress who writes the most beautiful and expressive poetry. She is very caring and sensitive, just not a walker. And although Catherine was understandably full of apprehension, she did train with Ian and Rachael and absolutely refused to let them go without her.

At first Catherine was reluctant but as she grew fitter she began to enjoy being out on the fells. One evening Ian heard the girls talking upstairs in their bedroom about the forthcoming C2C. Catherine was clearly fearful.

'Don't worry, sis,' comforted Rachael. 'Daddy and I will help you all the way!'

And they did.

ST. BEES TO PATTERDALE, C2C2

Almost before they realised it, the Moseley family: Rachael, Catherine and Ian were standing by Wainwright's Memorial that marks the beginning of the C2C at St. Bees. Photographs duly taken, they all went to dip their boots in the Irish Sea and Rachael and Catherine each selected a pebble to carry all the way – 192 miles – to Robin Hood's Bay and throw

C2C1 completed.

into the North Sea. The weather was glorious, bright sunshine and really hot. They were both very excited.

Catherine enthusiastically led the way up the cliff-path towards the lighthouse just as Rachael had done the year before.

Somewhere between St. Bees and Ennerdale, Ian initiated their 'Post Van Challenge'. He noticed that they had seen seven Post Office vans (or possibly the same van seven times!) so he decided it would be a good idea to have a competition. The rules were that Rachael, Catherine and Ian each had to decide how many Post Office vans they would see before they reached the beach at Robin Hood's Bay. Catherine reckoned twenty-three, Rachael twenty-two and Ian decided on twenty-one. All sisters compete, and this challenge proved invaluable in terms of diverting Catherine's concentration from her aching legs and blisters. And of course Rachael, ever competitive, was up for an extra challenge.

Throughout the Lake District section of the C2C, they followed the same plan as the previous year, walking out each day from Old Water View and re-turning each evening, with one exception: Rachael had decided that she wanted to celebrate her 8th birthday back at her beloved Black Sail Hut in Ennerdale Valley, so Ian booked an overnight stay for the three of them. Having looked at the weather fore-cast, Ian decided to walk this section of the route in reverse (east to west) so they could walk across the high mountain route in the predicted nice weather and then drop down via Haystacks to Black Sail. The following day, if bad weather arrived as anticipated, they would be able to walk down the sheltered valley to Ennerdale Bridge with a gale blowing high above them in the mountains.

I was staying with them at Old Water View so I was able to drop them off at Honister Quarry and watched them (fortified by large ice creams) excitably climb the steep, rocky path from the quarry to Fleetwith Pike. In his rucksack Ian was carrying a surprise birth-day cake, cards and presents as well as all their gear – after all, that is what daddies are for, isn't it?

Bless her! Rachael soon ran out of energy as she had really been really poorly with a stomach bug and was still quite weak. She sank down exhausted on a rock near the path. But nothing stops that little girl for long – a few words of encouragement from Catherine and Daddy and a drink and she was up on her feet again. Eager to help, Catherine, very kindly, carried Rachael's rucksack.

Sheer grit and determination got Rachael to Black Sail where she had a huge surprise: birthday balloons were bobbing merrily outside the hut. Actually they had been put up to celebrate the warden's birthday the day before but naturally Rachael thought they were for her! It was just the boost she needed. Soon she was racing around with Catherine, tummy-ache forgotten, jumping and laughing with joy – both of them were absolutely elated. Ian was delighted to see that Catherine clearly loved Black Sail as much as we all do.

The warden blew up some more special balloons just for Rachael and cooked a delicious meal for everyone. Fortunately another family was staying at Black Sail so they all shared Rachael's birthday cake and had a fantastic time. What a wonderful, memorable way for Rachael to celebrate her 8th birthday.

The next day they all walked happily together in fleeting sunshine down the long forest road towards Ennerdale Bridge. Rachael was sporting two balloons tied to her rucksack and because it was now devoid of the birthday cake, Daddy's rucksack looked too small, so Catherine and Rachael stuffed another balloon inside his bag making it look impressively large and heavy!

The girls skipped for joy hand in hand most of the way so they hardly noticed just how long that track is. As anticipated, there was indeed a gale blowing high above them in the mountains.

I picked them up just outside Ennerdale Bridge and took them home to Old Water View. They chatted excitedly all the way full of their wonderful shared experience.

PATTERDALE TO THE END OF C2C2 AT ROBIN HOOD'S BAY

To avoid unnecessary repetition, from Old Water View, Patterdale to the end of the C2C at Robin Hood's Bay, I will just record highlights and humorous incidents.

Rachael, Catherine and Ian had to make two attempts to reach Bampton Grange. The first was almost a disaster as, although they set out in sunshine, high winds were forecast for the end of the day. Ian judged that they would be over the high ground and down to safety by Haweswater so he decided that they would take the high route over to Kidsty Pike (the highest point on the C2C) and then down via Haweswater to Bampton Grange. This was a new route for Rachael.

Unfortunately weather forecasts are not always accurate because as they climbed past fabulous Angle Tarn towards Satura Crag, the wind suddenly rose and huge gusts battered them. The situation rapidly became dangerous as even Ian had problems staying on his feet and poor Rachael was blown over several times. The girls were very frightened but comforted by the presence of their dad – they trusted him implicitly to keep them safe. Sensibly, he turned them round and, after sheltering behind rocks at Angle Tarn on the way down, from here they managed to descend slowly, waiting for lulls in the gusting wind by the more sheltered Martindale back to safety at Old Water View. En route, one big gust picked Rachael up and deposited her on her bottom; she was not amused at all!

Undeterred they set out next day, but mindful of the unpredictable weather, Ian led the girls over Askham Fell, a beautiful but lower moorland route to Bampton, a village just before Shap (Wainwright's winter route). As they looked back towards Patterdale, they were all amazed to see dark heavy clouds hanging over their home and yet they were walking in T-shirts in bright sunshine: the vagaries of the capricious Lake District weather!

To encourage Catherine (a true chocoholic) to walk with more enthusiasm from Bampton to their next destination Orton, Ian and Rachael promised her a chocolate reward at the famous chocolate factory in Orton.

Catherine did not believe them so she was overjoyed to find that the factory really *did* exist and was open. They both rushed happily in to buy their well-earned rewards. They each chose a white lollipop thinking it was made of white chocolate – it wasn't! It was white rock and the girls felt cheated; after all a chocolate factory should only make chocolate sweets! But there is a bonus in everything if you seek it; the lollipops lasted for ages and kept them quiet all the way home.

From Kirkby Stephen – their next destination – onwards, they would stay in B&Bs as Rachael and Ian had done the year before. Unfortunately both girls suffer from carsickness, Catherine in particular, so by the time I dropped them off at Orton the next day, they were both feeling rather ill. Rachael recovered quickly and was soon back to her usual bouncy self but poor Catherine really struggled all that day and the next as they set off for Keld. Head down she trudged on doggedly up a gradual but very long hill at about half her normal walking pace, seeing nothing. She was still exhausted after lunch so Ian thought that he would play a joke on her to cheer her up.

Although their next stop, Keld Lodge, was hidden only a few hundred yards away, Ian thought that if he could convince Catherine that there still was a long way to go, she would be overjoyed when she realised Keld Lodge was in fact just ahead. A good idea … ? No! His plan backfired – badly! Even the best of dads can get it wrong and Ian did. When he pointed to a barn miles away on the horizon and told Catherine that was Keld Lodge, he had expected her just to grumble. Instead, Catherine burst into tears and sobbed. She was totally distraught!

Ian felt dreadful; he had completely misread the situation because normally Catherine has a fantastic sense of humour but the result showed how worn out she really was – bless her! Ian apologised quickly and gave her a big hug and after seeing that they were almost at Keld Lodge, Catherine's tears soon dried up.

They had a super evening there and after a delicious meal, Catherine was feeling much better and eager to

continue their walk the next day – so much so that when Ian gave her the option of stopping and going home, she adamantly refused:

'No Dad, I want to walk with you all the way,' she said.

Brave girl!

Remember the farmer who did not like walkers? Well that particular year he had increased his plastic deterrents on the stile: the skull was still there but the rats had increased to three (I didn't know plastic rats could breed, did you?) Of course the girls were undeterred and posed for lots of photos.

At Ingleby Cross, Rachael introduced Catherine to the metal sculpture of 'The Chain Lady' outside The Bluebell Inn –more photos! (Actually this 'Lady' now adorns Ian's patio at Old Water View and points the way to the C2C.)

Ian got it wrong again the morning they were leaving Ingleby Cross. Actually it was the first morning of the Olympic Games, when the girls were rudely awakened at 5 a.m. by a fully dressed Ian, shaking them.

'Come on, lazybones, get up! It's 7 a.m. already!'

Ever eager, Rachael leapt out of bed and was soon half dressed when Catherine, still in bed, looked at her watch, then at Ian and protested emphatically.

'But Dad, look at my watch – it's only 5 a.m.!'

Ian had to admit that this was true but not wanting to lose face, he added, 'Our watches could be wrong … '

Sensibly, Catherine switched on the TV and sure enough it was still only just past five o'clock. She smugly snuggled comfortably down in her cosy bed while Rachael and Ian had to undress. Back to sleep for another two hours.

Fortunately the weather that morning was brilliant, warm sunshine with a gentle breeze and ideal for walking, so the girls forgave Ian with the kind of condescension that makes all parents feel they are the child.

This day from Ingleby Cross to Clay Bank Top is quite an arduous one as it involves a steep climb up to Carlton Moor then a sharp descent to the unusual Lord's Stone Café. Unfortunately this year it was closed so there were no extra treats to encourage Catherine to tackle the lengthy climb to Cringle End.

She had enjoyed the walk along the moorland and marched along happily keeping up with Rachael but felt less enthusiastic about the next ascent. Ian and Rachael promised her that when she reached the top she could rest on a sofa. Needless to say, Catherine did not believe them. Actually there *is* a large stone sofa on Cringle End with a fabulous panoramic view. Ian took lots of photos of both girls resting in the sunshine and enjoying the wonderful views before they crossed Cringle Moor and Cold Moor.

They stopped to have their lunch on the top of Hasty Bank before they tackled the winding, steep descent to the enclosures on the saddle before they climbed yet again up to the spectacular Wainstones. From where they were sitting, they could see a herd of probably around thirty Galloway cattle milling around the gate of the enclosures far below. It was a gate they had to use.

All the way down, Ian schooled them about how they must behave as Galloways have a reputation for being quite awkward: they must approach the cows steadily and quietly, not a single sound. They obeyed to the letter, then, as they were in the middle of the herd – potentially the most dangerous place – Ian's mobile rang! (I'm afraid the culprit was me, Grandma Joyce, just phoning to see if they were okay. Sorry! The girls have since reminded me frequently about this.) Ian quickly hit the silence button and fortunately the cows just looked nonplussed and carried on eating. Disaster averted!

The steep ascent to the Wainstones was quickly overcome and, like Rachael the previous year, Catherine was completely overcome by the incredible shapes and natural sculptures of the rocks. Excitably, they scrambled over them, posed by them and jumped from them. They were in heaven – two gloriously happy girls. Ian's camera never stopped clicking!

While they were descending the awkward path to Clay Bank Top, Ian remembered that the small B&B where they stayed last year did not take bank cards so he needed some cash. He knew that there was a shop with a Post Office at Great Broughton two miles away down a considerable hill in the opposite direction, so instead of turning right to walk down to Chop Gate they had to turn left which, with the return journey, added an extra four miles to their day.

The girls were not impressed: they had already done a long tough walk so they were really looking forward to some rewards when they finally reached the shop – possibly ice creams and sweets. They were all to be disappointed in fact because the Post Office part of the shop had closed and the shop shelves were almost empty. No cash, no sweets and no ice creams. Embarrassed, the girl behind the counter explained that the owner was away and she had not been able to stock up.

The girls were not happy as they climbed back up the hill, particularly when Ian stopped at a nearby pub to buy them a drink but discovered the pub didn't

even sell crisps. Could things get any worse? Yes they could, because then it started to pour down with typical Lakeland style rain – it was incessant!

Soon they were all soaked. Actually Rachael didn't mind, ever cheerful she just skipped along completely oblivious to the rain, so quickly in fact, that she reached the Chop Gate sign and waited there merrily chasing raindrops until about twenty minutes later, when Catherine trudged miserably down to join her. Catherine was completely soaked; her face an absolute picture. Ian tried hard not to smile.

When they finally arrived at Rachael and Ian's favourite B&B, Forge House, Rob and Jenny made a huge pot of tea and big cups of hot chocolate for the girls. After a lovely hot shower, Catherine cheered up and graciously forgave Ian. At the local pub, they all had a substantial, delicious meal, which tasted even better for knowing that they had thoroughly earned it.

Catherine and Rachael had a fantastic start next morning before they all set off for their next destination because Robin and Jenny took them to their smallholding and let them feed the chickens, goats, sheep, their cows Nelly and Doris, and the bull calf whose name was Gizmo. They were completely engrossed and did a very good job and, this time, both girls were able to sit on Nelly.

Thankfully after this, Robin and Jenny gave them all a lift to the nearest town where Ian was able to withdraw some cash and pay their bill. Then they dropped Ian and the girls off back at Clay Bank Top at the beginning of the walk to the famous Lion Inn on Blakey Moor. Catherine and Rachael, with superior looks on their faces, did point out that, thanks to Dad, this was their third visit to Clay Bank Top in less than twenty-four hours!

Just after Rachael spotted the remote Lion Inn in the distance, the footpath suddenly disappeared into a wide, deep muddy morass. This gave Ian an opportunity to redeem himself. He searched in the heather and found a large flat boulder, which he deposited in the middle of the mud making a perfect stepping-stone for the girls – a virtual modern-day Sir Walter Raleigh! (Of course, his chivalry meant that he didn't get his shoes full of mud either …)

The next few incidents show how Rachael, aided by big sister Catherine, plotted to ensure that the next year she and Ian would be doing C2C3. (Poor man, he never stood a chance!)

After the Lion Inn they posed at the Fat Betty stone for yet more photos, left one of their chocolate bars and picked up the one left on the monument – a tradition of the C2C Walk. They marched on, thoroughly enjoying the walk to the monument on Fryup Head. Here Rachael asked Ian for a 20p coin and promptly buried it at the base of the monument.

'What are you doing?' asked Ian.

'I'm burying it to see if it is still there when we come again next year,' replied Rachael with an angelic expression.

Ian responded firmly, 'We are *not* coming back that soon. There will be no C2C in 2013!'

Then he added, 'I suppose because you have buried it so well, no one will think to look there and your 20p could still be waiting for you, *if* we do come back again several years from now. But definitely not in 2013!'

Rachael, of course, had other ideas. Catherine said nothing, as she knew something that Dad did not know … Rachael had already buried another coin under Fat Betty as double insurance. She was a little girl with a mission!

When they reached the bookshop at Grosmont, knowing how much Catherine liked to read, Ian gave her some money to buy a book. She came out with a huge grin on her face – guess what she bought? A book entitled *How to Train a Boy* (part of the plot, one wonders – you'll see!)

The next day, after climbing the 1 in 3 hill from Grosmont, which Rachael had christened the 'Huff and Puff Hill' and Catherine 'a huge mountain', they were all walking down to Littlebeck. Ian was about twenty feet in front of the girls who were walking arm-in-arm. Gradually he realised that there was a lot of giggling behind him. At first Ian thought that it was just the girls having fun but then he picked up exactly what they were giggling about. Their conversation went something like this:

Rachael: 'Catherine, how can I convince Dad to do this again with me? I really, *really* want to do a hat trick of C2Cs. You have to help me to find a way of doing it with Dad again next year. Please!'

Catherine: 'Why would you want to do it again? It's a nightmare – you must be mad!'

Giggling, she added, 'Besides, you have absolutely no chance – you only got to do the C2C again this year because I was jealous and wanted to do it like you and now I wish I hadn't. My poor feet are positively killing me!'

Between them they obviously hatched a cunning plan – perhaps that book gave them some ideas – and about ten minutes later came the ambush. They caught up with Ian and walked very close to him, one either side. As she gazed up into Ian's face, Rachael donned her most appealing, sorrowful look.

'Daddy, you are being really mean and unfair to me and it's not very nice!'

She really is just as good an actress as Catherine when she needs to be!

Astonished, Ian replied, 'Why? What have I done?'

'Well!' came Rachael's response, 'You know that all the people who do the C2C – when they have thrown their pebble into the sea and wet their boots – get to stay overnight at a B&B, meet up in the pub and celebrate their success. We don't even get to stay overnight. That's why it isn't fair!'

Good tactics – just wait for the rest of the master plan …

She continued after a suitably pregnant pause to allow her words to sink in.

'I know just how you can make it up to me.'

Ian waited silently; well aware he was being manipulated.

'You know how you let me celebrate my 8th birthday at Black Sail this year? Well I really, really want to celebrate my 9th birthday in a B&B at Robin Hood's Bay; *please, Dad!*'

'That seems a reasonable request,' answered Ian smiling. 'Yes, you can have your 9th birthday at Robin Hood's Bay, I promise.'

On hearing this promise, Rachael said excitably, 'Wow, Catherine! You see Dad has just agreed that I can spend my 9th birthday in a B&B at Robin Hood's Bay. He doesn't know yet that we are going to be walking all the way there from St. Bees!'

'Well, he does now!' Catherine pointed out with a huge grin.

Every sensible dad knows when he has been beaten – what could he say?

'I have been out-manoeuvred by two experts,' Ian thought, 'and they are only eight and ten – the future is going to be very interesting!'

Now for the result of the Post Van Challenge: on the last day Ian was confident that he would win as they had seen twenty-one – the number he had chosen. He knew the last stretch of their walk was along the cliffs to Robin Hood's Bay, so there was little chance of seeing any more vans.

Suspecting that Ian had somehow adjusted the rules to suit himself, the girls again came up with a plan to defeat him. Rachael suggested that it would be very nice to go a different way from last year – not over the cliffs, but by the fields (from which the road was visible) and then follow the road into Robin Hood's Bay. Catherine agreed enthusiastically. I'm sure you can work out their cunning plan: yes – more road walking meant there were more chances of seeing red post vans!

When Ian spotted a road sign saying Robin Hood's Bay ½ mile, he pointed to it and said proudly, 'Look! Only half a mile to go – you've no chance either of you – I've won!'

What do they say about pride coming before a fall? Just as he was proclaiming his victory, a red post van came round the corner! Number twenty-two, so Rachael had won: she laughed her head off! Poor Catherine however was quite upset.

'It's not fair!' she groaned. 'I can't beat my sister at anything no matter what I do or how hard I try!'

However the fates decreed otherwise because five minutes later, just as they reached the sign for Robin Hood's Bay, another red post van came past – number twenty-three. Catherine had won! She was ecstatic and marched through the village to the top of the steep hill that leads down to the beach with an enormous grin on her face – not because she had almost finished the C2C – oh no – but because at last she had beaten Rachael … and Ian as well!

Then the girls reminded Ian that one of his rules had been that the person who lost by the most bought the ice creams. Of course that was Ian himself so he bought them both a huge cone each.

Rachael raced down the hill and on to the beach, shouting for sheer joy with arms outstretched.

'I've done it – I've done it again!'

Catherine trudged down more sedately but soon joined her sister. Ian said you could see she was really happy and quietly proud of herself; she had overcome all her problems and fears and succeeded. She had achieved her goal; she had walked the C2C at ten years old! A fantastic achievement for her and one that she will remember with pride forever. We certainly will!

Full of joy, together two delighted girls threw their pebbles into the North Sea and jumped excitably into the waves. Then they went into Wainwright's Bar to sign the register and Ian bought them all a well-deserved drink. Sitting outside, Catherine and Rachael chatted happily about their amazing experiences. Ian, a very proud dad, listened to them fondly and reflected on what had been a challenging

C2C2 completed.

but unforgettable C2C. What stars his girls were – life was very good.

Ian had phoned ahead and arranged with Packhorse to give them a free lift home to Old Water View. The only problem was they had to climb back up the steep hill so they could be picked up! You can imagine Catherine's face when she heard that.

'Oh no!' she protested, 'Not climbing *again* – I don't believe it!'

On their way home, Catherine informed Rachael and Ian emphatically that she had retired permanently from 'pointless walking', as she called it. Although she had completed the C2C without a single blister and was really quite proud of herself for doing so, it was definitely her last long walk; she was never, *ever* going to do anything like that again. And she hasn't: it's just not her thing.

Each time Rachael and Ian embarked on another adventure, they tried to persuade Catherine to join them but she steadfastly refused. In fact she gave her boots to Rachael to wear on her future explorations, which Rachael did until they were finally consigned to the dustbin.

Ian however made sure that Catherine had her special time with him doing the things that she loved. He took her on long weekend city breaks, including trips to Edinburgh and Glasgow, where they stayed in luxurious hotels and Catherine was thoroughly pampered. She did a little sightseeing, ate in superb restaurants and the two of them shopped till they dropped.

This was Catherine's ideal treat and although Ian wasn't keen on cities, crowds of people and dressing up to eat in posh hotels and restaurants, he loved to be able to spend time with his bright, intelligent and amazingly funny daughter. She is a very entertaining companion and he loves her to bits.

C2C2 FOR GRANDMA JOYCE

My second C2C was completely different from the one undertaken by Ian and the girls. For once I wasn't walking alone, but planned to walk the trail with my dear friends Derek and Margaret. I had met them on my first C2C and we had spent many happy hours exploring the Peak District together. We decided to walk east to west: Robin Hood's Bay to St. Bees.

We booked all our accommodation before Christmas as we intended to start C2C2 at the beginning of the following September (2007) and we knew from experience that all the good B&Bs and hotels get booked up very quickly.

I had been back to trek in the Himalaya twice since my epic trek on the Everest Circuit to Everest Base Camp with my guide, friend and 'adopted' Nepalese son, Chandra Prakash Rai (C.P. for short). We trekked to Annapurna Base Camp and the following May (2007) we had completed the challenging Annapurna Circuit together.

I would never have completed any of these treks had it not been for the fantastic help and support I had from C.P. He had always wanted to see the UK so to thank him I decided to bring him over from Kathmandu to my home for a holiday. As he did not need to go back to Nepal until November when he had some treks booked, I thought that walking across England from C2C in September with my friends and me would be really interesting for him and give him a wonderful chance to see some very varied and breathtaking scenery; beautiful snapshots of the best of Britain. Luckily I managed to book him into most of our accommodation and waited eagerly for him to arrive in July.

What do they say about the best laid plans of mice and men? Yes – mine were almost wrecked. A few weeks before C.P. was due to arrive at Manchester, I was walking along the road at the side of Ladybower Dam in the Peak District, determined to maintain the good level of fitness I had reached by doing the Annapurna Circuit. It was raining hard and I slipped and fell in some deep mud, breaking my right ankle and right wrist. I couldn't believe it! I had trekked for three weeks in the high Himalaya, crossed the difficult Thorung La Pass and not had a single accident or health problem and I had fallen on a road in England!

You can imagine the look of horror on C.P.'s face when I met him at the airport on crutches with my leg and wrist in plaster! Eventually I had both plasters removed but then had very little time to train for our C2C.

Thanks to some sterling work by my physiotherapist, Ted Morgan-Jones who has put me back together for over twenty years of injuries, I decided that I would attempt my C2C2 because I did not want disappoint C.P. or, indeed, Derek and Margaret. Ted warned me that my right foot would swell up with all that constant rough walking and advised me not to take that boot off until we reached our accommodation at the end of each day or I would not get it back on again.

And so we all started off and, amazingly, I managed reasonably well thanks to some very strong painkillers and the odd wee dram in the evening. Of course my ankle was painful but my lovely supportive companions kept me going. I went the easier but pleasant route by the River Swale from Reeth to Keld whilst Derek, Margaret and C.P. did the high moors' route but otherwise we all walked together. We had two difficult and potentially dangerous days: the first when we were climbing up to Greenup Edge in the pouring rain and high wind and found an American lady who had fallen and appeared to have broken her ankle. We called out Mountain Rescue and spent a long cold time with her making her comfortable and preventing her from becoming hypothermic.

When the Mountain Rescue team finally arrived, we continued on our way up to the quagmire of the saddle, squelched across it and then headed down towards the Langstrath valley. By this time the mist had come down and with all the rain, the paths became water-falls especially around Lining Crag. We had great difficulty crossing the streams, which were raging torrents, and all four of us were blown off our feet several times.

Soaked, frozen and exhausted but thankfully safe we staggered into the Langstrath Hotel where we were given welcome hot drinks and even more welcome huge dry towels.

The next day when we had to reach Ennerdale Bridge proved to be our second difficult day, especially for me as my ankle had become very swollen and painful. We had decided the previous evening to take the Mountain Goat bus to the top of Honister Pass to cut down on the climbing and distance.

Unfortunately, when it arrived it was full so later than planned we had to start walking. To me, climbing that pass seemed more like trying to reach Everest Base Camp and the tricky steep descent from Haystacks had me in tears. C.P and I persuaded Derek and Margaret to go on ahead as by now I was limping badly and the path down Ennerdale valley is very long.

Bless him! C.P. stayed with me and patiently encouraged me all the way. It was dark by the time we reached the Shepherds Arms where, to our delight, the substantial meal that Derek and Margaret had ordered for us was waiting – a good job as the kitchen had closed. Never was a hot meal more welcome and reviving, with several well-deserved drinks, of course!

Understandably, the next day we decided to take the shortest route possible to St. Bees via Nannycatch Valley and Cleator entering St. Bees from the south. My lovely Steph was waiting for us on the beach with the celebratory bottle of champagne as usual and some doughnuts. And yes – she did forget the glasses again!

Of course, I was delighted to have completed this difficult challenge but my main feeling was one of relief – no more days of walking! At last I could take my boots off and leave them off; my sandals felt like soft padded cushions – sheer bliss!

In bed that evening at pleasant Stonehouse Farm, I thought about my C2C2: a marathon on a diet of painkillers, whisky and huge doses of stubbornness (or 'sheer bloody-mindedness' as my daughters call it!) I reflected on just how true my dad's maxim was:

'When I die I want to be able to say I'm glad I did – not I wish I had.'

Thanks Dad! He had lived all his life like that and so would I. You can always do far more than you or anyone thinks is possible. All it takes is a little courage and grim determination. Rachael, bless her, has these virtues in spades, as you will discover in the following account of her C2C3.

COAST TO COAST 3

Two weeks after C2C2, when Ian had added up all the sponsorship money, they took a cheque down to the Patterdale Mountain Rescue Team Centre. All the members made a terrific fuss of the girls, thanking them profusely for such a welcome donation. Rachael asked when she could become a Mountain Rescue Team member and was a little disappointed to be told that she was a bit too young and that you have to be at least sixteen years old because the rescue work can be very dangerous. However, she cheered up a lot when they promised that if she was still interested when she was fourteen, she could go and train with them. Wow! Training with that famous rescue team would be awesome and it wouldn't be too long to wait.

There was better news to come: In October 2012, Rachael received a letter from The Patterdale Mountain Rescue Team making her a lifetime member of their Supporters' Club. She was ecstatic! The surprises did not end there for this brave and inspirational little walker: at Christmas, members of the Patterdale team gave her a special Mountain Rescue Team jacket and a warm base-layer shirt.

'Wow!' she exclaimed, 'Now I feel like a proper member! Thank you – thank you so much! I just love them. I'll wear them all the time!'

And she did. She was so proud and could hardly wait to wear her 'new uniform' on their C2C3.

As you may have guessed, Ian had admitted defeat and had booked all the B&Bs along the C2C again. How could he deny his incredible little walker the chance to become a Record Breaker? He planned their C2C3 to coincide with the early Easter holidays in 2013 and this time they would not use Old Water View as a base but stay in B&Bs all the way.

From St. Bees, they would walk together for seventeen days and, magically, would reach Robin Hood's Bay on Rachael's 9th birthday, just as she wanted. Well she'd earned that treat, hadn't she?

She had another Christmas present to help her on her way. I had bought her a special mascot: a little bear proudly sporting a red jumper just like the mascot I had taken that September when I trekked in the Himalaya. However this bear had special gold embroidery on his red jumper. On the front it said, 'RACHAEL C2C3 2013' and on the back it said 'with my Dad'. Rachael named her bear Willy.

Rachael was so excited; the end of March would soon come and she could start her C2C3 challenge. What Rachael did not know was that I had planned an extra surprise for her when she stopped at her beloved Black Sail Hut on her way through Ennerdale. Years ago when my dear friend, Brian Wilkinson, was warden at Black Sail, I had spent many happy weekends and holidays climbing and walking the fells there.

Brian had given me a special Black Sail mug potted by a friend of his at Whitehaven: it is unique and much prized. As a reward for being such an amazing walker, I planned to give it to Rachael so that she could use it for her drinks when she reached Black Sail. Ian was going to carry it hidden in his rucksack and produce it 'just like that!'

NEARLY BEATEN BY THE BRITISH WEATHER

As you would expect, Rachael's 2013 C2C3 was planned by Ian with his usual meticulous attention to detail, especially regarding safety, as the start date – Saturday 30th March – was much earlier in the year than two previous C2Cs. This was to make sure Rachael completed her incredible three C2Cs at Robin Hood's Bay on her 9th birthday – April 17th.

However as readers might remember, the weather in March 2013 was horrendous: freezing temperatures, unceasing snow and incredibly high winds, which whipped snow into huge drifts across the Pennines, Wales and the Lake District in particular. People were cut off for days and the traffic was paralysed – it seemed that no one was going anywhere.

No one had anticipated that it would be so dreadful and last for so long – the worst conditions for over twenty-four years. Walkers were just not walking; the snow was tremendously deep, the wind chill was unbelievably high and paths were icy and dangerous. Guests kept arriving at Old Water View scared stiff and exhausted having battled their way from Grasmere over Grisedale Tarn.

Just below the Kirkstone Pass, eighteen red deer were found frozen to death in a huge impenetrable snowdrift – something that none of the locals ever remembered happening before. The severe weather conditions just continued; the cold biting wind and icy snowstorms were relentless.

Understandably, Ian was a very concerned dad. He had an enthusiastic eight-year-old, who was completely oblivious to all the dangers and could not wait to start her C2C3, yet he was responsible for her safety and wellbeing. He did not want to disappoint Rachael but he was intensely aware of difficulties and additional hazards that the dreadful weather had brought and was really worried – what should he do? He thought long and hard and decided that he had to give Rachael her opportunity to achieve her dreams.

Using his experience of the C2C and the Lakes, Ian was able to modify their route so that most potential dangers could be avoided and he knew that he would be able to protect his precious daughter. They would go but he was well aware that at any time dreadful conditions might prevent them from completing the challenge. Safety was paramount.

Sadly Rachael's beloved Black Sail Hut had to close. It was buried in a snowdrift and the snow had blown inside and affected the electricity and other power supplies. So Ian booked them in at the Youth Hostel at Buttermere – a good compromise because this meant that they did not have to cross the impassable Loft Beck trail. However this added an extra seven miles to the C2C: 192 + 7 = 199 miles!

He still planned to carry the Black Sail mug that I was giving her as a surprise but Rachael would be drinking out of it at Ennerdale Bridge instead of Black Sail. She would be just as thrilled; Rachael has such a joyful outlook on life, she can deal with small disappointments and remain upbeat – after all, she was walking with her dad!

THE BEGINNING – ST. BEES TO ENNERDALE BRIDGE

And so, on Easter Sunday, I drove them back to St. Bees again. Rachael was so eager, she kept urging my little car to go faster: if she could have flown there, she would! She leapt out of the car, dashed on to the beach to wet her boots in the Irish Sea again and was nearly caught by waves driven up the beach by the stiff onshore breeze; there were lots of squeals and much excitement!

We all selected pebbles, and Rachael chose extra ones for all the family. She popped all these in Ian's rucksack. After all, that is surely what dads are for: to carry extra things! As she posed for the obligatory photo by Wainwright's monument, the sun came out and continued for most of the day as they walked towards Ennerdale Bridge. Rachael soon shed some of her walking gear. She was dressed like a Himalayan explorer because, wisely, she had borrowed a lot of my trekking gear. They both knew just how capricious the weather could be; warming sunshine that changed quickly to icy biting winds and driving snow – challenging and dangerous conditions for the best of walkers.

It had actually snowed a little as we left Old Water View but at St. Bees the weather was utterly bizarre: sunny and warm, more like Spain, yet the distant fells were completely covered in snow!

As they headed towards the lighthouse where they would turn east for Robin Hood's Bay, they started their 'Tractor Challenge'. Ian had decided that it would be one point for spotting a blue, yellow or green tractor but two points for a red one – with a bonus point for one with a flashing light on top.

Just as Rachael expected, Ian soon cheated saying that he had seen two tractors with flashing lights just ahead. However when they rounded the corner, his tractors

had mysteriously disappeared. Rachael fined him two points for cheating and then she spotted a barn in which there were *nine* tractors – she was ecstatic.

'See Daddy, cheating does not pay! Now I am eleven points in front of you!'

(In Ian's defence, he knew that Rachael would cheat if she could but perhaps not so blatantly or so soon!)

As she skipped happily up the cliff path, Rachael suggested an additional challenge – counting phone boxes. As she pointed out, they are very important in case of emergency. Somewhat humiliated by being caught cheating on the Tractor Challenge, Ian readily agreed so that was two challenges on their C2C3, giving ever-competitive Rachael more chances of winning at least one. Two, of course, would be even better.

Ian had planned a short first day for them so they returned to Stonehouse Farm via the pretty path near to the railway line – a route unknown to Rachael. For the first time ever, Rachael had a small blister apparently caused by Grandma Joyce's woollen socks.

After a pleasant meal in the Queen's Head they were treated to a fabulous sunset over the sparkling Irish Sea. It was breathtaking: every shade of gold, orange, red and purple filling the darkening sky. Wheeling and diving overhead in a noisy chorus, the seagulls seemed to be greeting Rachael and wishing her good luck for her incredible challenge.

Next morning, having had an hour's less sleep due to the clocks going forwards, they set off towards the snow-covered mountains to re-join Wainwright's path. It was so warm and sunny that they were walking in T-shirts.

To vary the route from the previous years, Ian decided that they wouldn't climb

Dent Hill again but would instead walk the picturesque path around the bottom and then join the Nannycatch Valley at Nannycatch Gate. This was the last place where, looking backwards to the west, they could still catch a glimpse of the Irish Sea. Rachael was completely enthralled by this pretty secret valley and skipped along, absorbed by the scenery, until they reached the Shepherds Arms at Ennerdale Bridge.

She spent the remainder of the afternoon playing happily on the swings in the park, her blister entirely forgotten. She had spotted seven phone boxes already – four that day and three the day before.

A long time before Rachael began her C2C3, she had asked Ian if there really was an Easter Bunny. As always, when asked about such things as the Tooth Fairy or Santa Claus, Ian had replied, 'If you really believe in the Easter Bunny, then it is true.'

So Rachael had written a letter to the Easter Bunny asking for an Easter egg to be delivered to Black Sail on Easter Monday. Now, of course, the next venue had been changed to Buttermere Youth Hostel instead of Black Sail. Rachael was very concerned.

'I really, *really* want an Easter egg at Easter, Daddy, but the Easter Bunny thinks I am at Black Sail so she'll take it there!'

Ian, you will remember, was carrying an Easter egg for Rachael, along with my Black Sail mug so he answered somewhat smugly.

'Don't worry, darling, write another letter to the Easter Bunny. She is very clever: she will deliver your egg to Buttermere instead, I'm sure she will.'

'Okay!' replied Rachael and cheerfully began to compose her letter.

What do they say about 'the best laid plans of mice and men'? Everything was going well until Ian decided that he ought to give Rachael my present – the Black Sail mug at Ennerdale Bridge (the nearest they would be to the Ennerdale Valley and the path up to Black Sail.) She was overjoyed and unbelievably proud of her unique mug and immediately had a drink in it, carefully holding it by the body and not relying on the handle.

Coast to Coast Walkers

LOFT BECK, Ennerdale

If you intend to walk up Loft Beck (east of Black Sail YH) as part of your coast to coast walk, only do so if you are an experienced mountaineer. There is snow and ice on the path and a cornice at the very top. Scarth Gap is a good alternative, but again, please take care.

See pictures below taken on 25/3/13

Near top of Loft Beck — At start of Loft Beck — Deep snow on path

Black Sail YH — Cornice at top of loft beck

Unfortunately Ian neglected to close his rucksack properly so Rachael found the hidden Easter egg.

'Daddy!' she exclaimed accusingly. 'You were carrying that Easter egg for me, weren't you? Which means that one is from you and I want one from the Easter Bunny too. Please, please!'

'You'll have to wait and see,' replied Ian, privately thinking, 'How do I get out of this one?'

For once he did not have a cunning plan; clearly he needed a miracle!

ENNERDALE BRIDGE TO BUTTERMERE YOUTH HOSTEL

Beautiful sunshine greeted them the next morning as they set off on their long walk to Buttermere: a route that, due to the necessary diversion, was seven miles longer than the one originally planned.

As they left the Shepherds Arms, they noticed a large poster put up by the Mountain Rescue Service that really highlighted the still-dangerous conditions on the high fells. There were photos of Black Sail Hut

almost buried in the snow and Loft Beck, just above Black Sail, was completely blocked. The poster warned walkers not to attempt the climb as the conditions were extremely hazardous with snowdrifts, ice and hanging cornices. It was a different world from where they were yet amazingly it lay only a few miles away.

Chatting happily, Ian and Rachael were walking towards Loweswater when a man in a white van drew up beside them. Apparently he was the support driver for family friends doing the St Beda's Walk, which follows a similar route in this area. He was carrying Easter cupcakes – lovely little cakes topped with small multi-coloured Easter eggs – which he was delivering to the children at Ennerdale Bridge.

He had several spare cakes and was genuinely pleased when he recognised Rachael from the pub the previous evening. He duly gave her a cupcake and wished her every success and a very happy Easter. Excitedly Rachael thanked the man and with a 'Wow!' bounced on ahead. As Ian said, 'It was as if she was walking on air.'

'This is yummy!' she cried, munching happily. 'You see, Daddy, this is how the Easter Bunny does things. Although that man didn't look much like an Easter Bunny, did he?'

'He probably works for the Easter Bunny,' Ian explained.

How lucky was that? Ian had his miracle and a thoroughly satisfied little walker to boot.

Ian had borrowed a video camera so that he could record significant incidents on Rachael's attempt to become the youngest Triple Coast to Coaster. When they first caught sight of lovely Loweswater, Ian urged Rachael to sit on a gate so he could interview her on camera with the fantastic background of the shimmering water and the snowy fells behind her.

As she tried to climb down, she got caught up on the gate and fell off in a heap – Whoops! She looked so funny that they both had a fit of giggles.

And so on to enchanting Crummock Water, probably one of the most picturesque of the lakes. The scenery was breathtaking: the sun was shining on the glittering water and the high snowy fells were mirrored on its still surface. Both Rachael and Ian stood there silently in wonder – they were spellbound. It was one of those magical moments that live in your memories forever. To add to the enchantment, three buzzards circled lazily high above in the clear blue sky. In spite of the seemingly endless miles, Rachael said that this was the best day's walk of her life and her favourite view of all she had seen on her C2Cs.

'What a marvellous, amazing day, Daddy!' she murmured blissfully, 'I might not have a big Easter egg but I had something far better – a yummy Easter cupcake with lots of little eggs on it, brought by a random man in a white van. My blister has gone and I'm so glad that Black Sail was closed because I will be able to go back there with you another day!'

Rachael certainly sees the positive side of all situations!

The hostel at Buttermere proved to be a great success too: all right, it was not our beloved Black Sail but it was a really friendly, pleasant place with good food and a warm welcome. They would certainly return there one day.

On my C2C3, I had to stay at Buttermere Hostel as Black Sail was closed for renovations. I had a great meal there and the drying room was superb. Unlike Ian and Rachael, I was able to cross Floutern Pass from Ennerdale to Buttermere because the sky was reasonably clear. It is a useful short cut but good weather is needed as it has steep climbs and rough descents mainly on grass and scree and the ground underfoot is very soggy and the path indistinct in places with many streams to cross. (Surprisingly, I did not fall in any of them!) Just before you reach the 'Coffin Route'[1] from Buttermere, you pass the fabulous waterfall of Scale Force: a very picturesque place for a welcome rest, a drink and sandwiches.

BUTTERMERE TO ROSTHWAITE

It was very cold and windy when Ian and Rachael left the Youth Hostel next morning and walked through a tunnel and down to the lake edge, intending to follow the interesting lakeside path. They were about half-way along when Ian realised that his mobile phone was not in his pocket and he didn't know where it was. As the weather was much harsher and would be increasingly so as they climbed higher, a mobile phone was a necessity so they turned back to the hostel. After searching for some time, Ian found his mobile in the pocket of the trousers he had put in the dirty laundry bag in their luggage awaiting transport. Lucky man! Mobile phone located, they would be safe to carry on.

Next came the long steep road climb up to the summit of the Honister Pass. Fortunately there was very little traffic. By now they were surrounded by snow and the wind was bitingly cold. The beck, which normally tumbles in a cascade of bubbling water down to the valley bottom, was completely frozen over. They were in an entirely different world from that of the previous two days.

At last they reached the top of the pass and paused to gaze at the magnificent panoramic view that opened up before them: snow-covered fells surrounded them and high white mountains glistened in the distance. Spectacular green patches of grass began to peep through the snowy banks as their route descended steeply towards the Borrowdale Valley below.

It was too cold to linger so they ate their lunch quickly in the café at Honister Quarry and were soon on their way down the snow-covered but easy pack-horse trail to Rosthwaite.

When they arrived at Gillercombe – their B&B – Rachael had two unexpected surprises: the owner's

---

1 The Coffin Route or Corpse Road was the path followed by coffin or corpse bearers who respectfully carried the dead from Buttermere to Lamplugh Church and onwards to St. Bees Priory.

I too stayed with Rachel on my C2C3 but that friendly parrot wasn't so friendly to me: it pecked my cheek and did a messy whoopsie on my shoulder!

ROSTHWAITE TO KESWICK AND THEN GRASMERE

Their next destination was Grasmere and normally to get there, they would have climbed up Greenup Edge and down the valley of Far Easedale but the snow-drifts were so deep on this route, as Rachael observed, they were even higher than Dad (and would certainly have buried Rachael and Grandma Joyce) so a safe route via Keswick was necessary.

They walked along the Cumbria Way, a beautiful riverside walk and a path around superb, scenic Derwent Water, where Rachael posed by two giant wooden hands. Ian also took a photo of an acrobatic sheep, which much to Rachael's amusement kept jumping up and standing on its hind legs so it could eat from a tree!

From Keswick, they caught a bus to Grasmere. Sadly it was not the open-air bus that Ian had hoped was running but Rachael cheerfully accepted this and commented on the lovely scenery she could see through the windows. That evening she wrote in her journal.

'We walked the correct number of miles today but because of safety we ended up in the wrong place and it was so hot that I got a bit of sunburn because I did not wear my sunhat. Four more phone boxes to add to the total.'

Please note: she never mentioned Ian's score!

The weather conditions and temperatures on the high fells and those down in the valleys are so unbelievably different that even experienced and well-equipped walkers can be caught out.

GRASMERE TO PATTERDALE – A DAY OF DANGER

Rachael and Ian left Chestnut Villa, their overnight B&B in Grasmere, in bright sunshine. They spent a relaxed half hour watching a helicopter carrying bags of boulders to repair the eroded paths on the surrounding fells. The walking conditions were idyllic

name was Rachel and she had a very friendly African Grey parrot called Pip. Rachael soon had the bird perching on her shoulder.

In her journal she wrote the following:

'The view from my bed is amazing. There is a massive window and the view through it is absolutely stunning – I can see everything – what a great place! And I saw three more phone boxes today.'

They had dinner at the Langstrath Hotel and went to sleep quite early; it had been quite a hard, cold day but to Rachael it had seemed easy.

with warm sunshine and a gentle breeze, until they climbed up to the snowline some three miles from Grasmere. Ian was able to take lots of photos and interview Rachael – she is a real little star and loves performing for the camera.

But now the serious and potentially hazardous part of the day's walk began. Ian made sure that Rachael was correctly kitted up in all her warm, windproof clothing and had her walking pole and sunglasses to protect her eyes from the glare of sun on snow. They both wore spikes on their boots.

Initially Ian took some really dramatic shots of Rachael jumping up and down in the snow and filmed her tackling the steep snow slopes with determination and laughter. As the ground grew even steeper, he put the video camera in his pocket; this was the time to concentrate completely on the conditions underfoot and ahead. In such terrain, meticulous observation and previous knowledge are vital to ensure safety.

As they approached the saddle between Helvellyn and Fairfield, Ian was dismayed to see that it was still impossible to distinguish between the path and the margins of Grisedale Tarn. Everywhere there were snowdrifts and ice; critically, there were no footprints to show where others had gone.

Ian held Rachael's hands tightly and with a confident, calm, reassuring and loving voice guided her every step. What Ian did not know until later, was that the video camera was still switched on and was taking unusual footage of the mesh lining of his pocket! But more importantly it recorded all his comforting words to Rachael and, bless her, it also recorded her trusting and brave responses. By the tone of her voice you could tell that she was clearly scared but had implicit faith in her dad.

Slowly, patiently and skilfully, Ian guided her around where the entirely frozen tarn should be – one step at a time. Frequently, they could see the water under the ice, and down through the treacherous icy and snowy boulders beneath. Rachael's pole kept getting stuck in the ice and it was incredibly slippery but their spikes were really effective. Their progress was painfully slow but Ian was determined and experienced enough to keep his precious daughter safe. When they were back at Old Water View, Ian admitted to me that at this point he had felt that he was at the very edge of his ability and resources; the responsibility was enormous and would continue to be so, all the way to Robin Hood's Bay.

They were both concentrating so hard, neither of them noticed that Rachael's scarf had slipped down her face leaving her right cheek exposed. This was to cause her problems days later when she developed a cold.

Gradually Rachael grew more confident as they descended to more stable, safer ground where they did not have to watch every step and so were able to look around a little. Rachael was amazed at the size of the huge shining icicles hanging off Eagle Crag – they were bigger than Dad! The views were spectacular: huge mountain ridges covered with glistening snow and ice; patches of green beginning to appear between the rocks and, in the distance, the sparkle of the stream released from its icy prison tumbling down the valley with yet more shimmering, snowy fells ahead and a glimpse of gleaming Ullswater.

Soon Ian realised that although, emotionally, Rachael was still very excited and thrilled to be walking with her daddy, she was physically drained: the cold had really affected her and although spikes were no longer needed, her steps were still a little laboured and unsteady.

However our brave, resilient Rachael is never down for long: a rest and lunch sitting outside Ruthwaite Lodge and she became more like her bouncy, happy self as they both trekked down Grisedale Valley to Patterdale and home to Old Water View which was bathed in winter sunshine in the valley bottom.

In spite of a rough day, Rachael was ecstatic and triumphant: she had conquered her fears and overcome all difficulties and, although she was tired, she insisted she felt fine. She had experienced her first snow hike and it was just great to be home.

Next day was a rest day at Old Water View … at least for Rachael it was! Not for Ian or Grandma Joyce because Ian had a wedding booked there. It all went very well and the bride, groom and all the guests were thrilled.

When everything was cleared up, Ian had all his gear and Rachael's to sort out for the next morning when they were walking to Bampton. He had decided, because of the ice, snow and high winds on the fells, not to attempt the climb up to The Knott and Kidsty Pike and the high route to Bampton but to follow instead Wainwright's alternative winter route: the picturesque path through Howtown and up over Askham Fell. A walk along the pretty lanes would lead them to their comfy B&B – Bampton Village Store and Post Office.

For this part of their adventure, they were joined by Ian and Jackie and their friendly black Labrador, Jack. He certainly kept Rachael amused and although her cold was very clearly developing, she marched on cheerfully in the sunshine, simply glad to be walking with friends and Daddy again in the beautiful countryside.

Although this route is not as spectacular as the path over Kidsty Pike, the views looking back towards Ullswater are fabulous – particularly so on this walk, as mighty Helvellyn, Fairfield and all the surrounding fells were completely covered in snow and shone like huge beacons among the fluffy white clouds scudding across the blue sky.

Ian's friends remarked that they had recently been trekking in Peru but had not seen anything that matched the awesome beauty of the scene before them. Rachael was simply entranced.

It was only later, when we read Rachael's journal, that we realised although she had walked and skipped with her usual enthusiasm, she hadn't been at all well that day. She wrote, *'It was an easy walk today but I felt poorly. I saw one phone box.'*

BAMPTON TO ORTON

The weather was sunny as Rachael and Ian set out for Orton the next day but the wind was bitterly cold – the kind that takes your breath away. Rachael found the first four miles into Shap easy and she spent some happy moments standing on the M6 motorway bridge waving to the truck drivers who responded by beeping their horns at her. Then she discovered that she had lost the back off one of her earrings.

'Oh, dear!' she exclaimed, 'Daddy, it must have dropped on the back of one of those trucks so either it's on its way south to London or north to Scotland!'

A quick phone call to Grandma Joyce and a replacement was sent to Orton via Sherpa.

They had lunch in as sheltered position as they could find on the limestone plateau – Rachael describes this in her journal:

'We had to have lunch outside because we could not find the café.'

There wasn't one. This is an example of a Rachael joke – like Ian, she has a weird sense of humour!

However as the high, open limestone plateau is very exposed and extremely windy, soon poor Rachael began to struggle; walking against the wind is very tiring and clearly her cold was getting worse so she had problems breathing. Ian became increasingly concerned for her as he could plainly see that his little girl was rapidly becoming drained of energy. He asked her frequently if she wanted to stop but Rachael, as always, bravely insisted that she wanted to carry on and, putting her head down, she battled ahead; her determination and sense of humour keeping her going.

She observed later in her journal:

'Dad plotted a whole new route and didn't look at a map and we didn't get lost. Wow!'

About a mile away from Orton, Ian took another small diversion across some fields and they were both surprised to see a man fast asleep in the grass. He had no rucksack or other walking gear but was just stretched out on his back with a Stetson-like hat over his face. Apart from a few giggles, they walked past him quietly but they must have disturbed him, because when Ian looked round, the man was following them.

'Look, Rachael, there's a bear following us!' exclaimed Ian, and, indeed, the man was really hairy and resembled a bear.

'Don't be silly, Daddy!' answered Rachael with a toss of her head. 'It's that man who was asleep.'

'Oh no, it isn't', insisted Ian, 'It's a bear and it's going to overtake you and beat you to Orton!'

'Never!' was Rachael's reply and she marched on with renewed vigour and determination, triumphantly reaching Orton first. Bear or man, she'd beaten him! Although obviously not at her best, Rachael was still unbelievably competitive. Ian had a secret smile on his face – clever Daddy!

The lady behind the counter at the George Hotel recognised Rachael from photos and articles in the local press and gave her a warm welcome.

'You're famous, Rachael! Well done!' she said.

Although Rachael had perked up somewhat, her cold was getting worse so there wasn't a single protest when Ian suggested that they went to bed early. Hopefully a good night's sleep would help her.

ORTON TO KIRKBY STEPHEN

Before they left the George Hotel for Kirkby Stephen, Rachael confessed that she really felt poorly and didn't even seem very bothered about selecting some chocolate from the chocolate factory – totally unlike her. Obviously Ian asked her again if she wanted to stop but Rachael would not admit defeat. Tenacious as ever, she battled on stubbornly. Unusually for her though, she frequently asked Ian for rests.

Ian realised that Rachael was becoming increasingly exhausted and, crucially, close to the end of her ability and endurance. He knew that this was not going to get better and was really worried about the situation; keeping his precious daughter safe was his priority now.

It was absolutely freezing: the icy wind grew stronger and they could both feel and see the tiny particles of ice that were battering against them. Rachael was wearing all of her warm wind and waterproof clothing with scarves covering her face like a mask, but she was still shivering. When, at last, they reached Sunbiggin Tarn, Rachael collapsed at the foot of a wall unable to walk any further.

'I can't do it, Daddy! I really can't do it!' she cried, utterly distraught.

Ian was heartbroken to hear her admit this and to see what a state she was in. He was devastated – it was obvious Rachael could not carry on so he made the difficult but sensible decision that for this year their C2C was over. They were going home immediately, but how?

Unfortunately, at that moment, they were in a fairly isolated spot though Ian knew they were not too far from help. Rachael however was too heavy for him to carry any distance and he knew that he somehow had to get her up and moving or she would get hypothermia.

This is the situation that all parents dread – when you have to be cruel to be kind. He shouted loudly at her and forced her up onto her feet. Holding both of her hands tightly and with many urges of 'Come on, Rachael!' he managed to walk her to the nearest road which, thankfully, was only a few hundred yards away, hidden in a fold of the hills.

Luckily, he was soon able to flag down a kind lady in a car who, seeing Rachael's obvious distress, gave them a lift to a café and garden centre about two miles off their route. Here Rachael would be warm and comparatively safe for a while. Ian quickly bought her some hot blackcurrant juice, gave her some medication and, leaving her with her drink, tried to make arrangements for a taxi to take them home. When he turned around, Rachael was stretched across the table fast asleep. Half an hour or so later, she woke up and Ian told her about the taxi.

'Please, Daddy, I'm feeling much better now, so I don't want to stop. Please can we go on to our B&B in Kirkby Stephen and decide in the morning whether or not we should go home? I really, *really* want to try and carry on. Please!' she begged.

This seemed like a sensible suggestion and clearly she had bounced back – mentally at least. Knowing how much this C2C meant to Rachael, Ian agreed to delay the decision until the next morning. Fortunately the lady with the car was going to Kirkby Stephen so she gladly gave them a lift to their B&B – Fletcher House.

After giving Rachael a drink and some further medication, Ian put Rachael to bed and she slept soundly all that afternoon.

In the evening Rachael got up for a meal at their usual pub but, sadly, unlike previous years, she was too tired to play in the sandpit. They returned to Fletcher House and Rachael went straight back to bed. She slept all through the night without waking. As he watched her sleeping peacefully, Ian felt humbled and proud of his courageous little girl. He wondered what tomorrow would bring. He was almost in tears as he read her journal for the day:

'The weather today was very cold and very windy so I was feeling really ill – most of the way I felt dizzy and sick and my head hurt so much that I could not see or walk properly. I felt so ill I honestly thought I was not going to finish the C2C3 … a kind lady gave us a lift … I slept all afternoon … I feel a bit better and hope we can carry on tomorrow!'

Even though she had been very ill, her mind was completely focussed on trying to complete this C2C.

KIRKBY STEPHEN TO KELD

Joy! Next morning, Rachael looked much better: her cold had dried up and she was bright-eyed and ready for a challenge.

'Can we walk to Keld today, please Daddy?' she asked. 'I know I can do it and I love that walk and we can come back another day and walk the miles I missed yesterday.'

As always, Rachael was very concerned about doing the 'correct' mileage! Ian pointed out that because of the necessary diversions they had already done, she had walked about ten extra miles already, so the few miles lost yesterday did not matter. This seemed to satisfy Rachael as she didn't mention it again.

As she skipped joyfully ahead, admiring the scenery and pointing out unusual cloud shapes and the sparkling snow on the trees, walls and grass verges, Ian now knew they would finish this C2C3. He had his happy, wonderful little walker back – what a lucky dad, he was!

It was a fantastic day in so many ways: above all Rachael had bounced back and although there were a few short flurries of snow, the bitter wind had dropped a little. The snowy scenery was spectacular: gleaming snow-capped hills, huge wind-driven snowdrifts and trees and hedgerows garlanded in luminous white lacy raiment.

Not long after they set off, as on the previous C2C, Rachael paused briefly to have a swing on a tyre, but then she strode swiftly ahead, obviously feeling she had to make up for yesterday and prove she really *was* better.

The snow on the grass verges was very deep – up to six feet in places – so, inevitably, Rachael decided to leave her footprints there. There was lots of fun and giggles in the snow.

A little further on, the snow was even higher, covering a C2C signpost to within three inches of the top – higher than Rachael herself!

Ian was able to point out lots of birds that were new to her, including curlews, lapwings and oystercatchers. In fact when they spotted an oystercatcher in a nearby field, they decided to see how close they could get to it. They crept silently behind a long low wall peering over it now and again – like a pair of SAS soldiers on a mission. They managed to get within a few yards of it before it flew away so Rachael was able to store its vivid image in her memory.

Not once did Rachael ask for a rest and would not stop even to eat her lunch. When they reached one particularly steep hill that is marked by posts, Ian thought that she must slow down. Not Rachael! Exuberantly, she sprinted to the top and stood there, arms uplifted like the winner she is. Marvelling at her guts and determination, Ian, with a proud smile on his face, followed her to their destination for the day – Keld Lodge – the halfway point of the C2C.

In her journal, Rachael proudly recorded the following:

'I did not have **one** *rest today and I was a lot better. We got to Keld about lunchtime. I saw two phone boxes.'*

KELD TO DANBY WISKE

Rachael woke up early next morning, lively and eager to begin the walk to Reeth but first she had a full cooked breakfast. She had certainly bounced back and was her usual bright, cheerful self, an absolute joy to be with.

The sky was a little overcast and cloudy so it was cold and misty down on the path by the River Swale but Rachael was obviously so thrilled to be able to walk as normal that she laughed and skipped joyfully; she was brimming with excitement and wonder.

Incredibly, as Rachael recorded, they had not had any rain since they left St. Bees. About halfway along when they stopped for a snack, they spotted a very strange creature in the river. Rachael described it very well in her journal:

'It was an octopus-like creature – it had a salmon-pink body and tentacles about 30cm long and Daddy says it is definitely not a crayfish. It is a mystery.'

Even now, in spite of investigations, it still remains unidentified – perhaps readers can help.

When Rachael and Ian reached the pub at Gunnerside they were dismayed to find that it had closed down and that Sid – the friendly, greedy cat, that had been such a favourite, was nowhere to be seen. So they had to sit down outside the empty pub and eat their own sandwiches.

They plodded happily on to Reeth where their lovely hosts at their fab B&B – Springfield House – were absolutely delighted to see Rachael again. In fact, the lady had a large Easter Bunny with a stack of Easter eggs that she has been saving for Rachael.

'Wow!' exclaimed Rachael, 'The Easter Bunny really does keep her promises, doesn't she Daddy?'

As Rachael wrote later, *'I love this B&B because the owners are lovely people and they have a frog pond in the garden.'*

She quickly went to inspect the pond to see if there were lots of frogs like the year before. Unfortunately, although there had been lots of frogspawn, the lady owner told Rachael that the naughty cat next door had eaten most of them, as cats will. Consequently there were only a few frogs.

Later on Ian and Rachael walked down to the Buck Inn for another well-deserved pizza; Rachael really was back to full bounce!

REETH TO RICHMOND

It was a warm, sunny day as Rachael and Ian set out for Richmond. It was still windy but not the cold, biting wind they had experienced earlier. They walked up the road and climbed the hundred and one steps past Marrick Priory – Rachael rushing past Ian to beat him to the top so she could wait for him. Then they followed the same route as previous years to the path under the spectacular Applegarth Scar.

A little later, Ian decided to change the route and follow the Swale into Richmond. He soon realised however that Wainwright's route was far better because this river walk, although very pretty, involved using a few busy roads. And so off they marched

towards their B&B – The Old Brewery Guest House, which is owned by Sherpa. But … where was it? For once, Ian, a well-organised, meticulous man had to ring me up to find its location. Well, even Ian can't be perfect all the time!

Later they met up with 'Dad's crazy friend' – Steph – who was to walk with them for the next four days. They all went for dinner in a rather unpleasant, tacky pub where the tables were sticky and the food not too good either. Rachael, full of beans, was very disappointed and cross when Ian would not let her join in the disco and karaoke; she wanted to sing and dance the night away. Ian wasn't being a spoilsport; he was very mindful of just how ill Rachael had been quite recently and knew how much she needed to conserve her energy for the remainder of their journey.

ON TO DANBY WISKE, INGLEBY ARNCLIFFE AND THROUGH TO CLAY BANK TOP

The following morning didn't start too well: Ian and Rachael were up early and organised. However, Steph was missing. Eventually she was found in Boots pharmacy so much later than planned, they were all ready to carry on to Danby Wiske.

Traditionally, whenever they leave Richmond, they always have an ice cream for breakfast (a strange custom!) and so they began their walk across the Vale of Mowbray clutching their cones.

Most Coast to Coasters say they dislike this part of the route as they think it is boring. It *is* certainly different but it has a gentle varied beauty all of its own. For instance if you walk in summer, everything is green and lush with fields, hedgerows and trees bursting with life. In early autumn the golden cornfields have blood-red poppies scattered within their shining, breeze-blown waves. It can be a wonderful journey.

Jean at Ashfield House.

But that particular year, as it was really early and the weather had been so dreadful, even Ian who (like Rachael) looks for beauty everywhere, had to admit that the landscape did look very drab, uninteresting and lifeless. However the journey was enlivened by Rachael and Steph, who simply had a ball: they giggled and laughed at the silliest things all the way, while Ian listened, amused.

'No wonder Rachael calls her "Crazy Steph"!' he thought.

They walked on under the busy A1 road and into Bolton-on-Swale. Rachael was fascinated by the memorial stone to a man called Henry Jenkins who reputedly died at the age of 169 years old.

'I don't think I believe that!' Rachael wrote in her journal.

At last they reached Jean and Brian's home and their B&B – Ashfield House at Danby Wiske. Brian was away so, again, not wishing to break with tradition, they took Jean to the nearby White Swan for a beer. Ian had one himself while Rachael had her customary hot chocolate.

Undeservedly, the White Swan has had a bad press due to it being closed when both Wainwright and Julia Bradbury stopped there. But Ian has been there six times

Meet Gizmo the bull.

on his C2C journeys and Rachael three times and each time they have had really good food there. In fact this time they all thought that it was the best meal they had ever had in a pub on the C2C.

It is always great to start the day with a good laugh and this happened next morning when they passed an amusing sign on a gate that said, 'No guard dogs – the cat ate them!'

Clearly someone else owns a cat like mine!

Again, fits of giggles ensued as they journeyed joyfully on towards Ingleby Arncliffe. The walking was easy over comparatively flat ground and eventually they climbed over the stile that had the skull, owls and rats attached to the top. As it was early in the year for Coast to Coasters, the unwelcoming farmer had not yet added any more gruesome trophies.

Surprisingly, Ian lost his way when they were crossing an empty, ploughed field – he didn't recognise anything. The terrain was completely different at this time of the year; there were no paths through the crops or indeed any footprints to show where others had gone. A little shame-faced he had to consult his map and quickly found the correct direction.

Next they crossed the busy A19 and Rachael's dreaded railway lines and arrived at their B&B – the Blue Bell Inn – without any further incidents.

A little later they went to see their friends, Ruth and Gerry. Sadly since Ian and Rachael's previous visit, their lovely blind dog, Leader, had died.

Rachael soon cheered up when they went to the fabulous Ingleby Arncliffe Play Park. This wonderful park was opened in 2010 in memory of sixteen-year-old Andrew Phillips, a local schoolboy who had lived in the village and campaigned tirelessly for a safe place where the children could play. He had died of a rare form of cancer but his spirit lives on in this remarkable play park. All the villagers, including Gerry, helped to build it and create the fantastic features, many of which were designed by the children. There are dens, a secret garden, several climbing frames, a huge zip wire and many other exciting things including the Logs Ness Monster! Rachael, Steph and Gerry had a ball playing there and trying everything out.

Next day, although it was reasonably sunny and clear at first, the wind was really strong and quite cold. They climbed up through the pretty woods to the wide, open, heather moors of Carlton Bank and walked along the paved footpath of the Lyke Wake Walk and Cleveland Way buffeted by huge gusts of wind. Part of the moor here still looks rather like a lunar landscape as the heather has been cleared for the runways of a gliding club – an ideal spot for this sport.

Whenever there was a lull, Rachael pointed out to Steph interesting landmarks from this wonderful panoramic stretch of the C2C. In the distance of course, there is Roseberry Topping: that well-known spectacular mini Matterhorn.

They all descended carefully towards the place where the unusual Lord's Stone Café used to be sited under a bank and were delighted to see that it was being rebuilt. This news will gladden the hearts of many Coast to Coasters as it was such an amazing haven of good food, warmth and shelter.

Because of the strength of the wind, Ian decided to take the lower safer route and not to ascend Cringle End and cross Cringle and Cold moors and the Wainstones. In such conditions Rachael could easily have been blown off her feet. At first Rachael was a little grumpy because she had been looking forward so much to climbing on the spectacular Wainstones again but she quickly accepted that this year it would be very dangerous. Her awareness, knowledge and experience were growing all the time; she was maturing into the most marvellous and responsible walker.

As they approached Clay Bank Top by the beautiful path through the forest, it actually rained for about fifteen minutes – their first rain on the C2C3,

as Rachael noted in her journal, adding, '*And we had to walk two* **extra** *miles because our B&B is down at Chop Gate like last year!*'

TO GROSMONT

Rachael and Ian actually stayed at Forge House at Chop Gate with Robin and Jenny, who gave them a lift up to Clay Bank Top next morning. This meant that Rachael's total mileage for the C2C3 was 201 miles!

Rachael had recorded in her journal just how much she enjoyed staying at Forge House:

'*Robin and Jenny have lots of animals on their farm (smallholding). They have two cows, Doris and Nelly – Doris is pregnant with a calf – one baby bull called Gizmo, four chickens, a few sheep and four lambs. One was born at the exact moment that we arrived there. I got to hold one of the lambs and watched Jenny bottle-feeding them. We are coming back in three weeks when Doris' calf is born. This place is fab!*'

By now Rachael was so used to the next section of the C2C to Blakey Ridge that something spectacular would have had to happen to merit a mention in her journal. As it is, all she wrote was the following:

'*The walk over the moor to the Lion Inn is mostly flat – no phone boxes or tractors!*'

At Bloworth Crossing Rachael posed for several photos on the gate and then laughed and skipped her way ahead, determined to catch at least one of the many baby grouse that were squeaking and scurrying in the heather. As in previous years, she was completely unsuccessful but thoroughly enjoyed chasing them, much to the annoyance of their loudly clucking mums!

With Rachael sprinting in front of Ian and Steph and racing the wind on the moor, it was not long before they reached the Lion Inn at Blakey Ridge. They had a very pleasant meal at the inn and an uneventful evening. This did not stop Rachael and Steph making everyone smile with their jokes and giggles: two crazy 'kids' together.

Steph left them next morning heading back to Richmond, so Ian and Rachael set off in threatening weather towards Grosmont. Rachael noted in her journal:

'Steph left this morning and I met "Fat Betty" again and someone had nicked my coin. Then we walked to the Fryup monument and someone had nicked my other 20p too!'

(Readers will remember that the year before, with Catherine's help, Rachael had secretly buried a coin at each monument to make sure she had to return the next year to collect them.)

Actually while Rachael was searching the ground around Fat Betty, a couple who had been staying at the Lion Inn went past them and disappeared into the distance, walking rapidly down towards Glaisdale on the path called Cut Road. At that point Rachael and Ian, just as in the previous year, were walking in a bubble of sunshine whilst huge black rain clouds gathered on every side of them. Soon it began to pour down but not on them! How lucky can you be?

Further down, the speedy couple were getting soaked and stopped to put on all their rain gear, whilst Rachael and Ian were completely dry. As you might imagine, Rachael thought that was really funny.

'Serves them right for passing us!'

They stopped at the Arncliffe Arms, Glaisdale for a drink, and soon, friendly as ever, Rachael was chatting happily to another couple with two dogs. Unfortunately (for Dad) Rachael had a minor disaster. This is a quote from her journal:

'Whoops! I had an accident. I tipped a whole glass of cola into Daddy's lap. He was very wet and cold because there was ice in it. I was sorry but I couldn't help laughing – he looked so shocked! Mac and Archie, the dogs, thought it was very funny too because they jumped up and down and barked.'

Before Rachael and Ian left, this lovely couple sponsored Rachael for £20 – she was ecstatic.

'Aren't I lucky, Daddy?' she exclaimed proudly.

'You certainly are!' responded a very damp, Ian. 'And *dry* too!'

Rachael did not comment.

Just before Egton Bridge, Rachael and Ian overtook the speedy couple, who had stopped for another snack, so it was a very happy and triumphant Rachael who reached Grosmont first.

Right on time, the steam train waiting in Grosmont Station greeted her with a loud whistle and a huge bellowing cloud of steam. Later Rachael and Ian met the speedy couple again when they had a drink together sitting outside the Station Tavern and found that they were all staying at the same B&B.

At breakfast next morning, after hearing all about Rachael's amazing adventures, they gave Rachael a birthday card they had bought for her and sponsored her for another £20 – what a generous gesture! Rachael was absolutely thrilled.

In her journal is the entry:

'People are so kind to me – another £20 to help my school and our Mountain Rescue Team. So that is £40 since we left the Lion Inn. And we didn't get wet and I saw two phone boxes. What a fab day! I love this C2C!'

THE LAST DAY – GROSMONT TO ROBIN HOOD'S BAY

They set off in torrential rain. What a way to start your last C2C day and your 9th birthday as well. They went back down to Grosmont Station because Ian wanted to film Rachael there and record her feelings about her last day of C2C3. Because of the delay, the speedy couple were far, far ahead up the dreadfully steep hill from Grosmont. This is the hill that all Coast to Coasters dislike with a passion.

'Come on, Dad!' urged Rachael, 'We can beat them!'

And she actually began to sprint up the 'Huff and Puff Hill' in her determination to overtake them.

'Where does she get all that energy from?' thought a bemused Ian. 'Particularly after the terrible conditions she has overcome and her dreadful days of sickness when any ordinary person would have given up.'

He was so proud.

Did she overtake them? Of course she did – just as the couple reached the top of 'Huff and Puff Hill', before beginning to cross the moorland. It wasn't long before it stopped raining so, amazingly, they only had one hour and fifteen minutes of rain over the whole seventeen days of C2C3.

They walked on through Littlebeck and up the beautiful woods of Sneaton Forest to the Hermitage Cave where Rachael, as always, posed for several photos.

They stopped for refreshments at Falling Foss Tea Garden – that fabulous, tranquil little haven and children's playground nestling near the top of the magnificent Falling Foss waterfall in a magical fairy glen. Rachael and Ian didn't indulge in one of the sumptuous cream teas but did enjoy delicious ice creams. As you may imagine, Rachael did not spend long playing there as she had a goal to reach: Robin Hood's Bay.

They wound their way up through the enchanting woods and on to the open moorland in bright sunshine.

Time for a quick snack so, as she did the first year, Rachael climbed a tree there and sat perched in it eating her lunch. Not far to go now …

They carried on through High Hawsker and the caravan park and were soon on the 'last lap' – the spectacular cliff path to Robin Hood's Bay. Rachael barely noticed the beautiful scenery before her or the white-capped waves of the wind-driven North Sea far below. She was truly bursting with excitement and could hardly wait to finish.

The pair paused frequently so that Ian could take photos – after all this was an historic event: the remarkable achievement of his brave little daughter to be the youngest *ever* Triple Coast to Coaster!

Eventually they saw a little figure in the distance, wearing a bright pink fleece – me, Grandma Joyce. I could hear Rachael shouting with delight high on the cliffs above me. I had promised Rachael that I would come to Robin Hood's Bay to welcome her and meet her on the cliff path so we could all walk into Robin Hood's Bay together. She was ecstatic; so full of joy and triumph, she just glowed.

We all struggled against the wind, which was really strong. Ian held onto Rachael and I held onto whatever was around – fence posts, gates and walls! As we all looked across the North Sea for our first glimpse of Robin Hood's Bay, I was in tears. It is such an emotional moment for anyone who has walked all the way from the Irish Sea at St. Bees.

Before long, we reached the gate that marks the end of the C2C path and the end of Rachael's amazing challenge. She had done it – overcome tremendous obstacles and triumphed. It is hard to describe how she looked or indeed, how Ian and I felt; words are totally inadequate for such an occasion.

We all walked jubilantly to the top of the hill where we met her mum, her sister Catherine and Rachael's elder sister, Emily, who had travelled up from London. They had all come to greet her and celebrate her fabulous success and her 9th birthday. They congratulated her and gave her huge hugs.

We walked down the steep hill to the beach with an elated Rachael, as always, running way ahead of us, arms raised, shouting with happiness. She was incandescent with joy and pride. Naturally, she was first on the now familiar beach and ran around excitedly, arms outstretched, jumping and splashing like any ordinary little girl delighted to be at the seaside. But as we know, this is no ordinary little girl!

The sea wasn't too far out and the waves, blown by the wind, kept rushing up the beach nearly soaking our feet. Eventually, Rachael gave us the pebbles that Ian had carried all the way from St. Bees – one for each of us – and we all threw them into the North Sea and completed the tradition by 'officially' dipping our feet in the water. Rachael tried her hardest to pull Daddy into the sea and managed to get his feet and the bottom of his trousers thoroughly wet!

There were lots of photos, hugs and congratulations and then, as is the custom, we climbed up to Wainwright's Bar so that Rachael could sign the register of the Coast to Coasters again.

We had all brought birthday cards and presents for Rachael, and Catherine had made her a fantastic poster congratulating Rachael on her success. She was clearly very proud of her little sister – what a kind girl she is! I had been to my local chocolate shop and they had made a unique chocolate champagne bottle for Rachael to celebrate her success. On it were the following words:

Happy 9th Birthday
Rachael
c2c3 – 17.4.2013

Rachael was overjoyed. Deservedly, she was the centre of attention. She just loved it and her face shone with happiness. As she signed the register, the man behind the bar, looking at all her presents and cards said, 'Obviously, it's your birthday and you have just finished the C2C – how old are you?'

'I'm nine today', answered Rachael.

'Oh!' replied the man, somewhat smugly 'Then you are not the youngest person to walk the C2C – I've heard of a seven-year-old girl who walked it.'

Triumphantly, pointing at Rachael, I had the greatest pleasure informing him that the little miracle sitting in front of him *was* that seven-year-old and she had done the C2C *again* at the age of eight. And so now, at the age of nine, she was a Triple Coast to Coaster and a Record Breaker!

'Oh my God! Really? Congratulations!' he replied astonished and humbled.

We celebrated with a lovely meal and several drinks then climbed the steep hill from the beach to our B&B – Thackwood – a lovely welcoming place at the very top of the hill.

Rachael had always wanted to stay overnight at Robin Hood's Bay after completing the C2C but on each of their previous two walks; they had come straight home to Old Water View. This time however, to celebrate Rachael's 9th birthday, she had her special treat – her overnight stay, sharing a room with Daddy. Catherine slept with me. Bless her, Catherine was genuinely happy about her little sister's achievements and I was really proud of her for being so supportive and considerate, especially as she was only ten.

For readers who may be wondering who won the Phone Box Challenge – well, I bet you can guess … Rachael, of course, by a huge margin! She also won the Tractor Challenge, in spite of Ian's repeated attempts at cheating! Will he ever learn? Of course not!

Next day, we drove home to Old Water View in my little red car. After all the excitement and effort it was hard to come down to earth. Rachael was very happy to be home but was soon planning what they could do next.

Sometime later, Rachael said to me, 'You know Grandma Joyce, you are letting me down.'

Astonished I asked her why.

With a twinkle in her eye Rachael replied, 'Well, I have done three Coast to Coasts and you have only done two. I think you should do it again!'

There is no answer to that really, is there? Just like Ian, I was being out-manoeuvred by an expert! So, as readers will have realised by now, I did just that!

COAST TO COAST
& OTHER EVENTS

BIKE & WALK
CERTIFICATES
&
PLAQUES
AT
WELLS

C2C3 plus three world records completed!

THE STORY OF GRANDMA JOYCE'S C2C3

The following July, in 2014, ten years after my first C2C, I began my third challenge. Age completely forgotten, I felt really happy and excited especially as my dear Canadian friend Scott, whom I had met on that first C2C, had decided to do the walk again to celebrate 'our tenth anniversary'.

We had a great reunion at Ian's Old Water View and the next day I took my dear Scott on the steamer to Howtown and then guided him to the path over Askham Fell, which he followed to Bampton Grange and then on to Shap.

Scott had left his knee supports at the Langstrath Hotel in Borrowdale and did not want to risk his knees on the steep descent from Kidsty Pike. He thoroughly enjoyed the wide-reaching views and gentler nature of this alternative route, which is actually Wainwright's safe winter route as it is rarely covered in mist. Luckily for Scott, when he reached The Greyhound at Shap, Packhorse had delivered his knee supports along with his luggage.

Scott and I met up again at Kirkby Stephen but from there we had different venues and routes planned. However we were determined to meet up at the Lion Inn on Blakey Ridge to walk the last sections together.

I took the same route from Kirkby Stephen to Keld, Reeth and on to Richmond as Rachael and Ian did because it poured with rain almost every day and anyway, I had never walked the quiet country road to Keld, nor indeed followed the beautiful River Swale to Reeth in this direction. I carried on to Richmond and I was enchanted; the scenery is less spectacular but so lovely and peaceful.

I did get a few strange looks as I walked happily along because I was wearing a shocking pink Hello Kitty Buff scarf! It was Rachael's. When packing for her third C2C, we just could not find it despite a thorough search, so she borrowed one of mine. When she realised that I really was going to do the walk again, she pleaded with me to wear it because as she pointed out:

'I've done three C2Cs Grandma Joyce but my Buff scarf hasn't. So please, please will you wear it?'

How could I say no? Grandmas never can! I did however feel obliged to explain the situation to several bemused people and, as often happens, the story spread along the trail: the scarf and I became something of an embarrassing legend!

It was a really hot day with no breeze when I tackled the tough stretch from Ingleby Cross to Clay Bank Top. Whether it was the heat, the climbing or just a loss of concentration, I do not know, but somehow I took the wrong path around the Wainstones and got stuck among some large boulders hanging over a steep drop to my left. My little legs proved to be far too short to scramble over them or around them in spite of many earnest attempts.

Luckily for me, two very handsome and athletic young men who were actually climbing on the Wainstones spotted my plight and offered to help. One lovely young man pushed up from behind while the other took my hands and pulled from above. Success! I was soon back on the correct path. I thanked my valiant rescuers profusely and with renewed energy and a smile on my face, I marched on my way. I reflected that it was a long time since I'd had two such young handsome men handling me so expertly. You see, there is a bonus in everything – even at my age!

I thoroughly enjoyed the next day as after the steep climb up to Urra Moor the path is undulating but comparatively level and the views far reaching, especially over Rosedale from the route of the former Ironstone Railway. It is an undemanding, peaceful walk especially in such lovely sunny weather so I sauntered along taking my time stopping frequently just to gaze over the ever-changing patterns and colours of the moorland and indulge myself with several snacks and drinks – absolute heaven and solitude!

I knew that I would reach the Lion Inn well before Scott as he was walking through from Osmotherly. You can imagine my surprise when I entered the bar to be told that Scott had arrived before me. How? He hadn't passed me, had he? Had I somehow gone to sleep in the sunshine?

The manager explained that Scott, along with his luggage, had been given a lift by Packhorse because he was injured. Apparently as a result of walking a huge distance the previous day, he had sustained a stress fracture of his lower right leg, which was swollen and very painful. He was gutted!

After accepting my Voltarol cream, some Tubigrip and allowing me to ply him with several pints of Guinness and a few wee drams, Scott vowed that he was going to walk with me the next day. We'll see, I thought …

Surprisingly, next morning some of the swelling in his

calf had subsided and his ankle was not so painful so no amount of persuasion was going to stop him fulfilling his ambition. Naturally I was thrilled to be walking with my dear friend again, especially as it was drizzling and very misty – having a companion over the North York Moors in those weather conditions was great. However as the day wore on, it became increasingly obvious that Scott was in agony. He bravely struggled on, limping badly, but the descent on the road into Glaisdale was just too much; he was beaten.

I tried to cheer him up with a pint at the pub, before I loaded him onto the train at Glaisdale Station with the instructions to stay on the station when he reached Grosmont and wait for me because I had a surprise for him. As a treat, I had booked two return tickets on the steam train down to Goathland, the real-life village that doubles as the fictional village of Aidensfield in TV's Heartbeat. I knew that this was one of Scott's favourite British TV programmes – one he had always watched with his beloved mom who had died the previous year. He was thrilled and for a while managed to forget most of his pain, helped, I'm sure, by a drink in the Aidensfield Arms; photos in front of Scripps Garage and by the side of the famous Ford Anglia that was used in the series. As Scott said, 'It was a wonderful end to a painful day!' One he would always remember.

Sadly, next day I had to walk on my own as poor Scott could not bear any weight at all on his injured leg. I wasn't looking forward to the long climb up the 'Huff and Puff Hill', which seemed longer than it had ten years before and I was so disappointed not to be walking with my dear Scott.

When, eventually, I reached High Hawsker, I had decided that as a change, because I had walked the cliff path innumerable times, I would nip along the disused railway line to Robin Hood's Bay. This route has the added advantage of being shorter and not so undulating. However, my plans were thwarted by a friendly Australian couple who had heard on the C2C grapevine about 'this old lady who was walking the C2C for the third time' and asked if they could walk with me. I had to agree, so we marched happily along the many ups and downs of the coastal path to Robin Hood's Bay. They were delightful companions. I must admit that I shed a few tears again when,

from the cliffs, I saw that wonderful beach: the goal of so many weary walkers.

Scott was waiting for me outside our B&B and insisted on struggling down the hill to the beach where we threw our pebbles into the North Sea and celebrated with a wee dram from Scott's hip flask. This lovely man had filled it with Bowmore whisky, one of my favourites. We duly signed Wainwright's current record book, in which Coast to Coasters register their success (I wonder how many books there are now), had a pleasant meal and walked slowly up the path from the beach back to our B&B.

Scott went on to Liverpool next day by train to do the Beatles Tour and Packhorse, bless them, took me back to Kirkby Stephen where Ian picked me up and took me home to Old Water View. Everyone – family, guests and staff – was thrilled with my achievement and congratulated me.

I was so happy to be able to tell them that throughout my C2C3, everywhere I had stayed overnight or stopped for refreshment like the Falling Foss Tea Garden near Littlebeck, people remembered my wonderful granddaughter, Rachael, and her heroic efforts to complete three C2Cs by the time she was nine years old! Justifiably, they were all full of admiration and respect for our brave and determined little girl. We are so proud of her; she is, indeed, a superstar.

Her third C2C had been very difficult for Rachael, largely because of the dreadful weather, but she battled on tenaciously through snow and ice; through high and bitterly cold winds; through extra miles and sickness and she triumphed – an incredible achievement.

It took a while for us to realise that at the time I finished my C2C3, I was the oldest lady to have done three Coast to Coasts, and so – as Rachael was the youngest ever Triple Coast to Coaster – we had *two* Record Breakers in our remarkable family. Magic!

Find out what Rachael, our wonderful child explorer did next and the subsequent challenges she faced in the following chapters.

CHAPTER

**THE WEST HIGHLAND WAY
IN SCOTLAND** – APRIL 2014,
AGED TEN YEARS

HOW RACHAEL'S NEW ADVENTURE BEGAN

Not long after Rachael's record-breaking achievement of completing three C2Cs by her 9th birthday, she had a wonderful surprise.

Fran McCann, Marketing Executive of Macs Adventure Holidays based in Glasgow, rang Ian to say that she had just read a copy of the book *Rachael: A Remarkable Record Breaker* and that she and the whole Macs team were so impressed by Rachael's courage, sense of fun and adventure that they would like to sponsor her to walk The West Highland Way.

They had watched the video clips of Rachael's third C2C that her dad Ian had taken and agreed that she had such a bubbly, engaging personality. She was a natural at presenting, in fact, one day they thought she could become more famous than Julia Bradbury – Rachael's idol.

They hoped that she would make a four-to-five minute video documentary that they could use on their website as an invaluable incentive for anyone wishing to join one of their adventure holidays.

If Rachael agreed, they would send her a video camera so she could record all her experiences. Ian said that he would ask Rachael and let Fran know as soon as possible. I'm sure you can imagine Rachael's joyful response.

'Wow! Dad, of *course* I want to do that – I'd love it! Please, *please* say yes, yes, **yes** to Fran!'

Ian had to smile – obviously his famous little walker had lost none of her innate enthusiasm. He reflected, as he had done so many times before over the last seven years, that Rachael had been born with a love of walking and exploring that called incessantly to her soul, as it did to his. In this, they were soulmates.

Proudly he contacted Fran who was delighted with Rachael's positive response and said that they would despatch a video camera immediately so that Ian and Rachael could practise before they set off to walk the West Highland Way. They had lots of fun practising: Rachael is just so photogenic and relaxed and loves being in front of a camera that they both became 'experts' very quickly – well, at least Rachael did! The camera really does love her.

Rachael could hardly wait to start; she was so elated, she bounced with enthusiasm and Ian too was excited. They planned to end the walk at Fort William on Rachael's 10th birthday so that, if the conditions were suitable, Rachael would have the opportunity to climb Ben Nevis, the highest mountain in the United Kingdom the next day to celebrate being ten years and one day old – a fitting climax to another of our intrepid explorer's adventures.

So on April 9th Rachael and Ian travelled by train to Glasgow and then caught the local train to the town of Milngavie, the beginning of the West Highland Way. (Milngavie is pronounced 'Mullguy' – how and why is a Scottish mystery to me and, I'm sure, to many others. In fact, to date, no one seems to have come up with a rational explanation.)

They stayed overnight at the Premier Inn and Rachael had her first taste of Irn-Bru with her meal. After all, she was in Scotland and Irn-Bru is said to be

Scotland's other national drink … after whisky, of course! It is a soft carbonated drink – a rusty, bright orange colour with a distinctive 'iron taste' – hence the name. It is supposed to give you strength and energy but Rachael was not impressed. Urgh! She emphasised that she would manage *very well*, thank you, to complete the walk without drinking that Scottish speciality ever again!

They decided to go to bed reasonably early that evening as tomorrow was the first day of walking the ninety-five miles of the challenging West Highland Way.

DAY 1 – MILNGAVIE TO DRYMEN – TWELVE MILES

It was raining when they woke up but by the time they went down to breakfast, the skies were clearing and shafts of sunshine promised a fine day for walking. Rachael was amazed when someone in the breakfast room greeted her.

'Hello Rachael! I recognise you from your book. Congratulations you are a becoming a famous young adventurer.'

They asked her what she was doing and when Rachael explained that she and her dad, Ian, were walking the West Highland Way, everyone wished her good luck and a safe journey, to which Rachael replied enthusiastically, 'Thank you so much – I am going to love it!'

As they sorted out their backpacks ready for the day's walk, Rachael asked, 'Dad, am I really famous? I feel quite silly and embarrassed when people say that.'

'Well, darling,' replied Ian, his heart brimming with pride and love, 'You'll just have to get used to such remarks because you are a famous young walker now and you should be very proud of yourself. You know how proud we are of you.'

'Wow!' gasped Rachael, 'I can't wait to get started – hurry up Dad! Don't forget we are meeting Fiona at the start.'

Indeed they were. The previous evening Fiona Outdoors had phoned them to ask if she could accompany them on the first few miles so she could interview Rachael. Fiona is a well-published Scottish journalist, blogger and copywriter, who combines her work with a passion for outdoor adventures, sport and fitness. Obviously to her Rachael was an ideal interviewee.

They headed toward the little town square of Milngavie where they met Fiona by the splendid granite obelisk. It is carved with the thistle in the hexagon emblem and marks the beginning of the West Highland Way: Scotland's first official long-distance path. Time for a video of the start, although Ian needed a quick revision of the essential techniques – what a surprise!

Full of fun and mischief, and with a broad grin, Rachael pretended that she had the map upside down, and marched off in the wrong direction!

'Whoops!' she exclaimed with a chuckle. 'Wrong way! Let's turn round and go. Come on Dad and Fiona – keep up!'[1]

The first five to six miles give the walker a gentle but interesting introduction to the West Highland Way, being on easy paths through amenity parks and woodland, which lead you quickly out of the suburbs into picturesque countryside.

With Rachael leading the way, they walked along the path beside the small river – Allander Water – and

---

1 You can see this amusing and informative video on Rachael's website www.rachaelexplore.com

continued following the course of the stream until they left the buildings of Milngavie far behind. The air was filled with the sweet scent of pine trees and budding rhododendrons, and the surrounding countryside was green and wonderfully peaceful, broken only by the excited chatter between Rachael and Fiona as their interview progressed. Ian could hardly get a word in edgeways!

Interview over, Fiona left them as they reached the area of open rough scrubland, dotted with delicate, fluttering silver birch trees, that leads slightly uphill to rough moorland brightened with patches of brilliant yellow gorse bushes shining in the sunlight. Rachael was really excited by her first glimpse of the distant misty hills that promised further adventures to come.

The countryside on this first day was so varied and picturesque that Rachael was entranced by her surroundings: the first glimpse of tiny bluebell buds that shortly would become a vast deep-blue carpet and delicate white anemones nodding beneath the canopy of birch in Mugdock Wood. This delicate woodland was alive with birdsong and the hammering of woodpeckers adding their percussion accompaniment.

The river now became a tinkling mountain stream gurgling over falls and the beautiful views over the lovely Craigallian Loch were enhanced by the sight of buzzards patrolling overhead, riding the air searching for prey – their plaintive mewling cries giving a sense of space and loneliness. In fact, the abundance and variety of birdlife amazed them both especially around the small, quiet but charming Carbeth Loch.

Although they are very interested in nature, neither Ian nor Rachael are expert birdwatchers but they easily recognised other birds of prey, such as swiftly swooping peregrines and hovering kestrels. A lonely heron stood immobile, patiently waiting in a majestic pose for its fish dinner. Many more common birds like cheerful warblers and colourful chaffinches danced and chattered in the bushes while noisy squawking crows and rooks occasionally interrupted the beautiful music.

To the right of this loch, they admired the lovely view of the terraced Campsie Fells which always look like a huge layered cake with the strange-looking hill

named Dumgoyne at the end. Rachael thought that looked like a big bun!

When they reached the higher ground beyond the farmland grazed by cattle, Rachael was delighted to see that, through the gap between the rugged Kilpatrick and Campsie Fells ahead, she could catch a glimpse of the wonderful panorama of mountains that surround Loch Lomond. Her vision is so acute that she spots so many things we would miss.

'Wow Dad!' she cried. 'Really high mountains. Look! They even have big patches of snow on the tops. Now I know why they call this the West Highland Way!'

Ian agreed that the scenery was breathtaking and promised that it would become even more spectacular and challenging further on. They crossed yet more moorland where they were accompanied by the lonely mournful call of the curlew before descending to rolling grassland drained by tiny streams. Here the gentle but massive Highland cattle with their gingery coats grazed peacefully.

Rachael observed, 'they could do with a brush and haircut, Dad!'

Over the next few miles they walked on the bed of the disused Blane Valley Railway with lovely Blane Water nearby – 'easy-peasy walking' according to Rachael as she skipped joyfully ahead.

As they passed beneath the spectacular wooded cliffs of Dumgoyne Hill, Rachael reminded Ian that it looked very much like Applegarth Scar on the way to Richmond on the C2C – she has a wonderful pictorial memory.

Eventually to their right they spotted the white buildings of the Glengoyne Distillery. Wisely Rachael observed that if Grandma Joyce had been with them, she would definitely be visiting it. (How well she knows me – I must admit, I do enjoy a nice single malt!)

Just beyond the turn-off to the distillery on the Way itself, is a pleasant pub that has a miniature zoo in the garden. Rachael and Ian stopped for a quick meal and drink there.

Our intrepid travellers ignored the distillery and walked on through gentle pastureland. This placid countryside of green fields was dotted with small woods carpeted with early daffodils. These were just

beginning to open their enchanting heads and there were banks of shy violets and creamy yellow primroses. Among the quiet, grazing herds were yet more long-horned shaggy Highland cattle, such an iconic breed in Scotland – fierce-looking but gentle giants.

Eventually they reached the river called Endrick Water and its sparkling bubbling falls. Beyond the small, pretty hamlet of Gartness, they climbed the last hill on this their first day of the West Highland Way. Rachael was enthralled to see the stepped outline of the Campsie Fells again to her right but more importantly to her left, her first brief glimpse of Loch Lomond – their target for the next day.

On their way into Drymen and their accommodation at the Buchanan Arms Hotel, they had a really upsetting experience: a kamikaze ginger cat ran out from a cottage garden just in front of them, straight into the path of a car. One of the back tyres of the car went right over the cat, which miraculously struggled up (leaving clumps of ginger hair on the road) and ran away.

Ian quickly knocked on the door of the cottage and told the owner what had happened. The man thanked them profusely and immediately set off to find his reckless cat. Apparently he must have searched for a long time because much later, when they looked out of the windows of their hotel, they saw him go by

with the cat in his arms. They assumed the poor ginger cat had died because it was not moving.

Of course Rachael in particular was very upset as she has a naughty cat of her own at home called Mischief, who is always getting stuck up trees and into all sorts of trouble. Aware of this, Ian promised that before they set off the next day, they would find out what had happened to that foolish ginger moggy.

They were very impressed by the facilities and atmosphere of the Buchanan Arms Hotel, where despite the fact that renovations were being carried out, this in no way detracted from their warm welcome, great service and delicious food.

A rather funny and embarrassing event took place later that evening when Ian and Rachael tried to get back to their room. Ian led the way down a long corridor and through a door, only to find himself and Rachael among some of the renovations. It took some time before they finally arrived back in the sanctuary of their bedroom. Rachael did remind Ian (in a somewhat superior voice that many parents will recognise) that although he was a fantastic navigator when they were walking – no matter how difficult and confusing the terrain may be – he was no expert when it came to finding his way in buildings!

Readers of Rachael's first C2C will remember that before they started out from St. Bees, Ian got them lost in Booths supermarket in Keswick. Strange how children always remember your mistakes … especially the embarrassing ones!

When Rachael was snuggled down in her bed that night, she thanked Ian and said that their first day's walk had been one of the best ever and she had loved everything that she had seen.

'It was all so beautiful and different – so many exciting surprises! Can't wait for tomorrow, Dad. Goodnight – I love you,' she added sleepily.

Ian gave her a kiss and reflected on how lucky he was to have such a delightful, eager companion who, like him, had a true traveller's soul. Life was so good!

DAY 2 – DRYMEN TO ROWARDENNAN – FIFTEEN MILES

Next morning, when they went down for breakfast, Rachael and Ian were very relieved to be told that the ginger cat was okay. Unbelievably, it had escaped without any serious injury but had clearly lost one of its nine lives. That was one very lucky cat!

Rachael was really looking forward to the route this particular day as much of it is by the side of Loch Lomond – a fantastic introduction to the real rough Highland walking of the Way.

At first they enjoyed a picturesque ramble through bright gorse bushes and the chance to look back at the now distant Campsie Fells before plunging into a dense

conifer plantation enlivened by cheerful birdsong and the scurrying of numerous rabbits across their path. Of course Rachael wanted to chase them but they were far too quick even for her. Breaks in the forest gave brief tantalising views of Loch Lomond and, as the trees become less dense, they could see glimpses of the craggy peaks ahead.

Eventually they escaped briefly from the wood and Rachael had her first proper view of Loch Lomond.

'Wow, Dad, what a fabulous lake!' she exclaimed. 'It looks much bigger than our Ullswater but it's just as beautiful.'

She celebrated with one of her famous star jumps!

Now they had the attractive bulk of Conic Hill to negotiate. Fortunately Rachael and Ian were able follow the track that climbs steadily through the increasingly dense trees until they reached the end of the forest and the rough bracken-covered moorland beyond the high stile.

Walkers who choose a slightly later start date than Rachael and Ian are obliged to take an alternative and less spectacular route around Conic Hill, which is closed for a month or so during lambing season.

As they crossed the bridge of Mar, a footbridge which crosses the sparkling, tumbling burn[2] in its little gorge, shaded by beautiful rowan and birch trees, they spotted a pied flycatcher and several dippers busily bobbing up and down searching for insect larvae in the glittering spray. Rachael was enchanted.

Now came their first real climb of the Way: up some steps and then straight up the heather-covered ridge with its wide-reaching moorland views towards the top of Conic Hill. Of course, they deviated a little from the path, which passes just below the summit so they could enjoy the fabulous panoramic views over Loch Lomond. They could see the whole string of its beautiful islands, south to Glasgow and north to Ptarmigan, Ben Lomond and the Arrochar Alps. Rachael clapped her hands in glee.

As they descended the rocky and pebbly path, Rachael still managed to skip for joy. She would soon be walking beside Loch Lomond, facing more challenges.

They finally reached the shores of Loch Lomond, where a cluster of small, colourful boats was anchored in the lovely safe haven of Balmaha Bay. Much to Rachael's amusement, the path was now on duckboards at the edge of the loch and continued to hug the loch all the way around the bay. At the end, she had to clamber up some steps and climb the steep path that leads to the top of a knoll: a marvellous natural viewpoint called Craigie Fort.

'It just gets better, Dad!' she cried. 'Just look where the Way leads next!'

At this point many walkers would be quaking in their boots as they viewed the very rough path ahead – a series of steep climbs and descents, many of which overhang the loch. Was Rachael apprehensive? Of course not! She welcomed the challenge: that to her was *real* walking.

After admiring some of the densely wooded rocky islands nestling in the loch, they descended to the shoreline and walked along the winding woodland path. Under the canopy of lovely deciduous trees, bluebells, snowdrops, shamrocks and primroses decorated the woodland floor – it was absolutely enchanting. Along here the Way is marvellously managed and well drained; unobtrusive little stone water channels keep the path dry in a perfectly natural way. Rachael observed that the long right-hand-side path up her local Ennerdale Water would be far better if it was like this one – wise girl.

They thoroughly enjoyed their walk along this part of the Way which wanders mainly near to the loch side with superb views across Loch Lomond to the hills on the far side, dominated by the well-known anvil shape of the Cobbler: a truly aptly named mountain.

Underfoot, the path is rough in places with occasional boulders, gnarled tree roots and many short yet steep ascents where the crags fall sheer into the water – exciting but not fearsome to Rachael who enjoys every challenge – even the high

---

2 A burn is a stream.

ladder stiles that require energetic climbing. She pointed out to Ian some of the many nesting boxes that have encouraged a wonderful variety of interesting local birdlife in this lovely oak woodland, from which dominating conifers have been removed.

Eventually after following the Way as it squirmed up and down through hilly Ross Wood (which covers the promontory ending in Ross Point), they glimpsed Ben Lomond through the trees and, briefly, the Rowardennan Hotel, their destination for the night.

It was time to relax and talk about a great day. After a pleasant meal, they retired to bed reasonably early as it had been quite a strenuous trek of just over fifteen miles and they had yet another exciting challenge tomorrow.

DAY 3 – ROWARDENNAN TO INVERARNAN (ARDLUI HOTEL)

Next morning they woke up to typically grim, grey, wet Scottish weather. Huge rain-leaden clouds scudded across the brooding sky, driven by a biting wind that flung heavy raindrops onto their window. Below them the gloomy sullen surface of Loch Lomond was being whipped up into hundreds of white horses, which surged up the shoreline. In short, not ideal walking weather!

After breakfast, and suitably dressed in all their waterproof gear, Rachael and Ian set out on what is considered to be the most strenuous part of the Way along Loch Lomond. Its reputation for difficulty is due to the terrain: gnarled and tangled tree roots, large boulders and shattered crags, frequent streams and many steep and rocky scree-covered descents. Of course, they were hampered by waterproof trousers and gaiters, as well as waterproof jackets with hoods that obscured their vision. These combined to make the walking and scrambling very challenging at times, especially as the rain made all the rocky surfaces greasy and slippery and swelled the numerous cascading streams.

Rachael ploughed on undeterred, followed closely by Ian. Brief glimpses through the trees gave captivating views across the loch but when the wind and rain are driving in your face, the pauses to admire those views are few and far between.

Ian carried the video camera in his pocket, ready to record special moments, but the weather made it virtually impossible to hear or see anything. Whilst clambering up one of the many high ladder stiles, Ian dropped the camera and gasped in horror as it rolled downhill towards the loch. Fortunately Rachael retrieved it. Readers of her previous book may remember that she is very good at recapturing escaping apples and equipment, so this was one disaster averted, thanks to her swift reactions.

The rain began to lessen as they passed beneath the impressive crag known as Rob Roy's Prison. Legend claims it was here he held prisoners and hostages in a cave in the rocks. The position, just to the northwest of the foothills of Ben Lomond, is remote so there may well be some truth in this folktale.

Gradually the Way became easier as they followed forest tracks. They were able to enjoy some of the lovely fauna of these woodlands – lemony primroses, shy celandines and violets; bright green shamrock and budding bluebells as well as the cheerful chorus of birdsong accompanied by the hammering of woodpeckers.

Although they were more sheltered from the elements, the wind made far too much noise for any successful recordings to be made. Of course the momentary easing of the terrain did not continue as the Way continued to switch back between the shore and the boulder-strewn hillside, crossed by many tumbling, burbling streams and choked by twisted contorted tree roots. It was not enhanced by the distinctive, musky smell of the feral goats that roam this area. Rachael tried very hard not to breathe deeply and wrinkled her nose in disgust. Phew!

At last the Inversnaid Hotel came into view so, after admiring the spectacular sparkling waterfalls as they crossed the footbridge, they decided that they had earned a short stay for refreshments.

Fortified, they continued through the Inversnaid Nature Reserve where initially the walking was less demanding. However, as soon as they began climbing again, the path narrowed and became steadily rougher until it was almost blocked by huge boulders and overhanging crags and cliffs. Ian's long legs proved to be very useful as they scrambled over the many obstacles here. Rachael was undeterred and uncomplaining: this was just another challenge to overcome with her usual enthusiasm.

The Way never left the lochside for long and eventually, after crossing a whole series of fords – some quite deep because of the recent rain – they finally reached the little bay from which the ferry to Ardlui is summoned. Rachael was ecstatic to

find that she could raise the large orange ball on a signal mast by the jetty and the ferry would come to take them across Loch Lomond to their destination for the night: the Ardlui Hotel. What a great surprise! She jumped up and down for joy.

'Wow Dad!' she exclaimed in delight, 'this is so cool! What a wonderful end to a super day!'

She cheered and waved all the way across the loch.

Their room in the Ardlui Hotel was really warm and comfortable and the views from the dormer window over Loch Lomond and snow-capped Ben Lomond were absolutely stunning. As Ian said later, they were some of the best he had ever seen from a hotel bedroom window.

Later, when they went down for dinner, Rachael was amazed to find that two ladies, who were also walking the West Highland Way, recognised her and gave her their congratulations and best wishes for the rest of her adventure.

'Thank you so much,' Rachael responded, somewhat embarrassed. 'Good luck to you too and I shall definitely finish the Way. I'm loving every single minute – even when it rains and blows like it has today.'

'That's my girl!' thought Ian proudly. Nothing and no one was going to stop Rachael achieving another dream.

DAY 4 – ARDLUI HOTEL TO TYNDRUM

After breakfast next morning they crossed Loch Lomond on the ferry again, back to the jetty with its orange ball – what an exciting way to begin day four of their West Highland Way.

However as they had feared, because of the uncompromising leaden sky, it soon began pouring with rain so they had to struggle into their waterproofs once more before joining the Way exactly where they had left it the previous day.

The terrain changed initially to grassland grazed by some soggy-looking sheep and then the steep path led them up the side of a hill where they paused to look back on Loch Lomond for the last time. Ahead of them towered the row of peaks that rise above the top of the loch – Ben Lui, Ben Oss and Beinn Dubhchraig – their summits shrouded in mist, as was the snow-covered summit of Ben Lomond.

'Goodbye, Loch Lomond!' sang Rachael with a

regretful note in her voice. 'I'll be back one day when I'll climb Ben Lomond!'

'Why not?' thought Ian.

Now the Way was up a delightful narrow glen surrounded by rock-strewn hills with a hidden burn

gurgling loudly deep within a gully beside the track. From the top they had a splendid view of the picturesque Glen Falloch and the winding river with its succession of sparkling falls below. But it was not a day to linger in this fascinating wild landscape of hills, rocks, scattered oak woodlands and reedy bogs, especially as the wind and rain were increasing, and so they ploughed along as quickly as possible.

A steep stony descent led them to the footbridge over the Ben Glas Burn from where they could have walked into Inverarnan and called at the infamous eccentric Drovers Inn. Ian would have loved to show Rachael this unusual 18th century inn where visitors are greeted by a range of moulting stuffed animals, including a somewhat moth-eaten bear guarding the entrance and a dummy dressed in a red-coated soldier's uniform. However it was still quite early in the morning, it was throwing it down with rain and they had many miles to walk before they reached Tyndrum so

consequently Ian decided they should bypass the inn. But when he described this place to Rachael, perhaps you can imagine what she said:

'When I come back to climb Ben Lomond, Dad, maybe we can stay there? Please! It sounds great!'

She never misses an opportunity to suggest further adventures!

Although the next part of the route was shared with road and rail traffic, the noise was generally masked by the sound of the river as it roared down its rocky gorge in a series of waterfalls. The narrow path was criss-crossed by numerous streams but due to the incessant rain Rachael and Ian found that large stretches were flooded. They had to wade through, ending up with very wet feet as the water sloshed over the tops of their boots.

Did Rachael moan? Of course not! She is very resilient and has such a joyful outlook that she can find pleasure in even the most awful situations … like squelching along with cold water between her toes! Ian just trudged on doggedly – bless him!

Eventually they left the riverside as the path climbed up a small hill where a rusty broken-down waggon reminded them of the nearby railway. Then they had to go through the railway embankment via a sheep creep: not too difficult for Rachael but she laughed aloud at her dad who had to bend double and even then scraped the roof with his larger pack.

After another easy tunnel that went under the main road, they climbed up the very steep path, joining the old 18th century Military Road, which is followed intermittently from Inverarnan northwards by the West Highland Way.

The frenetic building of many such roads began in 1725 under the supervision of General Wade, as better roads were needed to move English troops quickly through the mountains to suppress the Jacobite rebellions of 1725 and 1745. Although the roads are known as Wade's military roads, it was his successor, Major William Caulfeild who completed the most difficult Highland roads that the Way now largely uses.

The path continued uphill but on a more gradual gradient towards a conifer plantation, which they entered by a kissing gate. At this point three paths meet – the one on the right leading to the pleasant village of Crianlarich, which is significant as it is marks roughly the halfway point of the West Highland Way.

Rachael and Ian continued ahead through the conifers, which, whilst affording some shelter from the wind, were so laden with water that huge amounts rained down on their heads at intervals. When they had initially looked at the map it looked as though the next two miles or so would be through this dense plantation. They soon found however that although the Way was very tortuous, winding up and down, it was mainly through more open woodland.

Finally they climbed to a grassy summit, a magnificent viewpoint, for straight ahead they could see the massive ramparts of snow-capped Ben More and views over Strath Fillan, the river and the viaduct that carries the railway to Fort William – their ultimate destination. However when the wind is driving rain into your face, admiring views is not a priority!

They squelched their way quickly down the path, under the viaduct, past the remains of St. Fillan's Priory to yet another riverside track. Further on there were many lovely waterfalls deep in a rocky gully surrounded by graceful birches and heather but these did not merit even a comment from Rachael or Ian; they had both had enough of the dreadful weather. As Rachael pointed out later in her only video clip that day,

'It just rained and rained and rained and then it rained and rained and rained!'

After trudging over twelve miles in relentless rain, they finally reached their destination, Tyndrum, and their accommodation – Glengarry House. They were absolutely soaked and looked like a pair of drowned rats!

They were given the most enthusiastic welcome and were delighted to find that the owners catered for their every need. There was a great separate hot drying room where they deposited their soaking boots, waterproofs and other wet clothing and were soon relaxing, warm and dry, enjoying wonderful hot drinks. In fact, Rachael had two mugs of hot chocolate, her favourite hot drink, which, you must agree, was thoroughly deserved. (There is always something very satisfying about giving yourself a little treat, especially when it has been earned the hard way!)

After a pleasant meal, they both snuggled down in their warm, comfortable beds and agreed that this B&B was superb – the best ever!

DAY 5 – TYNDRUM TO THE BRIDGE OF ORCHY

This was to be a shorter day than the last: only eight miles. And they were delighted to see that the sky was bluish – a kind of watery blue – but nevertheless with no rain and the wind appeared to have dropped. Magic! Better still, when they went to retrieve all their gear (which had been absolutely soaking the previous evening), they found it was all completely dry – even their sodden boots. That drying room at Glengarry was fabulous!

'It's as good as our drying room, Dad, at home at Old Water View!' Rachael pointed out and Ian agreed.

Old Water View is famous on the C2C for getting all the gear of every walker dry, ready for the next long leg over the mountains to Shap.

They were looking forward to this section of the Way as most of it is on the old Military Road, which, although cobbled and stony, provides a good walking surface; at last they would be able to stride out. The scenery too was reputed to be some of the finest on the whole Way, really wild with mountains, wide valleys, bridges and a splendid stone-arched viaduct. In fact the only downside was that there was little shelter so it was lucky it wasn't raining! They could hardly wait to get started.

As they headed northwards, the sun came out and it was soon hot enough for them to walk in T-shirts. What a bonus! Rachael skipped gaily ahead. They passed by a group of unattractive bright blue tanks that serve as reservoirs for the water supply for Tyndrum and on to where the valley narrowed so that the Way, the road and the railway ran close together.

Soon however the valley widened and they gasped with joy as the shapely cone of Beinn Odhar reared up before them. Their path led along its contours and an artificial terrace carved out of the hillside around this massive mountain. To their right rose a steep rock-strewn slope while to the left the river meandered lazily below. Ahead they caught their first glimpse of the mountains of Glencoe. Spectacular scenery and beautiful sunny weather enveloped them – it was the kind of day you feel just so glad to be alive.

The Way began to dip towards the deep cleft of the narrow valley carved out by the river Allt Kinglass, which is crossed by the railway on an impressive single arched viaduct with massive stone buttresses.

'Wow, Dad!' shouted Rachael excitedly, 'isn't it fab here? I just love it!'

Ian smiled with joy and pride; what a wonderful, happy companion he had.

Once over the river, they continued up the glen on the gently rising Military Road that wound its way along the rough stone-scarred foot of the bulky mass that was Beinn Dorain. This huge wide-spreading mountain with a gaunt, bare, rocky summit seemed far

Leaving Tyndrum.

lower than its actual height of 3,228ft. because it covered such an immense area, but it is actually a Munro being over 3,000ft.

As they neared their destination for the day, the Bridge of Orchy, the landscape became rougher with cliffs, crags and long drifts of scree running down the hillside, but the vistas ahead promised true highland grandeur and a fascinating following day.

The station at the tiny hamlet of the Bridge of Orchy looked like it belonged in one of those old-fashioned toy train sets as did the small cottages around it. They crossed the line by the subway to their accommodation, the popular Bridge of Orchy Hotel. Here they met a fourteen-year-old boy who was walking the West Highland Way with his mum and grandma: he was boasting about his achievements, which did not impress Rachael at all. His grandma invited Rachael

and Ian to join their party but she declined with unbelievable grace:

'I don't like him at all, Dad,' she said, 'why is he boasting about what he has done? He is at least four years older than I am.'

'He is probably scared that you are going to beat him,' explained Ian.

'Well, of course, I am,' responded Rachael emphatically. 'There is no way he is going to beat me – I'll show him! Just you wait and see!'

Ian had to smile – what a competitor his daughter was. He had not the slightest doubt that the next day that fourteen-year-old boy would have nothing to boast about. He would get his comeuppance!

DAY 6 – BRIDGE OF ORCHY TO KINGSHOUSE

After breakfast the next morning Rachael and Ian went to see the Bridge of Orchy to take some photos and a video of the beautiful view from the bridge as it crossed the river. They read the plaque there, which explained that the bridge was built in 1750 to the design of Major Caulfeild who, you will remember, took over the task of road construction from General Wade.

'Just look at that!' said Rachael angrily.

She pointed at the fourteen-year-old boy who was posing on the bridge whilst his adoring mum and grandma took photos. He had a huge rucksack on his back and stared at nine-year-old Rachael in a condescending way. Then she overheard him boasting to his mum.

'I'm going to beat that girl to our next stop at Kingshouse.'

Big mistake!

'So he thinks he is a better walker than I am, does he?' Rachael remarked. 'He is not going to win – I am going to beat him!'

Ian pointed out that it was not a competition but Rachael rightly responded, 'but Dad, he has turned it into a competition, not me! And, I am absolutely going to win, so there! He will soon learn that he cannot compete with me!'

Here we go again thought Ian – another challenge. Just like on her first Coast to Coast, Rachael was determined never to be beaten!

She noted with satisfaction that after having his photos taken, his mum took the big rucksack while the boy only carried a small bum bag (our American readers will know this as a fanny pack). Rachael, of course, carried the same rucksack that she had at the start.

Rachael had some videos to take so she lingered on the bridge. The boy took this opportunity to set off on the trail while she was preoccupied, determined to be in front of her by at least five minutes. Not for long! Rachael (and Ian when necessary) can walk really quickly so they soon caught up with the boy and his family.

It was a real slog all the way up the Military Road as it climbed steeply up through the pine forest. Rachael did not overtake the boy initially but stayed quietly close behind him, which made him climb quicker than he normally would. Clearly he pushed himself beyond his capabilities and soon he was exhausted and ran out of steam. With a beatific smile on her face and a small wave, Rachael nipped past him at the end of the forest and he never caught up with her again.

'That's my girl!' thought Ian proudly. He knew that this success would sustain her as she faced the 'delights' of Rannoch Moor just ahead, which had to be crossed before they reached Kingshouse.

From the crest of this hill, they had one of the most fantastic views of the whole West Highland Way. Although the summit is only just over a thousand feet, it is surrounded by a panorama of mountain peaks (up to eight Munros can be seen), with Loch Tulla and the wilderness of Rannoch Moor stretching out before them. The lonely cries of curlews drifting up from the margins of the loch added an air of mystery to the scene.

'Absolute magic, Dad!' exclaimed Rachael.

Ian had to agree. This was what the healing solitude of the Highlands was all about.

They zigzagged down the hill, past the Inveroran Hotel to begin the mammoth trek across the wilds of the remote, challenging Rannoch Moor. Fortunately for our intrepid travellers, it was warm and sunny with very little wind so they were not faced by the challenges weather can throw at walkers, like gales, driving rain, mist and boggy paths with no shelter whatsoever. I remember this stretch clearly, as I crossed this desolate moor in violent thundery rain, sleet and gale force winds that constantly blew me off the path into a mixture of deep bogs and pools of greasy putrid water; it is a day forever etched on my memory.

Rachael and Ian were so lucky. What have I said before? 'The sun shines on the righteous.' Well it did – all day! Although they were surrounded by peaty bogs occasionally interspersed with small clusters of wind-blown trees and rhododendrons, the path underfoot was comparatively dry, so they were able to stretch out their legs and make good progress. The Way began to climb steadily with grassy hummocks, heather and reed-choked bogs to one side and a plantation to the other.

Once clear of the plantation, they had a fabulous view of the awesome emptiness of Rannoch Moor; its rough hummocks interspersed with black peaty pools, tussocks of grass and clumps of heather, all surrounded by an endless series of hills. Here they stopped for a break to eat their sandwiches and have a welcome drink while they surveyed this unique, unforgettable landscape: a thin layer of vegetation resting on a great mass of black peat. Rachael searched for some shelter from the sun under the shadow of a rock where she cheerfully munched away. Even the most squashed and inedible-looking sandwiches seem appetising when surrounded by breathtaking scenery.

As the path levelled out, they were able to gaze over the wide expanses of Loch Tulla, the shapely hills of Black Mount and the glittering streams that danced down the hillsides. Hidden reedy lochans, sturdy patches of heather and deep squelchy quagmires were ready to trap unwary walkers who dared to step off the path. Everywhere there was interest and variety, and walkers who declare that Rannoch Moor is endless and boring have clearly walked it with their eyes shut or hidden deep within their waterproof hoods. There were a number of enchanting burns that galloped their way down from the now rugged hills and crags at the edge of the moors, like the lovely River Ba, which tumbles and sparkles its way over the rocks and under Ba Bridge – a favourite resting point for weary walkers.

Of course our walkers were not tired at all, particularly as when they climbed the next small summit

they could see beyond the endless moor. Their view was breathtaking, encompassing the outlines of the Grampian Mountains, the rugged hills of Glencoe and the famous cone shape of the fabulous mountain,

Buachaille Etive Mor: guardian of the entrances to Glen Etive and the gloomy valley of Glencoe.

More importantly for our walkers, at its foot nestled their destination for the day: the Kingshouse Hotel which is at least 200 years old and known for formerly offering shelter to honest drovers and less honest smugglers.

'Come on, Dad!' urged Rachael, 'Let's hurry – we're nearly there!'

There is no stopping or even slowing down our little adventurer. She was always so eager to complete each day's walk in a lively, spirited way.

'I wonder where she gets that energy from,' mused Ian proudly, not for the first time.

As they approached the hotel surrounded by protective conifers, Rachael noticed a small herd of deer, which, oblivious to human presence, were casually eating grass and scattered leftovers from the kitchen. As soon as they had deposited their rucksacks in their room, Rachael and Ian went outside to admire the wonderful views and look more closely at the deer. Rachael was enchanted and not scared in the least when one of the stags came up to her and accepted food from her hands.

'Magic, Dad!' she whispered.

With tears in his eyes, Ian looked at the rapt expression of wonder and delight on her shining face and knew that this was one memory she would treasure forever: a precious moment she could pluck out of time and press into her soul like a flower into a diary. Something that would always be there to look at, to touch and recall especially when, inevitably, in the future she would be faced with hard, lonely moments that are part of everyday life. What a gift!

Before they went down to the restaurant for their meal, they admired the magnificent view from their room overlooking the sheer dark face of Buachaille Etive Mor. It was crowned by a scattering of snow that glistened in the evening sun. To their right was gloomy Glencoe, which of course is well known for the infamous massacre in February 1692 when the MacDonalds were slaughtered by the Campbells, to whom they had given food and shelter from the blizzard.

This shocking episode is part of Scottish history and folklore. Today many scholars question 'the facts'. It is hard to establish the truth but the legend adds to the sombre air of the valley, which is hemmed in between tall murky hills. Often dark clouds form a kind of roof over Glencoe so that the road that follows the route of the old Military Road seems to vanish down a dim endless tunnel. It is certainly the kind of place that sends shivers down the spine of imaginative people.

When Ian and I, in different parties and – although we did not know it at the time – only a day apart had walked the West Highland Way some years before, we had occupied the same room – one at the back of the hotel, with a 'magnificent' view of the dustbins. The service we had was reluctant and the whole place was dilapidated. It had not improved, Ian noted. If anything it was even more tired and run down. Clearly people only stayed there because of its wonderful position.

When I wrote these words, I checked to see what current reviews said about the hotel: one that was posted only two weeks previously said that it was worth staying there for the views alone but the whole place was neglected, tired and gloomy. It would seem that nothing has changed – how disappointing. The owners were clearly missing a fantastic opportunity to improve and expand their business.

The fourteen-year-old boy and his family had arrived at Kingshouse an hour or so after Rachael and Ian, and the young lad did not even acknowledge her. Rachael raised this with her dad as they snuggled down in their beds:

'I wonder why he didn't even speak to me,' she mused.

'Probably because he is too scared to challenge you in case you beat him again,' Ian replied dryly. 'Remember, tomorrow you have to climb the Devil's Staircase.'

'Wow!' came the excited response. 'I can't wait!'

'I wonder if that poor lad thinks the same,' thought Ian sympathetically.

He genuinely hoped that the young man was enjoying the Way in spite of being humiliated by a nine-year-old girl!

DAY 7 – KINGSHOUSE TO KINLOCHLEVEN

After a disappointing breakfast where a 'waitress' watched carefully to ensure guests did not have porridge *and* cereal (only one choice was allowed), Rachael and Ian collected their rucksacks and set off in bright sunshine to walk the nine miles to Kinlochleven.

First they crossed Victoria Bridge over the River Etive and were astonished to see lots of trout swimming gaily below in the clear water. It would seem that they too, like the deer, benefitted from scraps thrown from the kitchen. Ian observed that fortunately most of them seemed too small to end up (immediately at least) in the chef's frying pan. Then they spotted a dancing dipper bobbing up and down, busily searching for food among the stones on the river bed: a lovely start to the day.

The Way now followed the original main road and soon they had a fabulous view down Glen Etive – a deep valley surrounded by wild mountains. They continued on an undulating path that wound its way alongside and above the main road with its noisy traffic and exhaust fumes. This was not their favourite type of terrain so they were delighted when at last they crossed a footbridge over a tumbling stream and began to climb out of Glencoe up the Devil's Staircase.

Rachael soon found out that this was not as fearsome as its name suggested. (The total climb is less than 850ft. and the gradient is never really severe, nor are there any frightening drops.)

'This is easy peasy, Dad!' she cried, climbing eagerly up the numerous and increasingly steep switchbacks of the stony path.

It became quite windy but this was a blessing as the sun was really hot – too hot for any energetic climbing. It was not long before they reached the summit cairn where they stopped to admire the view. They looked back over the rugged mountains of Glencoe then walked over the saddle between two peaks, where they were welcomed by a vast panorama of the majestic mountains to the north. They agreed that this was one of the best views of the West Highland Way. Unfortunately some of the northern summits were shrouded in mist so they were unable

to identify which one was Ben Nevis. On a really clear day you can easily recognise the hunched-up shoulder of Ben Nevis as even at that distance it rears up above the other peaks. Ian pointed this out to Rachael.

'Somewhere among those misty peaks is Ben Nevis, the highest mountain in the UK – it is such a shame that we cannot see it today.'

When Ian mentioned Ben Nevis, he missed the secret smile that crept over Rachael's face. I bet readers can guess what she was planning. Read on to find out …

The wind was blowing quite hard now and it was becoming chilly so Rachael donned her wind and waterproof jacket. Soon they began the long, slow descent towards Kinlochleven.

For the first time on the Way, they were disappointed to find that the scene was dominated by necessary industrialisation. The Blackwater Reservoir was constructed by thousands of navvies between 1902 and 1909 to supply what, at the time, was one of the biggest hydroelectric schemes in the country. Huge water pipes still carry water from the dam down to Kinlochleven.

Fortunately the delights of the surrounding hill scenery soon captured their attention. From a rocky ledge, which formed a ridge round the hill, they caught their first glimpse of the houses far below. They crossed a footbridge over a tinkling burn and followed the contours round the next hillside. The view from here was mainly of those impressive water pipes as they snaked across the landscape. Ben Nevis and the mountains to the north had disappeared behind the hills that bordered Loch Leven.

The path wound downwards through initially sparse woodland of delicate dancing silver birches and then in great hairpin bends as it descended more steeply through increasingly dense birch wood with a small dark reservoir to their left. This section gave our travellers a delightful contrast to the mountain and moorland scenery of previous days and was enhanced by the cheerful chorus of birdsong. The gradient of the track eased and became more direct and they had a close-up view of the six immense water pipes, which now looked strangely attractive, swooping down the hillside.

'They look just like one of those great big theme park slides, don't they Dad?' said Rachael.

Ian agreed – what a wonderful imagination his daughter possessed.

On their approach to the village they passed the now disused Kinlochleven aluminium shelter and processing plant that still provided electricity to the grid and straight down to the bridge over the River Leven bounded by spectacular salmon-pink and white rocks. Kinlochleven was originally built as a 'model village' to house the workers at the aluminium plant. They walked past really attractive houses, soon reaching Allt-na-Leven, their guest house for the night, where they received a wonderfully warm welcome.

After depositing their rucksacks and cleaning themselves up a little, they set off to find some food. They decided to have a pizza at the huge Ice Factor centre, which they had passed on the way in. They were amazed to find that besides a well-stocked café, the centre housed what was described as the biggest ice wall in the world: 500 tonnes of real snow and ice that rose upwards for twelve metres. Besides this giant, there were endless climbing walls of different degrees of difficulty as well as bouldering ones.

Rachael was so excited she ate her lunch far too quickly and ended up with hiccoughs! Ian watched her face: the eager, pleading look that shone in her eyes and heard her gasps of amazement.

'I don't suppose you would like to have a go on one of the climbing walls, would you Rachael?' he enquired. 'You've never done any climbing before.'

'Oh Dad, you have to be joking!' Rachael cried. 'You know I would absolutely love it! Can I have a go? Please, please, *please?*'

'Of course you can – as a special treat for being such a wonderful walker!' replied Ian with a knowing smile.

Soon she was kitted up and, with the help of an instructor, was ready for another adventure. Ian got out the video camera but she climbed up the wall right to the top so quickly that he was unable to film her first ascent and had to settle for filming her coming down.

For the next hour or so Rachael fearlessly tackled several more walls rejoicing in the new challenge. The instructor commented that she was a great natural climber and after this introduction to the joys of climbing, when she got home, Rachael joined a climbing club. She is now a regular climber with a helmet, ropes, harness and shoes of her own.

She was still buzzing with excitement when they finally arrived back at their guest house, after enjoying a super meal at the Tailrace Inn. The lovely couple there listened avidly as she described her fantastic experience and then questioned her about her adventures on the West Highland Way. They were so impressed that they congratulated her enthusiastically and the lady decided that Rachael deserved another treat. She disappeared into the kitchen and soon emerged with a huge mug of hot chocolate topped with whipped cream and marshmallows. Rachael's eyes were like saucers: two special treats in one day!

'Wow, thank you!' she exclaimed. 'I just love walking with my dad and I always get to do really exciting things!'

Ian watched his daughter with pride and reflected on how lucky he was to have such a joyful and brave companion.

Resting in their comfortable beds that night, ready for sleep, they both agreed that this guest house, Allt-na-Leven, was absolutely outstanding.

DAY 8 – KINLOCHLEVEN TO FORT WILLIAM

This was a landmark day in many ways: it was Rachael's 10th birthday and the last day of their walk.

Fortified by a large tasty breakfast, they set out reasonably early in the morning as they had fifteen hard miles to walk to the end of the West Highland Way at Fort William. They carried some delicious sandwiches made for them by their generous hosts and several other treats, as there is nowhere to stop for refreshments on this last section of the Way.

It was cloudy, cool and still quite windy so Rachael wore her jacket which, to celebrate her birthday, sported a large 'I'm 10!' badge. The first section followed the north shore road to the head of Loch Leven and then turned onto the old Military Road again. Now however the surface was more broken and stony and crossed by numerous streams. They walked through pleasant birch woodland and then the path began to climb quite steeply initially up a flight of rough stone steps.

The going became much harder as the road zigzagged up the hill to ease the gradient but at intervals they had lovely views through gaps in the trees. After a hairpin bend, they finally emerged from the trees to a breathtaking view of mountains to the south, including the easily recognisable Pap of Glencoe and the whole glorious vista of beautiful Loch Leven. They rested for a moment on the summit knoll to admire the far-reaching views and realised they had actually just climbed to the same height as the summit of the Devil's Staircase.

The Way now undulated down a broad glen bounded on the south by the hills of Beinn na Caillich and Mam na Gualainn and to the north the spectacular rocky summits of the Mamore Hills, three of them being Munros. They strode out westwards, occasionally climbing gently over foothills and crossing numerous clear bubbling mountain streams that raced each other as they tumbled down the hillsides. Rachael skipped happily ahead with arms outstretched shouting, 'It's my birthday! And I'm ten!'

This was the only sound that broke the silence and solitude of this remote high glen, apart from the occasional muted baaing from straggling groups of sheep roaming the hillsides and the haunting cry of buzzards circling above. Here and there lay the scattered ruins of several long-abandoned farmhouses with their sad rusting machinery, broken fences and old shielings that once provided shelter for clansmen during the summer grazing period.

Ahead the glen seemed to be closed in by the western hills but as they walked on they realised that the whole valley was just gently climbing northwards to more woodland. The path now became a rough broad forest track with firebreaks giving them welcome wider views of the wonderful scenery and the end of Lochan Lunn Da-Bhra far below. At this point they could have taken the quicker easy route into Fort William as the modern road follows the line of the old Military Road but Rachael and Ian were determined to follow the Way as it plunged back into the woods: no short cuts for them! They climbed over a very high stile and straight up a small hill, from which they had a wonderful view of the whole of

the lochan, surrounded by wild moorland and distant misty mountains.

Before they reached the dark conifer woodland ahead, their whole scene expanded and suddenly – quite unexpectedly – Ben Nevis reared up dramatically above the trees.

'Wow!' exclaimed Rachael, jumping up and down in excitement. 'My very first view of Ben Nevis! I hope it's fine tomorrow!'

Ian and our readers can guess why!

He gazed at her face, full of eager anticipation.

'We will have to wait and see, darling,' he explained carefully. 'It all depends on the weather. Look – you can't see the summit today because it is covered with thick mist so it could be raining tomorrow and too dangerous to climb.'

'It's going to be glorious!' was Rachael's response and with that she skipped ahead once more.

They were now in the dim conifer plantation where the stony path twisted and turned to avoid the worst of the gnarled tree roots and rocks. After crossing a wooden footbridge over a clear sparkling mountain stream, the Way seemed to head straight towards the foothills of Ben Nevis just as though it (like Rachael) was determined to climb to the summit.

There was a patch of more open ground before they re-entered the woodland where they were cheered on by songs from a remarkable number of chaffinches and thrushes.

The woodland was less dense now so they had enticing views of the surrounding mountains and hills. Soon however the trees began to close in again and the landscape became more rugged and challenging. This is one of the hardest parts of the Way: the rocky, twisting path plunged rapidly downwards towards a bridge which crossed the deep, boulder-strewn gorge of a mountain stream lined with silvery birches dancing in the breeze. Thankfully the steepest part of the headlong descent was eased by a series of wooden steps but still, great care was needed. For once Rachael was quiet as she concentrated on her footwork. Ian reflected proudly that his ten-year-old daughter was becoming a really skilled, experienced walker.

They were very lucky because, although extremely rough, the path was comparatively dry, so not too slippery. When it rains, this section becomes a perilous skiddy waterfall, which the author knows to her cost! Of course when they had crossed the bridge, inevitably they were faced with yet another undulating scramble up through the trees to a craggy ridge. However the gradient was easier and they were encouraged by lovely glimpses of rugged mountains through the trees, which made the route really interesting.

On their right they passed the remains of an Iron Age hill fort, Dun Deardail, from which there was not only a magnificent view of Ben Nevis but as they looked down Glen Nevis they caught sight of some houses that, excitingly, were on the outskirts of Fort William: their final destination.

The Way now followed a broad track through the Nevis Forest where they saw that many of the trees had been felled, leaving bare lonely stumps scattered over the scarred hillsides. As they tackled the long looping path that descended towards the bottom of the glen, they passed a man walking with his young teenage son. When she realised that they too had walked the West Highland Way, Rachael chatted with them enthusiastically about her adventures. Then, pointing across the narrow strip of fields that separate the Way from the slopes of Ben Nevis, she informed them that the next day, if the weather was fine, she was going to climb Ben Nevis with her dad to celebrate her 10th birthday, which was today.

Instead of wishing her a happy birthday that miserable man turned on Ian and accused him of child cruelty. What a horrible thing to do! One can only assume that he was jealous; clearly Rachael was far younger than his son and perhaps neither of them had the courage to tackle the long, long climb to the summit of the UK's highest mountain.

Ian was astonished – why did so many people choose to denigrate Rachael's achievements and infer that Ian was an uncaring, exploitative dad? No one on this earth could have given their child the wonderful opportunities that Ian had given Rachael while ensuring her safety – that was paramount. How unjust!

Rachael's new friend Bob

He pointed out to the man that obviously everything would depend on the weather conditions the next morning but, if these were conducive to climbing Ben Nevis, that is exactly what they would do. He added that he had vast experience of guiding and knew exactly how to keep his daughter safe but was determined to give her every chance to develop her skills and achieve all her dreams. With that, they continued on their journey towards the outskirts of Fort William.

Finally they reached the official end of the West Highland Way in front of the Travelodge on the High Street. Here 'Bob' – the bronze sculpture of a smiling, seated, contemplative man – marks the finish. Rachael flung her arms around him in triumph.

'This is my new friend, Bob. I met him at the end of the West Highland Way!'

Ian took lots of photos and made the video you can see on Rachael's website. Obviously he was really proud of his brave, adventurous daughter – what a superstar she was!

They walked into the centre of Fort William and had a snack and a drink to celebrate Rachael's birthday and the end of the West Highland Way. Then they did some essential shopping – presents for her mum and her sister, Catherine and one for herself.

Eventually they went to find their accommodation – Myrtle Bank – which had a fantastic view over the interesting bay of Fort William. They were delighted with their room, which was attractive and comfortable, and happy to find that their luggage had already arrived.

When they had freshened up, they went back into Fort William and had a superb meal before returning to Myrtle Bank. While they were there, Fran from Macs Adventure rang up to ask about Rachael's experiences on the West Highland Way; had she enjoyed it and liked the accommodation they had provided?

'Wow Fran!' Rachael exclaimed. 'It has all been fabulous and everywhere we have stayed was great – thank you so much. Oh, and Fran, if it is good weather tomorrow I am going to climb Ben Nevis with Dad! Isn't that wonderful?'

On hearing this, Fran asked if she could join them.

Ian pointed out that it was approximately a three-hour drive from Glasgow, Fran's base, to Fort William and if the weather was good, he and Rachael planned to set out at 8 a.m.

'That's fine,' responded Fran. 'I'll see you in the morning.'

It was very difficult for Rachael to settle down to sleep that night because, understandably, she was on such a high.

Eventually she settled, realising that, should the weather next day be okay, she would need a good night's sleep in order to be able to face her ultimate challenge: climbing the highest mountain in the UK – Ben Nevis.

CLIMBING BEN NEVIS – APRIL 18TH 2014

As soon as she woke up next morning, Rachael dashed to the window of their bedroom and eagerly looked out.

'Dad! Dad!' she cried, 'I can see beautiful blue sky and not a single cloud! Aren't we lucky? We can climb Ben Nevis today, can't we Dad?'

'If it stays like this, yes, darling – we can have a go,' responded Ian.

He was determined to give his brave, adventurous daughter the chance to conquer the UK's highest peak: 4,406ft – 1,344m.

They had an early breakfast and packed Ian's rucksack with all the gear, food, snacks and water needed for their ascent for although the weather promised to be sunny he knew just how long the haul would be to reach the summit. It would, most likely, take them around seven hours to complete and, as always, Rachael's safety was paramount in his mind.

He had decided the night before that he would carry everything in his rucksack so Rachael could just concentrate all her efforts on reaching the summit.

Fran did indeed keep her word and arrived at Myrtle Bank before 8 a.m. Rachael was overjoyed to see her; this really was a fabulous way to end her West Highland Way adventure by climbing Ben Nevis with her beloved Dad and Fran of Macs Adventure, whose sponsorship had made all this possible.

They set off through the quiet town and climbed easily up the picturesque Glen Nevis. Initially there was a nip in the air so they were glad of their fleeces. Ian was quietly confident that Rachael would be successful because, although the climb was strenuous, demanding a good level of stamina, he knew Rachael was very fit and had the necessary determination, endurance and tenacity to achieve her goal. She had proved this over and over again since she first started her walking challenges.

The day was absolutely glorious and soon it grew so warm that they shed their fleeces and continued walking in T-shirts. Rachael remarked how strange she felt without a rucksack to carry; she had become used to its comforting weight on her back. However the freedom certainly appeared to give her extra energy as she led the way with Fran and Ian behind her. What a girl!

They crossed the bridge over the River Nevis and, by Achintee Farm, started the real climb up the clear bridleway that would eventually lead them to the summit thousands of feet above. Originally the bridleway was built in 1883 as a pony track to provide access to a weather observatory on the summit.

They climbed steadily up the stony path with its occasional patches of scree and larger rocks but the gradient was never too severe so in beautiful sunshine it was an absolute joy. Rachael was so exhilarated that Fran and Ian caught her infectious enthusiasm and they all chatted happily about their experiences on the West Highland Way. They stopped occasionally to gaze back at the fantastic views behind them, which expanded magically as they gained further height.

They passed under the rugged face of Meall an t-Suidhe and climbed the steepening path as it turned left up Red Burn Gully. As the path swung round further to the left, the gradient eased somewhat and the climbing became easier for a while. They emerged by an attractive lochan nestled in the hollow below the majestic crags of the Ben; they were now halfway up the mountain.

They paused for a well-earned drink and a snack before crossing Red Burn and tackling the immense stony and seemingly endless zigzags that led up the steep mountain ramparts to the summit plateau. Not once did Rachael complain about sore legs, loose rocks or the steepness; she climbed steadily with a doggedness and resolve that amazed both Ian and Fran.

Although the sun was still shining brightly as they approached the last of the zigzags, inevitably because of the increasing height, the air became cooler and the path icy in places. Long tongues of glistening snow ran down the mountainsides from the summit blanket; it looked like a huge, white iced bun with icing overflowing down its edges.

Because of the ice and patches of snow on the main path, Ian led them up a more direct rocky route towards the summit plateau. This was beset with boulders and rocks at crazy angles but vitally, was free of ice and snow and so was much safer.

To their horror, an Australian man, who had been climbing all morning ahead of them, suddenly screamed, started sliding on the treacherous ice and snow and disappeared over the precipitous cliffs that guarded the summit. This potentially fatal accident reminded them that even in the best of conditions climbing on high mountains anywhere can be so dangerous; success can turn into disaster in the blink of an eye.

Once they had recovered from the initial shock, Ian, followed by Fran and Rachael climbed safely towards the bewildering wilderness of rocks and boulders that made up the summit plateau to see if they could help. They were very careful to avoid any ice and deep snow. Fortunately there were quite a few people already on the summit, some of who had witnessed the fall and immediately called the Mountain Rescue Team. One man, carefully anchored by a rope, crawled towards the edge of the cliffs over which the Australian had vanished.

He reported that, amazingly, the victim's fall had been arrested by a huge boulder. However he was quite a long way down and wasn't moving so this brave rescuer declared that he was going to try to climb down to see if he could help. Ian quickly took his Kahtoola spikes[3] out of his rucksack and offered them to this courageous man, who accepted them gratefully and pulled them on over his climbing boots.

Soon they heard the welcome sound of the Sea King helicopter carrying several members of the Mountain Rescue Team. Rachael, Ian and Fran watched it, mesmerised, as it rose from far below them to hover over the summit. Swiftly and professionally they sent down a winchman with a scoop stretcher and in an unbelievably short time the patient was winched safely into the helicopter and transported to the nearest appropriate hospital. The whole operation only seemed to take minutes: what fantastic efficiency! Our wonderful Mountain Rescue Teams

---

3 Kahtoola spikes are small crampons on a stretchy, thick rubber band and give fantastic grip on snow and ice. Ever mindful of safety, Ian had put his and Rachael's in his rucksack.

provide a fabulous vital service, absolutely free. They are all volunteers and complete heroes and I believe we should support them at every opportunity.

Mindful of Rachael's safety, Ian decided that they would stay on the edge of the snowfield and not risk clambering over the icy rocks and boulders that were rearing up through the deep snow around the ruins of the observatory and the Peace Cairn that adorns the highest point of the summit plateau. This cairn was erected to commemorate all those who died in the Second World War, a fitting site for such a tribute.

Rachael by now had recovered from all the drama and realised suddenly that she had actually climbed Ben Nevis. She raised her arms and shouted in triumph:

On top of Ben Nevis.

'I am on the top of the UK's highest mountain – I have climbed Ben Nevis! Hurray!

She was bursting with pride and joy, as were Ian and Fran. What an incredible accomplishment for a girl who was only ten years and one day old. What a superb way to celebrate her birthday and completing the West Highland Way – crowning her achievements with a successful climb of Ben Nevis. A perfect day: it could not get better!

Kahtoola spikes safely back in his rucksack, Ian led the way back down the path they had ascended. Fran and Rachael were in deep conversation behind him. Actually Fran, totally impressed by Rachael's performance, was asking her what she would like to do for her next adventure and informed her that Macs Adventure would sponsor her again – probably for the next one or two treks.

'Wow! Thank you, Fran. I will think about it carefully, I promise,' replied Rachael.

Ian kept looking at his amazing daughter: clearly she was thinking about something. He wondered if she was sad because this adventure was nearing its end; she wasn't her normal exuberant self.

Fran explained her offer to Ian and he realised that although Rachael was still watching carefully where she was putting her feet (like a true, experienced walker), she was making future plans in her head and was in a little world of her own.

Of course, he was right: Rachael was thinking back to all the conversations she and Ian had had over many months about other Triple Challenges – like her famous record-breaking three Coast to Coasts achieved by the time she was nine. What could she do that would be *really* adventurous and exciting – the worthy beginnings of a new Triple Challenge?

As she reached the bottom of the mountain path, Rachael's face suddenly lit up like a beam of sunshine.

'Dad! Fran! I have decided – I know what I would love to do next. I want to walk Hadrian's Wall because that is another Coast to Coast. And then I've always dreamed about trekking in Iceland and seeing all the volcanoes and geysers. Can we do those two treks, please Fran? I know Dad will love them too, won't you Dad?'

'Of course I will!' responded Ian with a wry smile.

He didn't really have a choice. His future was being planned by his ten-year-old daughter and he didn't mind in the least. He loved walking with his brave and amusing companion, Rachael – she was a joy to be with.

Fran couldn't help smiling too at how easily a ten-year-old could out-manoeuvre her dad.

'Well Rachael,' she replied, 'I'm sure at Macs we can work this out. When I get back, I'll put your ideas to the team and you know how everyone there is proud of you – our little adventurer. I'm sure you'll hear something exciting soon.'

Rachael thanked Fran profusely and gave her a big hug. To celebrate a successful day, they went into the Ben Nevis Inn for a drink. What did Rachael have? I'm sure readers can guess … yes, her favourite: hot chocolate with lots of cream on top.

While they were relaxing, Ian remarked, 'Rachael you've chosen Hadrian's Wall and an Iceland trek but that's only two challenges. I thought you were planning another Triple Challenge like your three Coasts to Coasts?'

'Silly Dad!' responded Rachael patiently, as if she were explaining to a young child. 'We have just done the West Highland Way, haven't we? That was number one, so when we walk Hadrian's Wall that will be number two. Our Iceland trek will be number *three*. We will have completed another Triple Challenge!'

'That's true,' agreed Ian. 'Why didn't I think of that?'

'Really, Dad! And perhaps I should mention it,' Rachael stated, a gloriously innocent look on her face, 'After Iceland I am going to Nepal to trek in the Himalaya with you. When I do *that* three times, it will be another Triple Challenge!'

There was a pause then she added, 'The last of those three treks could be going to Everest – the highest mountain in the world. Isn't that a fab idea?'

She really had been thinking deeply! Ian who was used to Rachael talking about her dreams and ambitions was totally astounded. Rachael had dropped this bombshell in such a casual way but then, she *had* just sent texts to her mum and sister Catherine to say that she'd just 'nipped up' Ben Nevis (as if it had been a walk in the park!)

Completely bewildered, all Ian could do was nod in agreement.

'Of course that *would* really be three wonderful challenges, darling. What a good idea!'

He and Fran raised their eyebrows and smiled knowingly. Rachael really was a true adventurer.

Did Rachael successfully complete these three amazing challenges? Readers, you will just have to read on to find out …

CHAPTER

HADRIAN'S WALL – APRIL 2015
AGED TEN YEARS

Early in the new year, Rachael received some eagerly awaited news: Fran of Macs Adventure rang Ian to say that they would sponsor Rachael to walk Hadrian's Wall and if she was still willing, they would send another video camera as before so Rachael could record the highlights of her new adventure.

Willing? Rachael was bouncing with enthusiasm.

'Tell her yes – yes! *Please* Dad! I can't wait to start,' was her fervent response.

Smiling, Ian told Fran that indeed his adventurous daughter was certainly up for it. So Fran asked for the dates of Rachael's Easter holidays as that would be an ideal time to tackle Hadrian's Wall. After some discussion, it was decided that the start date would be April 6th. This was perfect timing because it meant that Rachael would still be only ten years old when she completed the walk: two great achievements in one year. Amazing!

Ian pointed this out to Rachael emphasising that she would have successfully walked the West Highland Way and Hadrian's Wall in one year, reminding her that Hadrian's Wall was another Coast to Coast walk so at the end she would have completed four Coast to Coasts.

'Wow! Magic!' was the excited reply.

It was not long before Fran sent Ian the proposed itinerary for Hadrian's Wall. As soon as he received it, Ian posted the information on Rachael's website[1] so her followers would know what her next adventure would be and when it was going to begin. This had a surprising and welcome result: Craig and Brenda Littlefair, avid supporters of Rachael and frequent visitors to Old Water View, rang Ian and asked if he had arranged any transport to Wallsend – the beginning of the walk. When Ian replied that it was something he still had to do, this generous couple offered to drive down to Old Water View, pick them both up and take them back up to Newcastle to their overnight stay at the Hotel Indigo and onwards to the start at Wallsend the next morning.

Rachael and Ian were overjoyed and very grateful; they thanked Craig and Brenda profusely. Problem solved and another step towards Rachael's next adventure – the second of another Triple Challenge.

To help Rachael understand the historical significance of the walk, Ian borrowed a pictorial guide about Hadrian's Wall from the library. She soon had her nose in the book and eagerly read about the Romans and viewed all the photographs. She was especially interested in the forts so Ian decided that they would visit as many of them as possible. From previous experience, he knew that some of the best remains of forts are astride the Wall such as the ones at Housesteads and Birdoswald. For Vindolanda, they would have to descend a considerable distance southwards from the Wall so time would dictate whether or not it was practical to visit the site of that particular fort.

At this point it may help readers if I include some background information about this interesting and unique National Trail that stretches eighty-four miles between the Tyne and the Solway Firth.

---

1 www.rachaelexplore.com

The origin of the National Trail began in the 1970s when the need to control the overcrowding and frightening erosion at various sites became paramount. The realisation that Hadrian's Wall was a sensitive and fragile ancient monument that once damaged could never be the same again led to increasing efforts to conserve and preserve it while still giving access to the public: a massive project.

Its global importance was recognised in 1987 when UNESCO awarded Hadrian's Wall the status of a World Heritage Site (WHS) 'because of its uniqueness as the most complex and best preserved of the frontiers of the Roman Empire.'

It became the fifteenth National Trail in May 2003 so now, perhaps for the first time since the Roman occupation some 1600 years previously, it is a public right of way. However the necessary restrictions imposed by its status ensure that it is protected and no longer can the Wall be used legally as a walkway. The official path runs at the side of the Wall; the only exception being within Housesteads Wood to the west of the Roman fort where the public can walk a short distance on top of the Wall.

HADRIAN'S WALL

Built in the time of the Roman Emperor Hadrian, it was never intended to be some ancient Berlin Wall to keep out the barbarians – those hairy Scottish tribes to the north; that is a myth. It was built to control the movement of people north and south and allow the disciplined Roman legions stationed on the Wall to march out quickly to subdue any possible trouble.

Another advantage was that messages could be quickly passed to the bulk of the army in the forts to the south. The fortified gateways or milecastles are evidence of this and these allowed trade between people living either side of the Wall. It was simply part of a system controlling movement across the border but not preventing it.

Construction was started in AD 122 and was completed within sixteen years. The forty-five miles of Wall from Wallsend (Segedunum) to the River Irthing was constructed of stone and the next section through to the Solway Firth was initially made of turf. It is thought that the stone wall was probably around four metres high and three metres wide but it is known that later it was rebuilt at a reduced height and width.

FORTS

The Romans constructed forts at regular intervals along the Wall. Here they garrisoned the main part of their legions and all the support workers and artisans needed to maintain their army in first-class condition and provide a good comfortable standard of living, especially for the centurions and commanders. The remains of some of the forts lie astride the Wall, like Housesteads, which is thought to have been a civil settlement too and some to the south of the Wall, like the extensive, well-preserved sites at Corbridge and Vindolanda. There are also remains of other camps separate from the Wall.

MILECASTLES AND TURRETS

The fortified gateways were built every mile and so became known as milecastles. Two turrets were built between each milecastle as watchtowers so the whole length of the Wall was guarded vigilantly.

THE VALLUM

This was a deep ditch estimated to be at least three metres deep and six metres wide dug on the south side of the Wall with all the excavated earth piled up in mounds to either side. These huge earthworks are thought to have been dug to protect the soldiers manning the Wall. There still seems to be no clear reason for the construction, only several suppositions put forward by a variety of scholars over the years.

THE MILITARY WAY

This was a road constructed between the Wall and the Vallum to allow rapid troop movement. One cannot but admire the skill and dedication of the builders and sympathise with the Roman soldiers who manned the exposed Wall diligently in all weathers. Some of them, especially those used to the warm sunny climes of their native homelands, must have hated living in this cold, hostile landscape with its frequent wild swirling winds and incessant rain and, above all, the freezing wind-driven sleet, hailstones and snow of the icy winter months.

Perhaps, as was recently discovered, these particular Romans sensibly wore woollen socks with their sandals – a male fashion disaster today!

Rachael could hardly wait to begin this historic and atmospheric adventure: her Roman Odyssey.

'Just think, Dad,' she said, 'all the time we'll be walking where all those Roman soldiers used to be guarding Hadrian's Wall – that really will be magic. I wish the Easter holidays would hurry up and come!'

DAY 1 – OLD WATER VIEW TO NEWCASTLE

On April 5th, Rachael woke up early and as soon as she realised what day it was, she jumped out of bed.

'Hurray! Hurray! Today I'm going to Hadrian's Wall!'

'Can't you be quiet?' pleaded her sister Catherine, 'I'm trying to sleep!'

Her pleas went unheeded; when Rachael is excited, the entire world knows about it! She quickly ate her breakfast, cleaned her teeth and hastily gathered all her gear together. Ian watched fondly and reflected how different this was from a school morning, which was usually chaos. Not only did Rachael need several wake-up calls she always managed to misplace essential school clothing and equipment which Ian had to find and take into school later.

Rachael went into the breakfast room to make sure that Craig and Brenda were up. She beamed with joy when she saw they had almost finished their breakfast.

'Good morning!' she cried, 'Isn't it a great day? We'll soon be going, won't we?'

And she gave them both a huge hug.

'I guess someone can't wait to begin another adventure,' said Brenda with a knowing smile.

Rachael just nodded happily and bounced up and down. However they all had to wait until Ian had finished cooking for his guests. Some waited much more patiently than others. I bet you can guess which one was like a coiled spring!

It wasn't too long before they were all on their way to Newcastle, where Craig and Brenda lived. They had actually driven down to Old Water View in Patterdale

the previous evening and stayed at Ian's hotel because they knew Rachael would be very eager to set off as soon as possible the next morning. As they had arrived fairly late, Rachael had not seen them, hence her urgency to check that they really had arrived and were ready to drive her and her dad back to Newcastle.

Craig and Brenda dropped them off at the Hotel Indigo in the centre of Newcastle where Rachael and Ian were staying overnight, promising to pick them up next morning and take them to the start of Hadrian's Wall at Wallsend (Segedunum).

After depositing the gear in their lovely hotel room, Rachael and Ian set out to explore Newcastle and find somewhere to eat. The weather was fine and sunny, as it always seemed to be for our intrepid walkers. Eventually they reached the banks of the River Tyne and were amazed at the wonderful array of shops, displays, restaurants and cafés whose brightly covered tables spread out over the wide brick-paved Tyneside waterfront. It was such a lively, happy, bustling scene – just the place to sit and have a meal and a drink. When they spotted one of Rachael's favourite eating places: a Wetherspoon's pub, they went in and had a good meal and a drink – a pint for Ian and, of course, Rachael had her favourite hot chocolate. What a surprise!

Afterwards they strolled up and down in the beautiful evening sunshine admiring all the renovated and carefully preserved buildings that signified Tyneside's heritage of industry and trade and the magnificent historic bridges that spanned the river.

Rachael was especially fascinated by the Gateshead Millennium Bridge, which was opened in 2001 and is the only footbridge over the River Tyne linking Newcastle to Gateshead. It is nicknamed 'The Blinking Eye' because of its shape and when it tilts open to allow shipping to pass up and down the river, it does indeed, look as if it is blinking. Unfortunately no shipping needed the bridge to tilt open so they did not see it in operation. However they did walk into the centre of the bridge and took some fabulous shots from it of the water shimmering red and gold in the glowing evening sunshine. The wonderful reflections of the other bridges and buildings danced on the rippling surface of the river creating a magical scene – one they would remember for a long time.

Eventually they wended their way back to the Hotel Indigo and while Rachael had a shower and prepared for bed, Ian went out onto the balcony of their room, which was at the very top of the hotel. It was now dark so he was hoping for a view of all the city lights but disappointingly the view was only of a side street. Nevertheless he did get an unusual and somewhat entertaining view: the man occupying the adjacent room had not closed his curtains and was just about to climb into the bed as Ian turned that way, treating Ian to an expansive view of a large naked backside! He smiled to himself thinking how fortunate it was that Rachael was still in the bathroom … !

Waking up and ready to go!

DAY 2 – WALLSEND TO WYLAM – FIFTEEN MILES

True to their word, Craig and Brenda picked Rachael and Ian up from the Indigo Hotel next morning and gave them a lift to the beginning of Hadrian's Wall at Wallsend or Segedunum.

Craig and Brenda – at this point Ian and Rachael have asked me to thank you again for all your help and support. It made such a difference being able to rely on you for transport and enabled Ian to relax and concentrate on planning their route: you are really great friends!

Unfortunately the museum and excavated site of the fort of Segedunum was closed that morning so Rachael and Ian had to settle for peering through the surrounding railings. Such little setbacks however never dismay Rachael as she has such a positive attitude and the determination to thoroughly enjoy all her adventures with her dad.

She was thrilled to find just outside the fort, close to the west gate, the part of the Wall that had been excavated and rebuilt to a height of twelve Roman feet (three and a half metres) immediately south of the original foundations. It gives visitors a good idea of what the Wall may have looked like when it was first built as there is evidence that it may once have had a plaster render. Parts of it have been treated to show different versions of its construction. Of course

Rachael was eager to make full use of this historical vantage point to pose for several photos to mark the beginning of her new and historical Coast to Coast.

As they were about to start walking, a frog hopped across the path and croaked at them. It gave Ian an idea. Pointing to the frog, he spoke triumphantly to Rachael.

'You know how on all our C2C Walks we had some sort of counting competition and I was really fed up because either you or Catherine always beat me? Well, we are going to start a Hadrian's Wall competition now – counting frogs! And I bag that one, so it's Dad: 1 Rachael: nil!'

'That's not fair!' cried Rachael shaking her fist fiercely, 'There will be no chance of seeing any more frogs on Hadrian's Wall – you're cheating again!'

'No,' Ian responded smugly, 'I'm not and I saw it first so I'm claiming it!'

In high dudgeon, frowning and with head held high, Rachael marched ahead and Ian had to step out to keep up with her. She is never grumpy for long however and soon she became her joyful self again. In fact she had a secret little smile on her face because she knew that somehow Ian's cunning plan would fail, as it always did. Really, her dad would never learn. Silly Dad – she did so love him!

The first part of the path does not keep to the line of Hadrian's Wall as it is mainly hidden under the streets of Newcastle. Instead it uses the track bed of an old railway, which has a surprising rural feel as its banks were sown with wild flowers that now form a multi-coloured carpet. In glorious sunshine, Rachael was now skipping gaily ahead of Ian, enjoying the easy walking. She paused now and again to examine and identify some of the bright, nodding flowers.

Inevitably as the railway was originally built through an area of heavy industry, goods yards, sidings, shipyard cranes and gasholders are also part of the varied scenery. After they crossed a small area of parkland the Way divides so they turned left down the ramp and towards the riverside.

Rachael remarked that she was sure she could smell the sea and she was right because here the river is tidal and as the water was low they could see the skeletal remains of old wooden barges poking up through glistening mud.

They were delighted to spot many shoreline birds like waders, oystercatchers and redshanks while early butterflies flitted among the patches of birch and rowan on the grassy bank above the path. Enchanting: this pleasant scenery contrasted greatly with the landscape of endless grey tower blocks across the river at Gateshead.

After leaving the Walker Riverside Park, the buildings of Newcastle including St. James' Park football stadium soon came into view. Rachael pushed on enthusiastically past the area of new development named The Ropery with its bewildering variety of different styles of houses. Next they walked past St. Peter's Marina, busy with a wide range of craft from modest dinghies to grand yachts; then came several offices and the still impressive building that was Spillers Flour Mill. When it was built in 1938 it was the tallest flour mill in the world.

'Come on, Dad!' urged Rachael, 'Hurry up, please! I want to get to the exciting quayside part that we explored yesterday evening – that was so cool!'

And truly it is. This stretch of the quayside of the River Tyne is so full of interest with an enthralling variety of structures, that many walkers of Hadrian's Wall, like me, who initially hated the idea of walking through Newcastle, are overwhelmed. The planners of this area, in my opinion, have achieved a fantastic result balancing a pride in Newcastle's industrial past with a marvellous array of necessary modern facilities.

There are so many things to admire and examine especially the many famous Tyne bridges. The unique 'blinking eye' of the modern Millennium Bridge, the 1925 Tyne Bridge that looks like a scaled-down version of the Sydney Harbour Bridge and the magnificent historic High Level Bridge of Robert Stephenson which took four years to build (1845–1849). There are many more including the unusual Swing Bridge built by William George Armstrong in 1876.

In addition to the sheer variety of the architecture, the structure and range of building materials and styles attract and maintain your attention. All the needs of visitors are catered for by innumerable facilities including shops, pubs and cafés with bright awnings and parasols shading attractive outside tables.

Delightfully, many of the more modern buildings are faced with everything from brick cladding to classical columns, pitched roofs and stepped Dutch gables so they blend seamlessly with traditional buildings such as the Jacobean timber-framed houses of merchants and the exotic 19th century fish market. This has an intriguing carving of majestic Neptune gazing down somewhat smugly on some glum-faced fishwives gutting herring. This carving deservedly pays homage and is rightly dedicated to those hard-working women. When Ian explained about the harsh, difficult, dirty and smelly job the fishwives did, Rachael wrinkled up her nose in disgust but quickly affirmed that she thought they were all heroines: she would certainly hate to do their job!

Even the numerous information boards, strategically placed at interesting viewpoints, display exactly the correct balance of historical facts and attractive illustrations, greatly enhancing the whole experience, as do the exciting and diverse sculptures along the quayside.

Rachael was so animated and bewildered by the wealth of intriguing sights, that she clapped her hands and danced along, her eyes darting here and there in wonderment.

As the day was so hot, eventually even Rachael ran out of steam so they paused for a brief rest and much-needed refreshments at one of those attractive cafés – relieving their burning feet and sheltering from the fierce sun under one of its gaily coloured parasols. This was café culture more akin to a French boulevard than the grim north of England.

'This is all fab, Dad,' exclaimed Rachael, 'I'd like to come back one day and spend more time here. There is such a lot to see – I must have missed loads.'

She then added with a bewitching smile, 'And across the river in Gateshead is that super Metro Shopping Centre!'

Ian smiled, shopping indeed! His young walking companion was certainly growing up. Apparently shopping was now competing with her interest in history and scenery!

Throughout their quayside walk, Ian of course took endless photographs. Rachael particularly enjoyed posing for a special one in front of a superb tall intricate sculpture that is conical in shape and is presumably a tribute to Newcastle's former industrial furnaces. It is inscribed with a quotation from Longfellow:

Gleams through the trees: the red light of the forge.'

Gradually they began to leave the huge density of buildings of the city behind, although the Way was never far from houses. After a while, it joined the cycle track and footpath marked by strange tall iron posts covered with sculptures of chains, hawsers and other industrial implements.

'Goodbye Newcastle! We'll be back!' shouted Rachael waving madly as she raced through this pleasant landscaped area planted with a wide variety of shrubs.

'That's another place we have to revisit,' thought Ian. 'Great … we will be walking forever!'

Eventually this path led them to yet another one on a former railway track – The 1876 Scotswood, Newburn and Wylam line. As this part of the Way is higher up, it gave them good views over the open ground to the Tyne valley. The area around the track became increasingly rural with views out to the

Tribute to Newcastle's former industries.

distant hills, patches of bright gorse bushes and coarse grass, which was being nibbled enthusiastically by several horses. They were now following the Trail on the Old Wylam Waggonway, the scene of some of the earliest and somewhat hazardous experiments with steam locomotives – some of which had fascinating names like 'Wylam Dilly' and 'Puffing Billy.'

Soon the sparkling river became their companion once more but by now Ian was really suffering with his feet, his right ankle to be precise. It had been badly broken years ago when he fell down a mountain path while walking on the Appalachian Trail. The hard surfaces, over which they had walked for over twelve miles and the constant heat, had made it swell considerably. This was mainly due to the fact that because of the horrible break, he'd had to have metal plates inserted into his ankle and these were expanding in the incessant heat. His pain was becoming increasingly unbearable – he was in real agony.

You can imagine by the time he had hobbled past the Boathouse pub (unfortunately closed) and reached the Visitor Centre beyond the Tyne Riverside Park, he was extremely grateful to spot an ice cream van.

'Dad, Dad!' cried Rachael, 'Let's stop here and you can rest your poor ankle and we can cool down with a lovely big ice cream and a drink. Don't you think that's a good idea?'

Ian readily agreed and limped off to the ice cream van while Rachael took off her socks and boots so she could dangle her feet in the cool river and have a paddle in the shallows. She thought she had left her boots and socks in a safe place on the riverbank to dry but, as socks will, one of them escaped and started floating to freedom down the river. Fortunately Ian returned just in time to rescue it by means of a long stick. He wrung it out as much as possible and put it on one of the nearby bollards to dry while Rachael held the refreshments. They both perched on the bollards taking the weight off their feet while they devoured their ice cream cones. Then a curious dog started sniffing at Rachael's bare feet. Normally Rachael loves dogs – not this one because it cocked up its leg and peed all the way down her leg!

'Arrrrgh!' screamed Rachael, thoroughly and understandably incensed. 'Go away you dirty disgusting dog – how dare you pee on me!'

Handing her ice cream to Ian, she dashed into the river and washed her legs. Ian tried very hard not to laugh and failed miserably while Rachael continued to chunter, moan, shake her fists and jump up and down in anger. She was absolutely incandescent with rage. You could hardly blame her but she did look very funny!

Eventually she became more stoical as they got ready to tackle the last three miles mainly on the Wylam Waggonway. However, after she had put on her dry sock and struggled to pull on her wet one, she blamed the poor dog vociferously for her wet foot. (You will remember that sock had taken a dive into the river totally unaided by the dog!)

By now Ian was limping badly. Afterwards he said that it was just like walking on sharp pieces of glass that were digging into his ankle. Rachael was really concerned so instead of running ahead as she normally did, she stayed close to his side to give him help and encouragement. She gazed anxiously at his face and though Ian desperately tried to hide his pain, Rachael soon realised he was in agony.

'Don't worry Dad – it isn't far now and we have plenty of time so we can walk slowly,' she said sympathetically. 'You always help me so now I'm helping you!'

These thoughtful words brought tears to Ian's eyes – what a lovely caring girl his youngest daughter was. He was so proud of her!

Eventually they passed by the whitewashed cottage that was the birthplace of the famous railway engineer, George Stephenson who, it is said, was inspired by the early steam locomotives passing by to make engineering his lifelong career.

It wasn't too long before they reached their destination – the beautiful, picturesque Wormald House in the centre of Wylam. A lovely couple welcomed them warmly and suggested that Ian should soak his ankle in the en suite bath, to which he could add some muscle-relieving salts. Gratefully he took their advice and did find some slight relief from his tormenting pain.

After relaxing on the bed for a while, he felt able to go out for a meal. By now both he and Rachael were, understandably, very hungry.

On that particular evening, there was no place to eat in the village, so that wonderful couple drove them four miles to the nearest pub that was serving meals and returned to collect them later after they had a really tasty meal and several drinks.

Sadly, even the beer did little to reduce the pain in Ian's ankle and, Ian being Ian, absolutely refused to resort to painkillers or anti-inflammatory capsules: a brave macho-man but not necessarily a wise one!

The heat had certainly taken its toll on both of them: Rachael, unusually for her, was suffering slightly from heat exhaustion and needed no persuading to retire to her bed quite early. Ian sank gratefully into his soft mattress trying in vain to find a position in which his ankle was comfortable. They both lay there reminiscing about their interesting and challenging first day.

'Thank you for a marvellous day, Dad,' said Rachael sleepily, 'I hope you feel better tomorrow.'

Rachael crossed her fingers and wished and wished that her brave dad would be able to walk the next day. As she kissed him goodnight she gave him an extra hug for luck.

Ian was gutted: although he had indeed put on a brave face for Rachael, he was really afraid that, unless there was some miracle, this was going to be the end of their Hadrian's Wall walk. He was distraught: he loved walking with his wonderful young explorer, Rachael and he hated the thought that most likely he was going to have to let her down. Anxiously he clung to a little gleam of hope that tomorrow may bring some relief and luck. Please God!

DAY 3 – WYLAM TO CHOLLERFORD – EIGHTEEN MILES

When Ian woke up next morning, he cautiously flexed his right ankle and gasped as a sharp pain shot straight up his leg like a flash of lightning.

Gradually it subsided a little so he was able to gingerly lever himself into a sitting position with his legs over the edge of the bed. He gazed through the window and was dismayed to see that it was another bright sunny day. Normally he would have welcomed such ideal walking weather but it was not what Ian had hoped for: the sunshine and heat would make the plates in his ankle expand again. Soon he would be in crippling pain and totally unable to walk.

As soon as Rachael woke up, she immediately enquired how he was. As you would expect, Ian replied that he was okay. After dressing, Rachael took over the packing of their rucksacks to let Ian rest his ankle and she did a very good job. Ian smiled proudly; his young explorer was really becoming an experienced, skilled and responsible walker, apparently able to take care of herself *and* him!

Packing finished, they went downstairs and soon they were enjoying a splendid tasty breakfast together.

After breakfast, Ian managed to put on both of his walking shoes and lace them up but his right ankle was really sore so he realised that walking eighteen long miles to Chollerford that day was just not practical or possible. Above all he needed to keep Rachael safe so he decided that they would walk up towards Heddon-on-the-Wall, where they could join the Hadrian's Wall Path again.

More importantly, for most of the way, the trail that day ran very close to the road so Ian knew that he would be able to pick up a lift or order a taxi at any point. He decided that he would sit Rachael down and explain his plan to her when they re-joined the Old Wylam Waggonway.

They said goodbye and many thanks to their lovely hosts and set off back through the village. When they reached the Waggonway, Ian sat down on the bank and beckoned Rachael to come and join him. He explained his plan and bless her, although by looking at the tears in her eyes Ian knew how upset Rachael really was, she smiled bravely.

'That's okay, Dad, honestly. We can always come back and do the walk another time – it really doesn't matter!'

And she gave him a kiss and huge hug.

Ian was so proud of her: she was only ten years old and she had dealt with this massive disappointment with courage, understanding and love. What a lucky man he was.

As they left the Waggonway and began to walk up the path on the Golf Course towards Heddon-on-the-Wall some three miles away, Ian noticed that Rachael was dragging behind, head down. She was kicking her heels and grumbling and muttering in a very strange manner. Never before, throughout all their adventures together, had she ever lost her determination to reach their next destination. Readers will remember her valiant efforts in dreadful conditions during her third C2C, even when she was really ill, so why now? Ian was really puzzled especially when she cried out.

'I just don't want to walk – I really don't! I want to stop, Dad!'

Ian thought that she was still a little tired from the previous day's long walk in all that heat and was finding it difficult to get going. (How well all walkers know that feeling – especially those who tackle the long-distance walks – I certainly do! Some mornings your legs just seem to seize up and refuse to function, but with a little determination and persistence, you manage to get your 'walking legs' back and all the aches, pains and stiffness disappear.) So Ian encouraged her to pick up her pace:

'Come on, Rachael!' he urged, 'You are always in front of me. Hurry up or I shall beat you to the first real stretch of Hadrian's Wall just up there at Heddon.'

She trudged on not really making any effort. All her spark and enthusiasm seemed to have evaporated like the morning mist. Hoping that her mood was temporary, Ian kept chivvying her and trying to make her smile with some of his usual inane and cringe-making jokes, all without much success. At times, to motivate her, Ian was even reduced to speaking quite severely – a tactic he had rarely needed to use.

Then he realised there was probably something else behind her uncharacteristic grumpy behaviour and surmised, as I did later, that this was probably Rachael's ten-year-old way of dealing with the huge disappointment of having to abandon her Roman Odyssey. He imagined that she had lain in bed the previous night worrying about her dad being in so much pain and had accepted that they would not be walking the next day. She had convinced herself she must accept the inevitable so when it actually happened next day, she would be able to show Ian that it was okay with her. Bless her! She had realised that Ian would be devastated and simply did not want to add to his misery. Knowing Rachael, as I do, I'm sure that Ian's supposition was correct. She is a very caring girl who adores her dad.

Ian took hold of her hand and smiled down at her.

'Come on, love, we'll climb this last bit and reach the Wall together – okay?'

Rachael beamed up at him: 'Of course we will Dad. Thank you!'

It wasn't long before they reached the top of the hill and after turning right then following the road to the left they met Hadrian's Wall again. Fantastic! They were absolutely delighted because although the Wall here is not very high, this section is quite impressive being long and broad with the Vallum below like a deep depression. They were back on track in more ways than one.

Rachael was completely back to her old joyful self, clapping and jumping up and down and, amazingly, Ian suddenly realised that his ankle, though a little sore, was no longer painful and he told Rachael so. He had been concentrating so hard on trying to motivate Rachael that he had completely forgotten his injury.

They walked along thoroughly energised, enjoying the lovely sunshine: it was superb T-shirt weather with a welcome breeze so the overall heat was not oppressive, as it had been the previous day.

As they travelled westwards, the Path, now a road, dipped slightly as here they were walking on the filled-in Vallum and then actually on top of the buried Wall itself. All around them lay arable farmland, teeming with a variety of birds. It was a very pleasant stroll indeed, sometimes at the edge of fields. Towards the end of one of these fields Ian pointed out their first experience of a milecastle. Good imagination is certainly required here as all that is really visible is the raised, grassy platform defining the shape and a sign that identifies it as the site of Milecastle 13.

For quite a distance the Path now frequently switched from road to field walking with many gates to be negotiated with pleasant views opening out across the Tyne Valley wherever there was a slight climb. Although there was nothing spectacular to see, Rachael and Ian had a ball! All tiredness and pain forgotten, they laughed and joked, sang silly songs and went completely bonkers – a welcome release of all the tensions of the morning.

In one field they spotted some quite extensive earthworks and went to inspect them more closely. Actually they were the remains of the Fort of Vindobala or Rudchester, which apparently in the 18th century had been described as a well-preserved fort. However builders of the Military Road had taken away most of the stones and farming had destroyed much of what was left. Undeterred, Rachael insisted that she posed on one of the few remaining stones for essential photos because, as she pointed out, this was the site of a real Roman fort. Ian, of course, obliged.

The switchbacks continued but although the traces of the Wall were scarce and hard to interpret, the walk was really pleasant with grassy fields bright with many flowers. There were tremendous views over the countryside to the south and areas of deep yellow-flowered gorse and early flowering fragrant hawthorn.

In places the Vallum was close at hand, sometimes impressive but mostly hardly recognisable, while in others the Wall ditch to the north was more clearly defined indicating that the Wall was once again under the road. Further on the reservoirs either side of the road (surrounded by some exotic wild flowers that looked like orchids) gave them the chance to pause and watch the prolific birdlife on the water while drinking some of their very necessary water. And, of course, Rachael indulged herself with a chocolate bar.

In the distance now, they could see Halton Castle beyond an area of shallow quarries. When they reached the castle they were impressed by the building – a strange mixture of a gaunt medieval castle keep and a domestic yet stately house, built much later. The oblong pattern of the earthworks centred around its driveway represents the outline of the fort of Onnum. The striking gateway which marks the formal approach to the castle is the starting point for the circular walk to Corbridge with its fantastically preserved important Roman fort and military headquarters.

Because of their time and itinerary restrictions Rachael and Ian were unable to visit this significant site as it adds at least an extra day and eight extra miles to the walk.

But for readers considering walking Hadrian's Wall this is a fantastic diversion and one well worth considering, for it adds greatly to one's knowledge; there are many features of Roman occupation not easily seen elsewhere. All are preserved in such a way that it is easy to imagine what living in the original fort was like.

Ian explained all this to Rachael and when he added that I had done this circular walk to Corbridge as part of my Hadrian's Wall Path some years before, I'm sure you can guess just what Rachael said.

'Can we come back one day please, Dad and go there as well?'

Ever the competitor, she didn't like to think that Grandma Joyce had done something she hadn't.

The next section (in grey) is for those readers who may think of following in my footsteps by adding this circular walk to their itinerary.

FROM HADRIAN'S WALL TO CORBRIDGE AND BACK

Although the main object of this detour is to visit the important fort of Corbridge, its military headquarters and eventual development into a garrisoned civilian town, there are many points of interest on the way.

Take the driveway and then the attractive Leazes Lane, brightened by many patches of red campion down towards the castle and you will see a small church dating back to Saxon times which served the village of Halton. It is said that some of the large stones at the end of the south chancel are from a much earlier Roman temple. Once beyond the high hedge to the right, you should look back at the frontage of Halton Castle and you will see how the impressive stately house with its high fine chimneys has been 'tacked on' to the medieval keep. Past some woodland to the left is another grand house, Aydon Castle. Further on, at the foot of the hill, you will cross a ford by a footbridge and carry on into Corbridge, where you may be surprised to spot a pair of beautifully shaped bottle kilns and admire how the bricklayers managed to achieve that wonderfully sinuous shape.

Corbridge is a lovely, prosperous-looking historic town with attractive stone houses, many of which have delightful water features with taps, fountains and ancient stone troughs called pants. It is easy to imagine that possibly, in much earlier times, some of these troughs were 'borrowed' from the extensive remains of the Roman fort's water supply.

There are many inns and B&Bs in the town where visitors can stay overnight such as the Golden Lion Inn, where my friend Graham and I stayed. After all, if you have walked to Corbridge from Heddon or further still from Wylam, you may well be ready for a rest and on the next morning, you can spend two or three hours, as we did, exploring the fabulous Roman site to the west of the town. It is not a place to hurry round.

It is advisable to visit the interesting museum first as it does an excellent job of explaining the complex history of the site and its excavations, as well as displaying a rich collection of the many finds and providing superb informative guides. It is thought that the original fort was built by Agricola between AD 70 and 80 but, of course, over many years was rebuilt several times and extended to become an important military headquarters and supply depot for the soldiers manning Hadrian's Wall to the north. Later still, it developed into a large garrisoned civilian town with all the sophistication of Roman life.

The fort was strategically placed at the intersection of one of the principal routes, Dere Street, between England and Scotland and a line of communication between the Tyne and the Solway, hence its continuous occupation and development.

There are so many intriguing and fascinating remains of all the different stages of Roman occupation to be seen and interpreted, that visitors can explore for themselves. I will highlight some not to be missed: after the museum, it is advisable to walk down the main street of the site to view the remains of two large stone flagged granaries where the corn was kept cool and dry by a series of wall vents. One has a central stone mullion, the only one in situ in the whole of the UK.

To the east of the granaries, at the centre of the town, is the fountain house, the main distribution of the public water supply. Careful exploration will reveal remains of an aqueduct and conduit, water and aeration tanks, drains and troughs. In addition there is a large courtyard building thought to be the site of an enclosure containing the commandant's house and headquarters with an underground strongroom.[2]

The later development, when the site became a garrisoned civilian town, is evidenced by the remains of temples and many workshops with furnaces to house all the artisans working there such as potters, leatherworkers and smiths who used both iron and bronze. In general all glassware appears to have been transported along Dere Street from elsewhere.

Truly there is such a wealth of interesting structures and artefacts to be discovered that you could spend a whole day exploring and learning so please – do not hurry!

At some point you will need to get back to the Wall, so after leaving the site, turn left, cross the A69 and head for Sandhoe and the long steady climb back to the Path through lanes and endless fields. (A warning: if you are vertically challenged as I am, you too may get lost in the high corn – at one point Graham backtracked to find me as, to him, I was completely invisible!) Eventually you will reach the driveway to Halton Castle and be back on track.

Rachael and Ian continued for the next few miles much as before, crossing from one side of the road to the other, sometimes on the verges and other times through fields with the Vallum now generally more clearly visible to the south. Gradually the landscape changed from arable to moorland and, to Rachael's delight, was evidenced by a pair of partridges suddenly shooting up with a whirr of wings from the wiry tussocks of grass.

'Wow, Dad!' Rachael exclaimed. 'This is just like when we were walking the C2C on the path towards the Lion Inn at Blakey Ridge and all those grouse kept flying around and I chased them but couldn't catch them!'

---

2 Most larger Roman forts had strongrooms in which were kept valuables, artefacts, money for trade and to pay the soldiers and artisans. Also plans, maps and written commands and procedural instructions for the commandant.

'I don't think you have any chance of catching these birds either,' observed Ian.

'I'm too old for those sorts of things now, Dad!' Rachael stated emphatically with all the wisdom of a ten-year-old.

Now part of the trail was thankfully on flagstone walkways as the ground was very soggy and muddy and mainly in a straight line. Soon they reached the well-defined outline of Milecastle 24 which stuck out from the side of the road: photo time again. Further on they could clearly see the really deep Roman ditch to the north and enjoyed walking on the soft turf surrounded by the joyful chorus of many lively birds. Although some of them were difficult to see, the sweet song of the skylark, the call of the lapwing and the mournful cry of the curlew encouraged Rachael and Ian to push ahead at a good pace.

Later, to Rachael's joy, they finally reached a section where they could see the foundations of both the broad wall with a section of the curtain wall rising above it, and the narrow wall. They also spotted a culvert where the whole Wall narrowed and Ian explained that these were built to stop the water collecting and undermining the foundations of the Wall.

'The Romans were very clever, Dad!' Rachael observed. 'This bit is much more interesting and really feels like at last we are walking Hadrian's Wall.'

Ian readily agreed.

Being used to more rocky paths, they were happy that the countryside now was more rugged with a line of crags to the south and then magically the earthworks of the whole Wall emerged from under the road. Rachael clapped her hands – this was more like it!

The path to the right then led them to Brunton Turret where the Wall rises to a considerable height – six courses of stone, still standing in places – and the turret itself, in places, to an impressive height of *eleven* courses.

Rachael did actually count these, commenting, 'Wow, this is great! But I don't think I'd like to be in that tower in winter, Dad. It must have been freezing!'

As they looked westwards from the elevated position, they saw in the distance the outline of some houses and Ian, mistakenly, assumed that this was their destination – Chollerford. Actually, when they reached this point they discovered that it was the village of Lower Brunton with Chollerford some three miles further on. It was very unusual for Ian to be confused like this but he had in his mind the mileage of the original itinerary provided by Macs, which showed that the distance from Heddon-on-the-Wall to Chollerford was fifteen miles. This fact had lodged in Ian's memory but by the time they reached Chollerford, he realised that they had actually covered over eighteen miles because they had started in Wylam.

They walked over the handsome five-arched bridge into Chollerford and found the public telephone from which they had been instructed to phone the owner of their B&B to come and pick them up. They were both pretty exhausted, Rachael especially because she had started the day feeling tired and it had taken some time for her to find her 'walking legs'. She was clearly flagging and Ian was quite concerned about her – it had been a very long, challenging day in many ways. However when Ian went to use the phone, Rachael was absolutely furious.

'Dad, Dad,' she protested, 'We have never ever had a lift before – we are walkers and it's not right! We should walk to our B&B – we are not going to cheat!'

While Ian thoroughly admired her courage and commitment, he realised just how tired she was and walking another three miles northwards was simply not practical or safe: that would be twenty-one miles – a distance Rachael had never walked before. Calmly and sensibly he reasoned with Rachael, pointing out that when Hadrian had made his plans for the building of his Wall, he had not taken into consideration the needs of people like themselves who would be walking his Wall some 2000 years in the future. Hadrian had planned it to be protected by his soldiers who never left the wall but lived in milecastles on the Wall itself. However, now there was no accommodation on the Wall so *everyone* had to be transported north or south to their evening destination. It was not cheating but necessary and people accepted that.

He also added that he really did not want to walk any further because he was worried that it would make his sore ankle really painful again, meaning he wouldn't be able to walk at all the next day. (This was a masterful deception that completely fooled Rachael as obviously she was very concerned for her dad.)

She accepted, somewhat grumpily, that they needed a lift so Ian phoned the farmer at Hallbarns Farm who was very happy to pick them up. Whilst they were waiting for him, they walked down from the bridge to a wonderful picturesque little area at the side of the river where there was a huge sparkling weir. The water tumbled and frothed and threw up sprays of glistening drops just like diamonds hanging in beautiful necklaces. It was such a relaxing spot, that Rachael's innate good humour was restored and she became her usual sunny, happy self.

Hallbarns Farm was attractive and comfortable and they were welcomed warmly. After freshening up, they were treated to a wonderful home-cooked meal before they retired to bed early, both really tired. It had been a long, hard day for both of them.

Before she drifted off to sleep, Rachael said, 'Honestly Dad, I know we have walked a really, really long way today but I have so enjoyed it and we are going to carry on tomorrow, aren't we?'

'Of course we are, darling,' Ian confirmed. 'My ankle is fine now and we are going to finish Hadrian's Wall together – I promise!'

'Great!' responded Rachael sleepily, 'I always knew we would! Goodnight, Dad – I love you.'

'Love you too and I am so proud of you,' said Ian happily. Bless her, Rachael never heard his loving words because she was fast asleep.

DAY 4 – CHOLLERFORD TO STEEL RIGG – THIRTEEN MILES

Next morning, incredibly, Rachael was up, showered and dressed, with her rucksack packed before Ian even woke up! She couldn't wait to face the challenge of Hadrian's Wall and show her dad that she was completely up for it. All the tiredness of the previous day was just a memory and she was bouncing with enthusiasm again.

She shook Ian awake and, after she had made sure his ankle was okay, urged him to hurry up.

'We do need some breakfast, darling,' Ian pointed out, 'because although we have only thirteen miles to walk today, the terrain is much more challenging.

There are lots of steep climbs and even steeper descents.'

'Great!' was her only response.

So after a splendid breakfast their considerate host took them back to the Path. Again it was a lovely sunny day and almost as soon as they started walking, they reached a well-preserved section of the Wall that led to the fascinating remains of Chesters Fort. Magic! What a promising day it was going to be with endless exciting discoveries to be made.

This is certainly a site to be explored at leisure and Rachael and Ian did exactly that. Video camera at the ready, Ian let Rachael be her exuberant self: he was contented just to film her antics. Well, she skipped crazily up one side of the Wall and down the other and repeated this several times shouting and clapping with glee. Eventually she posed in a hollowed out space in the Wall that resembled a stone armchair. Unfortunately one of the stones she sat on had a pool of water in the centre so when she leaned back, her bottom got soaked! She leapt up screaming and waving her arms in the air while Ian laughed out loud but, of course, he kept on filming. They managed to brush some of the water off her trousers but she was left with a huge damp patch! Was she upset? No! She laughed as much as Ian did and marched in front of him proudly wiggling her bum as they made their way towards the important fort of Chesters. What a girl!

Ian planned for them to spend some time looking around the museum and the well-preserved remains of this site. Giving her clues from his information booklet, he encouraged Rachael to try to identify some of buildings as the plan of this particular

fort is typical of many Roman forts. The two barrack blocks are made up of several rooms designed to accommodate eight soldiers with a larger room for the centurion – an arrangement that has been copied by Roman armies ever since. As in Corbridge, the headquarters building has an underground strongroom while the commanding officer's house had the luxury of a personal bath house and hypocaust to provide central heating, both clearly evident.

When Ian explained how the hypocaust worked, Rachael marvelled that 2000 years ago those clever Romans invented central heating! She thought the main bath house was best as its walls rose above her Dad's height and there were changing rooms and a number of latrines.

'Wow Dad!' exclaimed Rachael, 'I would not like to use the toilets here – it would be very cold and windy and, I bet, very smelly too!'

'Yes, it would,' agreed Ian. 'And to think, they didn't have toilet paper.'

'What did they use then?' asked Rachael full of curiosity.

When Ian, with a wicked smile, informed her that the Romans used a sponge on a stick, she gasped and shuddered.

'Urgh, Dad! How gross! I hope they didn't share it!'

Ian didn't reply – he had a huge grin on his face and Rachael's eyes were like saucers.

Before they left the site, they walked down the river to the remains of the Roman bridge and guardhouse.

'That was all really cool, Dad!' Rachael enthused. 'What a lot of great things to see and we've only just started our day!' She was buzzing.

They continued to follow the Path past farms, barns and single-storey village houses, sometimes on quiet lanes and other times through fields. For a while they left the Wall itself and followed a sunken track past a prominent tree, a quarry and earthworks of the Wall ditch.

The next section of their walk was within the Northumberland National Park and soon, ahead, they could see on the approach to Black Carts, the first really long section of Hadrian's Wall they'd seen for some time, turrets and the deep V shape of the Wall ditch. As they climbed up to the trig point – a fantastic viewpoint over miles of open country – the stonework of the Wall disappeared and became a big hump in the ground.

Before Milecastle 30 however, the Wall reappeared so they followed it southwards along the natural contours of the land. As they reached the road they could see the Vallum again as the Wall here is built on an outcrop of limestone and the first part of the Wall ditch to the north had to be cut through solid rock. This proved to be too difficult even for the Romans so for a while the construction of the Wall ditch was abandoned. This spectacular rocky area is rightly known as Limestone Corner.

Their next highlight was the site of the fort of Brocolitia, which is unusual in that it was clearly built after Hadrian's Wall, being perched on top of the infilled Vallum. Near to this is the gloomy windowless temple to the Persian god Mithras, which would have had statues of the god and lamps inside – now there are

effective reproductions in situ. There is also a well, sacred to the goddess Coventina. The whole site has an air of mystery and intrigue.

Like Ian, many years before I took several interesting photos but left my camera behind on one of the statues. I didn't miss it until Graham and I had walked a further mile along the Wall. This meant backtracking to retrieve it – fortunately it was still there. However this added a couple of miles to my walk while Graham basked in the sunshine enjoying a drink and a snack. I did wonder at the time where chivalry had gone!

The undulating upland miles over wild rough grassland sped by with Rachael skipping and singing, full of joy and accompanied by the musical calls of skylark, curlews and lapwings. From their lofty track, they could often see the Military Road below. This provides a smooth, comparatively level path so Rachael and Ian could see several walkers taking advantage of this easier ground.

'They are cheating, Dad!' protested Rachael. 'We aren't going to do that, are we?'

Ian smiled – he would not have dared to suggest as much to Rachael!

Later, they paused briefly at Milecastle 33 as this has been partially restored, with new turves protecting the masonry, before reaching the lovely woods perched above the rocky slopes of the spectacular Sewingshields Crags. Initially it is a stiff climb but well worthwhile for the fabulous panoramic views the crags afford.

As they gazed in wonder at the magnificent scenery, a welcome breeze cooled them down. Ian reflected how different the conditions had been for him some ten years before when he had walked Hadrian's Wall in thirty hours, training for his forthcoming attempt at completing the 2000-mile Appalachian Trail down the eastern side of the USA.

They sat down for brief well-earned rest and refreshments and while Rachael munched happily on a chocolate bar, Ian told Rachael of his horrible experiences at this very spot in spring 2006.

He had already completed the 1100 miles of Land's End to John O'Groats as part of his training but decided that he would walk Hadrian's Wall in as little time as possible carrying the 30lb pack he would have to carry throughout the Appalachian Trail. (His friends in the Lake District called this pack 'the giant tea urn' because it had a silver waterproof cover and from the back it did indeed look as if Ian was carrying a huge tea urn on his back.)

Ian deliberately chose the Hadrian's Wall Path because it was undulating and exposed in places but most importantly there was no accommodation on the Wall itself so was very similar in that aspect to the Appalachian Trail.

Previously he had explained to his wife that in the interests of safety he needed a good reliable waterproof jacket and had purchased a splendid black Berghaus jacket that was completely waterproof and Gore-Tex lined to prevent sweating. It had cost £200. She had not been impressed at that huge cost because, not being a walker herself, she had little understanding of necessary safety measures.

Ian had started off from Wallsend a little later than planned so by the time he reached the top of Sewingshields Crags, it was beginning to grow dark, the rain suddenly started to pour down and the wind increased in its ferocity. Quickly he struggled to extricate his Berghaus jacket from his rucksack as, although he is a pretty big, strong man, the howling wind was threatening to blow him off his feet and the rain hitting him in the face was blinding him. Just as he was holding up his precious jacket in order to shake it out, a huge gust of wind viciously snatched it out of his hands and it spiralled up into the sky like a massive black kite. The last he saw of it was a tiny black speck as it disappeared towards Scotland: poor Ian had never even worn the jacket, as he hadn't been caught out in the rain before! There was no way he could follow it as the weather was growing increasingly worse and he was on the top of very steep cliffs in poor visibility.

Very soon he was absolutely soaking wet through and his teeth were beginning to chatter, he was frozen. He knew that soon he could become hypothermic,

so sensibly he decided that he must seek shelter back in the woods below the crags. He found some protection from the wind and rain under a stunted but thick tree and quickly donned all the warm clothing from his rucksack. Of course, he did not have another waterproof so he snuggled beside his rucksack and stopped his watch as he settled down for a cold, wet and uncomfortable night.

He woke very early next morning and was delighted to find that the rain had abated. After a snack and a drink, he set off southwards to try and find a shop in the distant village of Haltwhistle, where he hoped he could buy a waterproof in case the dreadful weather of the previous evening returned. After walking some ten miles, all he could find was a shop that sold cycling gear so he had no choice but to buy a £2.99 brilliant yellow waterproof cape. Well, at least, no one could miss him in that!

Somewhat shamefaced, he hid the violently coloured cape in his rucksack, started his stopwatch again and continued his walk back to Hadrian's Wall. However this enforced detour added an extra twenty miles to the overall distance.

In spite of all his mishaps, he actually completed the walk in thirty hours, a magnificent achievement considering the circumstances.

Actually he never used that abominable yellow cape but bought another Berghaus jacket like the previous one he'd never had the chance to wear. He speculated that it was now probably adorning the back of some very fortunate Scotsman: good luck to him!

'Your mum was not very pleased with me when she realised I had spent £402.99 (£200 + £200 + £2.99) on waterproofs,' Ian now confessed to Rachael.

'Well she wouldn't be, would she?' responded Rachael thoughtfully. 'Mum still doesn't understand how vital proper equipment is when you are doing long walks. You taught me that didn't you, Dad?'

Ian just nodded: how wise and knowledgeable his lovely young companion was becoming.

'And,' said Rachael, looking up at Ian with a mischievous grin on her face, 'Mum spends that much on shoes anyway!'

'Well, you'd better not let Grandma Joyce's waterproof blow away,' added Ian with a straight face. 'That cost a fortune and although she might be little she can get really cross!'

Because she was growing so fast, since her third C2C, sensibly Rachael had always borrowed some of my equipment for her walks.

'Don't be silly, Dad!' Rachael stated adamantly, 'Grandma Joyce loves me. Besides, she is a walker and if it was an accident she would understand. Come on we need to get going!'

So that was that – suitably chastised but with a wry grin on his face, Ian led the way down the steep path from the crags. His attempt to wind Rachael up had failed miserably.

Soon they were back on the Wall itself and at Milecastle 35. They were pleased to find that the outline of this was clear and the rooms within well delineated. Unlike most milecastles, this had no gateway to the north, as that would have led to a suicidal fall down those crags.

Next they had the joy of beginning to march ahead along a splendid section of the Wall as they climbed to another trig point and viewed the dramatic scene ahead. The countryside was open and beautiful with the picturesque Broomlee Lough nestled in a fold of the land. The Wall itself protected by the crags to the north, snaked away into the distance, following the natural defences of the higher ground. Of course, this meant that the next few miles would have a switchback character: dropping down steeply into hollows and then climbing just as steeply back up the other side – a real rollercoaster of a path. Undeterred, Rachael clapped her hands in glee: this was her sort of walking country.

Just past Knag Burn, the site of one of the main gateways through the wall, they were thrilled to realise that they had reached Housesteads Fort – one of the most popular places on the Wall. It is a magnificent site, actually on the Wall itself and looks exactly how you would expect a fort to look: it has well-defined ramparts and possibly the best preserved remains of a whole hypocaust system. The Romans called

Housesteads 'Vercovicium' – 'the place of good fighters' – and you can imagine that only the toughest troops would be sent to this bleak, isolated spot.

Rachael was entranced and Ian kept the camera clicking. She eagerly explored the site but then, like all children, she had a fit of giggles when she spotted the communal latrines. It is obvious that these were very sophisticated, with water fed from a cistern to a channel at foot level to wash the 'business' away through a duct in the walls. Housesteads was obviously an extensive fort with many streets, gates and what is thought to be the remains of a hospital.

The section of the walk beyond Housesteads is the only place where walking on the wall is actually allowed. Well, you can imagine Rachael's delight – she walked on it, skipped and danced on it, sat on it and bobbed up and down like a jack-in-a box! Ian was entranced as he proudly filmed all her antics. She was the epitome of life and joy, she would have made the most miserable person smile and feel happy.

This whole area is stunning: the surrounding woods are beautiful, the Housesteads Crags spectacular and there is the interesting archway (probably originally some fifteen feet high) of Milecastle 37 built by the Second Legion.

Many more climbs and descents followed but at least these were easier as they have rough stone steps. Although this part of Hadrian's Wall Path is rough and challenging, there is so much of interest (and awesome views) that your mind is full of wonder; you scarcely realise all the distance you have covered and the obstacles you have overcome.

Rachael and Ian climbed to the brow of the next steep hill and were stunned by the view over Crag Lough: the sheer crags drop spectacularly straight into the shining water. Eagerly they followed the path down to the side of the lake then climbed up through the woods to a truly beautiful view over the water. The wonderful tranquillity of this spot encouraged them to pause for a while to watch a swan lazily drifting across the lake and marvel at buzzards and other birds of prey hovering high over the rough landscape.

Thoroughly enlivened, they descended to the famous
Sycamore Gap marked by that iconic tree. Of course,
there were lots of photos to be taken including some
with Rachael posing with arms raised up in triumph.
Then they faced yet more steep climbs and sharp
descents as they ignored the easier route of the old
Military Road.

They added 'Castle Nick' (Milecastle 39) to their
list of achievements and then came one of the steepest
descents of the whole Wall, winding down the engineered rough stone path to Peel Gap and a sturdy turret.
A little way further they reached the car park at Steel
Rigg where they left the Wall and turned south towards
the hamlet of Once Brewed and stopped at the pub
there bizarrely called the Twice Brewed Inn. Strangely
there were no cars parked there and the whole place
looked deserted and ghostly, so you can imagine Ian
and Rachael's surprise when they went into the pub to
find it packed with drinkers and diners. Where had
they come from?

After buying a couple of Cokes for Rachael and
himself, Ian phoned the owners of their accommodation, Hunter Crook Lodge at Bardon Mill, to ask
for a lift. For once, Rachael did not protest but eagerly
climbed into the car when their lady host, Julia
arrived. It had been a fabulous day but a hard one
too and she had realised that everyone walking the
Wall had to take advantage of lifts, as much of the
available accommodation was miles away from the
line of the Wall.

Hunter Crook Lodge was outstanding: the setting,
the rooms, food and facilities were out of this world.
And there was a hot tub … oh dear! When packing
for their walk, Rachael had wanted to include her
swimming costume but Ian had said there was absolutely nowhere on Hadrian's Wall where she would be
able to use it so it had been left at home.

'Dad!' said Rachael crossly with hands on her
hips, 'This is the second time I'm very upset that you
banned me from bringing my swimming costume
because – if you remember – there was a pool near the
Hotel Indigo in Newcastle and now I can't go in that
superb hot tub either! It's not fair!'

'Sorry darling,' replied Ian. 'I really didn't think that you needed one – I'm truly sorry. We'll bring it next time.'

As always, Rachael soon recovered from her grumps and was delighted when she discovered that Hunter Crook Lodge was on a smallholding: that meant animals! After a quick shower and tidy up, she dashed to the bottom of the garden to explore the wooden enclosures from which exciting noises were coming.

She quickly made friends with some of the animals: the happy clucking free-range hens, noisy ducks and the enchanting gambolling spring lambs. Even though she must have been starving, Ian had to call her in for her dinner.

Seeing that Rachael loved animals so much, Julia suggested that when they had eaten, Rachael might like to go into the pens and play with the animals (as long as she cleaned her shoes before coming back into the house) – they were all friendly. Might like? Rachael was ecstatic!

All the way through the wonderful meal she chatted excitedly to Ian. Among other things, she told him that when she grew up, she was going to work with animals.

'Well, if you want to do that,' Ian explained, thinking that Rachael meant she wanted to become a vet, 'there is a problem because you do not like school very much and it will mean that you will have to stay there until you are eighteen and then spend seven years studying at university.'

'I'm not doing that!' was her rapid response. 'I only want to be with animals.'

'But darling,' Ian explained patiently, 'you really will have to train a very long time.'

'Well I will marry a farmer then!' Rachael stated emphatically, tucking hungrily into her dinner. Ian was gobsmacked; he hadn't expected that remark. Rachael certainly had her own way of ending a discussion.

The meal was outstanding – really tasty and beautifully presented. It had been cooked by Robin, Julia's husband, who loved to use the fresh produce from their smallholding. Apparently he was a former professional chef with an absolute passion for food. Early in his career, he had won the prestigious Chef of the Year competition so no wonder the meal was fabulous!

As soon as she had finished hers, Rachael asked to be excused so she could play with the animals. She rushed down the garden and climbed into the pens while Ian enjoyed a welcome glass of wine and relaxed gazing over the lovely countryside. From the squeals of delight and laughter, Ian knew his daughter was having a ball. What a wonderful end to a fantastic day!

When it grew darker, Ian called Rachael in. They soon went to bed as by now they were both really tired and they had over fifteen difficult miles to walk the next day.

Rachael was soon fast asleep but Ian lay awake for a while thinking about plans for the following day; what should they do? He knew that the superb fort of Vindolanda was nearby, a site well worth visiting but he eventually decided that on this occasion they would give it a miss. To do the fort justice, they would need to spend a couple of hours exploring it and it would also involve a considerable detour. Rachael was only ten and they still had many hard, undulating miles to walk on the Wall. Ian rightly surmised that at her age Rachael had probably had enough experience of Roman forts for this outing so they would delay visiting Vindolanda and perhaps return at a later date when they could combine this with an exploration of Corbridge Fort. Decision made, Ian fell asleep thinking of how lucky he was to have such a brave and joyous young companion: Rachael was a star!

DAY 5 – STEEL RIGG TO LANERCOST PRIORY – FIFTEEN MILES

After a superb breakfast, Julia drove Rachael and Ian back to the car park at Steel Rigg and Rachael was just bouncing with joy to be walking again: what a trooper she was.

They made good progress across fields climbing gently to a trig point, which at 345 metres is the highest on the Wall. Cue more photos! From here they could see that, in general, the Path was downhill however there were many dips and climbs to come much to Rachael's delight.

It was a joy to be walking across this fine, wild and rocky landscape on short, springy turf – so kind to the feet and, excitingly, the Wall soon reappeared in a substantial form.

They soon passed Milecastle 41 standing on top of one of the steep slopes and then, yet again, a descent and climb to where there had obviously been a turret. From here the Wall could be seen snaking its way into the distance with the Vallum clearly visible down in the valley.

Rachael and Ian had a ball, laughing and chatting, with Rachael, as always, full of the joys of spring, skipping and clapping her hands enthusiastically. This whole section of the Wall is also part of the Pennine Way; it follows Hadrian's Wall for some way until it turns northwards. At this point, Rachael reminded Ian, that the Pennine Way, which starts near Grandma Joyce's house was on her 'bucket list'. Ian pretended not to hear … selective hearing can be useful at times!

Soon they climbed up to the impressive ridge of Cawfield Crags, below which is a former quarry – now a lake. Rachael was soon to have a wonderful surprise regarding their frog competition.

As they approached the lake, Rachael was ecstatic because in the shallow water and on the banks she spotted hundreds of croaking, hopping frogs of various sizes.

'Wow, Dad!' she shouted, 'Frogs and frogs and *frogs* and I saw them first. So it's Rachael: 100 and Dad: only 1!'

'They are toads so they don't count,' Ian quickly responded. (He had no idea whether they were or not. Amphibians are not his strong point but he was not going to give up easily!)

'The are are frogs!' stated Rachael emphatically. 'We have studied them at school only a few weeks ago so I know – I really do!'

Then she added, giving Ian a hug, 'You know Dad, you really shouldn't always try to cheat because you are rubbish at it and you lose every time. When will you learn? It is a good job I love you!'

Ian had to smile as the last sentence was one of Grandma Joyce's frequent expressions. He had got his comeuppance and appeared to accept it almost graciously.

But, ever the optimist and a formidable competitor (just like his daughter) Ian answered, 'Okay, darling. You are winning up to now but we have still got lots of miles to walk.'

He was clearly hoping that as there were lots of stretches of water before the end of the Wall at Bowness-on-Solway, there would be a lot more frogs and he

would a have a chance of winning. Rachael didn't say anything but marched on with a triumphant smile on her face.

At times the Wall disappeared as they walked over gentle pastureland and eventually they reached the site of the small fort of Great Chesters or Aesica. They did not linger as little remained of the fort apart from the outline of the outside walls. However Ian did notice the squat, indistinctly carved pillar that is the only real altar still surviving in situ on the Wall – all the others are replicas.

The sheer variety of terrain from rocky outcrops and knolls to occasional patches of woodland, solitary trees and banks of turf maintained their interest and the miles sped by. All the time the Wall, Vallum and Wall ditch appeared and disappeared and high rocky ridges like Walltown Crags and turrets afforded fantastic panoramic views to the north and south. Just past these crags the builders of the Wall must have faced many difficulties as they had to fit the construction in between the many rocky knolls and the escarpment. The result is very impressive as in places the Wall stands above head height.

The area round Walltown Quarry has been transformed into a National Park recreation area with waymarked trails and reedy pools, home to a great variety of wildfowl. Ian really expected to see some frogs among those pools, but unfortunately, there wasn't a single one! They paused a while to look around and have a refreshing drink and, of course, Rachael had her customary chocolate bar.

At this point, they could have made a short diversion to see the fort of Carvoran and the Roman Army Museum, which holds some interesting reconstructions and artefacts illustrating all aspects of military life. However, Ian decided that Rachael had probably seen enough forts and so on for the time being and besides, he hadn't enough money with him to pay the museum entry fees!

Instead they walked happily over the fields on the north side of the Wall ditch towards the ruins of the 14th century Thirlwall Castle perched high on its steep-sided grassy motte. Most of the castle walls were built with stones purloined from Hadrian's Wall.

They continued on field paths and the occasional lane past farm buildings and the houses at the edge of Gilsland and dropped down to the Poltross Burn which is crossed by a single arched viaduct carrying the train line linking Newcastle and Carlisle.

The Path now crossed the stream, which bustled along over little sparkling falls and, to their joy, the Wall now reappeared and the remains of the important Milecastle 48. Inside this particular milecastle are some steps of a staircase which archaeologists think led up to the Walkway and they estimate that where the staircase meets the Wall, its height must have been a spectacular fifteen feet! Parts of the Wall past the village of Gilsland and Turret 48A had collapsed down into the river but in other places it was still well-preserved at a height of over one metre.

Rachael and Ian really enjoyed this gentler section through farmland with the River Irthing as a close companion. As often happens to walkers during a long, less demanding part of a trail, neither Ian nor Rachael spoke for a while: each one was completely occupied by their own thoughts.

Ian reflected that ten years ago when he had walked the Wall, somewhere around this area, he had had an intriguing and thought-provoking experience. From this, just like a little seed that eventually grows to become a huge plant, the episode lodged in his mind and years later grew to fruition.

He had been walking along with a high hedge to his right and open countryside to his left, when he noticed that a substantial hole had been cut through the hedge. Curious, he approached the gap and spotted a small wooden sign stuck into the ground near the entrance. On it, along with a large arrow, were the following words:

'HONESTY BAR AND TRAIL MAGIC'

Now thoroughly intrigued, following the direction of the arrow, he walked cautiously through the gap and at the bottom of what appeared to be a cottage garden, to his amazement, he saw a small wooden summerhouse. He opened the door and went inside.

There was a glass-fronted fridge containing all sorts of necessary goodies: bottles of water, juice and Coke and a huge variety of chocolate bars, trail munchies, flapjacks and crisps as well as eggs, crackers and a selection of different cheeses in little vacuum-packed polythene bags.

On a table beside the fridge, was a small box on which was the label, 'Honesty Box – please pay what you think is appropriate.'[3]

Ian gratefully helped himself to a Coke and put all his change – two pound coins – into the box. Then he noticed that pinned up on the walls of the summerhouse, were many drawings, obviously done by young children, of walkers at various stages of exhaustion! There was also a well-thumbed visitors' book and a pen: people had written glowing, thankful remarks inside. What a fabulous idea!

Ian had stored the experience in his memory and, as readers of the first 'Rachael Book' will remember this idea was reinforced years later when on the approach to Bolton-on-Swale, Rachael was fascinated to see a table full of similar essentials and another honesty box for payments. When they arrived home, they had adopted the idea and, outside Old Water View for many years, Catherine and Rachael had kept a large green container stocked with walkers' essentials and an honesty box, the proceeds of which were given to Patterdale Mountain Rescue Team.

Moving on to the present, the bar of Old Water View is now run in a similar way with guests paying for drinks and snacks by adding their items to a list to be settled on leaving or putting the price of their purchases in an honesty jar on the bar.

Rachael and Ian continued alongside the Wall towards the fort of Birdoswald. Soon Rachael's keen eyes spotted some inscriptions carved into several of

---

3 While Ian has a very clear memory of the hole in the hedge and the summerhouse, he cannot truly remember where it is situated and I must admit that when Graham and I walked Hadrian's Wall some years later, neither of us can recall seeing it and there is no record on the Internet. So … over to you, dear readers – please can you help identify where this lovely summerhouse actually is or was?

the Wall stones and she tried, without a great deal of success, to decipher them. Fortunately she ran out of enthusiasm before she reached the large brownish stone, the centurial stone of Julius Primus, which has engraved upon it a well-defined phallus! This is not the Roman equivalent of graffiti but a charm to keep the evil eye away. Ian heaved a sigh of relief – he was saved a potentially embarrassing explanation!

Birdoswald is very different from a lot of forts along Hadrian's Wall as the excavations there have revealed evidence of continuous occupation extending on a long time after Roman rule came to an end. There is a superb museum with a cinema where you can view a film about building and manning the Wall and see many interesting artefacts and illustrations. There is also as a very well-stocked shop. However you will remember that Ian hadn't sufficient money with him so he and Rachael could not go in this museum either but – particularly for people fascinated by Roman history – it is certainly worth a visit.

Ian decided that as Rachael was only ten years old, she had probably absorbed as much as she could about the historical aspects of Hadrian's Wall so they just had a quick look around the fort, noting particularly later additions like the pele tower and the remains of the fortified farm built on the site.

They followed the route past the front of the fort and walked with determination on through Banks past Pike Hill Signal Tower 36 and over Hare Hill towards their B&B at Abbey Farm House near spectacular Lanercost Priory. They actually left the line of the Wall just beyond Milecastle 54 and walked southwards down the side of Abbey Gills Wood to their destination.

They would have liked to visit beautiful Lanercost Priory as many people do but when they arrived there, they discovered it was closed: it was probably too late in the day. Normally you can visit the spectacular ruins – some of the best-preserved in the whole of Cumbria, the Visitor Centre and the nave of the church which still lives on as a parish church with triple arches and interesting monuments.

The Priory, nestling in the lovely wooded valley of the River Irthing, now has a wonderful air of tranquillity and peace however this belies an often turbulent history. As it is sited near Hadrian's Wall, it suffered frequent attacks during the long Anglo-Scottish wars, once by Robert the Bruce himself. The mortally sick King Edward I rested here for five months before his death in his final campaign. Founded by Robert de Vaux, Lord of Gilsland, Lanercost Priory was originally built around 1166 as a monastery to house Augustinian canons.

Somewhat disappointed, Ian and Rachael carried on and very soon were warmly welcomed by their hosts at Abbey Farm House.

DAY 6 – LANERCOST TO CARLISLE – FOURTEEN MILES

It was a glorious sunny day again as Rachael and Ian walked from their B&B accommodation back up to the line of the Wall again. This was their penultimate day of the Hadrian's Wall walk. Unfortunately from now onwards, right through to the end at Bowness-on-Solway, walkers need to keep memories of the Wall uppermost in their minds as further surface evidence of its existence have all but disappeared; only in places is the line of the Wall more obvious, as are the Wall ditch and Vallum.

However walking with a lively, eager companion is a joy in itself, so Ian considered himself to be very lucky. As for Rachael, she is always supremely happy just to be with her dad. The countryside was really pleasant and very fertile with lush green fields and patches of attractive woodland, many carpeted with gorgeous bright bluebells beginning to flourish beneath a canopy of fresh spring leaves. The scent was exquisite and a myriad of birdsong accompanied them: it was good to be alive!

They marched onwards sometimes on field tracks and other times on farm tracks and quiet lanes sheltered by thriving hedges. After passing through Walton, a pleasant little village with a large green and a simple Victorian church, the path's surface underfoot varied between bark and stone slabs, for which our walkers were grateful as all around were patches of soggy grass and standing pools. There were many gates and stiles to be negotiated and footbridges to be crossed like the one over the Cam Beck where sandstone bluffs rise above the shining water and a noisy weir bubbles downstream.

It was undemanding but really pleasant walking and as the day grew hotter they were thankful there was no strenuous climbing or steep descents. Beyond Newtown, the flat grazing ground was dotted with sturdy oaks but a tantalising line of hills appeared through the haze to the south.

Further on, Rachael was fascinated to be beside the small Carlisle Airport: she had never walked so close to an airport before and watched eagerly for a plane to appear – disappointingly none landed.

In the distance, from the tiny hamlet of Oldwall, they caught a glimpse of the taller buildings of Carlisle, their destination for the day. A little later the last signs of the Wall, a complex pattern of earthworks, were visible with the line of the Wall clearly defined by a long ridge in the middle of the field. Ian pointed this out to Rachael and tried to explain what she was seeing.

'You need a good imagination to work it all out, don't you Dad?' responded Rachael with a puzzled look on her face. Ian readily agreed.

Eventually they reached Crosby-on-Eden where they stopped for a drink at the Stag Inn: Ian had a pint of Coke and Rachael a half. It was a tranquil, pleasant place with a pretty though somewhat gloomy church at the edge of the village, almost lost among the surrounding tall horse chestnut trees. Next door stood a 19th century school that looked more like an estate lodge.

As they walked further on, the increasing sound of traffic on the A689 to the north began to assault their ears. They had become used to quiet and solitude with only the sounds of nature so this was quite an unwelcome shock: they were return-ing to civilisation, always a sad moment on a long trek.

They followed the track down to the River Eden and turned right to meet the path along the riverbank. A very pleasing section with open aspects and the lan-guid, placid river shining like glass, with occasional flurries of sparkling activity. Here and there they could see swans floating lazily and lots of other wildfowl in-cluding a considerable variety of ducks, moorhens and coots.

Just ahead were some bronzed copper beeches glowing in the sunlight but shel-tering an extensive rookery with the raucous cries of the rooks competing with the traffic noise from the nearby M6. Indeed the view ahead was mainly of traffic crossing the river by the Linstock motorway bridge.

As the river meandered away from them in a large loop, Rachael and Ian wandered down a fine avenue of trees and saw on the right a gaunt-looking house, Linstock Castle. It is not so much a castle as a pele tower, typical of border country. Local families would retreat here to safety with as many of their possessions as they could carry to escape the frequent violent raids of soldiers and the Border Reivers.[4]

Rachael and Ian crossed the motorway and were delighted to see in the distance the unmistakeable saddleback shape of majestic Blencathra and other mountains and fells to the north of Keswick on the outer edge of the Lake District: their home.

They continued on quiet lanes, a cycle track and footpath towards Carlisle. To their left they saw Tower Farm – aptly named as it is adorned by a square turret – and to the right a puzzling isolated tower in the middle of a field. Apparently this was built by an eccentric gentleman with the unlikely name of George Head-Head who lived in Rickerby House. He was obsessed by towers and turrets so when folly building was all the rage in the early 19th century, he had his own tower built to impress his friends and neighbours.

The cycle track now gave way to parkland and again the riverside path but sadly, because of its proximity to civilisation, this area was spoiled by litter. Rachael wrinkled her nose in disgust. The path now became more rural, hemmed in by all kinds of plants: hogweed, ransoms and ragwort predominating. Delightfully, the placid River Eden burst into a glistening series of falls just before it reached the impressively solid, stone road bridge. It really is a grand sight with its five arches and although it was widened in the 20th century, the style is still very much in keeping with its 1815 origins.

As Ian and Rachael crossed this bridge, Ian reminded her that this was the scene of the devastating 2015 floods when the road down which they were walk-ing was flooded to a depth of between four and six feet. The bridge itself had thankfully remained standing but the angry turbulent waters had reached the very top of the arches: a spectacular but frightening sight.

In fact when Graham and I walked Hadrian's Wall in 2005, a few months before, there had been similar destructive floods and we were unable to find accommodation

---

4 The Border Reivers were fierce, lawless Anglo-Scottish raiders who stole and plundered along the Border Country without regard for their victims' nationality between the 13th and 17th centuries. They often rode light, hardy ponies or nags and rustled cattle, stole portable household goods, clothing and valuables, took prisoners for ransom and ran profitable blackmail and protection rackets. There were usually around a dozen Reivers in each band but at times over a thousand would plunder together: they were greatly feared by the local population.

in Carlisle itself as so many guest houses had been flooded and were closed for renovation.

Rachael and Ian walked up Warwick Road, past Carlisle Football ground (Brunton Park) and soon found their B&B: a pleasant guesthouse called Howard Lodge where they were welcomed warmly by a lovely couple. Ian retrieved his wallet from their transported baggage, which awaited them in their pleasant room.

After freshening up, Rachael and Ian walked into the centre of Carlisle and found a pizza restaurant where they both enjoyed their favourite pizza with a drink. Ian's was a beer and Rachael's? I bet you can guess … yes – a huge mug of hot chocolate!

DAY 7 – CARLISLE TO BOWNESS-ON-SOLWAY – FIFTEEN MILES

Their last day dawned bright and sunny; whenever Ian and Rachael walk they always seem to have glorious weather – they are so lucky. I however, probably like many readers, always manage to get soaked as Graham and I did on our last stretch of the Hadrian's Wall Path: it rained incessantly all day!

After a sustaining beautifully cooked breakfast, they thanked their hosts and soon joined the next part of the Path, which coincides with the City Trail through Bitts Park (also spelt Bitz). Rachael was surprised by two huge armchairs, which sat by the side of the broad pathway. These were totally unexpected and fascinating as they were made of mosaics. (Possibly an homage to the Romans and their wonderful intricate mosaic floors and walls.)

One armchair had pink, orange and yellow designs of hearts and a huge, smiley face of the sun and the other had blue designs of faces and limbs. Rachael was enchanted and after examining them carefully, she eagerly posed for several photos in both of them. It had rained in the night so when Rachael stood up she discovered that, as before, she had a wet bum! She just laughed and rubbed her bottom vigorously; little problems like that never worry Rachael – she just radiates joy.

'What a great way to start our last day, Dad,' she enthused. 'I don't care if my bum is a bit wet again. Come on – let's get going!'

They had one brief glimpse of Carlisle Castle, looking suitably forbidding, before they left the city and re-joined the riverside path. For the next two miles, the path close by the River Eden was very muddy and messy due to the recent flooding so they had to pick their way carefully to avoid slipping and falling.

As they reached the first huge meander of the river, Ian, using his local knowledge and having walked Hadrian's Wall before, took Rachael away from the riverside onto a quiet road. Not only were they able to make far better progress but sensibly, Ian had planned the detour to avoid passing near to the sewage works and rubbish dumps that marred the outskirts of the city and smelled really unpleasant. Rachael would have hated that!

Soon her sharp eyes spotted a horseshoe at the side of the road so she went to pick it up.

'Do you really need that?' asked Ian.

'Of course I do, Dad!' she replied quickly, 'Horseshoes are lucky.'

And with that she popped it into Ian's rucksack before he could protest. She still has that horseshoe today.

On the approach to Grinsdale, they returned briefly to the pretty riverside path of the calm River Eden through fields bright with meadow flowers of many different species: a much better environment. However the walk then turned away from the river skirting a clump of trees and headed into the village.

The next part – over fields and along banks and lanes – was very boring, both Ian and Rachael agreed, with endless gates, stiles and footbridges to be negotiated. There was little to attract their attention other than the occasional dip in the land, showing where the shallow Vallum lay and indicating that they were still following the line of Hadrian's Wall.

It was around here that Rachael asked Ian if she could phone her mum. Understandably, she wanted her mum to come and meet her at the end of Hadrian's Wall. She called her mum thinking that she would be at home.

'Mum, please, please come – you are only about an hour away from Bowness so you will have plenty of time to drive there. I so want you to see me finish my fourth C2C walk.'

'Sorry Rachael,' was her mum's reply, 'I am very busy today: I've so many things to do.'

At this point her sister Catherine came on the phone and said very innocently, 'Hello sis, how are you doing? I hope you've had a great time. Mum and I are shopping in Carlisle and we are in Debenhams department store now looking at some clothes.'

Rachael replied with a knowing voice, 'But we passed Debenhams this morning on our way out of Carlisle so you aren't far away.'

She asked Ian just how long it would take her mum to drive from Carlisle to Bowness-on-Solway.

'About fifteen minutes – twenty at the most,' replied Ian.

However, when she told her mum this, her mum said that Bowness was much further away than that and she did not have the time. So, in resignation, after thanking Catherine and telling her that she'd had a fab time, Rachael handed the phone back to Ian.

She was rather quiet and subdued for a while but brightened up as they once more joined the riverside path, which climbed to the top of a wooded bank above the river and descended on an undulating course, twisted over the years by landslips. She was clearly determined to enjoy her last day of walking with her dad. They carried on until the path reached the road where they turned left up into Beaumont with Rachael skipping ahead of Ian as usual.

They paused by the church which stands on a mound: indeed, this is how the village came to have its name – 'beau mont' meaning beautiful hill or mountain. The Wall actually came through this site so the enterprising Normans used the stones to build the church. They continued down the road signposted to Burgh by Sands and then walked, climbing slightly, on a broad straight path set directly on the course of the Wall.

Although the climb was almost imperceptible, in this very flat landscape, it did afford views of the Scottish hills to the north. Ian and Rachael began to sing, chat and tell silly stories and jokes: believe me some of Ian's jokes make you cringe! But it was a case of trying anything to liven up this monotonous part of the Path.

The village of Burgh by Sands stands on the site of the Roman fort of Abavalla, which means 'apple orchard' however there is little trace of either the Wall or the fort. They stopped here for a nice meal and a Coke at the Greyhound Inn outside which is a bronze statue of King Edward I more commonly known as 'Longshanks' or 'Scourge of the Scots'. Readers will remember that he stopped at Lanercost Priory for five months trying to recover from a debilitating illness. However he died ingloriously just north of Burgh by Sands out on the cold wet marshes – not by the sword but of dysentery.

They looked at the historically significant building of St. Michael's Church, which is sited within the boundary of the old Roman fort and so was originally built with stones from the Wall. This Christian church is said to have the carved head of a pagan god inside the chancel on the east wall. However our two intrepid walkers still had quite a long way to go so they resisted investigating and plodded on down the main street, continuing down the seemingly endless road with fields either side. The only interest to break the monotony was provided by an unexpected

sign announcing that this part of the road was liable to flooding. In fact much of this section has extensive salt marshes both sides of the road, extending to the River Eden, so when exceptionally high tides flow up the Solway Firth, the whole area can be under several feet of water. No such tides were predicted at the time of their walk so they were safe. However, Rachael is never one to miss an opportunity to pose for a photo so Ian, obligingly, snapped her with her arms around the post.

The path was now below the line of the long, high embankment to the left of the road, which is a sea-defence barrier but soon the road again seemed to stretch in an interminable straight line to distant Drumburgh. Fortunately there were lovely familiar views to the south of the fabulous faraway fells of the Lake District, including the shapely cone of Skiddaw, rugged Caldbeck Fells and the magnificent mountain, Blencathra. To the north were the salt marshes frequented by grazing cattle and innumerable sandbanks in the River Eden, alive with many species of wildfowl. There were waders and many other seabirds but they were especially thrilled to see several oystercatchers with their eye-catching black and white plumage, bright orange beaks and attractive pink legs. This iconic bird has been adopted as the symbol of the Solway coast. However having walked this section of the Path myself, I can confirm that it is difficult to keep that seemingly ceaseless road from dominating your view: you plod along and never seem to get any nearer to your ultimate goal!

Eventually they reached Drumburgh, the site of a small fort and then walked in front of Drumburgh Castle, which is a fortified house with an entrance at the first level to make it easier to defend. They stayed on the coastal road, bypassing Glasson, and continued along the disused railway embankment into Port Carlisle. This was built in 1819 so the difficult waters of the Solway Firth could be avoided and was linked to Carlisle by canal. It had a short life however as the shifting sands of the estuary made the port virtually unusable.

Rachael and Ian did not linger as they were longing to reach the end of their historic walk so they marched along the final stretch of the road right down on the shoreline and up to Bowness-on-Solway where Hadrian's Wall originally came to an end, running straight down into the sea. Of course the Wall itself has long since been eroded away by the tossing waves but the vast broad waters stretching away to the horizon and Scotland (visible on the far bank) give this spot an ancient atmosphere. You can really feel that this was once a wild frontier: the most northerly of the Roman Empire.

The end of the Hadrian's Wall Path is marked by a welcome sign in a wooden gazebo down a back ginnel – a somewhat disappointing and anticlimactic way to end a fabulous trail full of interesting history and contrasts.

Rachael and Ian's adventure had started on the edge of the great city of Newcastle under the shadow of shipyard cranes and ended on a lonely shore with the cries of gulls and the gentle lap of the waves: truly magical.

As you can imagine, Ian's camera was soon clicking again as he took a host of photos of Rachael, with a huge grin, arms raised and outstretched, celebrating the completion of her fourth C2C. What a true explorer she was; Ian was so proud of her.

They soon found their accommodation, the Old Rectory Guest House (also called Wallsend House.) It was a superb, welcoming place with cheerful hosts, spacious rooms and, to Rachael's delight, a really friendly cat.

After a quick clean up and a drink, they went to eat at the nearby King's Arms pub about five minutes' walk away. Ian was astonished at the prices on the menu: all the meals were ridiculously cheap at around £4.95 and the beer over £1 cheaper than elsewhere. Understandably, Ian assumed that with such low prices their meal would be of poor quality but he was completely wrong – their meals were excellent, truly delicious.

When Ian went to the bar to buy another drink, he remarked that the lovely meals and the beer were far too cheap. The landlady explained that they had only just taken over the pub but she was sure that no one would want to pay any more. Ian tried to convince her she was wrong and set her a challenge: for the next customers, she should double the price of each meal and charge another pound for the beer.

If those people thought the prices were too high, didn't want to pay that amount and left, *he* would pay for the meals lost. She readily agreed, suspecting she was right but, with Ian's offer, she couldn't lose and so she altered the prices on the menu.

The next people who came in were a Dutch couple who eagerly ordered fish and chips and drinks at the new price and paid promptly without comment. Soon they were tucking enthusiastically into their meals, with no sign of displeasure. Ian gave the landlady a thumbs-up sign and smiled triumphantly. She smiled happily back. He couldn't resist an ironic chuckle when he went back to the bar to buy another pint and was charged the new price.

'Serves me right,' he thought, 'I deserved that!'

As they left the King's Arms and began to walk back to the Old Rectory, Rachael spoke to Ian.

'You know, Dad, that was the best evening ever that I have had in a pub! It was great and I really loved that big veggie lasagne, it was so tasty!'

'Why don't you go and tell them then?' Ian replied, never thinking that she would. How wrong he was! Without another word, she turned round and on her own, our surprising ten-year-old, pushed open the pub door and went inside. Ian stayed outside amazed.

A few minutes later, she emerged with a huge grin on her face and told Ian what had happened.

'I walked straight up to the bar, Dad, and I said, "thank you for a super evening – the best I have ever had in a pub. Your food is great and you have made the end of my Hadrian's Wall walk really special so thank you again. I want to come back very soon!"'

'Wow!' said Ian astonished. 'That was really nice of you, Rachael, and brave too.'

'Well they deserved it,' came her matter-of-fact reply.

At this point, dear readers, I would like to say that Ian told me that the King's Arms is a smashing pub with a good selection of food including vegetarian dishes. He would encourage anyone to go there and enjoy the experience as much as he and Rachael did. Even with the new prices it is still very good value and one of the cheapest and best on the whole of the Hadrian's Wall Path.

Happy and very full, our fab twosome walked back to their B&B and were soon in their beds. It had been a long, hard and hot day but an absolute triumph. They had completed their Roman Odyssey – Hadrian's Wall Path in seven days and more importantly, completed Rachael's fourth C2C. What a star she was!

Some months later, Ian phoned the pub's landlady to ask how they were doing and was thanked profusely for his advice.

'We are doing really, really well. You have made us a fortune!' she said gratefully. 'And I must tell you that when your lovely young daughter came in all on her own and thanked us, we couldn't believe our ears. It was the best thing that has happened to us all season: she blew us away – we were both in tears. What a fantastic girl she is – you must be very proud of her.'

'I am,' Ian responded. 'Very proud, indeed!'

DAY 8 – BOWNESS-ON-SOLWAY TO OLD WATER VIEW VIA CARLISLE

Next morning they enjoyed a splendid breakfast and thanked their hosts for a lovely stay. Rachael had several cuddles with the friendly cat while they waited for the taxi-bus to Carlisle. It soon came and they boarded it a little regretfully as this really was the end of their adventure. When they were sitting down, Rachael began chatting excitedly about parts of the walk that she had especially enjoyed: she was bubbling over with joy. It was then that she reminded Ian of the Counting Frogs Competition.

'I seem to remember, Dad,' she announced with a satisfied smile, 'that the last score at the lake below Cawfield Crags was Rachael: 100 and Dad: 1. So as you haven't seen any more and the competition ended last night, I have won, ha ha!'

Ian had to reluctantly admit that he had been beaten again but, being a fierce competitor just like Rachael, he added, 'But I will beat you next time!'

'We'll see … ' was her only response.

Only fifteen minutes later, they were alighting in Carlisle.

'So it is true!' exclaimed Rachael. 'Bowness-on-Solway really is only fifteen minutes from Carlisle.' And without another word, she gave Ian that knowing and slightly crestfallen look.

They too did some shopping in Carlisle before they caught the train to Penrith, the nearest station to their home at Old Water View, Patterdale. While they were on the train, Rachael thanked Ian for helping her complete another fantastic C2C.

'It was a great adventure, Dad, and I loved every minute of it but I feel a bit sad that it is all over. When is our Iceland trip? I can't wait to see those geysers and volcanoes!'

'It's only a few months away,' replied Ian. 'And that will be the *third* adventure of your second Triple Challenge – a sort of C2C5 in a different country.'

'Great!' Rachael replied joyfully with a magical smile that illuminated her face. 'I'm really *really* looking forward to that!'

Ian smiled contentedly: his ten-year-old daughter was always looking for a new challenge. She was a true explorer!

CHAPTER

ICELAND: DRIVE AND HIKE –
AUGUST 2015
AGED ELEVEN YEARS
FOUR MONTHS

Early in the summer Ian received the email from Fran that Rachael had been expecting for some time. Fran confirmed that Macs Adventure would sponsor Rachael to go to Iceland and offered two options: one was a drive and trek in the Icelandic Highlands and the other a drive and hike tour of Iceland's Scenic South Coast including the Golden Circle tour.

As you may imagine, Rachael, initially wanted to choose driving and trekking in the Icelandic Highlands as she adores hills and mountains. However, Ian pointed out that all the guidebooks say that walking in the Highlands in Iceland can be hazardous because of the frequent sudden changes of weather due to a huge variety of different weather fronts. It can be lovely and clear then, without any advance warning, the temperature plummets and solid mist descends so rapidly it becomes very difficult to follow even established trails. Ever mindful of Rachael's safety, Ian added that quite recently an active volcano in that area had erupted so he persuaded her that the drive and hike tour would be far safer, still very dramatic and thoroughly enjoyable.

Being very aware that safety is always paramount when planning any adventure, Rachael readily agreed but, of course, wanted to know all about the south coast tour. Ian explained that it was an action-packed drive and hike tour that started and ended in the capital, Reykjavik, and took in massive glaciers, thundering waterfalls, huge black lava fields and hot springs.

'Wow!' Rachael exclaimed. 'That will be really cool, Dad – a fantastic new adventure!'

Ian emailed Fran to thank her and inform her that they had chosen The Scenic South Coast tour. Fran was delighted and emphasised that they had made an excellent choice – she thought that it was the best introduction to Iceland: the Land of Ice and Fire. She added that she would send them some information about the tour, their itinerary and travel documents as soon as possible. Rachael could hardly wait and eagerly checked the post each day.

I must admit that I would love to spend some time in Iceland. A lucky and thoroughly enchanted teaching colleague of mine told me after a month's visit

Cheers – with Dad's pint!

to Iceland that it really is a mind-blowing experience: a geography lesson like no other. In her words:

'Soaring mountains, hidden valleys, huge glaciers and icebergs, dormant and active volcanoes, deep rocky fissures and rugged craters, basalt columns and dark canyons, roaring waterfalls and twisting rivers with plains of moss-covered lava fields reveal a raw, dramatic and often stunning experience and close views of the evolving formation of the landscape of this fabulous country.'

Iceland's spectacular natural beauty encompasses Europe's largest national park and the mightiest ice-cap outside the poles; a sea full of whales and the world's biggest puffin colonies.

For Rachael and Ian, their tour would include seeing huge glaciers one after another as Ian drove southwards: an awe-inspiring experience, as would be the bold, beautiful but somewhat alarming icebergs in the glacial lagoon at Jokulsarlon – a worrying example of how climate changes are affecting Iceland.

Every waterfall or foss would seem to be more stunning, higher, faster, and more picturesque than the previous one. The spectacular deep fissures in the landscape would show where the tectonic plates of North America and Europe are tearing away from each other: geography and geology in action. Rachael would be absorbing all this knowledge through experience without even realising it: the very best way to learn.

They would also discover that Iceland is a land of myth and legend. Besides all the ancient creation legends, many Icelandic people still genuinely believe in elves and it is not difficult to imagine such magical creatures living in this bewitching countryside. Years ago, they also believed in trolls who lived in the glaciers, lava fields and fissures in the earth's crust and, it is said, used the woolly fringe-moss that covers so much of the landscape as their troll blankets.

It was not long before the package from Macs came and Rachael spent many enthralling hours examining the itinerary and finding their route, overnight destinations and the promised exciting sights on the map of Iceland. She could not wait for the summer term to end!

With Grandma Joyce safely installed in Old Water View and trying her best to run Ian's guest house and maintain his standards of service, on Monday 3rd August 2015, Rachael and Ian took the 14.45 train to Manchester Airport to begin their Icelandic adventure.

Their flight next morning was very early – 6.10 a.m. – and they had to check in two hours before so they stayed overnight at the Carlton Hotel at the airport. This was a new, thrilling experience for Rachael: she was bubbling over with anticipation. However, because of their untimely wake-up time of 3 a.m. the next morning, after a light meal they were both in their beds unusually early that evening.

'Night, Dad,' Rachael murmured sleepily. 'Tomorrow is going to be fab – I can't wait!'

Ian had to admit that he was just as excited as she was.

DAY 1 – MANCHESTER AIRPORT TO REYKJAVIK, ICELAND – TUESDAY 4TH AUGUST 2015

The flight itself was approximately two hours so in no time at all, they were flying over the spectacular and remarkable scenery of Iceland. With the vast, treeless, black lava fields, it looked like an alien landscape full of mystery. Glowing with joy and expectation, Rachael took lots of photos from the plane window:

'Wow! Wow! Wow! Dad – what weird countryside – it looks like another world! I am longing to explore it all. Do we land soon?'

Ian had to smile at her eagerness and reflected on what a very different experience this drive/hike adventure in Iceland was going to be for Rachael.

The Land of Fire and Ice might be an overused marketing slogan but it is not hyperbole: serene majestic scenery belies Iceland's fiery heart. There are some thirty active volcanoes; many of them lie beneath the huge thick ice-cap and when their fire-breathing fury is unleashed, the whole world has to take notice.

As they descended towards Iceland's capital, they could see the fascinating, multi-coloured buildings of Reykjavik. In glorious sunshine, this whole gem of a city looked so pristinely clean and captivating that it truly invited you to explore its wonders.

Luckily it wasn't long before they landed at Keflavik International Airport where a coach picked them up to transport them to their overnight accommodation – Hotel Reykjavik Centrum.

On the way they passed through rugged deep craters and otherworldly black lava fields and, most importantly, the incredible Blue Lagoon. Although the coach did not stop, they were enchanted just to see a glimpse of this awesome famous spectacle. Set in a magnificent black lava field, this milky-tea spa is fed water from the futuristic Svartsengi geothermal plant; with its silver towers, billowing clouds of steam, and people daubed in protective, energising white silica mud, it really does look like a different world.

The superheated water is rich in blue-green algae, mineral salts and fine silica mud that condition and exfoliate the skin. Although this sounds more like a health spa advert, my fortunate friend did confirm that you emerge from this hot, colourful water thoroughly invigorated and with 'skin as soft as a baby's bum!'

Eventually they reached their charming hotel, Reykjavik Centrum situated on one of the oldest streets in the historic centre of the city, the liveliest and most charming part of Reykjavik. The central part of the hotel, built in bright red brick is said to be one of the oldest buildings in the city dating from 1764. However Rachael and Ian were in one of the more modern adjacent wings, which had been built in such a sympathetic style they blended in perfectly. In addition, there is a basement museum built around the archaeological remains of a Viking longhouse dating back to 871 AD – the oldest in Iceland.

Rachael was so eager to explore the city and the Old Harbour that they did not visit the museum but were delighted to find that in front of the hotel, there was a large, toughened, plate-glass flagstone set in the pavement, through which they could see a considerable part of the interesting remains. They soon found that the city was really quirky and stimulating with a huge variety of shops selling outdoor equipment and handicrafts with a wide range of Icelandic carvings and traditional clothing of all colours, sizes and designs.

There were various galleries and museums with exhibitions of everything from art and sculpture to an endearingly bloodthirsty saga of Icelandic history with lifelike models and a multi-language soundtrack of thudding axes and hair-raising screams. The vibrant café culture spilled out onto the pavements and there were many inviting restaurants with varied and comprehensive menus.

Next they made their way down to the Old Harbour, which used to be just a service harbour but had now blossomed into a real tourist hotspot.

It had quite a few restaurants and cafés and excitingly lots of different boats nestling in the harbour. Unfortunately there was also a massive whaling factory ship, which incensed Rachael and Ian – both committed vegetarians – as they had always been against the barbaric practices of the whaling industry.

Rachael soon spotted several signs advertising sea fishing, puffin viewing and whale-watching trips. Ian didn't need any persuading to book a whale-watching trip – he was just as eager as Rachael. They decided to choose Elding Adventures at Sea because it was the city's most established and eco-friendly outfit and the well-maintained boat was a good size with refreshments and a whale exhibition on board.

As they went out to sea, the owner came to talk to them and explained that the company was committed to saving these magnificent creatures and preventing their slaughter. He asked them to support Elding's efforts by not patronising restaurants and cafés that had whale meat on their menu. Both Rachael and Ian readily agreed that this was something they would certainly do.

The coast of Iceland quickly disappeared and soon they were out in the open sea. They were told to look carefully for water spouts emitted from the whales' blowholes and were soon rewarded by the electrifying sight of a blackish, streamlined, majestic humpback whale breaching the surface of the sea: how lucky! Cameras clicking, they followed it for some time until

it disappeared under the waves. The humpback is one of the larger baleen whales with a distinctive stocky body shape, long pectoral fins and a knobbly head; the knobs, called tubercles, are actually hair follicles. Sadly the humpback was and still is one of the species most hunted by whalers.

The owner explained to everyone on board that they would smell the minke whales long before they saw them: true enough because soon the most putrid smell assaulted their noses as several minkes breached the surface just in front of them. They really were 'stinky minkes': much smaller than the humpbacks, they had greyish-black backs with white underbellies and a distinctive white band on their flippers. They were quite attractive to see but their malodorous presence made everyone glad when they finally disappeared.

They were soon replaced by a school of delightful white-beaked dolphins leaping into the air, chasing the boat and playing with each other like happy children in a playground: a splendid sight. The whale watchers soon realised that, not only were the dolphins chasing the boat, they appeared to be chasing the humpback whale. At first it seemed that they were attacking the humpback but soon it became obvious that they were just playing with the whale: they leapt over it, circled it and splashed it just like naughty schoolchildren! The humpback was totally unperturbed, in fact, seemed to be enjoying the company but eventually decided that enough was enough and, with a flourish of its huge fluked wavy-edged tail, it disappeared below the waves. It was an absolutely magical experience. Rachael clapped her hands in glee; what a fabulous start to her Iceland adventure.

After thanking the owner, they left the boat at the harbour from which they had embarked and walked towards the centre of the city to find somewhere to eat. By now they were both starving but they were careful to find a restaurant that did not have whale meat on its menu. This is quite easy as all the eating places that do not use whale meat display a sticker prominently in their windows. Eventually they found a suitable restaurant, where they had a huge vegetarian pizza each accompanied by a very expensive beer for Ian and a Diet Coke for Rachael.

They didn't linger as they were both tired from a very long day that had started at 3 a.m. but they were both so fervently enthusiastic about their forthcoming adventure, they hardly noticed. They snuggled down in their beds still buzzing from their exciting day and full of anticipation for the even more exhilarating day to follow.

DAY 2 – THE GOLDEN CIRCLE – PINGVELLIR, GULLFOSS AND GEYSIR – DRIVE AND HIKE

Rachael and Ian were up early, eager to begin the next part of their Icelandic adventure. While they were eating splendid breakfasts, they noticed on the hotel's comprehensive and varied day's menu that whale meat was included in several dishes. They were really pleased that, in spite of the hotel having a superb, highly recommended restaurant, they had decided not to eat there the previous evening. Principles thankfully intact, they went to find their transport for the remainder of the tour.

They picked up their car, a Volkswagen Golf, at the National/Europcar Office in Reykjavik city centre. This car – unfortunately not a 4x4 – was their transport for the next six days and came with unlimited mileage, tax, collision damage and limited insurance: accidental damage excess was limited to £880.

They drive on the right in Iceland and the main roads are generally fine although, unusually, some are built on high embankments. Beyond these roads, however, some become rough dirt tracks littered with large stones and boulders. Ian thoroughly enjoys driving and is a very good, experienced driver and now Rachael loves sightseeing and journeying by car. When she was younger, just like her older sister Catherine, she suffered from severe travel sickness. Fortunately she had grown out of this so she was really looking forward to their drive to the beginning of the Golden Circle at Pingvellir twenty-three kilometres away.

Pingvellir is a fabulous national park of vivid beauty and a UNESCO World Heritage Site – a wonderful beginning to the second day of their Icelandic adventure. It was very interesting to be driving through such an unusual and alien landscape: a totally out of this world experience. Both Rachael and Ian were fascinated.

After an hour or so, they reached the Park Service Centre and car park so they quickly parked the car and decided that their first walk would be the two miles down the great Rift Canyon of the Pingvellir plain.

This is an awesome and unique experience to actually see where the land is ripping apart: the formation of the landscape of Iceland in front of you, below you and surrounding you. This may sound brutal and dramatic but Iceland is truly being pulled apart at the incredible rate of up to two centimetres every year. This is because Iceland sits over two major tectonic plates, the American and European plates which are pulling apart and creating a spell-binding and ever evolving scarred landscape of yawning fissures, lakes, ponds and cascading rivers.

Initially Rachael and Ian decided to walk above the intimidating canyon on the European plate side before they descended into the deep massive fissure of the fault. Dramatic rugged cliffs reared up either side as they walked slowly along the path. Massive moss-covered boulders that looked like huge solidified bubbles of lava with gloomy cracks and crevices seemed to have tumbled down there or been pushed up through the earth's crust from some Stygian depths. It was easy to understand how the myth of trolls living underground, hidden in their moss blankets had arisen. Both Ian and Rachael were completely awestruck. Imagine the astonished look on Rachael's face when she stopped, completely rooted to the spot as she realised that she actually had one foot in Europe and one foot in America – she was straddling two different continental plates!

'Wow! Dad!' she exclaimed in wonder. 'This is so cool: it's unbelievable! Aren't I lucky?'

Ian readily agreed and wondered how many eleven-year-old children had ever had or would have this fabulous experience. Of course, he took many photos with Rachael happily posing, arms stretched skywards and an enraptured expression on her face: she was enchanted.

From this fascinating site of geology in action, they walked towards Iceland's most important site of historical interest where the Vikings established the world's first democratic parliament in AD 930 – the Alping or Parliament fields. The meetings were held outdoors in a natural amphitheatre in the immense, fissured rift valley. Although you can only see the stone foundations of ancient encampments, you can truly feel the historic significance of this unique site. The Alping however was to play another important

Where the American and European tectonic plates join.

role much later in Icelandic history: apparently in 1942, when Germany invaded Denmark, Icelanders met at the Alping. Determined not to submit to Nazi control, they decided to declare unilateral independence from Denmark and establish the Republic of Iceland. This was ratified in 1944 although there have been many changes to the constitution since then.

Rachael and Ian paused for a while embracing the strange otherworldly atmosphere of this significant site before they set off on a path through heathland dotted here and there with bushes back to the car park. Their entire circular hike in beautiful sunshine had taken the best part of four hours – most of the morning – but it had been the most exhilarating experience. Rachael quickly jumped into the car impatient to embark on the next part of the Golden Circle Tour. Ian too was full of anticipation.

It was only about half an hour's drive to the car park and small Visitor Centre at Gullfoss. They could hardly wait to see Iceland's most famous waterfall – Gullfoss or Golden Falls – a breathtaking double cascade. It is an iconic Icelandic waterfall on the Hvita (White) River fed by the second largest glacier in the country – the Langojkull. It gives visitors a spectacular view of the forces and beauty of pristine nature. It is really like two small Niagaras – one below and lying at 90 degrees to the other: an absolute marvel.

Still in T-shirts in the glorious sunshine, they hurried from the car park above the falls down the fenced wooden walkway and broad path, eager to see this famous waterfall. They were not disappointed! The glistening fast-flowing water roared and plummeted down at least thirty-two metres in a stupendous two-tiered fall

before it thundered away down a narrow rugged canyon whose cliffs reach skywards for over seventy metres.

Huge clouds of spray were flung up into the air in magical shining curtains interwoven with shimmering rainbows. It was indeed breathtaking; they were both absolutely spellbound. Ian's camera was clicking continuously and Rachael clapped her hands in ecstasy. Because of the drifting spray, Rachael was wearing the authentic waterproof jacket presented to her by Patterdale Mountain Rescue Team for raising so much sponsorship money for them. You can see it on one of the photos in this book; behind her is a magical shining rainbow and she is also holding up Patrick Bear given to her by the Team to bring her good luck when she tackled the West Highland Way.

'Oh Dad, isn't it awesome?' she gasped.

Ian nodded. For once he was speechless but he told me afterwards that the scene was one of the best he had ever viewed. At the end of their adventure, Rachael confirmed that of all the wonders she had seen, Gullfoss was her favourite. Reluctantly they made their way back up the path and walkway to the car park[1] pausing frequently to look back in wonder at that fabulous scene. They still had another exciting place to visit so they were full of expectation.

Ian drove for about another half hour to their next destination – The Geysir Centre where they parked.

Geysir, in the Haukadafur geothermal region is supposed to be one of Iceland's most famous tourist attractions. (Geysir, meaning 'gusher', is the original hot water spout after which all other geysers were named.) Geysir is said to have been active for around 800 years and once gushed hot steaming water in a huge plume up to eighty metres in the air before it vanished down its enormous hole: another truly spectacular sight. However visitors are told that there have been periods since 1916 when it has not been so active or vigorous.

Full of anticipation, they waited and waited at the side of the hole for some action, as did other visitors. Eventually everyone decided nothing was going to happen that day so they went back to their transport.

---

1 What is impressive to note is that, as far as Ian could ascertain, all car parks and parking in Iceland are free: no annoying payment meters in sight. Come on UK – catch up!

What they had not been told was that the Geysir had not erupted for some considerable time because Icelanders did not want people to be put off from visiting the site.

Somewhat disappointed, Rachael and Ian set off to drive to their accommodation for the night – the Hotel Ork in Hveragerdi some distance away. What should have been roughly an hour's pleasant drive was about to turn into a nightmare.

At the end of the road from the car park was a T-junction and Ian turned left through some road-works instead of turning right. For what seemed ages, he followed a line of cars and a minibus through more roadworks, assuming he was on the correct road. The landscape grew wilder and the road deteriorated from tarmac to a rough dirt track. Ian thought this would stop any minute and they would soon be back on a tarmac road leading to civilisation. However, the dirt track seemed to go on forever and became more hazardous and undulating with steep climbs and drops; the surface became littered with big stones and occasional boulders: this required a 4x4 – not the ordinary car that Ian had hired.

Rachael was unperturbed as she had complete trust in her dad. Ian managed to hide his increasing anxiety but he was afraid they were completely lost. The terrain was growing more and more hostile and the track narrower. When a minibus stopped in front of them, Ian drew in behind it and asked where they were, adding that he was looking for Hveragerdi. To his dismay, the lady driver told him that he was heading towards the uninhabited central area of Iceland: definitely not driving country and she advised him to turn round and head back the way he had come.

Thankfully, after several scary attempts, Ian managed to turn the VW around and headed southwards back towards the turn off for the Geysir, at least an hour's drive away. Soon he had to negotiate his way carefully around an approaching four-wheel-drive car – not easy as the track was narrow and stony. In fact he clipped the wing mirror of the other car so he stopped, went to apologise to the driver and to see if any damage had been done. The driver was an Icelandic

gentleman who said there was no damage done but then, to Ian's amazement, took out his camera and photographed Ian and his car. Of course Ian enquired why the man had done this and was amazed to hear the explanation: apparently this very pleasant man had never seen an ordinary car like Ian's VW on that road before so he had taken the photo to show his friends for fun!

'Okay,' thought Ian, 'he clearly thinks I'm a mad Englishman!'

They shook hands and after confirming he was heading in the right direction, Ian set off again only to break sharply when Rachael yelled that there was a huge stone in the road – Ian had not seen it. He quickly got out of the VW to check for any damage and found to his relief that although the stone was the size of a football, there was only a small scratch like a tiny shaving cut on the bumper. That lovely Icelander came to make sure that Ian and Rachael were okay and when he realised they were safe, he waved them cheerfully on their way.

The stony dirt track seemed endless: it was like driving on a rough roller-coaster or a crater on the moon

waterslide, hot tubs and geothermal sauna. She was determined that before they left next day, she was going to swim there. They checked in and when they had freshened up, they decided to go into the nearby village to eat. They soon spotted an Italian-style restaurant and decided to go in for their favourite pizza. Sadly they soon discovered that the owners did not have any pizzas on their menu: small wonder there wasn't a single customer!

So Ian and Rachael left quickly and went to a nearby restaurant that was packed full of happy customers. Obviously this one served really good food. It was warm and welcoming with prompt, cheerful service, so soon they were each tucking into a huge tasty vegetarian meal: by this time they were absolutely ravenous.

When they got back at the hotel, Ian treated himself to a well-deserved but expensive beer – £5! I bet you can guess what Rachael did … yes! She went for a swim in that geothermally heated pool with water at forty to forty-two degrees and had an absolute ball. Both Ian and Rachael, yet again, had forgotten to pack her bathing costume so she swam in her pants and T-shirt.

As Ian watched her fondly as she swam lazily up and down the warm, rippling pool and slid gracefully down the waterslide, he reflected on how harrowing he had found the time when he was completely lost. He realised that, had he been on his own, he would have enjoyed the challenge of being off-road in the middle of nowhere. However, because he had the responsibility of keeping his precious daughter safe, he had been really frightened; understandably so, but he was angry with himself for unintentionally putting them at risk.[2]

Rachael stayed in that magical pool, now lit by the silvery radiance of the rising moon, until around 11 p.m. when Ian decided it was really time for bed. They both agreed that in spite of their 'slight detour' it had been a perfectly marvellous day.

but eventually they reached the tarmac road again and made good speed to the Hotel Ork.

They were very happy to find that the hotel was superb – a beautiful country hotel located in the 'greenhouse village' of Hveragerdi which has earned its name because it is situated amongst the spectacular lava fields and hills pierced by surreal but natural steaming vents. Hveragerdi's highly active geothermal field heats hundreds of greenhouses and is famous for its horticultural college.

The hotel had excellent facilities and, very importantly for Rachael, an outside swimming pool with a

---

2 He would have been even angrier had he known that when he took the car back at the end of their tour, he would be fined £400 for that tiny scratch on the bumper! He could actually have written the car off and because of the insurance limit on damages, would only have had £880 to pay – a ridiculous situation! Thankfully he did not know this yet so he relaxed and enjoyed his beer.

DAY 3 – SELJALANDSFOSS, GLUFRAFOSS AND SKOGAFOSS WATERFALLS – DRIVE AND HIKE

In spite of being up fairly late the previous evening, Rachael was awake before Ian.

'Come on, Dad, hurry up!' she chided. 'We need to get going. I'm really looking forward to walking behind that big waterfall.'

When they were at dinner the previous evening Ian had told her why Seljalandsfoss was very special so she was impatient to see it. Ian pointed out that they needed breakfast first as it was going to be another long, action-packed day. In no time at all, Rachael was tucking into another splendid breakfast, a large vegetarian one with toast and hot chocolate. She was always so active and eager to do everything that she certainly needed the calories. Every morning she had a huge breakfast while for Ian, a splendid breakfast when he is hiking is always black coffee, white toast if possible and plenty of butter.

Soon they were driving again along the safe tarmac road with a continuous line of distant mountains to their left towards Seljalandsfoss: one of Iceland's famous and most-photographed waterfalls because of its unique formation. As soon as they parked, Rachael sensibly picked up her waterproof jacket again from the back seat and jumped out of the car. She had heard that you could get very wet walking behind the falls and I think, knowing Rachael, she was secretly rather looking forward to getting soaked!

They were somewhat disappointed when they saw the waterfall from a distance as from the front it did not look particularly special apart from obviously being very high – sixty metres (two hundred feet). However as they walked nearer, through carpets of beautiful wild flowers, they began to realise that it was a very powerful cascade with something hidden behind the curtains of water and billowing mist.

As they neared the deep, serene pool into which it poured, they noticed the path that ran down the side of the pool and behind the waterfall itself. Magic! Rachael decided not to wear her waterproof because she wanted to get really wet under that massive natural shower. So, with Ian just in a T-shirt, they made their way carefully along the rocky path, which was greasy and slippery from the perpetual water spray. They chose to go anti-clockwise as there was a section where they had to climb some mossy rocks; it is always better to climb up slippery rocks than try to go down them.

Rachael was rather disappointed that she hardly got wet at all – only slightly at the very beginning but she soon became completely enchanted as she gazed through the huge curtains of glistening water and felt the droplets of spray on her face and hands. It was just like a giant's massive shower falling in front of her and she was actually hiding behind it! She gazed in wonder at the rugged cave behind the falls, which had been eroded into the cliff face by the power of the water. Every nook and cranny was shimmering and gleaming as the water droplets shone like diamonds in the diffused light created by the plumes of mist. The roar of the water reverberated around their ears like a huge, surrounding echo magnifying all their senses. It was a truly magical experience that would become a cherished memory:

the mighty power of nature up close. After taking endless photos, at last they forced themselves to move away from this awe-inspiring scene and followed the narrow path at the foot of the rugged cliffs towards a second waterfall not far away: Glufrafoss.

Suddenly between the cliffs and the path, they noticed that from the deep vivid-green grass, a spout of water was shooting up about eight feet into the air – could it be the world's smallest geyser? They fervently hoped so as they had not seen the famous Geysir erupt the previous day. Curious and full of expectation, they rushed over to investigate only to burst into laughter: their geyser was not romantic or surprising; it was only a prosaic blue plastic pipe with a large hole in it – how disappointing! It had probably been put there to collect water for some villagers. Still smiling, they carried on towards Glufrafoss.

Sadly most visitors never bother to view this waterfall, which is such a shame as it is truly worth visiting. It is hidden deep within a rocky canyon with a narrow entrance, more like a cleft or cave in the cliffs. Rachael and Ian followed the stream that emerged from a hidden opening, walking deep into the interior where it suddenly opened up into a kind of amphitheatre with a wide sparkling waterfall cascading some seventy feet over gloomy rocks: an eerie, mysterious place that sent a shiver down their spines.

When they had retraced their steps to the cliff path, Rachael asked Ian if she could climb up to the top of the cliffs so she could look down into this strange cavern-like hole and see the water falling downwards. Ever concerned for her safety, Ian reluctantly agreed and said he would wait for her on the path at the base of the cliffs.

He spent the next half an hour so with his heart in his mouth, worrying about her, as parents do when their child tackles something potentially dangerous on their own. Ian waited anxiously trying unsuccessfully not to imagine what could happen – he was determined to give Rachael the freedom and responsibility to have a little adventure on her own. You can imagine just how relieved he was, when eventually she ran back down to his side completely safe and with her face aglow with joy.

'You really, really should have climbed up with me, Dad,' she exclaimed excitedly, 'the view from the top of the waterfall was great! I could see all the way down that huge frightening hole and watched the water splashing down for ages. I was very careful – I didn't go too near the edge and I watched where I put my feet.'

'Thank God!' thought Ian – his teachings about safety when trekking and scrambling had clearly been absorbed by Rachael.

She added with a grin, 'I could see right over to those lovely mountains. I do so hope we can go and explore them!'

Ian had to smile: Rachael was indefatigable; always looking for a new challenge and experience – his daughter was indeed a true explorer.

'You'll just have to wait and see,' he responded. 'We've another superb waterfall to see first.'

It was about an hour's drive past several glaciers to Skogafoss, which many people believe rivals two-tiered Gullfoss in majesty. It certainly is absolutely spectacular being sixty metres (two hundred feet) high and twenty-five metres (eighty-two feet) wide and the sheer volume of water that thunders down the cliffs of a former coastline is breathtaking. The coastline has now receded seawards approximately five kilometres. This classic rectangular-shaped waterfall, Skogafoss, is visible though distant from the road and the roar of the massive falls increases as you approach: a true surround-sound experience. Its location, in eye-catching landscape with two towering snow-capped glaciers, adds to its allure, as does the folklore about the treasure of Prasi Porolfsson, a Viking settler who around 900 AD is said to have hidden a treasure chest full of gold beneath the falls.

By now it was really hot so Rachael left her waterproof in the car but Ian decided to carry his fleece as they planned to climb quite high to the top of the falls; if it grew cooler either he or Rachael could wear it if they felt cold.

Rachael and Ian were both mesmerised: the scene before them was awesome with thundering water, sheets of sparkling spray and billowing mist rising into the air which they hoped would soon produce magical rainbows. They watched and listened for a while and took lots of photos. Initially Rachael was rather cross that, because there were so many sightseers, she could not get a shot of the whole expanse of the waterfall without having people in it. (As she had shown a remarkable interest and developed considerable skill in photography, Ian had bought her a Canon professional camera.) Ian explained to her that having people in the foreground would give her photos more interest and show the true scale of those massive falls. This proved to be absolutely true because she took some great photos and was really proud of them especially the ones where she managed to catch a glimpse of a beautiful rainbow.

Ian took one absolutely stunning photo of Rachael in front of the falls with a wonderful look of enchantment on her face and arms outstretched. Magically, there was a rainbow behind her: a masterpiece!

Now it was time for them to climb up the path to the right of the falls: there were 527 steps to surmount before they reached the viewing platform at the top. (Rachael counted these very carefully on the way up and down and her tally agrees with the one recorded in a travel book I have.)

The spray hung above the falls like a silver cloud in the brilliant blue sky and the view down the falls was magnificent but somewhat precarious. The incredible raw power of the thundering water was truly amazing; the platform seemed to tremble under their feet as though frightened by nature's awesome display. The whole experience was overwhelming.

Rachael took a super photo looking down over a gull's nest perched on the cliffs and several others of the waterfall, the shining silvery mist and looking out

to the majestic Atlantic Ocean. Then they climbed the fence by a stile as they had decided to walk up the path beside the River Skoga. Passing smaller shining water-falls and deep pools with swirling eddies, they carried on for about an hour before turning round and retracing their steps.

On the drive to their overnight accommodation – the Icelandair Hotel Klaustur at the small village of Kirkjubaejarklaustur – Ian told Rachael about some of the things he had read on the information boards on the viewing platform. Apparently 'Skogur' means forest – so the name Skogafoss means Forest Falls. It is thought that this indicates that once, millennia ago, the area around that wonderful waterfall was forested. Also it had been the location of many films like *Thor: The Dark World* and in 2015, the Bollywood movie, *Dilwale*.

After they had checked in at their hotel, set in a lovely location between two glaciers, Ian, mindful of Rachael's earlier desire to explore one of the fascinating mountains, took her up the steep waymarked trail on the mountain facing their hotel. Rachael was supremely happy to be climbing and walking again. They explored for about two hours and were delighted to find a beautiful tarn – very like their favourite small mountain lake at home, Angle Tarn. They sat by it for a while then, as it was getting late, they walked down to their hotel, freshened up and changed.

They had to wear their waterproofs as it was raining heavily when they went out for a pleasant evening meal and afterwards walked to the local leisure centre where there was an open-air swimming pool. (Guess who spotted this first!) Completely oblivious to the rain lashing down on her, Rachael swam up and down the pool thoroughly enjoying herself in lovely, warm, thirty-eight degree water.

Ian waved and called to her frequently because some people in the pool were look-ing at him in a puzzled way; he wanted them to realise that his daughter was also in the pool and he was watching her. He had to admit that he probably did look rather peculiar, sitting in his fleece under a parasol and trying to keep dry. One day he would remember to pack his trunks and then he would be able to go swimming too.

At last Rachael had to admit that she was feeling a bit tired: it had been a long and energetic day so she showered and dressed quickly and was rewarded with a hot chocolate. Another fantastic day drew to a close.

DAY 4 – SKAFTAFELL NATIONAL PARK – DRIVE AND HIKE

After breakfast next morning, before they set off on their drive to Skaftafell National Park, Rachael and Ian visited the hotel gift shop. While Rachael was looking for possible little gifts to take home, Ian photographed two fantastic posters on the wall: one was of a humpback whale leaping high above the choppy surface of the sea and the other was of the famous Geysir gushing a huge plume of water some eighty metres up into the air. When Rachael saw what he was doing, she was incensed:

'You can't do that Dad!' she exclaimed. 'That's cheating!'

'No it's not,' explained Ian. 'I am not going to pretend I took the original photographs for the posters – it's just that we didn't have the chance to take the photo of the Geysir as it was inactive and the humpback whale we saw never jumped in the air. The photos are to remind us of what we might have seen had we been lucky.'

Rachael seemed to accept Ian's explanation but still muttered under her breath; she wasn't completely satisfied. Before long they were on their way and Rachael cheered up quickly when she looked out of the car window at the weird moonscape around them; her mood can change in a heartbeat when confronted by some wonder of nature.

The whole of the drive that day was through Eldraun, a massive lava field covered in luxuriant moss of every shade of green. It was just like being on another planet. The snow-capped mountains and glaciers to their left glinted invitingly in the sunshine. Rachael was so fascinated that she put her camera on the dashboard of their car and videoed the whole fabulous journey: the best yet! About two hours later, they parked at the Visitor Centre at Skaftafell.

Skaftafell is a well-known preservation area in southeast Iceland, called Oraefi. This name means 'wasteland' and was given to the entire district after the disastrous eruption of the Oraefojokull volcano in 1363 wiped out the entire local community and the productive manor farmland, leaving behind barren, stony, sandy land devoid of vegetation. It was established as a national park in 1967; however, in 2008 it became part of the much larger Vatnajokull National Park.

The scenery around Skaftafell is full of stark contrasts. Numerous rubble-strewn, crevassed glacial tongues emerge from the huge glacial ice-cap flanked by active and dormant volcanoes and jagged snow-capped mountains, with the spectacular glacier-topped peak of Hvannadalshnjukur being the highest. Volcanic eruptions, such as that from Grimsvotn, frequently burst out from under the ice-cap and give rise to destructive glacial floods (jokulhlaups) which scour the landscape and massively swell the River Skeioara. These in turn create and extend the sandy, stony outwash plain between the glacier and the sea known locally as a sandur. The last major glacial flood was as late as 1996.

In the whole area, evidence abounds of volcanic activity and the powerful erosive forces exerted by glacial ice and rivers; small wonder that Iceland is called the Land of Fire and Ice. It is a land constantly in flux and evolving: exhilarating geology in action.

Adding to the attraction of these wonders of natural forces in action, the Skaftafell is renowned in Iceland for its agreeable climate and the number of clear, sunny days in summer, uncommon in the south of Iceland. Also there is a great variety of wildlife including Arctic foxes, field mice, meadow pipits, ravens, merlin and snow bunting, and many plants like harebells, saxifrage, sea pea and Arctic beauty.

Rachael and Ian could hardly wait to explore this fascinating national park. Because they would be hiking all day on various waymarked trails and climbing quite high in the mountains, Ian decided they should take some extra sandwiches, snacks and drinks with them: a visit to the shop in the Visitor Centre was necessary. Rucksacks filled with goodies as well as essential hiking gear, they set off on the first part of the trail through grass and low birch trees and willow towards the unique and picturesque Svartifoss (Black Falls): a hike of well over an hour.

In fact their whole day would be spent hiking on rugged undulating ridges around that fabulous valley containing the Vatnajokull glacier, rivers and the outwash plain with wonderful views over to the vast Atlantic Ocean: the kind of day that they both loved. They scarcely noticed they were walking up hill all the time as the scenery was so interesting and they were chatting. They were actually planning a return visit to Iceland in the near future with Icelandair, staying where they had the previous night – the Hotel Klaustur. Using the hotel as a base, they could take a helicopter tour of Iceland and in particular, fly over and look down into an active volcano. After that, they hoped they could go on to Greenland.

'Wow, Dad – that would be fab!' cried Rachael. She was only about halfway through this adventure but, as always, was eager to plan another.

On the way to Svartifoss, they passed three smaller sparkling waterfalls – each with fascinating names: Pjofafoss (Thieves' Fall), Hundafoss (Dogs' Fall) and Magnusarfoss – (the Falls of Magnus.) Apparently Hundafoss was so named because when there was a flood, the bodies of farm dogs were swept over the falls.

Their first view across the valley of that extraordinary waterfall – Svartifoss – made them gasp with wonder. Even from a distance, they could see that it was beautifully framed in a superb heart shape of black basalt columns over which a glistening cascade fell some twelve metres.

Rachael was determined to get a close-up view of this fascinating waterfall, aptly named Black Falls.

'Come on, Dad!' she begged, 'Please, *please* can we go nearer – I want to take some photos.'

Ian pointed out that it was quite a long way off their route and would mean climbing down from the ridge they were on and up the other side of the mountain facing them. Rachael was undeterred: she was indefatigable and her determination was unbending. With a shake of his head and a knowing smile of pride, Ian agreed and led the way down, across a river and up the other side.

As they approached the falls Rachael rushed ahead, eager to take her photos. Although it had been quite a long detour, Ian had to admit that it was really worthwhile. The spray from the falling plume of water made the basalt columns gleam with every shade of black you could imagine and the shining water splashed over the smaller basalt columns and mossy boulders at the foot of the falls creating a breathtaking scene.

The whole heart-shaped basin was filled with small bright green birches and willows and huge tufts of grass waving in the breeze. Ian and Rachael took many photos of this truly bewitching scene.

After a while they re-joined the ridge where it curved around the huge ice mass that was the Vatnajokull glacier and gazed down awestruck on its ridged, boulder-strewn and crevassed surface. So many people expect glaciers to be a sparkling bluish-white colour but when you consider their massive erosive power, inevitably they carry along all kinds of debris, which discolours the ice.

Rachael and Ian continued climbing up the dramatic ridge until they reached a crag with a large flattish surface at the top of the mountain: a sensational viewpoint. They decided this was where they would eat their lunch and settled down comfortably in spite of having to share the crag with lots of people who obviously had the same idea. They had hiked all morning and had scarcely seen another person and now they were amongst a crowd but as everyone was clearly enjoying the scene and very happy Rachael and Ian didn't really mind. The view was panoramic and exceptional: not only could they see snow-capped mountains, rugged peaks, the verdant green valley and vast outwash plain, they could follow the line of that spectacular glacier right down the estuary that led to the sea.

Reluctantly they left that magnificent viewpoint but were delighted to find that wonderful sights accompanied them all the way down the ridge. About an hour before they reached the Visitor Centre, they ran out of water but fortunately they could actually see the centre and the car park with their car visible far below them so they knew they were safe. It had been a long, hard day of hiking but a glorious one. They were buzzing with excitement as Ian drove to their destination for the night, the Hotel Smyrlabjorg which, according to their itinerary, was 'a family-owned hotel situated on a working sheep farm in rural countryside west of Hofn.'

Naturally they thought that it would be a rustic farmhouse with outbuildings so they were absolutely astonished when they arrived there. Not only were the buildings modern but the facilities out of this world! Actually there were fifty-two lovely rooms, all en suite, with wonderful views either of the mountains or the ocean: a rustic farmhouse – I don't think so! Ian was completely astounded when he saw the luxurious dining room, which they passed on their way up to their comfortable spacious room. They were both looking forward fervently to the evening meal there – the first time they had actually eaten dinner in any of their hotels.

After a quick shower, they went down to the dining room and looked around in wonder. It was fabulous: beautifully set tables with shining cutlery, sparkling glasses and immaculate tablecloths with perfectly folded serviettes. They could have been in a five star hotel; it was that good! For once Ian was speechless; he could not find words to describe the sheer opulence of that dining room.

In their itinerary it had also said there was a large dining room with homemade meals using local produce. Well, 'large' was true but nothing had prepared them for the huge buffet with an unbelievable array of fantastic mouth-watering dishes awaiting their pleasure. It was obvious that each one had been meticulously prepared and was beautifully presented. There was a huge variety of meat dishes but they had never seen such a vast range of vegetarian choices for starters, a main meal and appetising desserts. They stood there mesmerised, unable to decide what to select. Of course Rachael wanted to try as many different dishes as she could and Ian made a valiant effort by choosing a small amount of each vegetarian dish. He did notice that Rachael's portions gradually grew smaller as she determinedly sampled every one of them.

They really deserved a good evening meal after all the hiking they had done in that wonderful national park but never in their wildest dreams had they anticipated having such a splendid banquet. Ian, who has travelled extensively in many countries, described it as 'absolutely world class.'[3]

When they were back in their super bedroom, Ian chilled out on his bed watching the TV with the sound

---

3 Readers you should really check out this hotel – it is beyond any expectations you might possibly have of a hotel in the middle of nowhere. It would grace any high-class district of a major city. Read about it at www.smyrlabjorg.is

turned down because Rachael, stuffed to the gills with food, went on her iPad to FaceTime her mum. She described in detail the fantastic day they had had, emphasised what an amazing holiday she was having in Iceland and filmed the room to show how luxurious it was.

Eventually the conservation turned to her forthcoming adventure: trekking with her dad and Grandma Joyce's Sherpa – Chandra – in Nepal. Ian had to smile: Rachael was always looking forward to her next exciting challenge – she truly had the soul of an explorer!

It was the end of another perfect day. Ian reflected that each day had seemed perfect but this day had reached beyond perfection into a different dimension.

DAY 5 – JOKULSARLON GLACIAL LAGOON – DRIVE AND HIKE

Next morning they went down for breakfast wondering what the menu would be like. They were not disappointed, as the breakfast buffet was almost as comprehensive as the evening one had been. In spite of the massive meal she had consumed the previous evening Rachael made a brave attempt to do justice to the marvellous spread. Ian however had his normal black coffee and, for once, instead of toast he had croissants, bread rolls and butter.

Completely fortified, they set off in glorious sunshine once again for Jokulsarlon Glacial Lagoon, one of the famous and most visited and photographed wonders

of Iceland. It was a fairly short drive on the ring road but the most spectacular yet: truly a heavenly stretch of road over black lava fields. Interesting rural properties lined the route and most of them had glaciers either in their backyards or nearby. To their right was the sparkling sea and to their left the rugged peaks of snow-capped mountains and gleaming glaciers.

Although theirs seemed to be the only car on the road, Ian had to break sharply as a herd of cows made their nonchalant, lazy way across the road from right to left. Obviously those cows had all the time in the world! Not Rachael: she had read so much about the icebergs in the glacial lagoon that she could hardly wait to get there.

Ian drove across a small suspension bridge and suddenly they were there at the fabulous Jokulsarlon Glacial Lagoon. Nothing, not photos or extensive reading, could have prepared them for the magnificent scene in front of them. It was utterly breathtaking: majestic, surreal and overwhelmingly beautiful. They were completely mesmerised.

For a while they just sat there looking at this miracle of nature then Ian quickly parked and they walked down to the shoreline of the lagoon to view all the wonders at close hand.

Jokulsarlon Lake or Iceberg Lagoon is testament to the climate changes affecting Iceland. When temperatures began to rise, the Breioamerkurjokull glacier, a tongue of the huge Vatnajokull one, retreated rapidly and continually forced icebergs of every shape and size to drop into the ocean. As the glacier drifted inland every year, it left glacial moraines exposed at both sides of the lake and deep gorges, which filled with melted water and large chunks of ice calved from the glacier.

These icebergs, in a vast array of colourful shades from milky white to azure blue, float around the deep lagoon eventually heading towards the sea. They gather at the mouth of the lake's shallow exit and in summer melt and roll down the channel, escaping seawards. In winter the lagoon freezes and locks the icebergs in place: a wonderland of mighty ice sculptures – some up to thirty metres (ninety-eight feet) high. It is said that the wonderful lagoon has doubled in size in the last fifteen years and is predicted to continue to grow.

Rachael and Ian explored the unusual black sandy beach, which was littered with splinters and chunks of sparkling ice. They gazed out in wonder at the myriad of fantastically shaped icebergs, unable to believe their eyes at the range of colours that changed according to the degree of reflected light and the amount of air and volcanic ash trapped in the ice crystals. They walked to where the glacier actually entered the lagoon and saw how the ice fractured, cracked and fell with a huge splash into the water. Magic!

Later, Ian found a small mound, which had originally been the moraine of the retreating glacier and sat there on a rock where he could see the whole of the shore. From here he could watch Rachael carefully whilst giving her the freedom to explore the whole area safely and take as many photos as she wished from various viewpoints.

Utterly amazed, he marvelled at the panorama of beauty and otherworldly strangeness of his surroundings and realised that this was probably the most spectacular setting he had ever seen. He was enchanted. His view out to sea was of the astonishing icebergs floating on a deep blue lagoon; landwards, the snow-capped peaks of verdant velvety green mountains and volcanoes. The outstanding view was of the mystic massive Vatnajokull ice-cap that stood 3000-feet high and from which numerous huge glaciers emerged.

It was not at all surprising to find that this area had been used as the set for many famous movies including two Bond films: *A View to a Kill* and *Die Another Day*, as well as *Tomb Raider* and *Batman Begins*. Apparently in *Die Another Day*, the lagoon was specially frozen and six Aston Martins were destroyed on the ice.

Ian never lost sight of Rachael, who was obviously having a ball. For about two hours, she wandered around here and there completely in a world of her own imagination. She snapped everything from every angle and, because of the quality of her camera, she was able to experiment with wide-angle views and close-up detailed photos. Seals, birds, icebergs, ice shards, rocks, the lagoon and the glacier came under her scrutiny. One fabulous photo was taken by Rachael as she lay prone on the beach, looking through a circular ring of ice that had been deposited there: she snapped a beautiful iceberg nearby and this wonderful image made it look as if it were framed by shining ice.

By now they were both feeling a little hungry so they went to the Visitor Centre for a light lunch. As they came out, Ian noticed one of the amphibious craft that took people on boat trips out into the lagoon had pulled up the beach. These boats are unique forms of transportation as they can drive on the land,

pick people up from the beach and take them into the water. Although sturdy boats, they are accompanied all the time by a small safety boat so Ian was quite confident they would be okay. He asked Rachael if she would like one of these exciting boat trips. I'm sure that you can imagine what she said.

'Wow, Dad! I'd love that. It will be really cool!'

Indeed the whole trip was breathtaking: for over an hour, they wove in and out of fantastic icebergs and spotted seals basking lazily on them. Some were more energetic and cavorted around flapping their flippers in the air as if waving to the passengers. Everyone waved back enchanted. Skuas, terns and other seabirds wheeled over their heads and as they neared the place where the massive glacier entered the lagoon, they were thrilled to see and hear chunks of ice breaking from it. Their cameras never stopped clicking. Rachael squealed with delight, her face aglow with excitement.

The views from the boat of the distant jagged snow-capped mountains, the velvety green hills and the huge ice-cap were amazing. Adding to their enjoyment, they soon discovered that the owner of the boat was very knowledgeable: he explained about the origins of the lagoon and the glacier and then picked up a piece of floating ice and broke it into pieces. He offered everyone 'a piece of thousand-year-old ice' to taste. Ian refused but, of course, Rachael eagerly sampled some; she really is up for anything!

When they were back on shore, Rachael and Ian took a short walk up the side of the glacier to see all the crevasses and ridges that scoured its surface. Then they went back to their car and drove to their next hotel on a hill just outside Vik.

The Hotel Dyrholaey was a lovely family-run countryside hotel surrounded by heath and productive farmland. Every room had a fabulous view either over snow-capped mountains or of the bay and sea beyond. After checking in, Ian drove into the small town of Vik to fill the car up with petrol, then they walked down to the fascinating basalt-columned bay. It was very large – a bit like Morecambe Bay near their home but the sand here was a spectacular black and very grainy.

Tasting 1000-year-old ice.

In the distance, they could see yet another wonder: the remains of an extinct volcano that many years ago had exploded violently and left a huge crater –a large caldera – surrounded by a ring of rugged hills and rocky arches. These arches were said to be the favourite sanctuary for puffins but to Rachael's disappointment, none were visible that evening.

When they were back at their hotel, they decided not to have any dinner as they were still quite full from the huge meals they had eaten the previous day and the menu did not have much choice of vegetarian dishes to tempt them. They settled on some comfortable sofas at the end of the dining room, had drinks and chatted about their phenomenal day. It was difficult for both of them to comprehend all the marvels

they had been privileged to see that day: miracles of nature. They looked through all their stunning photos and Ian was amazed at just how good Rachael's were; she really had a natural talent for framing a photo perfectly and finding an unusual and interesting view or angle, enhancing ordinary objects into images of beauty. She truly had captured the unbelievable wonders of the Jokulsarlon Glacial Lagoon.

Before they went to their beds, Rachael admitted she was feeling a little peckish so Ian ordered her a plate of chips. She had earned them many times over with her zest for life and her joyful, infectious sense of fun that made her the most delightful of companions. Ian was so proud of her and knew that he was one very lucky dad.

DAY 6 – HVERAGERDI AND ON TO REYKJAVIK – DRIVE AND HIKE

This day, the last of their Scenic South Coast tour, was mainly a long drive of 190km back to Reykjavik with a scheduled break at Hveragerdi, one of the most important geothermal sites in Iceland. Although Ian and Rachael were basically retracing the route of their outward journey, they were looking forward to seeing the landscape from a different perspective.

As the day was unusually cloudy, Rachael asked Ian if they could go back to the glacial lagoon at Jokulsarlon to see it in different weather conditions. Ian thought this was an excellent idea so the lagoon was their first stop.

Dull clouds of billowing fog were hanging over the whole bay: it was totally surreal – a gloomy, completely different atmosphere from the previous day. The fog had leeched all the colours from that spectacular scene and even the icebergs, emerging here and there from the drifting fog, had lost their pristine white and azure-blue sparkling colours. They were just huge chunks of dull greyish-white ice floating on grey cloudy water. Rachael and Ian were so grateful that they had seen the magic of that marvellous glacial lagoon in glorious sunshine.

They climbed back into the car and Ian drove through the weird black lava fields to the site of the infamously destructive Oraefajokull eruption, which took place in 1362 with a smaller eruption in 1727. Ian had promised Rachael she could select a piece of that special lava as a keepsake; a memory of her wonderful Icelandic adventure.

She took some time choosing exactly the right piece and with a triumphant smile, came back to the car. She still has that piece of lava today, displayed on a special shelf among all her treasures.

Ian drove on towards Hveragerdi, a town some forty-five kilometres from Reykjavik, well known for its geothermal springs and highly active geothermal field, which heats hundreds of greenhouses. Nationally, the town is famous for its agricultural college and naturopathic clinic.

They parked at the Visitor Centre where they spotted a bird pretending to be a member of staff! (see below) Then they went to explore the massive 5000-year-old

black lava fields: the vista was unbelievable. In spite of the lava, the surrounding area was green and verdant. There were some beautiful trees springing from the fertile volcanic soil – it was a really pleasant area to walk around. Unfortunately because they had already made two fairly lengthy stops, Rachael and Ian did not have enough time to complete the hike they would like to have done up to the Kambar mountain slopes, which are said to provide many wonderful viewpoints.

Really, they did not miss anything truly exciting as none of the numerous geothermal springs were erupting that day. Usually pillars of hot steam could be seen frequently and regularly emerging from the ground and stretching high into the sky. Even all the bubbling mud pools were quiescent.

Although a lot of the volcanic activity was not apparent that day, Ian and Rachael read on an information board that the powerful earthquake that struck the south coast of Iceland on May 29th 2008 had its epicentre less than two kilometres from Hveragerdi. It caused a new hot spring area to break through the ground of the hillside above the town. Several very active hot springs began to throw colourful mud and steaming water into the air: a spectacular sight. Sadly none of this was visible on the day they visited but neither of them was upset as they had unforgettable memories of fantastic experiences they had been blessed with throughout their tour, both driving and hiking.

Eventually they arrived back in Reykjavik and went to hand over their hire car. Ian was astounded when he was fined £400 for the really tiny scratch sustained when he had hit that stone on the road: a massive fine for such minor damage.

Somewhat disgruntled at this injustice, Ian and Rachael went to check into the lovely hotel, where they had stayed on the first evening of their fabulous Icelandic adventure – the Hotel Reykjavik Centrum. They freshened up and then went out to find somewhere to eat; of course, it had to be somewhere that did not use whale meat in their dishes. They wandered around and spotted the attractive-looking Bjarni Fel Sportsbar complete with multiple TV screens, so they went inside for a drink. It was heaving with noisy but well-behaved British football supporters avidly watching various football matches.

After all the serene silence, peace and solitude of the previous days, they found they could hardly bear the noise or the crush of bodies so they drank up quickly and went to find somewhere much quieter to eat and chat in peace. Initially, Ian wanted to find a new restaurant but Rachael pointed out that they'd had a great vegetarian meal in the Caruso Restaurant on their first night – why bother look anywhere else? Ian agreed this was sensible so they sought it out and settled down to a wonderfully tasty meal and drinks. Although the building looks a little dour and unattractive from the outside, the atmosphere inside is warm and welcoming and the food and service top class. In all, they actually ate there three times so you can surmise that it really was a superb place to relax and enjoy a lovely meal. What's more, the owners had a ban on the use of whale meat. Wonderful!

DAY 7 – REYKJAVIK – A TRIP TO HOSPITAL

While they were eating breakfast the next morning, Ian asked Rachael what she would like to do on their last day in Iceland. Obviously she had been thinking about this because she replied immediately:

'What I really, *really* want to do is to go whale watching on one of those speedboats. Please, *please* Dad – can we do that? It will be so exciting!'

'Of course we can, darling!' Ian responded happily.

He admitted to Rachael that he had secretly been hoping she would choose that trip because it was what just what he had been dreaming of doing. He had not liked to say what his preference was as he wanted Rachael to have a free choice.

They made their way quickly down to the Old Harbour and went to book with the same company they had chosen for their first trip – Elding: Ultimate Whale Watching Tours. However this time, they selected the exhilarating Express Whale and Puffin Tour. While they were waiting, they read all about what this exciting trip entailed.

'An exhilarating express tour in a RIB boat with a specially trained whale guide and certified RIB boat captain; only 12 people per boat. Search for the wildlife and explore the seas on the adventure of a lifetime on our express boats.

'Our specially engineered RIB boats get you closer and faster to the whales and puffins than our bigger boats. These stable and safe boats also allow us to search a bigger area, thus increasing your likelihood of viewing the whales, dolphins and birdlife.'

There was an additional note:

'This tour is not suitable for pregnant women and those with a history of back injuries.'

Dad before the speedboat trip ...

The warning was to prove utterly ironic!

Rachael was so excited she could hardly contain her joy: she jumped up and down and clapped her hands gleefully. She did not have to wait too long because they needed to be kitted up. Besides goggles and a lifebelt, they had to climb into rather stiff, waterproof overalls, which would protect them from the spray. They both looked very adventurous in their warm, bright, red, whole-body suits.

Eagerly Rachael and Ian climbed down some steps to the pontoon where their RIB boat was moored. They chose some rigid seats at the front, which they had to sit astride. It wasn't long before everyone was aboard and, with a roar of its powerful engine, their boat speedily left the Old Harbour. Rachael and Ian were full of anticipation and excitement.

At speed, the boat headed out towards the nearby islands, the natural home of countless puffins. Cameras clicked continually, as the passengers took endless photos of these wonderful comical characters with their clown-like eyes and brilliant red-tipped beaks. Some of the puffins flew down from their perches on the rocky outcrops and scooted amusingly across the surface of the sea; they seemed to be putting on a special show for the visitors.

Then the captain turned the boat, speeded up again and headed out to sea. Disastrously, a large wave confronted them and as the boat reared up and bucked over it, Ian was thrown into the air and came down heavily on his rigid seat. There was a loud crack, which made Rachael flinch. Ian was horrified, certain that he had broken something in his back. He gasped in agony as sickening pains shot up his spine; the pain was overwhelming, almost unendurable. Ian is a very brave man who can bear considerable pain but he was completely shocked and felt really faint and nauseous.

Rachael scrutinised her dad's increasingly pale face and quickly realised he was badly hurt.

'Are you okay, Dad?' she whispered in a caring but frightened voice.

'Of course I am,' replied Ian, not wishing to frighten her. 'I'll be fine.'

Rachael knew instinctively that this was just her dad being brave so she put her hand over his, held his wrist and spoke quietly and lovingly:

'Don't worry, Dad, you've always looked after me so now it's my turn. I'll take care of you.'

Ian was never more proud of her than at that moment: what a caring girl she was.

'Thank you, darling,' was all he could whisper.

With white knuckles, Ian gripped the sides of his seat, trying desperately to brace himself against the bouncing movements of the boat. He tried hard not to breathe deeply as each movement of his chest was torture; he took shallow breaths and panted lightly, like a woman in the last stages of a painful labour. (Considering the warning notice about pregnant women and broken backs, this was the ultimate irony!) Rachael kept looking at him anxiously, as did the other passengers and the captain, who asked Ian if he needed to go back to the harbour.

That proud, silly man, concerned that it would spoil the trip for everyone including Rachael, said that he would manage until the tour was finished, as long as he could sit at the rear of the boat. The captain slowed the speed right down and with many willing hands helping him and Rachael guarding his back, Ian managed to cautiously crawl to the back. He gritted his teeth as the least movement caused terrific shooting pains all over his body but he was determined to tough it out and let all the passengers enjoy their trip. Rachael just sat by her dad and watched him quietly, trying to protect him from the inevitable movement of the boat caused by the waves. She did this in such a mature, calm and caring way that it brought tears to Ian's eyes; she truly was a treasure.

Sadly, although the whale guide searched and searched, no whales or dolphins were visible so eventually the captain headed back to the Old Harbour. Slowly, in soul-destroying pain and holding on to Rachael, Ian managed very gingerly to climb

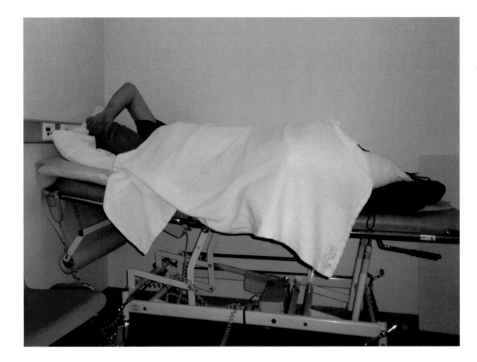

... and after!

out of the boat and up the steps to the pontoon. To this day, he truly does not know how he did this and cannot really remember with any degree of clarity what actually happened. Some people peeled him out of his overalls and guided him to the harbour wall, which he held on to, trying in vain to support his damaged back. The anxious captain advised Ian to go back to his hotel and have a long soak in a hot, deep bath with muscle salts and then see how he felt. He offered to ring for a taxi but Ian refused his kind offer. (Really some men – especially Ian – can be so stubborn, finding it incredibly hard to accept help.)

The captain was genuinely distressed and explained that this kind of accident had never ever happened before and apologised profusely. Despite his horrendous pain, Ian thanked the captain and said it was no one's fault; it was a freak injury, a complete fluke and he was just unlucky. The captain, obviously admiring Ian's fortitude and courage, said that if ever Ian came back to Reykjavik, he would take him out on a free whale watching trip again. (Ian still intends to return to Iceland one day and, of course, he also intends to take the captain up on his offer. Some people never learn!)

Ian knew he could not face trying to bend to climb in and out of a taxi, so when he explained this to Rachael, she quietly affirmed that she would help him to walk. Mustering all his courage and determination, step by painful step Ian, with Rachael's help, made his way very slowly back to the hotel. Each step was a small triumph for Ian in his battle against the pain that threatened to overwhelm him. Rachael walked closely by his side all the way, ensuring that no one pushed by her dad or got in his way. Vigilantly she watched out for obstructions and guided Ian safely back to the Hotel Reykjavik Centrum.

Once in the hotel, Rachael worked the lift and helped Ian to their room. He gazed longingly at the bath: he would have loved to have a soak in hot soothing water but he knew that if he managed to climb in, he would certainly not be able to get out. Ian decided that most of all he needed to rest: the excruciating pain had worn him out. He undid his belt, let his trousers drop to the floor and cautiously lowered himself into a sitting position on the side of his bed. After a considerable pause and holding onto Rachael's supporting arm, he was able to lower himself gradually until he was lying flat on his back. He closed his eyes not thinking for one moment that he would be able to sleep but exhaustion took over and for an hour or so slept soundly. Rachael did not fuss or talk; she propped herself up on her bed and played on her iPad.

As the dreadful pain resurfaced, Ian woke up and accepted that he was in real trouble and needed to go to hospital as soon as possible. Steadily, with Rachael's help, he levered himself back up into a sitting position on the side of the bed. He could not even bend to retrieve his trousers, so Rachael dressed him and patiently waited until he could stand up. Finally they managed to get down to reception where the poor gentleman on duty stared horrified at Ian: clearly this man was injured. Ian explained that he needed to go to hospital, so the receptionist ordered a taxi.

Very soon the taxi arrived and even with the awful pain gnawing away at his whole body, Ian soon had a wry smile on his face. In all the time they had been in Iceland, their taxi driver was the only one who did not speak a word of English! After many gestures, groans and Red Cross signs, drawn by Rachael, they managed to make him understand and before long they were in the Accident and Emergency Department of the hospital. Ian was quickly and efficiently assessed and sent on a trolley for an MRI scan.

While he was waiting for the results of the scan, Ian remained on the trolley with Rachael by his side. She looked a little glum so he tried to cheer her up by reminding her that he always kept his promises.

'I promised you that we would go to Nepal in your next half-term holiday and we will. I am not going to let my accident stop us from doing what we planned.'

Rachael rolled her eyes and replied, 'Oh, yeah? I don't think so!'

'Just wait and see. I'll be fine.' was Ian's response.

The results were what he had anticipated: he had two broken vertebrae in his back as well as extensive bruising. The doctor explained that Ian needed further investigations and would probably need an operation. He asked Ian if he had insurance and but Ian had to admit he had left his medical insurance card back in their hotel room. He could retrieve it later if necessary.

Ian was given two options: he could use Medivac and be accompanied by qualified medics on the flight but because of the way that organisation works, he would be flown to a hospital in the USA. Or he could be given strong medication – morphine – to reduce his pain. They would fit him with a spinal support and hopefully this would allow him to get to the airport and fly home early next morning for treatment in the UK.

Ian looked at Rachael's white, concerned face and knew immediately that he would go down the medication route: she had been incredibly brave, caring and capable but, nevertheless, she was still an eleven-year-old child who had been through an awful lot of trauma herself in the past twelve or so hours.

Option one was never a viable solution: it would mean that Rachael would be in the USA and, presumably, not be allowed to be with him in the hospital. They needed to be home.

Ian still does not know for sure, but he thinks he had painkilling injections and was given lots of tablets to cover him for the next few days. Also, he was fitted with a spinal jacket to support his back and found this reduced his pain level as it severely restricted his movement.

In the evening when he went to sign out of the hospital, he was presented with a bill. He dreaded opening it, as generally everything in Iceland seemed to be expensive. He had been in hospital most of the day, he had been given an MRI Scan, treatment and medication and fitted with a spinal jacket: he was expecting to have to pay thousands of pounds. Imagine his relief when he realised he was being charged only £300 for all that care and treatment. He quickly paid with his Barclaycard, ordered a taxi and soon they were back safely in their hotel room.

It was only when Ian noticed Rachael searching in their rucksacks that he realised neither of them had eaten since breakfast – now it was late evening. Ian was not at all hungry but welcomed one of the drinks they still had in their room and Rachael tucked into several different energy bars, a bar of chocolate, some crisps and a bottle of juice. Ian was still in considerable pain but perhaps because of the strong morphine medication, he felt as if he was floating above the ground and not really in full charge of his limbs or brain! When he did go to the bathroom, he walked like a zombie so decided that it would be much wiser and safer if he went to bed. Rachael told him to go to sleep; she would do all the packing and sort the room out. She promised that she would not forget anything.

Ian arranged for an early morning wake-up call and set the alarm to make sure they had plenty of time to get downstairs next morning. He reflected on how magnificently his eleven-year-old daughter had coped with the difficult situation his accident had caused. She had been so calm, controlled and sensible; for a while she had been the adult and he an injured child. He was so proud of her. Then he submitted gratefully to the power of the morphine and soon fell fast asleep.

Their transport had already been arranged for early next morning as their flight left at 6 a.m. Knowing that all the packing needed to be done before she went to bed, Rachael got herself organised, packing all their clothes and keepsakes efficiently and checking the rooms and drawers for any 'escapees'. She made sure that all the documents they would need at the airport were readily available in the front of one of their rucksacks, then she cleaned her teeth and went over to kiss Ian goodnight. He was sleeping soundly but had a little frown on his face so Rachael knew he was still in some pain. She made herself a cup of well-deserved hot chocolate and climbed into her bed. Bless her; she was completely wiped out.

DAY 8: THE JOURNEY HOME

Ian was awoken by the alarm call next morning and levered himself up groggily until he was sitting upright in bed. He had a drink of water and was pleased that his head gradually cleared. He was amazed to find that Rachael was already up, dressed, had eaten a snack and had all their luggage lined up by the door.

'Hope you are feeling a bit better this morning, Dad,' she said. 'Don't worry! Take your time getting ready while I take all our luggage downstairs to reception.'

It took her several trips!

'She a better organiser than I am,' thought Ian ruefully. 'Thank God I have such a wonderful daughter. She's a real trooper.'

Reluctantly he took some more painkillers because he knew he needed to be able to control some of his persistent pain in order to make sure they arrived home safely.

He vaguely remembers going down in the hotel lift and leaning up against the wall outside waiting for the taxi to arrive but not a great deal more. The whole journey passed in a strange blur: he was there and yet he wasn't. It was almost as though he was watching the scenario – a dad and his daughter travelling home – from the sidelines. It was a very strange experience. He does recall praying that the aircraft landed without a bump, which thankfully it did, but remembers little of Passport Control, Customs or Rachael retrieving and carrying all their luggage.

Unbelievably they managed to catch the train to Penrith without mishap and found a taxi to bring them back home to Old Water View.

The first we knew about Ian's dreadful accident was when Rachael, carrying a huge rucksack, burst through the kitchen door and announced loudly that they were home. She was followed slowly by a grey-faced Ian, clearly in dreadful pain as he gripped both sides of the doorway and levered himself inside.

'Why didn't you phone us?' we demanded, 'One of us would have picked you up at the airport!'

'We managed!' Ian stubbornly responded. 'It was fine.'

Fine, indeed! Famous last words …

Over the next twenty-four hours, we were told all the details of Ian's accident by Rachael and what had been confirmed by the Cumbria Infirmary in Carlisle when Ian went for a further scan. He had broken two vertebrae but, miraculously, his spinal cord had not been damaged. The doctor explained that at the moment, there was no need for surgery as trying to repair the vertebrae could be dangerous and damage the spinal cord. Ian was given some more painkillers and fitted with a more supportive spinal jacket. He was also given some crutches and told that complete rest was absolutely vital. However, to ensure Ian received the best advice possible, the doctor referred him to a consultant specialist at Newcastle Royal Victoria Infirmary.

Ian went on the train several times to Newcastle; the stubborn man would not let any of us drive him. Each time he was scanned and eventually measured for a tailor-made spinal jacket that would give him complete support (he simply would not rest as much as he was told!) In fact on his second visit to the consultant, his back had deteriorated.

I stayed on at Old Water View to run the place for Ian so he could relax and concentrate on doing all he could to heal his back. All the members of his staff were marvellous – really supportive – but poor Ian was completely frustrated and angry: a most impatient patient! Understandably so, to be fair, because not only was he battling a really painful back, he badly missed socialising with his guests. This was an aspect of the job he had always really enjoyed.

Rachael remained cheerful throughout his rehabilitation and both she and Catherine did their best to help. Ian, like Rachael, has never lacked courage, fortitude and determination; they have it in spades. They are both up for any challenge, no matter what it may be. Now Ian had a special challenge: to work hard to strengthen his back and get fit so Rachael and he could go trekking in Nepal in roughly two months' time. He had a target to aim for and he was determined to make it.

Did he succeed? Were they both able to trek in Nepal in the autumn half-term holiday? Read on and you will discover what happened …

CHAPTER

NEPAL 1: THE KATHMANDU VALLEY – AGED TEN YEARS SIX MONTHS

When planning the content and sequencing of the chapters in this book, I decided that as far as possible all the wonderful stories about Rachael would be in chronological order.

However, to make the whole book flow easily and to avoid unnecessary (and possibly boring) repetition, I came to realise that Rachael's three exciting explorations in the Nepal Himalaya, should be described sequentially in three separate chapters: Nepal 1, 2 and 3.

Fortunately this meant that the three trips sponsored by Macs Adventures could be written in sequence: The West Highland Way, Hadrian's Wall and The Drive/Hike Tour of Iceland's Scenic South Coast.

So, dear readers, at the end of the fabulous Iceland trip when Ian had his horrible accident while whale watching on that RIB Boat, he did, indeed, work unbelievably hard with tremendous courage and tenacity to overcome his pain, heal his back and recover his fitness. And he succeeded: some ten weeks after his dreadful injury, Rachael and he were walking again in Nepal in the spectacular Annapurna Region (Nepal 2).

So Rachael actually had three trips to Nepal: 2014, 2015 and 2016. The first trip took place a year before the 2015 Iceland Tour. However, I have grouped the Nepal trips together in this book to make the story flow better. Ian's accident happened in August 2015 and the walk in the Annapurna Region, (Nepal 2), at the end of October 2015. How he managed to get fit again, I will never know!

I sincerely hope that you will enjoy reading about Rachael's awesome explorations as much as Rachael and Ian loved walking every step.

Her three trips to Nepal meant Rachael actually spent almost two months in this incredible country and, as well as trekking, she learnt so much about the wonderful, friendly Nepalese people, their lifestyle and their culture: invaluable learning experiences in every way.

RACHAEL'S FIRST TRIP TO NEPAL – OCTOBER 2014

Although she had been abroad several times, Rachael had never visited a Third World country before so she could hardly wait to discover all she could about the lifestyle and culture of the Nepalese people. Of course, she was extremely excited about walking in the magnificent Himalaya: that was going to be a true adventure. She had heard a lot about the fabulous country of Nepal from Ian who had been there twice as a representative of the Rotary Club of Penrith and from me, Grandma Joyce. I have trekked to Everest and Annapurna base camps as well as several other treks so Rachael had avidly studied all my photos and videos and was really looking forward to her first visit.

Readers of my previous book about Rachael will remember her saying that because I had been to Everest Base Camp, not only was she going there but one day she would climb Everest and stand on the top of the highest mountain in the world!

An added bonus for Rachael was that she and Ian would be trekking with Chandra Prakash Rai (C.P. for short) whom she had met when she was younger.

C.P. is my dear friend, a mountain leader and guide. My success in completing many severe and difficult treks in the Himalaya was largely due to his expertise, dedication, encouragement and care. To thank him, I sponsored him to come to the UK to study English and develop his computer skills on a comprehensive three-year course. This would mean that when he grew too old to be a mountain guide and could no longer lead their treks, he could work in the office of Mountain Monarch Adventures, the company owned and run by his friends Pradip Limbu and Subash Rai. He would be able to help to design their website, plan and organise treks efficiently using the knowledge and expertise he had accumulated over the years. He could also offer advice on safety issues and this would prolong his earning capacity so he could provide for his family long term.

While he was living with me in the UK, we visited Ian, Catherine and Rachael frequently at Old Water View. Of course they were both young girls then, but grew to think of C.P as their older brother and he loved them as younger sisters. Even when he returned to Kathmandu, they kept in touch regularly. Rachael was very eager to meet him again, along with his wife Pari and daughter Khushi who was just a year younger than Rachael. Perhaps they would become good friends and keep in touch online: Rachael certainly hoped so!

RACHAEL AND IAN'S JOURNEY TO KATHMANDU, THE CAPITAL CITY OF NEPAL

On October 27th, they flew from Manchester Airport to Kathmandu on an Etihad Airways flight at ten past eight in the evening. It was the beginning of a very long journey but fortunately both Rachael and Ian thoroughly enjoy flying; a good job as the flight was over six hours and then they faced a long stop-over at Abu Dhabi Airport in the Gulf. (All travellers to Kathmandu have to change to a smaller plane for the next part of their flight as Tribhuvan, Nepal's International Airport, is quite small with short runways.) Rachael and Ian actually landed at Abu Dhabi at 7.20 p.m. and then had over a six-hour wait but they did not mind at all; strangely, to me at least, they quite enjoy exploring foreign airports, buying snacks and relaxing – Rachael on her iPad and Ian just snoozing.

They boarded their onward flight at 1.45 p.m. and landed at Tribhuvan Airport at 7.40 p.m. the same day. (Nepal is roughly five hours ahead of the UK, GMT, which accounts for the strange flight and landing times and the problems with jet lag.)

Magically, on their approach to Kathmandu, they flew over the Himalaya: Rachael was absolutely thrilled and announced that she was sure she had seen Everest. It was still quite hot and muggy when they landed and after they had safely negotiated passport control and customs – an interesting experience to say the least – they went to find a trolley and retrieve their luggage. Ian's height and long arms proved to be very useful here so it was not too long before they were outside and looking for Subash and the Mountain Monarch sign with their names on it.

'Really cool, Dad!' exclaimed Rachael still able to bounce up and down with excitement even after that long journey.

Subash greeted them warmly and explained that C.P. was on his way back from a long trek and would meet them the evening before their Kathmandu Valley trek. He loaded their luggage into his waiting taxi and soon they were on the ring road being driven towards their accommodation at the Hotel Shakti in Thamel, the trekking hotel district of Kathmandu.

The drive was an unbelievable experience: waves of noise assaulted their ears and the fumes of the traffic caught in their throats. Honking horns and shouts of frustrated drivers filled the air and the lack of traffic lights and darkness added to the confusion. In all my visits to Nepal, I have never discovered for certain which side of the road people are supposed to drive on! I believe, like the UK, it is on the left but I am not sure. It seems to be that whoever can blast his horn the loudest gets precedence: it is terrifying madness but somehow invigorating!

By now they were really tired so after checking in and having some refreshments, they went up to their pleasant twin-bedded room. After a quick wash, they sank into their comfortable beds and were soon fast asleep.

SIGHTSEEING IN THE KATHMANDU VALLEY: CULTURE SHOCK, A CHILDREN'S HOME AND A MAGICAL EVENING

Next morning they both felt thoroughly rested and eager to begin their exploration of Kathmandu. Ian had previously arranged with C.P. that the first day in Kathmandu would just be Rachael and Ian, wandering around the streets so that Ian could introduce his daughter to the very different life and culture in that city gradually. It was to prove more difficult than he thought.

After a light breakfast Ian decided that they should begin by exploring the Thamel district around their hotel and then walk further into the heart of the city. He thought that Rachael would enjoy spending some time looking at the immense variety of shops, buildings and little cafes. It did not quite work out that way …

Rachael was shocked and stared open-mouthed at the scene in front of her. Bless her; she was experiencing a complete culture overload. Initially it is difficult to come to terms with the narrow streets of Kathmandu with all the noise, overpowering smells and traffic chaos. Buses, lorries, cars, motorbikes, bicycle rickshaws, ordinary cycles, cows and pedestrians compete for space and walking is extremely hazardous as everyone and everything tries hard to progress down the street. Generally there are no continuous pavements, just high platform-like steps in front of the shops so you have to climb on and off these, desperately trying to avoid the traffic and people hurrying past you.

Rachael gazed at Ian with a bemused look:

'What are cows doing here, Dad? And that one had just done a huge poo on the road! Phew – it stinks!'

Ian had to smile at her disgusted expression and he explained that in Nepal most of the people are Hindus and to them the cow is a holy animal, worshipped as a sort of god so it is completely protected. No one would dream of hurting one – even less killing one to eat. As Rachael was a vegetarian she thought that this was a good and sensible custom but she still looked apprehensively at these beasts ambling down the street, especially those with long, sharp horns. They really did seem to know they were privileged animals: they had very superior and supercilious looks on their faces.

Ian took Rachael towards the start of the ring road so she could see all the crazy traffic in the daylight and the poor policemen who desperately try to control it: they really try to do a good job in an impossible situation. They seem to have a whistle permanently in their mouths and blast it constantly. All of them wear masks because of the pollution caused by traffic fumes, though C.P. assures me that all transport has to have a vehicle safety certificate like ours – I don't think so! The engine emissions smell truly lethal and cause a dense haze that stings your eyes and hits the back of your throat.

As they made their way back to the Hotel Shakti, Rachael looked up at Ian and asked why he had brought her to this madness of a city:

'I really hate it here, Dad!' she protested. 'I know that you said before I came here, I would either love it or hate it. Well I'm afraid I really hate it!'

She was experiencing a complete culture shock. Kathmandu is certainly a place that encourages strong opinions.

Ian decided to change tactics: after they had eaten a snack or two and had a drink, he would take Rachael to see the Surya Children's Home that he had visited on his two earlier trips. He was sure that she would enjoy meeting all the orphan children and the dedicated people who cared for them. Rachael was familiar with how children's homes were run in the UK as Ian, many years before she was born, had founded The Millers Homes for Children. As she and Catherine grew up, he had shared his philosophy and passion with them. Thus they came to understand a great deal about how vulnerable youngsters and teenagers should be cared for and given the experience of a real family life, probably for the first time in their lives. Rachael is really proud of her dad and his commitment to helping poor children of all ages.

She also remembered how many years later, Ian's compassion and commitment to help all vulnerable children worldwide came into fruition: he set up F.I.N.C.H. (Friends International Network of Children's Homes). This amazing, supportive network uses social media as a link between people of all countries, cultures and faiths who have one aspiration in common: a dedication to helping and caring for vulnerable children. Through F.I.N.C.H. they are able to access information and advice and share experiences.

Ian thought that it would be a good idea to walk the two miles or so to the location of Surya Children's Home. He knew the streets leading south to the home, would not be so busy and the noise and smells not so oppressive, giving Rachael time to recover from her culture shock and hopefully regain some of her spirit of exploration and fun.

A lady called Namita and her friend Milan, set up Surya Children's Home some years before in difficult circumstances, mainly to help the street children of Kathmandu but they also raise babies who have been abandoned. Sadly some of these babies had been left in boxes outside the gates of the Home by desperate mothers and fathers and had been rescued by Namita and Milan. They had chosen the name 'Surya' because it means sunrise in the Nepalese language; just as the sunrise brings light after the darkness of night, they hoped their home would bring light into the lives of their rescued children.

Nepal is such a poor country that there is no government or organised aid for these children who live on the streets and beg for food every day to keep themselves alive. Many of them are orphans or have been abandoned for a variety of reasons and have no family, no home and no schooling. At Surya they are loved and nurtured and attend a nearby school. Although all education has to be paid for in Nepal, the local school very generously gives Namita and Milan a considerable concession for each child.

Ian was sure that he and Rachael would be able to see Surya because although it was a school day in Kathmandu, the youngest children and the babies would likely still be at home. When they arrived, Milan was very excited to see them and welcomed them warmly.

He explained that, unfortunately, Namita was away trying to raise money to keep the home running. This was a very necessary exercise as the home relied completely on donations from caring supporters. He took them upstairs where a few younger children were around but as Ian and Rachael had expected, most of the children were at school. He showed Rachael and Ian all around the home: the bedrooms, the living room, the playroom with a good selection of well-worn books, games and toys, their small medical room and the kitchen. (In summer they cooked and ate outside on the roof terrace.) Although everything was sparse and worn as you would expect in a home with so many children, everywhere was scrupulously clean and the children were clearly very happy though, understandably, a little shy with visitors. They were

obviously well cared for and knew they were loved; the whole place radiated happiness and devotion.

Ian was delighted to meet the little girl he nursed in his arms when she was only ten months old. Now she was a lively, joyful toddler and was being cared for by several older children. They all clearly loved each other and naturally looked after all their 'brothers and sisters' in their big happy family. This enchanting toddler's heart-breaking but heart-warming story shows how a life can be saved and enhanced by hope, love, care and the invaluable advice and support given by members of F.I.N.C.H.

THIS IS THAT BABY'S STORY:

One night, around midnight, Namita had been woken up by loud knocking on the protective outside gate. She had rushed outside and found two policemen with a really tiny mewling baby. The policemen explained that they had been on patrol when they heard strange squeaky sounds coming from a dustbin. At first they thought that a rat or cat had become trapped in the bin. However to their utter astonishment, when they lifted up the lid, they had found this tiny baby girl lying amongst the rubbish crying weakly. They had quickly wrapped her up in one of their jackets and, because they did not know where to take her, had rushed to Surya to see if Namita could help them. She quickly thanked them and said that she would do her best.

Namita had taken the tiny girl inside, wrapped her up in warm blankets and held her, trying hard to comfort her. The baby was obviously extremely weak and thin:

not much more than a tiny parcel of bones. Namita was frantic: she really didn't know the best way to help; how and what should she feed the baby? How could she keep her alive? She needed urgent help. Then Namita remembered Ian who had visited Surya the previous year and told her all about his work with children and about F.I.N.C.H. She quickly phoned him and Ian put out an appeal on the F.I.N.C.H. website. To their amazement, almost instantly a childcare worker in Uganda, 6,256 kilometres away, who had a lot of experience nursing very sick babies, got in touch with Namita and told her exactly what to do. She warned Namita that the baby would probably die but the best thing to do immediately was to hold the baby between her breasts next to her heart – heartbeat to heartbeat – and keep her warm. She must just give the baby small warm drinks of boiled water from a bottle – not milk at first as the baby was probably too ill to digest it – she just needed to be kept warm and hydrated and if the baby survived for twenty-four hours then she had a chance of living.

Miraculously that tiny scrap of a child survived and thrived under the love and care of her new family and is a testament to what can be achieved by three people on three different continents working together to save a life.

When Ian went back to Kathmandu in 2012, he had gone down to Surya particularly to see this little miracle, then a chubby, engaging ten-month-old bundle of love. Completely bewitched, he had nursed her throughout his visit. Now, in 2014, Rachael, with her dad, was thrilled to meet this 'miracle child' who had grown into an enchanting toddler. Rachael gave her a big cuddle.

Before they left, Ian gave Milan a small donation that would provide essential rice for all the children for some time. While they were in the taxi taking them back to the Hotel Shakti, Rachael looked very thoughtful. Eventually she spoke:

'Thank you, Dad for taking me to Surya Children's Home. Now I realise just how important your work to help children is. I think that I would like to do something like that when I grow up.'

'That would be wonderful, darling,' Ian replied. He was very proud of his daughter's caring nature.

That evening Rachael and Ian went for a meal at the Rum Doodle, probably Kathmandu's most iconic restaurant and the favourite eating place of Ian's and mine. It is named after a mythical mountain called Rum Doodle: supposedly 40,000-feet high and the confabulated but very entertaining story of the climbers involved in trying to conquer it. Over the years the Rum Doodle has become a magnet for all climbers, trekkers and visitors. Climbers and adventurous trekkers are given two Yeti footprint-shaped cardboard coasters and are invited to record their successes with dates and names on them. These footprints are then displayed on the walls and ceiling of the restaurant. Apparently Rachael and Ian searched for mine but could not find them: hardly surprising as there are literally thousands! Then Rachael reminded Ian what she had said she was going to do when she was older:

'I am going to have my name on this ceiling like Grandma Joyce. But you know, Dad, one day when I come back to Nepal, I am going to climb Everest.'

Ian was not surprised. He just nodded in an encouraging way.

They enjoyed a superb meal, beautifully cooked, and served with a wonderful smile. Nepalese people consider that providing good service and taking care of people is an honour and a privilege. To accompany their meal they had a Diet Coke each but Ian reminded Rachael it was not a good idea to have ice. He had explained earlier that in some restaurants and cafés, the ice was made by freezing tap water and the water in Nepal, as in most Third World countries, was contaminated and could give her a really bad tummy ache and probably diarrhoea. (The infamous 'Delhi Belly' here is called 'Kathmandu Quickstep'!) He added that he thought the Rum Doodle would freeze bottled water for ice but it was better to be safe than sorry – while they were in Nepal she should to get used to refusing ice politely whenever she was asked if she wanted some.

Rachael was absolutely delighted with the meal and the setting on the atmospheric roof terrace with captivating Nepalese music drifting up into the cool night air. Although there was a crumbling wall facing the terrace, the subtle lighting turned the rooftop into a magical space: a wonderful place to eat in a city of dreams.

'This is the best restaurant in the world: I love it here!' enthused Rachael.

Ian agreed and said that he thought it was an enchanting place for a meal. To her surprise and joy, as they were leaving the restaurant, the owner gave Rachael two of those Yeti footprint coasters so she would have a record of her Kathmandu Valley Rim Trek, her first in Nepal. After her trek she filled them in and they are proudly displayed on her wall at home.

When they were back in their hotel room, Rachael said to Ian, 'I really, really loved the Rum Doodle, Dad! It was the best evening I've ever spent in my whole life!'

Ian had to smile: Kathmandu was clearly working her magic on Rachael.

EXPLORING TWO TEMPLES AND A CULTURAL EVENING MEAL

The very first words spoken by Rachael next morning were, 'Dad why did I say I hated Kathmandu? I absolutely **love it!**'

Kathmandu had certainly captivated her! And with this announcement, she bounced out of bed ready for whatever the day may bring.

Shortly after they had finished breakfast, Ram Raj Gurung, a city guide employed by Mountain Monarch Adventures, arrived in his car at the Hotel Shakti. He introduced himself to Ian and Rachael and explained that C.P. had not yet arrived back from his long trek with his client and friend, John Waldman, so it had been arranged that he, Ram, would take them to see two very important temples that day.

The first temple they were going to see was the fabulous Swayambunath Stupa, better known as the Monkey Temple which is perched atop a hill on the western edge of the Kathmandu Valley. On the way there, Ram told them a little about the history of this ancient and probably most important Buddhist shrine in Kathmandu. He explained that the sleepy, all-seeing Buddha eyes, which stare out in every direction from the top of the stupa, have become the quintessential

symbol of Nepal. It is a UNESCO World Heritage Site and is absolutely beautiful and awe-inspiring with an atmosphere of eternal peace and devotion.

Ram smiled as he told them two of the Buddhist legends about how the temple came into being.

The first legend tells of its founding some 2000 years ago when the Kathmandu Valley was filled by a huge lake that had a single perfect lotus blossom growing in the centre. When the prince of all Buddhist teachings, (the Bodhisattva Manjusri), came along, he drained the lake with a slash of his mighty Sword of Wisdom, and the perfect lotus flower settled on top of the hill and was magically transformed into the shrine over an eternal flame. Thus it is known as the Self-Created (Swayambhu) Stupa.

Alternatively, he told them, you may prefer the second myth, which explains how the stupa got its name – The Monkey Temple. This ancient story tells of how the Bodhisattva of wisdom and learning was raised on that hill. As he grew older and his hair grew long, head lice grew in it; these lice were transformed into the monkeys that now run and play all over the temple complex.

From the expression on her face, Ian could see that the second legend and head lice in particular did not appeal to Rachael at all, although she was eager to see the monkeys. Whatever you choose to believe, ancient scriptures and historical and geological evidence reveal that the Kathmandu valley was once submerged under water and that as early as 640 AD King Manadeva had building work done on the hill. In the 17th century, King Pratap Malla built the long steps known as the Pilgrims Steps that lead up to the very top. Most probably the current complex grew from the series of smaller temples into the large magnificent stupa of today.

Ram parked on the eastern side near the bottom of the Pilgrims Steps and, briefly, they watched all the devoted pilgrims and visitors steadily climbing the 365 ancient steps up the steep forested hillside; the most memorable and atmospheric way to the top. Rachael was eager to join them but first they paused by the brightly painted eastern gate at the bottom of the stairway. It contains a huge Tibetan prayer wheel nearly

27.05.2007

twelve feet tall: apparently it takes two people to turn it and ring the bell on the top. Although Rachael looked at this, she was keen to try spinning some small prayer wheels herself. Ram had explained the ritual to her: you always approach them from the left-hand side and spin each wheel in the line in sequence with your right hand. Not only is this a form of respect of the devotees releasing prayers to heaven but if you succeed in turning the last wheel when the first one is still revolving, then you will have a long, happy and healthy life. Rachael was overjoyed that after several attempts she managed to do this. Both Ian and Ram congratulated her.

At last they began climbing the steps past 17th century painted Buddha statues and endless mani stones which are inscribed with the Tibetan holy mantra, 'Om mani padme hum' ('Hail to the jewel in the lotus'). Merchants line the steps eager to sell tourists overpriced small versions of these stones and all the way you are surrounded by monkeys (macaques) that inhabit the trees lining the steps. Rachael was thrilled to see them and laughed out loud at their antics. However, Ram warned her to be careful, as they are dreadful thieves – stealing food, shiny objects and anything in your hand or your bag! Nevertheless there is no denying they are engaging.

Rachael and Ian gasped with wonder when they reached the central buildings and decorations that are unbelievably colourful with gold everywhere. You can imagine just how dazzling this scene is with the sun shining down on these temples and statues making them shimmer and glow. The main stupa is huge, overpowering and absolutely breathtaking. Ram explained that the whitewashed dome represents the womb of creation, complemented by the central phallic tower: both symbolising birth. This gold tower is surmounted by a spire of thirteen gold discs, representing the thirteen steps to enlightenment and heaven. In 2010, twenty kilogrammes of pure gold was used to re-gild this wonderful monument to the Buddhist faith and culture. Although this whole complex is Buddhist, because of its significant history and atmosphere of worship and dedication, Hindus too come to pray here.

They walked round the main stupa and marvelled at all the beautiful golden and copper-covered smaller temples that surrounded it: five of them are dedicated to the elements: sky, air, fire, water and earth. These five elements are also symbolised in the hundreds of colourful prayer flags or 'lungtas', which are suspended from the trees and buildings throughout the complex, fluttering and dancing in the breeze. Each lungta has a central wind-horse, is surrounded by a prayer or mantra and is a different colour: blue symbolises sky and space; white, air and wind; red, fire; green, water; and yellow, earth. These elements together are said to bring inward and outward peace and harmony and as the wind blows through the symbolic flags, it spreads peace, goodwill and harmony to people all over the world: an inspirational belief.

Between the temples, they gazed in wonderment at the chains of prayer wheels and butter lamps, votive structures and brilliant shrines and statues encased in intricate carvings with wonderful gilded copper repoussé work for which the Kathmandu Valley is renowned. There was so much to hold in awe and to marvel at that both Ian and Rachael found it difficult to absorb it all.

Ian told me later that although he was not a believer, he was profoundly aware of the holy nature and spiritual ambience of the site and Rachael too seemed to feel this at times as she gazed around and spoke in a respectful whisper. Their cameras never stopped clicking. They would have some fabulous photos to remind them of this very special visit: the sights, the colours and sheer chaos of some areas would remain in their memories. Rachael most delightful memory was of a monkey jumping out of a tree and landing with a big splash into a pool, much to the disgust of tourists standing near by!

Petitioners at the various shrines and temples, like the one dedicated to Harati, the Hindu Goddess of smallpox and other epidemics, toss flower petals, rice, coloured powder and holy water over the image to gain blessings. Unfortunately, monkeys, stray dogs and pigeons fight over the rice – the squeals, barks and shouts add to the overall chaos. Rachael and Ian found it all overwhelming and were grateful to pause by the school building where the monks and their trainees chanted quietly, completely absorbed in their studies.

Towards the end of their visit, Ram took them down to The World Peace Pool, which was built in 1998 to promote the ideal of World Peace. There is a meaningful inscription on its wall: 'May Peace prevail on Earth.' Again Rachael and Ian's cameras were whirring.

Their final fantastic vista was the panoramic view over the vast expanse of the Kathmandu Valley far below. All the streets, buildings, shops, roads and traffic stretched out below them like tiny models on a magnificent plan, spoilt to a degree by the pall of pollution that hung like mist across the valley, though still awe inspiring.

They made their way back to Ram's car and were soon being driven to their next wonderful temple, the glorious Boudhanath Stupa on the eastern fringe of the city of Kathmandu. At least for a little while they could sit and rest their aching feet though not for long! On the way, just as before, Ram told them a little about the history, legends and myths of this massive ancient Buddhist stupa, which towers majestically above the city skyline and is one of the largest in the world.

Boudhanath, (or Boudnath, the name generally used by tourists and Nepalese), like The Monkey Temple, is a UNESCO World Heritage Site. The influx of countless refugees from Tibet in the 1950s has resulted in the building of over fifty Tibetan gompas (monasteries) around the stupa and many Tibetans living in the vicinity. Thus it has become one of the most important and holiest centres of Tibetan Buddhism and culture: a vital place of pilgrimage and meditation for Tibetan Buddhists and local Nepalis – both Hindu and Buddhist – as well as being a very popular tourist site.

The stupa was probably built in the 14th century on an ancient popular trade route from Tibet. It is said to have been created just after the passing of the Buddha and to have the remains of Kassapa Buddha entombed in its base. So for centuries it was a powerful focal point of worship, meditation and offerings in the area for locals, merchants, travellers and pilgrims, long before the Tibetans sought refuge there.

Again there are two main intriguing legends about the Boudnath Stupa's creation, how it became such an inspiring, spiritual place, and how everyone will benefit from walking around it and keeping it clean and well swept day and night.

The first describes how a poor but extremely devout mother, Jadzima, petitioned the king of Nepal to allow her to build a stupa or chorten. Possibly affected by her air of holiness and spirituality (her karma), the king was amazed to find that he agreed to her request without thinking – the words 'okay, it can be done' just slipped out of his mouth. That is why Tibetans call Boudnath 'Jarung Kashor Chorten.' Jarung means 'it can be done' and Kashor is 'slipped out of the mouth'.

The mother died after she had completed the dome but her four sons finished the stupa. When they stood in front of it praying and making wishes, the story goes that all the spirits of the Buddhas and great monks who had ever been in the world, were absorbed into the stupa, which is why it is also called 'All-encompassing and wish-fulfilling'. From this grew the belief that anyone who prays there, whatever you pray for, will succeed, especially when you see the Boudnath Stupa for the first time. There are endless stories of how people's wishes have been fulfilled.

The second legend tells of a very grumpy, rude and irreligious man who lived in ancient Nepal. He hated everyone and so no one ever patronised his shop. When he died he went straight to hell because of his sins, but he was rescued by the Holy Buddha and given the chance to atone because he had once circled the Boudnath Stupa while chasing his dog – this alone gave him merit! After this happened, the belief grew that anyone would be forgiven their sins and given the opportunity to lead a better life if they circled the stupa.

Rachael gave Ram a disbelieving look and shook her head as if to say, 'It is very strange what some people think!'

Ram smiled at her wisely and warned Rachael and Ian that very shortly they were both going to be totally overwhelmed when they first saw the Boudnath Stupa: and so they were. After Ram parked his car, they walked

through the entrance in the north of the irregular sixteen-sided wall that surrounds that wonderful monument. The entrance is lined with small shops but Rachael and Ian scarcely saw them because suddenly they were confronted by the immense, powerful presence of the stupa. They just stood there gaping in awe at its sheer size and magnificence; Ram had been right! The huge eyes of the Buddha seemed to gaze straight down at them, almost through them, creating a really weird feeling: the all-seeing, all-knowing Buddha. Almost immediately Ram told them that he was going to pray as he always did when facing the Buddha and to Ian's surprise, Rachael joined him. She stood there calmly and respectfully, head bowed, eyes closed and hands together in prayer. Perhaps she had been influenced by the first story and the pervading spiritual atmosphere of this sacred site.

They paused for a while to regain their composure and then began their circuit of the stupendous stupa. Ram explained all about its structure and answered Rachael's excited questions. First she wanted to know about the Buddha's 'nose', which is like a huge question mark. Ram said that the question mark symbol is actually the Nepali character for the number one and signifies unity – one way to reach enlightenment and spiritual understanding through the teachings of Buddha. Above his 'nose' is the third eye, which denotes his wisdom.

Ram also told Rachael to look for the frescos of Padmapani in the niches of the surrounding wall: apparently there are 108 (this is a holy number for Hindus) but Ram confessed he had never been able to find them all.

All around the base of the stupa are prayer wheels

carved with the mantra 'Om Mani Padme hum'. Rachael learned this chant off by heart, often repeating it and, of course, insisted on spinning the prayer wheels whenever she could, remembering to use her right hand – clever girl!

Ram informed them that from above, Boudnath Stupa, looks like a huge mandala or diagram of the Buddhist cosmos and that, as always, five smaller Buddhas surround it – four marking north, east, south and west and one enshrined in the centre of the white dome. These Buddhas also represent the five elements – the sky and space, air and wind, fire, earth, and water just as they are symbolised in all the colourful prayer flags. They continued walking round the huge platforms that form the base: three of them decreasing in size represent the earth and these are surmounted by two circular plinths symbolising water.

Rachael and Ian stopped to watch some Nepali men reviving the lotus-leaf shapes that adorned the white dome. Initially it looked like a fairly primitive technique: they have buckets of yellow dye which they transfer to enamel bowls, then they swing the bowls up in the air and spray lines of perfect semi-circular leaf shapes around the dome. Both Rachael and Ian were mesmerised at their skill, as was I, especially as quite a strong wind can blow through the site. I remember when I first saw the men doing this, I was full of admiration and thought that, had I tried to emulate them, I would have been covered from head to toe in yellow dye and so would the floor! I doubted that one single spot would have landed in the correct space on that beautiful dome.

As at The Monkey Temple, a spectacular gilded tower rises above the dome and this is topped by a golden pyramid with thirteen[1] steps – the ladder to enlightenment. On top of this is yet another marvel – a gilded canopy, which represents air and wind, and finally a shining golden spire symbolising the ether: sky and space. From the stupa flutter countless prayer flags carrying prayers and good wishes heavenward in the wind and across the world, sharing their message of peace and goodwill with all people in all countries.

Everything is of such tremendous scale that it is a totally mind-blowing experience; one you never forget. Rachael and Ian's necks were aching from constantly gazing upwards. It is so difficult to embrace and understand all the ancient symbolism; it truly is an otherworldly experience, embodying utter faith and belief.

Eventually they completed their circuit of the stupa and went towards the entrance so they could explore the area around that spiritual monument.

Here reality and modern day hit Ian: he was approached by a young mother with a baby tightly wrapped-up. She begged him to help her as she had no money to feed her starving child. Ian couldn't actually see what sort of state the baby was in due to its extensive covers. She asked for the equivalent of £20 to buy two packets of milk powder from a nearby shop and assured him that the gods would bless him for his charity. By now, somewhat suspicious, Ian said that he would give her £10 to buy one packet and so she guided him towards a particular shop. Ian duly handed over the required money and the lady received her packet of milk powder, thanked him profusely and promptly disappeared.

A little while later, Ian noticed her talking with the shopkeeper who had sold the milk powder and some money exchanged hands. Ram smiled and confirmed that Ian had indeed been conned: he had fallen for one of the regular scams. Many poor-looking women pretend their babies are starving and persuade generous tourists to help them by buying milk powder. This powder only costs around £2 so the 'mum' and the shopkeeper share the profits. Ian was rather shame-faced and vowed never to be conned again – he had certainly learnt his lesson! However, although

she laughed, Rachael was really proud of her caring dad and gave him a hug.

They looked around all the shops, temples and other interesting buildings surrounding the stupa but did not go in any of them as, by now, they were all pretty tired. Ram drove them back to the Hotel Shakti, reminding them that C.P. was coming to the hotel early that evening to take them for a cultural meal at a very popular Nepalese restaurant nearby. Ram confirmed that after the meal, C.P. would talk to Ian and Rachael about the arrangements for their Kathmandu Valley Rim Trek, which they would be starting next morning. He wished them both good luck and said to Rachael that he hoped she would love her first trek in the foothills of the Himalaya. She replied with an engaging smile and her hands together in a traditional Nepalese greeting:

'Namaste, Ram. I am really going to miss you!'

She had formed a warm, friendly relationship with Ram and he respected how well she had embraced his beliefs and culture at such a young age. Rachael had already learned a great deal.

After Ram drove away, Ian and Rachael sank gratefully into two of the chairs scattered around the garden, ordered some well-deserved drinks and relaxed in the late afternoon sunshine. Ian hadn't noticed that Pradip, C.P.'s friend and Managing Director of Mountain Monarch Adventures, was sitting talking to a group of guests who were about to embark on a trek to Everest Base Camp.

Pradip introduced Rachael and Ian to the trekkers and they all chatted for a while. Rachael was eager to know exactly what they were planning to do because, as she explained to them, she was going to go to Base Camp when she was a little older and, one day, hoped to climb to the summit of that marvellous mountain. You can imagine just how delighted she was when Pradip gave her a book about a trek to Everest, especially as he had signed it – wishing her good luck overcoming yet another challenge. She just radiated joy: what a true adventurer and explorer this vivacious ten-year-old girl was becoming! Ian glowed with pride.

---

[1] Thirteen is another holy number in both the Buddhist and Hindu faiths.

As soon as they had finished their drinks, Rachael and Ian went upstairs to their room to pack their rucksacks for their trek the next morning. They would be able to leave any surplus clothes and equipment in the secure store at the Hotel Shakti.

It wasn't long before C.P. arrived and introduced them to John Waldman, the American friend he had guided for over a month on many different treks in Nepal. John was staying at the Hotel Shakti too. I had met him and his wife Nancy a few years before, when I had just finished the Annapurna Circuit and John and his wife were going to tackle the Everest Base Camp Trek. Rachael was very eager to

C.P. with John Waldman.

hear all about John's adventures with C.P. and soon they were all chatting happily. C.P. was overjoyed to meet his lovely 'little sister' again.

They did not have far to walk to the wonderful Nepalese restaurant called The Satkar. (Satkar means welcome and it certainly was welcoming!) It was built in the traditional Nepali style with intricate carvings and beautiful multi-coloured decorations. The table linen, cutlery and seating were immaculate and all the staff were warm and caring and provided prompt, efficient service. The authentic Nepalese cuisine was comprehensive and all the dishes looked very tasty and inviting: as the brochure said, 'We serve you with heart and our food is cooked with love and rich spices and herbs.'

There was also a well-stocked bar but Rachael settled for her favourite Diet Coke and Ian wisely avoided the local wine and, even more wisely, the local whisky or Rakshi; he settled for Everest beer as did John and C.P. They raised their glasses to each other in celebration of this happy evening with many good wishes for the following day. It was John's last day in Kathmandu as he was flying out very early next morning and it was the evening before Rachael's first trek in Nepal. Consequently, there was a little sadness but mainly an overwhelming sense of anticipation and joy. In the background lovely captivating music was playing, while on the stage beautiful Nepalese ladies and handsome men enchanted the diners with their intricate, expressive traditional dances.

They all chose a main meal of dhal bhat: the authentic staple meal of the Nepalese. It consists of a sort of thick, spicy, chunky vegetable soup full of lentils and as well as being very healthy and nutritious, it is truly delicious. This was accompanied by a huge variety of small spicy dishes that were really tempting and unbelievably tasty and were served in lovely shiny bowls that glowed in the soft candlelight. As soon as one bowl was empty, it was quickly replenished, as was their mound of dhal bhat. They were all so full that they could not manage a sweet so they settled for another drink, watched the fantastic cultural dancing and listened to delightful singing for a while.

Although C.P. told them a little about what each dance was about, Rachael, Ian and John genuinely wished that they understood what each of the ritual intricate hand gestures, complex facial expressions and bewitching movements represented. Obviously some traditional story was being told, so it would have added to their enjoyment if, before each dance began, one of the dancers had explained what they were about to depict. Rachael was particularly fascinated with the elaborate hand movements and tried hard to copy some of them. It was a wonderful evening: good food, good entertainment and good company.

Soon they all made their way back to the hotel as they had a very busy day facing them in the morning. Rachael and Ian wished John a safe journey as he headed up to bed, and then joined C.P. in the reception area. C.P. outlined what they were going to do the following day and was delighted that they had already packed their rucksacks. He said that he didn't need to check anything as he knew what experienced walkers Ian and Rachael were; he just made arrangements for their extra luggage to be safely stored before they left next morning.

C.P. told them that he would be picking them up about 7 a.m. so they could be driven up to Sundarijal from where they would start walking. Sundarijal stands at nearly 5000 feet and would be Rachael's highest elevation yet. She was bouncing with joy and anticipation and, for once, didn't need any persuading that it was bedtime. Next morning she was going to be walking with her dad, Ian and her 'big brother' C.P. Amazing!

THE KATHMANDU VALLEY RIM TREK

Rachael was awake really early the next morning and dressed before she shook Ian excitedly.

'Come on, Dad! It's time to get up! We're walking today.'

Ian protested, with very little success, that it was only six o'clock but had to smile as Rachael informed him they needed breakfast before setting out and they had to

be in the reception area by 7 a.m. to meet C.P. Not for the first time, Ian wondered who exactly was the 'boss' in their relationship!

Rachael managed quite a substantial breakfast – a Nepalese dish mainly consisting of potatoes – but Ian just had black coffee. The Hotel Shakti, like all trekking hotels, is accustomed to providing very early breakfasts for walkers and for guests flying home.

It was not long before they were sitting in reception with their rucksacks, having overseen their spare luggage being safely stored. C.P. arrived in a taxi accompanied by their porter, Sandip Rai, promptly at 7 a.m. and greeted Rachael and Ian warmly. Rachael was buzzing; as much as she had loved visiting Surya Children's Home and those magnificent temples, she was a dedicated walker at heart so she knew the next few days would be magical. She was going to climb up into the foothills and see fabulous views of the breathtaking high Himalaya.

They soon left the outskirts of Kathmandu and continued mainly northwards up towards the dappled-green forested hills of the Valley Rim. They passed through many small villages as the road climbed higher and C.P. told Rachael to take particular notice of the people's dress as they neared the starting point for their trek, namely Sundarijal. He explained that this was the beginning of Tamang settlements and that the ethnic group of Tamangs (who are Buddhists) have their own dialect, style of dress, customs and culture.

After a one-and-a-half-hour journey they finally reached Sundarijal and they all climbed out of taxi, collected their gear and Rachael and Ian sat outside a kind of shop where they had a drink of Coke – lukewarm but welcome. Rachael had never seen an open-sided shop before and stared at it with a puzzled expression – how did they lock it up, she wondered.

C.P. went off to the nearby Army post to collect their permits for the park: these are necessary when trekking in any national park anywhere in the Himalaya and are generally scrutinised by armed soldiers at Army posts.

C.P. was back very soon and so, in glorious sunshine, they started walking on a gradual uphill path that was a little rough with earth and stone steps in places but far better than some paths Rachael and Ian had tackled on their many adventures. To their right was a deep, wooded ravine with a gleaming, silvery river far below and all around them was a light forest with dark green pine trees interspersed with dainty silver birches and, of course, rhododendrons. These grow to tree-size in Nepal and are spectacular when covered with bright red blooms: they are one of the national flowers of Nepal along with marigolds.

Rachael remarked to Ian that the countryside around them was very like that seen when walking in the hills of their beloved Lake District or in Scotland. Ian agreed and, yes, I can confirm that wherever you trek in Nepal, the foothills of the Himalaya seem just like our native hills in the UK with very similar flowers and vegetation.

After about forty-five minutes from the start, they passed the now disused Nepalese Army barracks formerly occupied by the Gurkhas and the Sundarijal Water Treatment Plant, which C.P. explained, supplies all the drinking water in Kathmandu. Rachael wanted to know why there was an Army barracks in such a beautiful peaceful place. Ian explained that Nepal had not always been peaceful, so presumably, this was one of the reasons for the position of the barracks – to protect this vital water plant. He also reminded Rachael that when Grandma Joyce had trekked to Everest Base Camp many years ago, her small group had been stopped by a band of Maoist terrorists dressed in combat gear with Kalashnikov rifles and demanding a 'donation'.

Indeed that is exactly what they did! They had brandished their guns in a threatening way so we did not say no but wisely asked, 'how much?' We offered the equivalent of £10 and this was obviously acceptable because they took it from me with the words 'Wait, lady!' They actually wrote out a sort of receipt in Nepali on a grubby piece of paper and handed it to me saying, 'You show this and no more of us will stop you and ask you for more money.' Then they disappeared into the trees.

We had walked on, with me waving the 'receipt' in my hand just in case there were any more Maoists lurking in the bushes. Kevin, one of my companions, an SAS soldier and paratrooper, had a very serious expression on his face.

'Joyce, I should not wave that "receipt" about if I were you,' he advised.

Of course I had asked why not. Kevin replied, still with a very straight face,

'Because it says on it, "Shoot this woman on sight."'

Immediately, with very shaky fingers, I had thrust that piece of paper deep inside my trouser pocket. I completely believed him because I knew he had served with the Gurkhas and been to Nepal before, so I thought he could read Nepali. It wasn't until we reached Everest Base Camp that he admitted he had been pulling my leg all the time – he couldn't read Nepali at all and had no idea what was actually on that blessed piece of paper! I could have shaken him but instead I gave him a big hug because we had both just achieved a dream – to stand at the bottom of the famous Khumbu Icefall at Everest Base Camp.

Ian, Rachael, C.P. and their porter continued ascending the now steepening path and Rachael and Ian were delighted to meet some happy, chattering schoolchildren proudly wearing brightly coloured, immaculate school uniforms. This was the first time they had met any Nepalese schoolchildren in uniform. Then more and more children appeared: strangely, some seemed to be climbing agilely up the hill while others were running down. Ian must have looked very puzzled because one of their charming teachers explained to him that the younger children were going down to the infant school in Sundarijal while the older children were going up to the senior school in Mulkarka – a considerable climb both in distance and in height. Then, of course, they had to return home in the afternoon – yet more climbing or steep descending. Rachael was amazed.

'What on earth do they do if they forget their pencil case?' she asked.

Clearly she was thinking of her own antics at home: Ian had become used to getting phone calls from her most weeks asking him to bring in various items of school equipment she had forgotten!

'Well, for sure, their dads will not be delivering anything *their* children have forgotten,' Ian answered quickly, smiling at her. 'Perhaps they have better memories than you or they check their school bags carefully!'

Rachael was excellent at making sure she had all the necessary equipment in her rucksack when she was walking. However she certainly did not extend this skill to ensuring she packed her school bag with all she needed for that particular day. Wisely she did not reply to Ian's remarks but just sniffed and walked in front of him for a while with her head held high!

They carried on climbing, mostly through sparse mixed woodland and could hear a symphony of birdsong although they were unable to actually see the birds themselves. Nevertheless the cheerful sounds helped them on the steep ascent. Below they could see the narrow terraces of the strip fields covering the hillsides. Rachael was fascinated and asked C.P. what they were for and who had made them. C.P. explained that because the hillsides were so steep, the farmers had to terrace them in a series of narrow fields like huge steps because it was the only way to stop the rain washing all the soil away, especially in the monsoon. On those narrow strips they planted rice and all the vegetables their families needed to keep them alive. They paused for a while to watch one of the farmers ploughing his narrow strip field and marvelled how he managed to turn his ox and plough around when they reached the end of his patch. He was really skilful!

After around two hours, they reached the top of the village of Mulkarka at 6100 feet – much higher than Rachael and Ian had ever been before. They stopped for lunch at a small lodge/shop snuggled into the hillside and sat outside while C.P. went into the kitchen to cook dhal bhat for them all. They enjoyed a Coke each while C.P. was very busy cooking. While they were waiting, Rachael spotted some hens pecking around in the soil and asked Ian if she could try to catch one and if she succeeded, could she keep it? (Readers will remember that she had made a similar request when she was walking the English C2C: she had seen some baby grouse but hadn't managed to catch a single one.) Ian replied, as he had done before, 'Of course you can darling. Good Luck!'

Rachael dashed off but, to his amazement, she reappeared a few minutes later clutching a little black hen. That hen sat calmly on her knee while she stroked it – it even seemed to go to sleep.

Rachael was enchanted and said, 'Can I keep it then, Dad?'

'Well,' joked Ian, 'you have a problem: just how are you going to get it in your suitcase to take it home?'

Rachael didn't reply because that was a really bad dad joke!

Eventually C.P. came out of the kitchen carrying huge plates of dhal bhat for them. Rachael tucked in eagerly but Ian didn't really feel like eating. He didn't want to offend C.P. so he tried to eat as much as possible. Unfortunately because there was so much rice, Ian was really sick afterwards. C.P. was naturally very upset but Ian explained that when he was walking, he rarely had much to eat at lunchtime but usually managed with just a snack because he suffers from 'starch overload': his stomach cannot cope with lots of starchy food, especially when he is walking or working hard. He emphasised that the food had been delicious and that in no way was it C.P.'s fault. It was just his silly stomach. He confirmed that now he was absolutely fine and thanked C.P. for his care and concern.

While they were eating, that little black hen stayed asleep on Rachael's knee, completely contented and absolutely still. As much as she would have liked to keep it, and bearing in mind Dad's joking reply, Rachael sensibly decided that she ought to let it go to join the others. However as she popped it back in the garden area, she noticed there was a row of six goats tied in descending order of size behind the shack. Ever curious, she asked Ian why they were tied up like that. Ian explained that although the goats were kept for milk and for cheese-making, they were also killed for meat for the family to eat. They had probably been tied up in that order so that the largest would be slaughtered first. Rachael, who is a vegetarian just like Ian, was totally shocked at first. But then, with mature reasoning, she told Ian that she knew people in the UK ate meat, which meant that animals were killed: it was a choice people made. She didn't like the idea so she chose not to eat meat or fish of any kind but knew many people who did, including her mum. Ian was really pleased that his daughter was becoming such a thoughtful and tolerant young lady.

A little while later, they continued their steep ascent through the pretty woodland with continual views over those fascinating multi-coloured terraced fields and surrounding verdant hills with the breathtaking high Himalaya appearing like hazy white clouds above them.

At long last they reached the village of Bhorlang Bhanjyang, which, at over 7970 feet, was the highest point of their trek. From here they descended gradually on the twisting stone and earth path past Thulo Dhap towards their destination for the day, the small town of Chisapani at 7265 feet. Here they would be staying at the Dorje Lakpa Hotel and Lodge.

Rachael and Ian were quite surprised when they finally arrived at their hotel because it was much larger than they expected: most of the building was two-storey but it had a single extension to the side. It was nicely decorated and was surrounded by pots of beautiful flowers. The Nepalese love plants and flowers and utilise every kind of container as a flowerpot.

The loo!

Nothing is wasted: they really are experts at recycling. They decorate paint pots, buckets and polythene containers in bright colours and plant them up with brilliant geraniums, deep orange marigolds, orchids and busy lizzies (*impatiens*) of every colour, stately sunflowers, blood-red poppies and beautiful blue irises: a positive riot of colour. Around posts and hanging from roofs are variegated cascades of creepers like clematis, trumpet creeper, roses and lush bougainvillea: even the smallest and poorest houses have flowers that gladden the soul.

The view from the loo.

Rachael and Ian were given an en suite upstairs room: it was rather different from other rooms they had shared. Rachael was intrigued to find that the two beds were rather like deep wooden trays fastened to the wall with a hard mattress on each. She was certainly grateful that C.P. and their porter had carried up their thick duvet sleeping bags and liners – these would make the beds more comfortable and cosy. Ian suggested that Rachael have a shower first while the water was hot; he would have one later.

'Okay, Dad. Thanks,' she said, 'but I am going to the toilet first.'

She opened the bathroom door and went inside but came out very quickly.

'There isn't a toilet! There's only a hole in the floor!' she exclaimed in astonishment. This was Rachael's first experience of real Nepalese toilets.

'That's right, darling,' Ian replied. 'I'll show you what you have to do.'

He went inside the bathroom and explained to Rachael that you put your feet either side of the hole on the porcelain surrounding it and squat down over the hole to 'do what you have to do'. Then he took the blue bucket sitting in the corner and filled it up with water from the shower.

'You use the jug hanging on the bucket to ladle water down the hole to flush everything away,' he added, 'but please remember to put all toilet paper in the container near the hole or you'll block up the system.'

He expected Rachael to protest at the unusual facilities but she didn't. She just shrugged her shoulders and said, 'That's cool, I'll do exactly what you say.' However when she went to squat down, she realised she was looking out of a huge window that actually formed most of the facing wall.

'Dad!' she shouted, 'There's a big window and no curtains!'

Ian went back in the bathroom and gazed through the window at the magnificent view. He pointed out to Rachael that they were literally hanging over a very deep gully with huge green wooded hillside facing them, beyond which was a glimpse of towering Himalayan peaks – one of which must be Mount Dorje Lakpa after which their hotel was named. They certainly had the most wonderful 'loo with a view'!

'And,' he added, 'how is anyone going to be able to look in through that window?'

'I don't suppose anyone can,' agreed Rachael and, modesty satisfied, she asked another question: 'Where is the towel, Dad?'

'Whoops!' answered Ian apologetically. 'I should have realised that towels wouldn't be provided in trekking lodges. I'm afraid we haven't got one – sorry! But don't worry – I'll find something we can use.'

He searched desperately through his rucksack but the only thing he could find that was remotely suitable was his thick fleece hat. Rachael took it with a sigh and disappeared into the bathroom. Ian heard the shower running and soon Rachael was singing joyfully. She really was very good at adapting to unusual and unexpected situations so it was good that occasionally her clever dad made a little mistake!

After Rachael was dry and dressed, Ian decided they would have something to eat and he would have a shower when they came back; a wise decision as the water was now running cold and that fleece hat was sopping wet!

They went downstairs to find C.P. and a little while later he took them to a nearby café where, to their delight, they found pizza was on the menu: pizza and Coke – just what they needed!

On their way back to the hotel, they all marvelled at the beautiful sunset: Rachael and Ian took some photos of the spectacular vista of rose-coloured, snow-capped mountains above dark wooded hills and a fabulous sky of fiery colours from gold, through every shade of orange and red to a deep dark purple: magnificent!

It was Rachael's first close panoramic view of the glorious high Himalaya and her face shone with wonder. She was enchanted.

Later, when Ian went for his long-delayed shower, he took another photo of that wonderful sunset from their bathroom window. Fortunately the shower was hot as it was becoming really cold in their room. He dried himself quickly on that useful fleece hat (which thankfully was dry) and when he came out of the bathroom, was happy to see that Rachael had sensibly snuggled down in her duvet sleeping bag. He quickly climbed into his and was very grateful for the fleece liner.

While they were chatting, the electricity went off and they were plunged into darkness. Unfortunately this occurs often, especially when trekking, although there are many power cuts in Kathmandu City too. However Ian and Rachael were prepared – they had their headlamps safely stored under their pillows and so they put them on quickly. Rachael observed that most of her friends and especially her sister, Catherine, would absolutely hate their accommodation and be disgusted at the facilities but she *loved* it!

'I really, really do Dad. I absolutely love it. I am having the time of my life. Thank you!'

Ian smiled and marvelled at her enthusiasm and eagerness to accept all conditions; to find joy in exploring every new situation. What a wonderful companion she was! At this point, I think that I should inform our readers that when Rachael is at home, she is just a normal, pretty girl who loves nice clothes, attractive accessories in her beautifully styled hair, a little make-up and most 'girly' things. However when she is walking with Ian, she couldn't care less about her appearance! She copes with mud, dust, rain and whatever the weather and conditions throw at her with equanimity – she is at one with her surroundings.

After breakfast next morning, they set off again in beautiful sunshine to walk the long amazing ridge that led to Nagarkot through the Shivapuri National Park. The path was still mainly of impacted earth interspersed with stones but although they were on a high ridge, it was not level walking but very undulating with many uphill climbs and descents. However the fabulous scenery made each step a true pleasure. C.P. had told them that the vistas would be even more wonderful than any they had seen before and he was right. Gradually the wonderful views of the high Himalaya expanded until they encompassed a panorama of all the stupendous peaks from the far west Annapurna Region to the far east Everest Region and included the magnificent Ganesh, Mansiri and Langtang Himal, ending with the massive bulk of Makalu and challenging Kanchenjunga: far too many incredible peaks to name or even try to count. Rachael was utterly bewitched. C.P. could see she was captivated by the Himalaya and so he promised her that if she came back again with Ian to do another trek, he would take them into the high mountains.

The ridge was surrounded by low, sparse woodland and patches of bright wild-flowers covered the ground but for many hours they walked without seeing any villages, just occasional low crude houses with a few skinny animals grazing and hens scratching about in the narrow terraced fields. Rachael and Ian were really pleased to be greeted with smiles and the traditional 'Namaste' as they passed by.

Eventually after quite a steep climb, they reached their lunchtime destination – an unbelievably modern, clean and well-stocked little lodge at Jhule, set in a beautiful garden. They sat outside in the glorious sunshine enjoying the 180-degree panorama of stunning peaks and the peaceful ambience of that lovely place. After a while, they went inside to eat: C.P. advised them to choose a local dish that was made mainly of spicy vegetables and tasted absolutely delicious. Ian had a large Coke but Rachael thought that she would try a banana milkshake. She was really thirsty so she drank it all but confessed quietly to Ian that it was disgusting. From the smell, he deduced that it was probably made with goats' milk. In spite of this they both thought the lodge was really stunning and totally unexpected in such an isolated spot.

Before they continued, C.P. picked one of the pretty orange marigolds and put it in Rachael's hair so, of course, she had to pose for a photo. Gradually their path began to lead through more and more villages: each one very different in its style of housing, dress and custom, as this part of the ridge is settled by many varied ethnic groups. Besides Tamang, these include Gurung, Ghale Magar, Jaisi, Chetri and Brahmin people. They may belong to different ethnic groups, but all were smiling and welcoming and myriads of brightly coloured flowers adorned their houses. Rachael and Ian were enchanted by the sheer variety of costume and the immediate and genuine cheerful reception given by all the villagers, irrespective of ethnic differences. They felt surrounded by happiness and hospitality.

They had not been walking for very long, when Rachael complained that her left foot was sore. She sat down on a rock at the side of the path and took off her boot and sock: sure enough there was a small blister on one of her toes.

Normally Rachael never has blisters but the day was rather hot and possibly she hadn't put her socks on properly. With a huge grin on his face, C.P. opened up the large, bright-red Mountain Monarch First Aid kit that was being carried by their smiling porter, Sandip. C.P. carefully cleaned Rachael's toe and applied an appropriate plaster. She thanked him gratefully and, repairs complete, they all set off again.

A little further on, they passed a beggar sitting on the floor on the left-hand side of the path. Both Rachael and Ian noticed that one of his legs was missing from the knee downwards. All visitors to Nepal are warned about the massive numbers of beggars and advised never to give donations to them as many are not genuine but just too lazy to work and really are just conning travellers. You will remember the 'poor Nepalese lady with a starving baby' at Boudnath who had successfully conned Ian out of the equivalent of £10 for baby milk. Determined Rachael and Ian ignored this beggar and walked on up the path. After a while they realised that C.P. was not following them so they stopped and waited for him. When he caught up with them, he explained that he had been talking to that beggar.

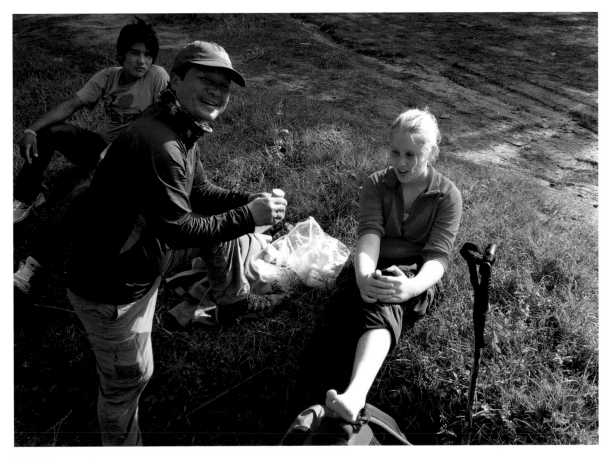

Rachael has a puncture.

Apparently he was an ex-colleague of C.P.'s with whom he had worked on several treks in the past. He had been a mountain leader just like C.P. but he had been badly injured in a fall while leading a group of climbers on a high expedition. The European company, for which he was working, had airlifted him out and paid for his hospital treatment. However, now he could no longer work as a guide and as there is no benefit system in the poor country of Nepal, he was reduced to begging. Rachael and Ian were really upset that they had ignored the beggar but C.P. assured them he had given his friend donations for all of them and so they carried on somewhat subdued towards Nagarkot and their accommodation for the night – The Sunshine Hotel.

Nagarkot is the best location on this ridge from which to see all the fabulous high Himalaya: the mountains seem so near, absolutely glorious and overpowering that they truly take your breath away.

Their hotel was very pleasant indeed: a red-brick, four-storey building with fantastic views and very helpful staff. The facilities were great and their en suite really comfortable. Eager to have a shower and change into clean clothes, Rachael headed first for the bathroom and to her delight found that this hotel supplied towels and a sit-down toilet – Western style – fantastic! However she did remember, as always, what Ian and I had told her: she must always keep her mouth shut when showering so she didn't get any water (which could possibly be infected) in her mouth. Also she ensured that she cleaned her teeth using bottled water: what a wise and knowledgeable trekker she was becoming. Even in hotels of a good standard, you cannot rely on a pure piped water supply. The hot water supply was continuous so for once, Ian was able to have a shower immediately after Rachael.

Nagarkot, at 7200 feet, is situated in a fantastic position high on the ridge overlooking the Kathmandu Valley. Numerous hotels are scattered all over the beautiful wooded hillsides and on the ridge itself. It is only thirty-two kilometres from Kathmandu and has the most spectacular panoramic vistas of the Himalaya from the ranges of the Annapurna Region and the beautiful peak of Manaslu to the Everest Range including a breathtaking view of majestic Everest herself. Inevitably, many tourists travel up to Nagarkot by car, taxi and bus just to view the magnificent sunsets and sunrises; they stay overnight and return to Kathmandu the next day. Hence the vast number of high-class hotels that have sprung up in what was formerly a farming village. It has the reputation that at sunset and sunrise, it is the most beautiful place on earth.

Originally, because of its strategic position, it was the site of an ancient fort built to monitor the activities of other kingdoms and later became a summer retreat for the Royal Family of Nepal. Later still it gained fame as an international hill station where rich people could escape from the heat and overcrowding of the Kathmandu Valley.

Rachael and Ian could hardly wait to explore this fascinating village and look at the wonderful views westwards to the vast expanse of the Kathmandu Valley below them and the panoramic 180-degree view of all the snow-capped Himalayan mountains. They both took a huge number of photos before going back to the Sunrise Hotel for a well-earned meal. Ian and Rachael persuaded C.P. and their porter, Sandip, to join them for dinner to celebrate the end of their brief but wonderful Kathmandu Valley Rim Trek. They most certainly would be back: in fact after a really delicious meal, they all held up their glasses and, not surprisingly, their toast was, 'To our next trek!' Rachael was ecstatic!

After their meal, Rachael and Ian went for a short walk while they waited for the famous sunset. They were not disappointed: as the deep orange sun slipped slowly behind the mountains the whole sky lit up with every shade of gold, orange, red, violet and deep purple imaginable and all those snow-capped peaks glowed a magical deep rosy pink, here and there, illuminated with flashes of gold and deep red. It was just as if all the mountains were on fire: a truly breathtaking vista! Their cameras were clicking for ages.

Eventually they decided that perhaps it would be a good idea to go to bed a little earlier than normal as they had walked a long way that day and needed to be up at 4 a.m. the next morning to watch the sunrise.

As they snuggled down in their beds, Rachael said sleepily, 'This has been a fabulous trek, Dad. Thank you so much. I just wish it could have been longer.'

'I promise when we come back again, darling,' Ian affirmed, 'we will do a much longer trek with C.P. and go higher into the Himalaya.'

'Wow! Fab!' was Rachael's reply: she was going to have another exciting adventure with her dad.

NAGARKOT TO KATHMANDU AND THE GARDEN OF DREAMS

Indeed they were up at 4 a.m. For once Ian was the first to wake as he had set his alarm. There were no complaints from Rachael when he woke her up although she had been fast asleep; she was just as eager as Ian to watch the sunrise over those fabulous mountains. They dressed quickly and climbed the staircase that led to the roof terrace. Ian cautioned Rachael not to lean on the surrounding balustrade, as in places there were large cracks as a result of an earthquake a while ago. C.P. had assured them that it was safe but Ian was concerned for his adventurous daughter: her safety and wellbeing, as always, were his priority.

It wasn't too long before the purplish, deep-blue sky began to lighten and gradually fill with all the amazing hues of an awesome dawn. The reds, oranges and bright yellow streaks of colour seemed far brighter and clearer than any Rachael and Ian had ever seen before: the whole sky was illuminated as though lit from within as the glorious golden sun slowly rose above the mountain peaks bathing them in a brilliant rosy glow. Our lucky pair was enchanted and took many memorable photos of every beguiling colour change. It was pure magic! Initially the wonderful clarity of the vistas was breathtaking, however as can happen in the mountains, gradually the mist that was blanketing the valleys drifts slowly upwards and by the time C.P. appeared, the sheer depth of colours had been leeched away. It is possible he had taken the opportunity to have a couple of extra hours in bed; in his long career as a mountain leader, he had witnessed many such wonderful sunrises in the Himalaya.

After breakfast, the car that had been arranged by Mountain Monarch arrived to take them back to the Hotel Shakti in Kathmandu. The two-hour drive was interesting to say the least: the views were spectacular and the drops from the edge of the road somewhat disturbing though exhilarating as well. It was rather like being on a huge rollercoaster with all the humps and bumps, horseshoe-shaped loops and endless switchbacks: both Ian and Rachael loved it!

C.P and Sandip took their luggage upstairs to the bedroom and then they all had a cooling drink in the lovely Shakti garden before Rachael and Ian had a shower and C.P. and Sandip went back to Mountain Monarch's office. Sandip was needed as porter on another trek and C.P. had lots and lots of washing to do! Ian had arranged that, after he and Rachael had showered and changed, he was going to take her for a pizza and then visit the exquisite Garden of Dreams, just a short walk from their hotel.

The Garden of Dreams, also known as the Garden of Six Seasons is located in Kaiser Mahal which is across the street from the former Royal Palace at the entrance to the Thamel tourist area of downtown Kathmandu. Completely surrounded by walls, it is an unbelievably tranquil oasis and haven of peace and beauty in the midst of the chaos, noise, traffic and pollution of the city. It is two minutes' walk but one million miles from central Thamel! It was created in the 1920s by Field Marshal Kaiser Sumsher Rana after visiting Edwardian gardens in England and is an

enduring legacy to his talent and vision. Apparently Kaiser Sumsher funded the building of his famous garden by winning an epic 100,000 rupees game of cowrie shells against his father, the Maharajah and Prime Minister.

This beautiful, serene, neo-classical enclave is full of incredible pavilions of many styles and designs, dazzling fountains, ornamental ponds full of tall reeds and huge water lilies, statues and urns, verandas, pergolas, decorative garden furniture, balustrades and birdhouses. Each of the six pavilions, which provide the Garden's architectural framework, is dedicated to one of the six seasons in Nepal: spring, early summer, late summer and monsoon season, early autumn, late autumn and winter. When Kaiser Sumsher died in 1964, he left his Garden of Dreams to the Nepalese government and for some decades it was neglected. However it was renovated and brought back to life over a six-year period ending in 2007 with the aid of the Austrian Government, the Nepalese Ministry of Education and Eco-Nepal. It now stands as a glorious testament to its creator and to what can be achieved when countries work together. Throughout the garden fascinating plants and trees from all over the world appear alongside Nepal's own vibrant and exotic flora: the whole area is so shady and peaceful, it is a true haven of serenity.

Rachael discovered a tall bamboo swing and spent a long time just gently swinging to and fro, completely relaxed and happy. Although these swings look fragile, they are remarkably stable and a great favourite with all Nepalese children and adults alike. They are made of four long bamboo poles set upright at the corners of a square and tied securely together at the top to a cross pole, from which the swing is suspended. Some have wooden seats but many, especially in the hillside villages, have improvised seats of tyres or thick material slings. The whole structure is about twenty feet high so while it might look frightening is perfectly safe. Ian watched her from one of the many garden seats utterly at ease. Rachael seemed lost in a little world all of her own. Ian wondered if she was thinking, as he was, of their lovely dream garden at Old Water View that cascaded down in terraces of verdant grass and bushes to the tree-lined sparkling Goldrill Beck. Or perhaps she was remembering her favourite book, *The Secret Garden*. Somehow the Garden of Dreams had entranced her and, he was sure, would stay in her memory forever.

Later when they were both snuggled down in their comfortable beds back at the Hotel Shakti, they reminisced about their wonderful experiences: a day that had started at 4 a.m. with an awe-inspiring sunrise over the high Himalaya and ended with a beautiful tranquil sunset in the Garden of Dreams. A truly perfect day!

EXPLORING BHAKTAPUR

Over a lengthy breakfast next morning, Ian explained to Rachael what he had planned for them to do that day.

'I thought we could hire a taxi and go to the city of Bhaktapur. It's very old and we could explore it together and discover why it is so popular with tourists and Nepalese people as well.'

Rachael readily agreed: she was always up for any adventure with her dad. They quickly packed Ian's rucksack with their bottles of water and some snacks and walked into Thamel to find a taxi. By now Ian was really adept at negotiating taxi fares, so soon they were in one of the iconic taxis so prevalent in Kathmandu: a whitish battered Suzuki. These are amazing and a ride in them is an experience to say the least. If you 'indulge' in this popular form of transport, you need to forget about luxury and be prepared for very hard seats and a complete lack of adequate suspension, although most of these Suzukis are fitted with very necessary handles

that you can grip with white knuckles! You will be tossed about as the taxi goes over the many potholes, humps and bumps that epitomise the majority of roads outside Kathmandu City: it is all part of the fun and experience of this amazing country. The spectacular views of the green foothills and snow-capped Himalayan peaks to the left enhanced their journey eastwards to Bhaktapur: a scenic if somewhat uncomfortable journey.

The whole of Bhaktapur is truly like an open living museum: the ambience here is so opulent and overpowering that you are immediately transported back centuries the moment you step into its magical territory. It is rather like stepping into a historical film set. Bhaktapur – locally called Khwopa – is world renowned for its elegant art, fabulous architecture, culture and indigenous lifestyle. Currently this ancient city is known variously as the 'City of Culture', the 'Living Heritage' and 'Nepal's Cultural Gem': all of which accurately describe its unique character. Understandably, it is a World Heritage Site listed by UNESCO.

The city's absolute gem is Durbar Square, strewn with incomparable palaces, temples and monasteries famous for their exquisite artworks in wood, metal and stone, which have bewitched pilgrims and travellers for centuries. Bhaktapur's situation in the Kathmandu Valley, surrounded by the fantastic holy Himalaya adds to the atmosphere of history, devotion and serenity: it is as though the mountains are keeping vigil over its purity, beauty and splendour.

Bhaktapur grew up from a collection of villages along the old trade route between India and Tibet. Founded in the 12th century by King Ananda Malla, it was the capital city of the Greater Malla Kingdom until the 15th century but it was not until the 1700s that it was designed in its present shape. Most of Bhaktapur's most renowned and distinguished monuments were built by the then Malla rulers. A ban on vehicles in Durbar Square was extended and enforced in 1992: the law forbids heavy vehicles to enter the heart of the city and all vehicles from any religious enclave. The endeavours of the Bhaktapur Municipality and the cooperation of the local citizens have resulted in

Bhaktapur becoming the least polluted city in Nepal – a great bonus for its inhabitants and visitors alike.

As Ian and Rachael slowly explored Bhaktapur, they were mesmerised by all the varied and intricate monumental masterpieces, each seeming delightfully more attractive and wondrous than the previous one. Mainly they are constructed of terracotta supported by fabulously carved columns and elaborately chiselled struts. Their windows and doors are intricately carved and they have shining gilded roofs and pinnacles, beautiful open spaces and courts. The fascinating divine and kingly images reflect the different religious beliefs and allegiances, social outlook and economic status of the builders. All illustrate perfectly the traditional rich artistic skills in wood, repoussé metal work and detailed and ornate stone carvings of the Newar people and the Malla rulers. There are far too many wonders to describe them all in detail but I will highlight the ones that Rachael and Ian found most memorable.

Durbar Square (Layaku) was their first fascinating destination. It is full of pagodas and shikhara-style temples dedicated mostly to Hindu gods and goddesses grouped around The Palace of Fifty-Five Windows – the royal palace made of wood and brick which was moved to Durbar Square from Dattaraya Square where it was originally constructed. Next to it is the world famous Golden Gate: an unparalleled specimen of re-poussé art. Rachael eagerly urged Ian through this wonderful shining entrance to the marvellous Taleju Temple Complex with courtyards and the Royal Bath with a huge golden water spout in the shape of sinuous snake.

'Fancy having a bath in that, Dad!' she said excitedly.

Ian pointed out that he would not like to have a proper bath in front of so many visitors – he preferred a little more privacy: this response made Rachael giggle!

The next object to amaze them was the massive Big Bell erected by the last Malla king – Ranajit Malla in the 1700s in honour of their particular goddess, Talaju. It is still rung twice a day to pay homage to her. However the bell that fascinated Rachael most, understandably because of her love of all animals, was the nearby smaller Barking Bell: apparently, when this

is rung by the caretaker, all the dogs in the vicinity bark and howl. To her disappointment, no one appeared to ring it so eventually Ian persuaded Rachael to move on as there was still so much to see. (It is said that there is scientific proof that the barking dogs are not just another myth: it seems that the pitch of the bell is such that it makes all dogs bark – I'll leave it to you to decide on the verity of this claim!)

The ostentatious golden effigies of the kings perched on amazing stone monoliths, the numerous guardian deities looking out from their brightly decorated sanctuaries, and fantastic range of intricate wooden carvings festooning every building should vie with each other but instead, amazingly, they all seem to form a well-orchestrated symphony. The whole scene is absolutely breathtaking and both our explorers took lots of photos but also often just stood there entranced, absorbing the incredible atmosphere: it is a cultural overload in the best possible way.

Their next wonderful highlight, and Rachael's favourite, was the pagoda-style Nyatapola Temple, which towers over Taumadhi Square. It was built in 1702 AD in a period of just seven months by King Bhupatindra Malla as a place where his people could worship the goddess Siddhi Lakshmi: the Hindu goddess of prosperity. This magnificent five-storeyed temple is the tallest pagoda in Bhaktapur standing some thirty metres high and thought to be one of the tallest in the

the same name. This beautiful three-storeyed pagoda is a temple dedicated to the Hindu Trinity: Brahma the creator, Vishnu the preserver and Shiva the destroyer and some claim it was built as early as the 15th century. However the exact date is uncertain, as is the claim that it was constructed from a single piece of wood from one tree. It is nevertheless undoubtedly spectacular and has statues of the same wrestler depicted at the Nyatapola Temple, as well as a chakra circle or spinning wheel and a glowing gilded metal statue of Garuda, a bird-like divinity. Ian noticed that all around the temple were detailed panels of explicit and erotic carvings but Rachael did not seem to notice these. She was staring at the monastery next door, which has the wonderfully intricate and brilliantly coloured 'Peacock Window' also aptly called the 'Mona Lisa of Nepal' – a masterpiece of incredible exquisite wood carving.

Ian decided that Rachael had probably seen enough of monuments and temples for the time being and suggested that they ought to find out more about the people who lived and worked in Bhaktapur. He guided her down the narrow, more tranquil side streets towards 'Pottery Square' where they watched very skilful potters producing a wonderful variety of pots on their primitive wheels driven by foot pedals.

As they moved on, they came across a series of small rectangular pools full of dye of every brilliant colour. This was where all the leather used by the dexterous accomplished artisans to craft the most attractive leather goods was softened and dyed. Rachael could hardly wait to explore the endless alleyways that housed fascinating little shops selling beautifully made traditional handicrafts of every description: from articles of exquisitely embroidered clothing to fantastic wooden carvings, brilliantly decorated pottery, intricately designed metalwork and jewellery, lovely wall hangings and woven goods, wonderfully soft leather articles of every kind and amazingly elaborate pictures, scrolls and thankas. Thankas are incomparably beautiful, minutely detailed religious paintings often done by artisans and Tibetan Buddhist monks on cloth: they shine with gold and highly colourful designs.

whole of Nepal. Intricately and beautifully carved with divine figures, it is an everlasting tribute to the immense skills of its Newar craftsmen and rests on top of five huge step-like terraces with four Ganesh[2] shrines at each corner. A long flight of steps leads to the top platform: each step has an ornate statue on either side. To make his temple strong and powerful, King Bhupatindra Malla also ordered huge guardians to be carved and placed in pairs on each level of the base leading up to the pagoda-shaped temple itself. The first level has statues of Bhaktapur's strongest man – the famous wrestler – Jaya mal Pata, the second level has two elephants followed by two lions, then two gryffons and finally Baghini and Singhini, the tiger and lion goddesses. The whole effect is completely stunning.

Rachael quickly climbed up the flight of steps pausing frequently to pose for photos taken by her loving dad; they would provide another memory to treasure.

The last landmark they visited was the much-admired Dattatreya Temple standing in the square bearing

---

2 Ganesh – the elephant-headed Hindu God, son of Lord Shiva and the Goddess Parvati – is the benevolent Hindu god of beginnings, wisdom and learning.

Those bought from monastery schools like the one in Boudnath are incredibly precise and executed as a mark of devotion solely by monks. The thankas, meticulously painted by a Master, like the ones both Ian and I have, are very expensive and take months to complete. Both Ian and Rachael were fascinated by the wealth and range of goods on display: they had nothing but admiration for the skill and devotion of the artisans; what a marvellous legacy they had inherited from their ancestors.

When Rachael found out that Bhaktapur was also famous for all the splendid festivals with their ancient ritual dances, many as unique as the city itself, she asked Ian if they could return one day when a festival was being held. This would not be difficult, she informed her dad, as each month a different festival took place. Ian smiled: his daughter was always so eager for new experiences. And, of course, another trek and cultural encounter would add greatly to her knowledge so he readily agreed that when they returned to Nepal, they would indeed attend a festival.

By this time, they were both pretty weary so Ian hailed a taxi, inevitably a grubby white Suzuki, and soon they were being shaken again as they travelled back to the Hotel Shakti. They decided that they would not go out for a meal that evening; they had all their packing to do because the following morning C.P. was going to pick them up and take them to meet his wife Pari and his daughter, Khushi (her name means 'happy' and she is the most delightful, happy child and a precious 'granddaughter' to me.) Ian and Rachael were going to stay overnight at C.P.'s home and Pari, who is an excellent cook, was looking forward to providing them with a traditional Nepalese meal. Rachael was absolutely delighted that she was going to meet Khushi the very next day.

Ian suggested that they went out to the nearby minimarket and bought some typical Nepalese snacks: Rachael thought that was a super idea. They bought lots of packets of different kinds of spicy snacks, some chocolate bars and Nepalese sweets. Ian treated himself to some beer: bottles of Gourkha, Everest and Nepal Ice and Rachael thought she would try some almond milk.

They piled up all their goodies on their beds, just like naughty schoolchildren having a secret midnight feast! Rachael thought it was great and thoroughly enjoyed sampling all the spicy snacks: real Nepalese junk food. Unfortunately she found that the almond milk really was disgusting but that didn't worry her as she still had bottles of fruit juice and water. Rachael is never upset when this happens because she is always eager to try new things and so expects that occasionally she is not going to like them; that, she realises maturely, is inevitable. They chatted for a while about their amazing day and looked through all the magnificent photos they had taken.

'Wow! They are awesome photos, Dad. Thank you for a fab day. I'm really looking forward to meeting Khushi tomorrow!' were Rachael's last words before she dropped into a deep sleep.

RACHAEL MEETS KHUSHI

When Rachael and Ian went downstairs next morning, they found that C.P. had left a message for them to say he would be picking them about 10 a.m. This was great as it meant they could have a leisurely breakfast before bringing down all their gear. Rachael was so excited about meeting Khushi at last, that she could hardly sit still: she was just bouncing with anticipation. While they were waiting in reception for C.P. to arrive, Ian pointed out to Rachael that when they arrived at C.P.'s house, Khushi would be at school but Rachael was not concerned at all.

'Well I shall see where she lives, won't I Dad? And I will meet Pari,' she said happily.

C.P. arrived promptly at 10 a.m. and greeted Rachael and Ian with a huge beaming smile and the traditional 'Namaste' to which they responded in kind. Then he and the driver loaded all their gear into the car provided by Mountain Monarch Adventures. Rachael was buzzing and Ian was really looking forward to meeting C.P.'s family. After saying goodbye to the staff of the Hotel Shakti and thanking them for their care, Rachael and Ian climbed into the back seat of the car and they were soon on their way. As always their journey was exciting: successfully navigating around the traffic in Kathmandu requires nerve, skill, liberal use of the horn and good luck! Their driver was excellent and before long, he was helping them out of the car and depositing their luggage in front of C.P.'s flat before he took the car back to the Mountain Monarch offices.

C.P. took Ian and Rachael inside his home and introduced them to his lovely wife Pari, who greeted them smiling happily. She is a gentle, caring and very pretty lady and although her English at this time was limited, there was no doubt she was absolutely thrilled to meet Rachael and Ian. Rachael loved looking round their home: she had been longing to see inside a typical Nepalese house and see how most people lived. She was amazed that there was a Western-style toilet and a shower in the small bathroom, a TV in the living room and she was delighted with all the bright colourful furniture, wall hangings and ornaments. There was no luxury but everything was immaculate and the whole atmosphere warm, caring and friendly. It was a real home in every way.[3] Rachael was really interested to find out how and where they cooked, so Pari and C.P. showed her the kitchen with a double gas ring that used bottled butane gas. Ian and Rachael were soon to discover what tasty meals and snacks Pari, who had been a very skilful chef, could produce.

They all had a drink, tasty snacks and chatted happily before C.P. reminded Rachael and Ian that he had promised to take them to the offices of Mountain Monarch to meet Pradip and Subash again and some of their staff. The offices were only a short walk away and while they were out, he explained, Pari would collect Khushi from school so that on their return they could meet his lovely daughter. He and Pari were obviously very proud of their daughter, as am I. My beautiful Nepalese 'granddaughter', Khushi, is a really lovely child, very modest, kind and polite; she is a little treasure.

---

3 When I first met C.P. he was living in a flat in one of the narrow alleyways in the centre of Kathmandu but when he and Pari married and had Khushi, they moved out of the pollution of the city to the outskirts. As a small child, Khushi had been prone to chest infections so living in the city was impractical and bad for her health.

Ian and Rachael accompanied C.P. up the steep track towards MMA offices, built at the side of Pradip's wonderful two-storeyed house – an amazing, elegant building with a lovely view over the surrounding hills.

I remember vividly when I first trekked with MMA that Pradip and his family lived in a small compound near to C.P. Their offices, storerooms and flat were crammed into a really small place. But later, through sheer hard work and enterprise, their company had grown to become a very successful organisation; thoroughly professional and with an excellent reputation, not only for caring for their trekking guests and climbers, but for their staff too.

Rachael meets Khushi.

Rachael and Ian were greeted warmly by Pradip and Subash and were introduced to some of the MMA staff including climbing and trekking Sherpas, medical staff and other trek leaders like C.P. They were all planning forthcoming treks so you can imagine that Rachael was really interested and asked them lots of questions. Eventually it was time to leave and after wishing Ian and Rachael a safe journey home, both Pradip and Subash expressed the hope that they would return another year to tackle one of the higher Himalayan treks.

'We are certainly going to do that, aren't we Dad?' exclaimed Rachael. 'We'll see you next year!'

Ian smiled: Rachael had definite plans for their future explorations and he was delighted to be part of them.

When they arrived back at C.P.'s home, Khushi was waiting for them. Rachael rushed across the room and gave her a huge hug. Khushi was obviously thrilled to meet Rachael and soon the two of them were chatting and playing together as if they had been friends forever. Rachael gave Khushi one of her special 'Rachael Explore' Teddy Bears, which sported a green jumper with Rachael's logo embroidered on the front. Ian had these made when he launched Rachael's website www.rachaelexplore.com which gives information about her adventures and offers clothing and a variety of other items for sale. Khushi was absolutely delighted as she collected teddy bears and soon took her new bear into the bedroom and sat him proudly on her shelf. They stayed in the bedroom playing happily for some time whilst Pari started to prepare the evening meal. Ian and C.P. went to a nearby shop to buy some Everest beer, bottles of cola for the girls and some snacks.

After a while Khushi's teacher arrived: C.P. was paying her to coach Khushi and help with her English so that she could achieve her potential at school. Khushi loved her teacher and Rachael was pleased that they allowed her to sit quietly in the spare room with them and watch and listen to Khushi's lesson. Khushi was an excellent pupil and wanted to learn everything she could: she worked very hard but very joyfully. (A little different from Rachael, Ian thought, who viewed school as something she had to endure!)

Children in Nepal must be a joy and privilege to teach as they all value education immensely. They are brought up to realise that a good education and good results are their passport out of poverty so they are all eager to learn. Although Nepal is a very poor country and most ordinary people earn very little, all schooling has to be paid for. Thus every family ensures that their children take full advantage of the sacrifice their parents often have to make to give them the chance to have a better life and a bright future.

By the time Khushi had finished her lesson, Ian and C.P. had returned with the Everest beer and Pari had just about finished cooking. Khushi, Rachael and C.P. set the small table and they all sat down to plates of delicious dhal bhat: the very best Ian and Rachael had eaten all the time they had been in Nepal. In addition, Pari had cooked lots of little spicy side dishes that were mouth-watering; it was a thoroughly enjoyable meal. Pari was delighted by their obvious pleasure and smiled

in acceptance when Ian insisted that she join them at the table. Often wives wait until their husbands and visitors eat before they have their own meal but Ian asked C.P. to make Pari understand that he wanted them all to eat together as a family.

After Pari's wonderful meal, Rachael and Khushi went back into the bedroom where they chatted and giggled together and plaited each other's hair. Ian smiled fondly as he watched them through the open door: one golden head beside a shiny black one – two girls from two different cultures, completely content and in consummate harmony. Besides all the fabulous scenery, this was exactly what Ian had wanted Rachael to experience in Nepal and he was so proud that she was embracing it with all her usual understanding and enthusiasm.

Pari cleared up in the kitchen while Ian and C.P. had several beers, chatted about many different things and looked at all the fabulous photos Ian had taken of their adventures in Nepal. Pari joined them and admired all the beautiful scenes and the lovely pictures of Rachael, who is very photogenic. Ian then took photos of them all, especially Khushi and Rachael as they made a really gorgeous pair. Although Khushi is only a year younger, she is very much smaller than Rachael who is tall for her age. Neither C.P. nor Pari are much taller than I am (at five foot) so it is no wonder Rachael towers over Khushi because Ian, who is well over six feet, towers over the three of us!

C.P. then put on a Disney video for Khushi and Rachael: although it was dubbed in Nepali, Rachael knew the story so both girls could understand the plot perfectly and discussed it quietly. C.P. and Ian continued to chat happily while Pari tried to persuade them to eat a variety of snacks. When visiting friends in Nepal, you will never go hungry! You will be constantly urged to try food of every kind. In their culture, feeding you really well is a sign of the affection and admiration so it is difficult to refuse. But in the end, even Ian had to admit he was defeated and could not eat another mouthful.

As the evening wore on, it became apparent that Khushi in particular was becoming tired, so after the video had finished, they decided it was time for bed. They had all had a wonderful day, a complete bonding of cultures. Ian and Rachael were very grateful for such friendly hospitality and thanked their hosts profusely. Ian slept on the large day bed in the lounge, while Rachael snuggled down in fleecy blankets on the bed-settee there.

'Goodnight, Dad,' said Rachael sleepily. 'I've had a marvellous day. It is fab here in Khushi's home. It is much better than any hotel. I just love it!'

Ian totally agreed.

RACHAEL'S LAST DAY IN NEPAL – NOT QUITE!

They were all up quite early next morning, as Khushi wanted to spend some time with Rachael before going to school. Pari cooked everyone a really tasty breakfast, a typical Nepalese dish rather like a spicy potato and vegetable omelette. After this, Khushi and Rachael sat down together to plan how they were going to keep in touch. They had bonded so well that they both felt like sisters rather than just friends. They decided they would use the Internet – a face-to-face video link that would enable them to chat and see each other whenever they had any news. Rachael promised Khushi that when she got home she would send her new friend an iPhone and charger. She explained that this would be in a parcel full of UK goodies that she and her dad planned to send to Pari, C.P. and Khushi.

A week later, Ian and Rachael did indeed post such a parcel and they had lots of fun selecting typical British items that they thought their Nepalese family would enjoy. These included selections of tea, shortbread biscuits and sweets including Kendal mint cake and lots of other things.

All too soon, it was time for Pari to take Khushi to meet the school bus, so both girls hugged each other warmly and a little tearfully. They had clearly formed a friendship that would never be broken.

When Pari returned, they all set out to walk up to the Budhanilkantha Temple that C.P. and Pari attended regularly to perform their pujas: a form of intense prayer and worship usually done in the morning.

Budhanilkantha in Nepali literally means 'Old Blue Throat' and is situated to the north of Kathmandu just below the Shivapuri Hill. It is about a forty-five minute walk from C.P.'s home. The temple is dedicated to Hindu God, Lord Vishnu, the Protector and is very unusual as it is open-air. Rachael really enjoyed the walk and gained a lot of knowledge about everyday Nepalese life as they passed by lots of ordinary small houses where women were washing clothes in outside tubs and carrying out other daily tasks. There were also quite a few open-fronted shops like the one that had amazed her in the hills. Rachael absorbs all different cultural experiences like a sponge and absolutely loves it.

When they arrived at the temple compound, Rachael and Ian were amazed to find that it was completely different from any of the temples they had seen before. The main statue of the Deity, Lord Vishnu, around five metres tall is elaborately carved from a single block of spectacular black basalt and is positioned in the centre of a recessed pool of water, thirteen metres long. Lord Vishnu is depicted reclining, as though he is sleeping, on the coils of the cosmic serpent, Ananta Shesha. As Hindus, C.P. and Pari were able to walk down the steps and touch Lord Vishnu's feet but all other visitors are not allowed to do this. There is a legend that, in the 17th century, King Pratap Malla had a prophetic vision that left him believing that if any King of Nepal visited the Budhanilkantha Temple they would die. This fear apparently persisted because from that time no Nepalese king has ever visited the site.

A typical Nepali temple.

As you might imagine, as soon as they arrived back at C.P. and Pari's home, she went into the kitchen to cook them some snacks and make drinks. Ian insisted that they all sat down together to celebrate and share this last meal. By now Pari had lost some of her natural shyness and laughed and chatted happily: she is a lovely lady.

Eventually Subash arrived to drive Rachael and Ian to the airport for their long flight back to the UK. He presented them with a kata scarf each; these are golden silk scarves which are placed around the necks of guests, friends and family to wish them good luck, good health and a safe journey. Just after their plane took off and they were flying over the fabulous Himalaya, Ian noticed that Rachael was staring out of the window, waving her hand and mumbling. Curious, he asked her what she was doing.

With a beaming smile that lit up her lovely face, Rachael explained:

'I am just waving goodbye to the Himalaya, Dad and promising that we will be back next year!'

CHAPTER

**NEPAL 2: POKHARA AND THE
ANNAPURNA REGION – 2015**
AGED ELEVEN YEARS
SIX MONTHS

It is something of a miracle that Rachael's second adventure in Nepal with her dad ever took place.

Readers will remember that their exploration of Iceland in 2015 ended in disaster with Ian breaking his back on August 7th at the beginning of an exciting whale-watching trip on a RIB boat from the harbour of Reykjavik. You will recall how much Rachael helped her dad to get home with no fuss, after hospital treatment and the agony that he suffered from his crushed and splintered vertebrae. Above all, he was determined to keep his promise to Rachael that they would return to Nepal that October half term to do the higher trek already organised with C.P.

Never once did Rachael remind him of this promise because she realised, as we all did, that the chance of Ian being able to climb and trek just ten weeks after injuring his back so badly (and being heavily sedated and having to wear a back-brace) were negligible. Of course, we had all not taken into consideration the intransigent stubbornness, guts, courage and sheer bloody-mindedness of Ian: he was not going to be beaten and he was going to keep his promise. As I said before he was the most impatient of patients! Nevertheless, in obvious pain, he gradually began to walk again, first of all with crutches and eventually without them, although his grim expression of determination showed the amount of effort this took. He had a goal: exploring Pokhara and the Annapurna Region with Rachael and C.P. towards the end of October.

Even now Ian will admit he does not really know how he managed to achieve his goal: it is complete madness to go trekking in the Himalaya when, only ten weeks before, you had broken your back. But he did it. At this point, I feel that it is important to emphasise no matter how determined Ian was to get fit enough again to trek in the Himalaya, he would never have taken Rachael to Nepal again, had he not been absolutely sure he could keep her safe and well. He would never put her in danger. Also he knew that, should there be an accident, (as can happen anytime to anyone) his Nepalese family, C.P. Pari and Khushi would take care of Rachael and make sure she was safe and happy.

MANCHESTER TO KATHMANDU

So unbelievably, on October 21st 2015, he and Rachael flew from Manchester Airport to Kathmandu via Abu Dhabi to fulfil a promise and a dream. Although Ian had flown many times before – both short- and long-haul flights – this time he experienced 'jet bloat'. It is a very uncomfortable and embarrassing condition, caused when an accumulation of air collects in your abdomen. Apparently it is due to the change in air pressure in the aircraft cabin when it flies above 30,000 feet and is exacerbated by the intake of alcohol and, in particular, salty food. It generally clears up a few days after your flight but can persist for several painful weeks, which unfortunately, is what happened to Ian, whose 'jet bloat' persisted for two weeks after they returned home.

It had never happened to him before. As always, he only had half a pint of beer before the flight, however his massive efforts to get fit and the amount of medication he had to take could have made him more vulnerable. Or, of course, it could have been sheer bad luck. Just as she had done on their Iceland trip, Rachael helped Ian whenever she could with things like supervising their luggage and keeping him amused with her witty comments.

When, very much later, they emerged from Tribhuvan Airport, Kathmandu, they discovered a taxi and driver waiting for them: C.P. had arranged this with Pradip, the owner of Mountain Monarch Adventures. The driver and Rachael loaded up their luggage and soon they were speeding towards C.P.'s home, which is not far from the airport. By now Rachael was used to the traffic chaos of Kathmandu so scarcely noticed the noise, horn blasts and smell of the polluted air. All she said was, 'Isn't it great to be back, Dad? I do so love it all!'

Pari, Khushi and C.P. were waiting eagerly to meet them again and welcomed them warmly. Khushi danced up and down with joy and Pari and C.P. beamed with pleasure. They had been so afraid that Ian and Rachael would not be able to come to Kathmandu that year – just ten weeks after Ian's horrible back injury in Iceland. They had all prayed earnestly for a miracle and that had certainly happened; they were overjoyed. When

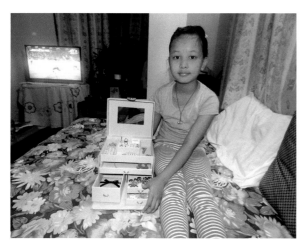

Khushi.

they went inside, Ubick, Pari's fifteen-year-old nephew, greeted Rachael and Ian enthusiastically. He had heard a lot about Rachael and was longing to meet her. He told Ian he was really happy because he was going to be their porter on the trek in the Annapurna Region.

There were tears of joy from Khushi, when Rachael gave her a very special present that she had chosen and bought herself: it was a beautiful, pale-pink jewellery box with gold handles. It had lots of little drawers, which Rachael had filled with pretty hair accessories, rings, bracelets, bangles, earrings and other treasures that she thought Khushi would love. Khushi was ecstatic and eagerly showed her parents Rachael's wonderful gift: Pari and C.P. were genuinely delighted. Then the girls went into the bedroom so Rachael could help

Khushi decide which drawers she should use for her own jewellery: it took some time! Decisions made, they played happily together and, as before, plaited each other's hair. It was just as though they had never been apart; their bond was very real and very strong.

Ian, Ubick and C.P. chatted in the living room while Pari went into the kitchen to cook a meal for all of them. Ubick explained to Ian why he was so eager to be their porter: it was a step towards becoming a top mountain and trek leader like C.P. He planned that when he was eighteen, he was going to apply to join the army so he could gain experience, skills and fitness. Then he hoped to join a company like MMA and progress from being a porter, to a sherpa and eventually become a leader like his uncle, C.P.

Almost like magic, Pari soon produced a very tasty meal with lots of snacks and extra rice for C.P. and Ubick, who both had excellent appetites. Because of his 'jet bloat', Ian tried hard to limit the amount he ate but that proved very difficult with Pari offering such superb food in such a caring way. I know from experience that this is a cultural trait of Nepalese people: the urge to ensure that their visitors and family never go hungry. I have always found it almost impossible to convince Nepalese people in general and Pari in particular that the only reason I cannot eat any more of their delicious food is truly because I am completely full! To do this in such a way that you do not cause these lovely people any offence is not easy.

When everything was tidied away, they all retired to bed early as Rachael and Ian were quite exhausted from such a long journey and the next day they and C.P. were flying to Pokhara. Ubick was travelling there by bus.

'Goodnight, Dad, I love you!' said Rachael drowsily. 'I am so looking forward to tomorrow when I will see all those wonderful mountains again. Thank you, thank you so much for bringing me back!'

'Goodnight, darling,' Ian replied. 'Tomorrow is going to be great!'

KATHMANDU TO POKHARA AND FEWA LAKE

Ubick was up early next morning as he was catching the bus to Pokhara. It is a long, interesting but quite exhausting journey that lasts for the best part of a day. Ian and Rachael had originally planned to travel by bus but Ian had sensibly taken C.P.'s advice to fly to Pokhara as the road there from Kathmandu is very rough in places with lots of switchbacks. In addition it is also prone to landslides, which make the surface very bumpy and uneven and the buses are not particularly comfortable and often very crowded. So around mid-morning C.P. took Rachael and Ian to the airport by taxi and soon they were flying westwards over fascinating countryside

on their way to Pokhara. The scenery is quite spectacular: verdant green hills surrounding multi-coloured fields of rice, buckwheat and vegetables with the fabulous snow-capped high Himalaya stretching invitingly into the distance. Rachael was enchanted: she took lots of photos through the window of the aircraft and managed to get the propeller and part of the wing in some of them. She kept up an excited running commentary, which amused Ian greatly.

'Just look at all those paths winding up the steep hills, Dad! I can't wait to climb up them. It's going to be fab!'

I must say this is not always the reaction of travellers and certainly wasn't mine the first time I flew into Pokhara. Those steep paths look very intimidating and endless, rather like the long twisting coils of huge snakes rearing up through the trees and scrub.

The flight is quite a short one, so less than an hour after boarding the plane Ian, Rachael and C.P. were climbing down the aircraft steps into beautiful warm sunshine. Pokhara airport is surprisingly attractive and welcoming with clean, neat buildings surrounded by trees and borders of grass and bright flowers. Multi-coloured flags fly above boards saying, 'Welcome to Pokhara', while the same greeting is picked out in white stones among the flower borders.

C.P. quickly found a taxi to take them and their luggage to the Hotel Tulsi, a really pleasant hotel set in a beautiful garden full of shady trees, brilliant flowers and bushes situated in the Lakeside area of Pokhara city. All the staff were very welcoming and soon Rachael and Ian were freshening up in their comfortable room. Rachael was pleased to find that there was a Western-style toilet and a lovely bath and shower: luxury in Nepal!

A little while later, they walked around the Lakeside shops with C.P. and then went for a light meal at an open-fronted vegetarian restaurant that was one of C.P.'s favourites. The food was very good. Rachael and Ian shared a splendid vegetarian pizza and a plate of vegetable momos – Nepalese steamed dumplings that are filled with vegetables and really tasty. C.P. had his customary dhal bhat and they all had drinks: C.P. a beer, Rachael a Coke and Ian a can of Red Bull – the non-fizzy kind as he did not want to aggravate his 'jet bloat'.

Then they made their way down to the highlight of Pokhara city; the wonderful Fewa Lake (Phewa Tal). It is a huge freshwater lake, the second largest in Nepal. The lake is stream-fed but a dam regulates the water reserve so actually it is classified as a semi-natural freshwater lake. It is located at 2434ft or 742m and covers an area of around two square miles, the average depth being 28ft (8.6m). This fabulous lake is a major attraction for all water sport enthusiasts and for families and visitors who simply love absorbing the breathtaking scenery. The clean warm water of the lake is really inviting and ideal for a trip in one of the small wooden boats.

The stupendous Dhaulagiri and Annapurna Ranges loom majestically in the distance with the iconic, holy mountain of snow-capped Machhapuchhare dominating the scene. This mountain is exactly what you imagine a mountain should look like: a magnificent sharp cone of a peak that shines and glistens in the sunlight. It is only when you have a closer side view of Machhapuchhare, (Fishtail Mountain), that you realise why it is so named: it is shaped like a fishtail – one peak behind the other with a high saddle in between. It is utterly beautiful and because it is a holy mountain, it is worshipped and respected and has never been climbed. On a calm day, all these wonderful mountains are perfectly mirrored on the surface of Fewa Lake. Away from the shore, the water is clean and deep and the dense forest on the south side of the lake is rich in wildlife while the buildings and lights of the northern Lakeside make a different but very attractive background.

Rachael was bewitched: she could hardly wait for her boat trip. C.P. selected one of the boats, skilfully rowed by a charming young man who took them on a complete circuit of that picturesque lake. Rachael and Ian's cameras worked overtime. There were so many attractions to photograph: not just the fabulous scenery but all the brightly coloured boats and people of all ages in their traditional costumes. Rachael was mesmerised by the paragliders circling overhead: she was really envious.

'Wow, Dad! They are flying just like birds!' she gasped. 'I would really, really like to do that one day. How do I get on one?'

'I'll find out,' replied Ian.

Rachael was so excited that he decided he would treat her to a secret paragliding flight when they returned to Pokhara: she deserved an extra treat!

Eventually they landed on the small, lush, tree-covered island in the middle of Fewa Lake. On this island is the lovely two-storeyed pagoda-like Hindu temple called the Barahi Temple dedicated to the Goddess Durga. She takes the form of a

boar called Barahi and protects the gods from demons by piercing them with her pointed tusks. She is depicted with a cup in one hand and a fish in the other. The temple is also guarded by statues of fierce golden lions and the elephant god – Ganesh. The Barahi Temple is an important centre of worship for all Hindu devotees and apparently on Saturdays, they can be seen making their way to the temple carrying animals for sacrifice. The whole temple is festooned with beautiful garlands of different kinds of flowers. Their brilliant colours of red, orange, white, yellow and pink glow and shine as they sway in the breeze creating an enchanting scene.

Ian was curious to know why all the trees have bands of red and then white at the bottom of their trunks: according to C.P. these colours represent the same elements as those on the prayer flags – red for fire and white for air and wind. Ian was also amazed to discover that he and Rachael, non-Hindus, could go inside the temple to look around. Perhaps this is because Buddhists are allowed to worship in the Barahi Temple too.

Rachael was overjoyed to see lots of plump pigeons squabbling and scrabbling around for seeds and scraps and, for once, she didn't ask Ian if she could catch one and keep it – wise girl! Although this lovely island can be quite busy, it still has a very peaceful and serene ambience. It really feels a very welcoming and joyful place.

While C.P. went to pray, Rachael and Ian explored the remainder of the island and were fascinated by the view of the shining white World Peace Pagoda high in the southern hills. They decided that one day they would climb up to it: Rachael thought that was a great idea; the view should be panoramic.

C.P. and Rachael.

There was an amusing incident before they landed back on the northern shore-line. They had just left the island when Ian noticed a log, approximately six feet in length, floating half-submerged in the water about twenty feet from the boat. With a completely straight face, he pointed at the log and said to Rachael, 'Look over there, darling, there's a crocodile!'

'Wow!' cried Rachael and immediately began to take photographs.

Ian and C.P. burst into laughter and Rachael looked at them suspiciously.

'Joke darling!' Ian explained, 'Look carefully and you will see it isn't breathing!'

'It's only a log! You horrible, horrible man – your jokes are getting worse!' Rachael shouted, thoroughly annoyed. However, she soon joined in their laughter. Her dad really had fooled her but she would get her own back when he was least expecting it.

After their interesting boat trip, they all walked back to the Hotel Tulsi. Although there is quite a lot of traffic, the roads in the Lakeside area are not as busy or chaotic as those in Kathmandu so it is quite pleasant just to wander around. They had a short rest then went out for an evening meal to the Fewa Paradise Restaurant. Besides delicious food, they were entertained by beautiful Nepalese dancers wearing fantastic costumes. The music and melodious singing, pretty lights and prompt friendly service made the end of their first day in Pokhara truly special. As they settled down in their beds at the hotel, Rachael reminded Ian that the next day they were beginning their trek into the high hills of the Annapurna Region. Ever mindful of the injury Ian had suffered, she enquired about his wellbeing in a caring quiet voice.

'You are all right, aren't you, Dad? You will be okay, won't you?'

'Of course, I am, darling,' Ian replied confidently. 'We'll be fine.'

POKHARA TO DHAMPUS

Next morning, Rachael was up, washed and dressed before Ian and began checking her rucksack to make sure that she had everything she needed for their trek. Ian smiled proudly: his daughter really was a developing into a responsible explorer. He quickly checked that he had packed correctly and then they went upstairs for breakfast, which was supposed be ready at 6 a.m. The previous evening, C.P. had made arrangements for them to have an early breakfast because the minibus was arriving at 7 a.m. to take them towards Phedi and the beginning of their trek to Dhampus. However when they reached the breakfast room all the lights were on but there wasn't a single waiter. Ian looked in the side-room and called out, 'Is anyone there?' but no one answered. Clearly Rachael and he were not going to have any breakfast that morning!

There was no point in wasting any more time so they went back to their room and collected their rucksacks. They went downstairs to reception where they found C.P. and Ubick waiting for them. C.P. would have been really upset had he known they had missed breakfast so Ian and Rachael agreed not to tell him. They were carrying lots of drinks and snacks that they could consume on the way so they would be completely fine.

The minibus arrived soon after 7 a.m. and C.P. and Ubick packed the luggage in the back along with the rucksacks. Ian kept a bottle of water handy as did Rachael but she had some snacks in her pockets too – sensible girl!

The dusty road wasn't too rough which was great because the suspension of the mini-bus was not exactly in the best condition, making the ride somewhat bouncy and uncomfortable. C.P. asked the driver to be careful and not to drive too fast because he did not want Ian to injure his back. The views ahead grew more and more picturesque as they travelled westwards. Small houses, fields of vegetables and lovely green, forested hills surrounded them while the distant snow-capped peaks of the Annapurna Range rose spectacularly in the distance.

Finally, around 9 a.m. they arrived at Labachowk, Phedi stopping in front of some shops. Eager to start their trek, Rachael jumped out of the minibus and started running around in sheer joy; she was so excited. Ian, C.P. and Ubick shook their heads and smiled at her antics – she really was such a joyful companion, she made everyone feel happy. C.P. went into one of the shops and bought some snacks for Ubick and himself but Ian decided he and Rachael had sufficient supplies for the day's walk so they shouldered their rucksacks ready for the climb up to Dhampus. As always, the weather was glorious, with blue skies and brilliant sunshine.

The path was made of hard earth and was stony in places, very like the paths at home in the Lake District and, initially, the ascent was fairly gentle. Rachael was really impressed by how strong Ubick was; he had fastened the duffel bags together to make a large pack, lifted that pack easily and placed the supporting strap (the namlo) around his forehead. With a huge grin on his face he carried his load effortlessly as if he had been a porter all his life, yet this was his first experience of that really hard job. He was fantastic!

As they climbed higher the path steepened and soon they were among the terraced strip fields that stretched up the hillsides. They could see rice, wheat, barley and lots of vegetables growing. Farmers were

Ubick.

using ponderous oxen to pull the primitive wooden ploughs. Rachael and Ian paused to admire how skilfully they ploughed the shallow stony earth and how easily they turned the oxen at the end of the narrow terraces, ploughing evenly in the opposite direction.

Groups of happy, laughing Nepalese children rushed down the track towards them then stopped and crowded around Rachael and Ian. They were curious about the digital cameras and begged to have their photos taken. They were absolutely fascinated by being able to see their faces in the viewer; to them it was magic. Then, with a happy greeting of 'Namaste', the children carried on down the path while Rachael and Ian followed C.P. and Ubick up towards Dhampus.

They passed lots of small houses bedecked with flowers, each having a productive vegetable garden with stacks of sweetcorn drying in the sunshine. All the people waved to them and smiled warmly. The Nepalese people living in the hills are obviously poor but they are so friendly and kind that it is a joy to trek in their beautiful country.

Occasionally our happy group stopped at narrow flat resting places to admire the views, take photos and have refreshments. At these spots there were usually tiered stone platforms, above which prayer flags flutter gaily in the breeze. The lowest platform is built so it is exactly the correct height for porters to lean their backs against. This is so they can take the weight of the packs off their shoulders for a while. It saves them from having to take the heavy pack off and lift it up again when it is time to carry on.

As they climbed higher, the majestic peaks of the Annapurna Range appeared ever more clearly over the wooded hillsides: they seemed to be beckoning our travellers to approach them. Eventually, around mid-afternoon, they reached the charming village of Dhampus where they soon found their hotel atop the steep green hillside – the Hotel Yama Sakura. C.P. reminded Rachael and Ian that I had stayed there

on the way back from Annapurna Base Camp. It was a lovely lodge with a nice shower room and a Western-style toilet at the end of the block of bedrooms. As I had done many years before, Rachael and Ian admired the beautiful garden full of bright orange marigolds, wonderfully perfumed roses, statuesque lilies and the many other flowers that surround the hotel. The long patio terrace was full of tubs and pots of bright red geraniums, golden marigolds and purple and white orchids. The patio was surrounded by a strong stone wall, which supported its overhanging position so the view from there was uninterrupted and spectacular. Our happy foursome relaxed on plastic patio chairs and enjoyed some welcoming drinks and a few snacks before they went for a shower.

Fortunately, Ian had remembered to pack towels this time; readers will remember that on the Kathmandu Valley Rim trek, Rachael and he had to use his fleece hat to dry themselves. Ian found Rachael's towel and toiletries in their duffel bag, which Ubick had put in their room. Rachael chose some clean clothes and went for a shower while Ian unpacked their gear and spread out their padded sleeping bags on the thin mattresses of the beds. He sat Patrick, Rachael's Mountain Rescue bear on her bed; that beloved little bear who had first done the West Highland Way and climbed Ben Nevis with Rachael, had been hiding in their duffel bag!

Rachael came back glowing.

Corn – not dead chickens!

'Wow, that was a super shower, Dad – really, really hot so you need to hurry up and go for your shower before anyone else goes in!'

Ian picked up his towel and said, 'Alright, young lady, I'll go now!'

He smiled to himself; sometimes it was far easier just to go with Rachael's flow than argue or protest!

While he was showering, Rachael was wandering around outside in a little world all of her own. Nepal had really captured her: she was enthralled with the scenery, the people and their culture. After his shower, Ian went to look for her and found her gazing upwards at the eaves of the lodge, a look of horror on her face.

He enquired what was wrong; why was she so upset? Rachael pointed up to some things hanging from the eaves and replied shakily.

'Dad! There are dead chickens up there. That is dreadful!'

Ian looked more closely and laughed.

'You silly, lovely girl! They aren't dead chickens – although I must admit that they do resemble them. They are cobs of sweetcorn that the owners have fastened up there to dry. Look carefully, darling, and you'll see I'm right!'

Rachael was hugely relieved. She knew that chickens, goats, cows and other animals were killed – some people loved eating meat even if she didn't want to do that. It was their choice but she had been shocked to think of dead chickens hanging from the roof of that beautiful lodge in a picturesque place.

They all had a lovely evening. Ubick and C.P. joined them and Rachael was highly amused by Ubick who had a great sense of humour. They giggled and laughed out loud together. Their meals were delicious too: Rachael and Ian had vegetable pizzas and C.P. and Ubick had their usual dhal bhat. Then they sat for a while on the patio terrace enjoying the fabulous sunset and watching the mist gradually blanketing the valley below: it was magical.

Rachael and Ian went to bed fairly early as their host had advised them to get up and watch the sunrise over the mountains; she said it was breath taking.

'I bet I'm awake before you, Dad,' said Rachael sleepily. 'Don't worry, I'll wake you up so you won't miss the sunrise – I promise.'

'Thank you, darling!' Ian replied but Rachael did not hear him – she had already dropped off to sleep.

DHAMPUS TO TOLKA

True to her word, Rachael was indeed awake before Ian. She dressed quickly and put on her fleece jacket because at 5 a.m. it was rather cold. She collected her camera and Patrick Bear and made sure that Ian was awake before she went outside to wait for the sunrise. Although the sky was beginning to lighten, it was still quite dark but Rachael could see the sky was clear so she was sure that the dawn and sunrise were going to be beautiful. She waited patiently, happy to be in such a wonderfully peaceful place. Ian soon joined her and together they waited for that promised spectacular sunrise. They were not disappointed. Gradually the sky brightened: at first with muted shades of purple and red but as the golden sun rose above the horizon, everything was bathed with brilliant colours of red, orange, gold and yellow. It was as though the whole sky was on fire. The windows of the lodge sparkled in the sunshine and the lovely flowers in the garden and on the patio lifted their heads to welcome the dawn. Below in the valley the mist drifted ethereally among the trees like magical smoke and the birds began to sing their cheerful dawn chorus. When the sun caught the peaks of the snow-capped mountains, they glistened and sparkled like huge rough-cut diamonds: the whole scene took their breath away. Both Rachael and Ian agreed that this sunrise was far better than the famous one they had seen the previous year at Nagarkot on their Kathmandu Valley Rim trek. They took some fabulous photos.

Ian went back inside to sort out their rucksacks and pack their duffel bag while Rachael spent another hour happily taking photos, content to absorb every aspect of that marvellous place. She posed Patrick Bear in various positions on the steps of the stone wall that surrounded the patio and took some charming photos of him: he really looked as if he were climbing! After all, he had been up Ben Nevis – the highest mountain in the UK – and now he was mountaineering in the Himalaya: what an adventurous bear! He spent the next few days sitting proudly in Rachael's rucksack.

It was soon time for breakfast in the pleasant dining room. Ian had his usual black coffee while Rachael tucked hungrily into eggs and toast. After thanking their hosts, our adventurous foursome set off around 9 a.m. They faced a very long uphill slog to Tolka with very few breaks in the steepness of the ascent. As you know this was the kind of walking that both Rachael and Ian loved so they were really looking forward to their day's trek. The trail was mainly on rough stone paving and after they passed through the pretty village of Deurali, they faced a really steep climb on the uneven stone steps to Pothana at 1,890m, approximately 6,200ft.

To their left the terraced fields gave way to a forest of rhododendrons which look particularly spectacular in the spring: in Nepal they grow into quite tall trees and, in spring, erupt with beautiful bright red blossoms. At the time of Rachael and Ian's trek, they were brightened further by clusters of multi-coloured orchids, hanging like garlands from their branches – breathtaking beauty that gladdened their hearts. The views through the trees down to the lush green valley below were phenomenal, rather like a series of brilliant postcards. The awkward steps of stone of many different shapes, sizes and angles seemed endless but the group developed a smooth steady climbing rhythm that helped them ascend comfortably. The time just sped by, aided by Rachael's obvious enthusiasm and happiness; she just radiated joy. Ubick continued to cope remarkably well with his heavy pack, and his cheerful engaging smile filled everyone with high spirits: he was becoming a superb porter. Ian was especially pleased to find that the steep climbing was easy for him too. This realisation was awesome and very welcome. Since his accident in Iceland, he had spent many weeks recovering on the sofa and then, gradually, he had begun to train for this Nepal trip. However, until he had tested out his fitness on this steep ascent, he had not been entirely sure how he would cope. He was elated with his performance.

Whenever the majestic mountains of the Annapurna Range appeared ahead of them, Rachael was truly excited and pointed them out eagerly to C.P. He confirmed that the main peak she could see was that of Annapurna South, a very dramatic and awe-inspiring mountain.

Eventually they reached Pothana – quite a large village with an attractive lodge and many small houses with pretty flower-filled gardens. The people here are mainly Gurungs and have their own traditional style of dress and a distinctive dialect – quite different from the Nepali language spoken by other tribes. One thing they do have in common however is the warm welcome they give to all guests and visitors. C.P. suggested that they pause here for a while and have some refreshments, so they stopped at a small wayside café built into the hillside. They had drinks and snacks and relaxed in the warm sunshine admiring the astonishing views.

Soon they were on the stone-paved trail again, climbing up northwards to the Gurung village of Bhichok Deurali – one of the higher points of their day's trek at 2,100m or approximately 6,890ft. From here, the path was along a really long undulating ridge with many rises and descents. To his delight Ian was able to stride out in comfort and at times, both C.P. and Rachael had to hurry to keep up with him. As you may imagine Rachael kept putting on energetic spurts so she could pass him: she was not going to be beaten by anyone, even her beloved dad! However they could all see from the expression on her face just how proud of him she was. Ubick, sensibly, kept up his steady even pace, thoroughly enjoying both the joyful company and the scenery.

Annapurna South.

Indeed the views from this elevated ridge were panoramic, varied and unbelievable; they were all entranced. It was as though they were walking on top of the world. When they paused to look backwards down over the forested hillsides and terraced fields to the lush green valley far below at Phedi, they realised just how high they had climbed. To their left and far below, the sinuous Modi Khola River meandered down its verdant valley glistening with silvery shimmers in the lovely sunlight. C.P. explained that the Modi Khola had descended in waterfalls and rushed over cliffs and boulders all the way from the glaciers of Annapurna and Machhapuchhare base camps.

Neat multi-coloured terraces clothed the lower slopes of the hills with trees and rocks rearing up sharply above them and scars where the inevitable landslides had swept their destructive way down the steepest slopes. These landslides occur every year, especially in the monsoon season when the sheer volume of water washes away villagers' houses and their valuable terraced strip fields, crops and soil, thus destroying their livelihood. Tragically, each year many lives are lost. The whole valley is a wonderful patchwork of sub-tropical to alpine zones illustrating the magnificent raw power of nature. It is crowned by shining snow-capped peaks of the mighty Himalaya thrusting their way through the clouds. To visit this area is truly an out-of-this-world experience.

Towards the end of the afternoon, just beyond the hamlet of Bhedi Kharka, the stone trail turned in a north-westerly direction and the group began to descend quite steeply towards their destination for that day: the village of Tolka (2,100m,

or 5,576ft). Ian and C.P. told me just how much this village had grown since I was there in 2006. It is now a popular place for trekkers to stay because of its position and spectacular views. Our party of four reached their overnight accommodation by 5 p.m. and were delighted that it was the super new lodge called the Namaste Guest House.

By trekking standards it was a fabulous lodge with immaculately clean bedrooms, a well-equipped dining room and kitchen and a large shower room with a Western-style toilet, all in separate blocks. The series of low stone buildings were set in beautiful gardens full of flowers in a myriad of colours, bright orange marigolds, bright red geraniums and banks of reddish-orange nasturtiums predominating. The flowerbeds and manicured lawns were edged by Everest beer bottles set upside down in the soil: a demonstration of how all Nepalese are experts at recycling.

Indeed the patios were full of flowers in containers of every shape, size and colour: painted recycled tins, plastic containers and simply any object that could hold enough soil to harbour a plant. Every post and trellis was covered by hanging vines and creepers such as bright-pink bougainvillea, the bright orange flowers of the trumpet vine – rather like honeysuckle – and fragrant roses. A real focal point was a huge, open, heart-shaped structure topped by a pair of praying hands. Winding all around it was a lovely prolific clematis that would be fabulous when in full bloom. Above all this splendour fluttered long lines of colourful Buddhist prayer flags carrying their messages of peace and goodwill all over the world. It was a haven and a sanctuary for tired trekkers and all visitors.

While Ubick took their bags to their pleasant room in the bedroom block, Rachael, Ian and C.P. admired the awesome panoramic view from the front terrace. The massive bulk of snow-covered Annapurna South and all its surrounding snow-capped satellite peaks reared up beyond the cliffs, trees and terraced hillsides while the Modi Khola gleamed below like a giant silvery snake coiling in its gorge. Ian was so overwhelmed by the sheer beauty and magnificence of the view that his eyes filled with tears; it was the most awesome vista he had ever seen. Rachael squeezed his hand and whispered, 'Isn't it wonderful, Dad?' She too was awestruck.

The view from Namaste Guest House.

Rachael went for a shower while Ian chatted to the owner of the Namaste Guest House. They talked about the differences of running a guest house in the Himalaya and where Ian's hotel was in the Lake District in the UK, and discovered they had lots of similar experiences and problems. The owner was so interested that he immediately found Ian's Old Water View, Ullswater on the Internet. He smiled and expressed his delight that it was such a lovely building set in beautiful surroundings. He informed Ian that he had a brother in the UK so he promised that, when he visited his brother, he would certainly try to visit Ian and his family at Old Water View. Of course Ian said he would be very welcome.

They were soon joined by Rachael, fresh and clean from her lovely hot shower and they chatted together for a while. Rachael expressed her desire to learn Nepali so the owner advised her to find a Nepalese community in the UK, perhaps a Gurkha family, and ask one of them to teach her. He explained that she would find it much easier and more satisfactory if she were taught by a Nepalese person and she would learn more about the different Nepalese cultures. Ian promised that he would do some research for her when they returned home.

Ian then went for his shower but had to make do with tepid water. There were so many trekkers staying at the lodge that they had used up most of the hot water.

He could have waited for it to heat up again but as the weather was still quite warm, he decided to brave it.

Rachael and Ian had a superb meal; a dish of very tasty spicy dhal bhat and Rachael was really pleased to find that she could have her favourite hot chocolate. Ian as before, had a still Red Bull because his 'jet bloat' had not subsided and he did not want to aggravate the condition. They had climbed and walked a huge distance that day so, although Ian's back ached a little, he was overjoyed that he had coped so well and had absolutely loved the experience. He was now really confident he would be able to finish their short trek and he knew Rachael would be thrilled too – she could stop worrying about her dad.

C.P. and Ubick ate together but after the meal C.P. joined Rachael, Ian and Patrick Bear on the terrace and they watched the beautiful sunset together: possibly an even more spectacular one than the evening before. Rachael thought it was the best yet as the colours seemed brighter and faded more slowly than at Dhampus. Of course the nearness of the high Himalaya and their situation near the top of their high ridge added to the drama. Rachael took lots of photos and made a video encompassing that amazing vista.

Meanwhile Ubick spent a long time chatting with his fellow porters, many of whom were on their way back from Annapurna Base Camp: he was eager to pick up some tips from them and learn about their experiences. As soon as the sun went down, it began to grow chilly, so after a last look at the wonderful night sky – a glistening tapestry of stars – Rachael and Ian went to their room and snuggled down in their sleeping bags. They looked at all their fantastic photos and chatted about their exciting day.

'You were great today, Dad,' said Rachael. 'You seemed to find those steep climbs really easy. C.P. and I could hardly keep up with you! You will be okay tomorrow when we have that long descent down to the river, won't you Dad?'

'Of course, I will, darling!' Ian confirmed quickly. 'I'll be absolutely fine.'

It was wonderful to be able to say that confidently. Ian was one very happy and grateful man.

TOLKA TO GHANDRUK

Rachael and Ian slept really soundly and were only woken when C.P. knocked on their bedroom door. He was carrying the bowl of hot water that he brought every morning so they could have a quick wash before having breakfast in the dining room. They then dressed swiftly and went outside to admire the last vestiges of the sunrise and gaze in wonder, yet again, at the magnificent views. Ian just had his usual black coffee but Rachael decided she would like a potato omelette and politely ordered that and her favourite chocolate drink. It was a very good choice because that omelette was delicious and the chocolate hot and creamy – a good way to start another exciting day.

As C.P. had already told them that they were setting off a little later than usual, they had left their packing until after breakfast. It didn't take long: Ian sorted out

his rucksack, rolled up their sleeping bags and put them, along with their clothes and toiletries, into their duffel bag ready for Ubick to add to the other bags that made up his load. He was whistling happily as he secured the pack, clearly looking forward to the trek ahead. Rachael popped Patrick Bear into her rucksack along with bottles of water and the obligatory snacks she loved, so soon they were ready and sat on the terrace waiting for C.P. to arrive. He had gone to the little ACAP (Annapurna Conservation Area Project) office to pay for the permits that allowed them to trek in the Annapurna Conservation Area. Permits are needed for entry into all the national parks in Nepal.

They waited and waited and still C.P. did not appear. Ian, in particular, was very puzzled as to why they were making such a late start because C.P. was usually eager to start as early as possible. He was to find out the answer later that day.

Eventually C.P. appeared so at around 10.30 a.m. they began their long descent towards the Modi Khola River far below. Again, the sun was shining brightly and fluffy white clouds driven by a light breeze drifted lazily across the clear blue sky. It was a superb day for walking. The rough paved stone path snaked in huge loops around the hillside, descending quite gradually at first. The scenery was breathtaking with fertile terraces, lovely trees and bushes and bright multi-coloured flowers. Here and there goats and clucking hens foraged around the small stone houses with corrugated roofs. All these interesting and picturesque features were set magically against a background of steep hillsides, topped by the high snowy peaks of the Himalaya. Our trekkers were enthralled: it was an unforgettable experience, one they would treasure forever.

As they descended, they must have passed the small, very basic lodge that I had stayed in when I climbed up to Tolka on my return from Annapurna Base Camp in October 2006.

The conditions there were completely different from those at the superb Namaste Guest House and the weather was horrendous. On the way up from Landruk, where we had hoped to stay, we were hit by a tremendous thunderstorm: high winds, thunder and lightning and torrential rain: it bucketed down! The path then was just rock, stone and earth, so it soon turned into a slippery mudslide up which we had to struggle until, eventually, it became a muddy waterfall. In spite of good waterproofs, we were soaked and so was all our gear. At that time Tolka was not much more than a small hamlet with very little accommodation for trekkers. C.P. managed to find some rooms for us in that somewhat dilapidated lodge. The people were wonderful and tried their best to help us and make us welcome. However the roof was leaking in places, many of the windowpanes did not have any glass in them and there was no heat or lighting as the meagre electricity supply had shorted out in the storm.

As you can imagine, the beds were damp, though reasonably clean so we were very grateful to discover that, although our bags that the porters had carried were extremely wet, the plastic bags inside which we had packed all our clothes and sleeping bags had kept most things dry. Never had those four-season sleeping bags been more welcome: being so wet, we were colder than we had been at Base Camp as the wind whistled through the broken windowpanes and showers of freezing rain were driven through the holes. We tried to dry ourselves and put on all our warm clothes including hats, scarves and gloves.

C.P. – bless him – hung up all our wet things on a line that crossed the open veranda and tried to dry our soggy boots. Our lovely hosts provided us with candles and made us hot drinks. They even managed to cook us some tasty dhal bhat, unusual 'chicken' soup, potatoes and hard-boiled eggs on the top of the earth oven, heated by wood in the tiny side-kitchen. Rajendra, C.P.'s brother and one of our porters, helped them and made his speciality: some delicious pakoras (a kind of fritter). And I bought some beer for all of us, so in spite of the conditions, we had a jolly night!

Unfortunately the toilet, located some way from the side of the house did not have a proper door and the loo itself was just a hole in some really unsafe wooden slats perched over a considerable drop. We all tried very hard

to use it sparingly as it meant getting wet again and it was understandably rather smelly: the joys of trekking!

We all went to bed early snuggling deep down into our sleeping bags, leaving just our eyes and noses exposed. We were very grateful that we all had our headlamps as we dare not take candles into the bedrooms and the night was inky black.

Next morning we were ecstatic to find the sun was shining and at least our gear had stopped dripping. Better still our boots, put in the kitchen overnight by our wonderful hosts, were almost dry. Fantastic! We thanked them profusely and after a breakfast snack were ready to tackle the steep hill in front of us. As we climbed up we were fascinated to see far below us a series of helicopters flying up the ravine towards Machhapuchhare and Annapurna base camps to rescue trekkers trapped by the deep snow. Our tremendous rainstorm had become a blinding blizzard up high in those mountains and wind-driven snow had piled up around the lodges in deep drifts making it impossible for the trekkers to escape. Apparently some of them had hypothermia and others had developed dangerous altitude sickness. This had been a sober lesson for us and graphically illustrated just how quickly dangerous and life-threatening conditions can develop at high altitudes: we had been very lucky. We watched mesmerised as those helicopters continued flying up and down the valley for some time; clearly lots of people were in trouble.

While we were watching, a smartly dressed Nepalese gentleman joined us and introduced himself. He was the headmaster of the local school and, as a retired teacher, I was very interested to learn about his school and how they educated the children, so we chatted for some time. Before we parted, we all gave him a donation and C.P. gave him some pencils for the children. It was then that I noticed an old tattered notice on a board that had informed the villagers of a forthcoming polio eradication scheme initiated by Rotary International and supported by the World Health Organisation. It offered life-saving polio drops for all infants and children and there was a picture of a small child with its mouth open swallowing the drops. I asked the headmaster if the campaign had been successful. His face lit up as he confirmed it had been marvellous. His father had been headmaster before him and at that time many children had contracted polio, were crippled by it and had to be carried to school by older siblings or their parents. Now, miraculously, no children in his school or in the whole of the valley ever caught polio: a heartening success story that made us all very happy and proud. As a committed Rotarian, I can confirm that polio has now been completely eradicated in Nepal and most parts of the world.

As the party continued downwards, they could hear lively music and lots of laughter and voices. Clearly some sort of social event was being held further down the hillside. They descended an uneven stone staircase and by lunchtime, they reached the Gurung village of Landruk where C.P. said they were going to stop. Neither Ian nor Rachael was very hungry but they had a drink and a small plate of dhal bhat while C.P. and Ubick had very much larger helpings that they ate quickly. Although Landruk is very much lower than Tolka, the views are still excellent. As they were all chatting, Ian began to realise that when C.P. said they were stopping, he meant staying overnight. Ian was quite astonished: they had only been walking for a few hours and although he had descended carefully he had not experienced any pain at all and was eager to carry on. He told C.P. that both he and Rachael wanted to continue and did not want to stay at Landruk; he was completely fine and needed to keep on walking. He stood up and put on his rucksack to show that he was serious and Rachael too begged C.P. to let them carry on.

Reluctantly C.P. agreed; he had planned the initial descent to be really short because he was responsible for Ian's safety and was very concerned about him. He knew that descending on steep stone paths – especially down large stone steps – is very hard on the knees and back, especially for someone like Ian who had sustained a serious back injury only just over ten weeks before. Although Ian was surprised, he realised C.P. was only doing his job as a leader and trying to care for him. However Ian was determined to carry on, assuring C.P. that he felt great. He emphasised that he would descend very carefully and slowly. Rachael and he re-joined the stone trail and were

The volleyball pitch.

soon followed by C.P. and Ubick.

They soon discovered what all the music, noise and the cheering shouts were about: further on it became apparent that some kind of volleyball tournament was being held to the right of the path. It was a hive of activity: there were beer tents, tables of food, stationary helicopters, police marshalling spectators, and music and a loud commentary over the tannoy system. It was just like a festival or country show. All the spectators were cheering, shouting and encouraging their teams; it was a very lively scene.

Rachael, C.P. and Ubick were really interested and stopped to watch the matches. Ubick told them that he played volleyball a great deal and loved it. He had actually played volleyball for his school team in Kathmandu. Ian watched for a while but it really didn't interest him so he told C.P. he was going to carry on down the stone path. He promised that when he was climbing down the steep steps to the ravine at the bottom, he would go slowly, take his time and ensure he would be okay. He would wait for them at the bridge over the Modi Khola.

He was really enjoying the solitude and freedom when he heard quick footsteps behind him. It was C.P. who had become afraid as soon as Ian disappeared round the bend and out of view. They carried on together but were soon overtaken by Rachael, who flew past them with huge grin on her face.

'I'll see you at the bottom, Dad!'

Ever the competitor, she could not bear anyone to be in front of her. Ian had to smile at the horrified look on C.P.'s face. Ubick followed more sedately and before long they were all by the side of the turbulent Modi Khola, waiting for a herd of goats to cross the bridge.

Eventually all the goats were rounded up and our foursome crossed on the bouncy Swiss-engineered suspension bridge. There are many of these in Nepal: narrow but beautifully constructed and totally safe, except when you meet animals – especially large ones – crossing them! You need, in particular, to avoid the big-horned yaks mainly used in the Everest region for transporting heavy goods, or strings of heavily laden ponies like those in the Annapurna Region. Their huge packs threaten to pitch you over the sides of the bridge if you are silly enough to try to pass them; then it's 'goodbye trekker!' Everyone soon learns to wait until the bridges are empty when it is perfectly safe to cross.

However, locally made bridges are often hazardous and very unsafe as pieces of wood and stones tend to drop off them into the swift, freezing water far below. Your stomach does somersaults; it is not a pleasant experience, but I suppose, an adventure!

They climbed up the huge steps on the other side of the bridge and soon reached the beautiful Beehive View Guest House and Restaurant. It had lovely accommodation, a comprehensive menu and a wonderful eating area with chairs and tables spread out under shady awnings. A myriad of beautiful flowers surrounded the buildings making it a pleasant place to eat. Ian wasn't hungry so only had a drink but Rachael, C.P. and Ubick had large lunches: pizza for Rachael and dhal bhat for the other two. Ian wondered how they managed to eat so much food when they were trekking. Throughout all his walking life, he had never liked to hike on a full stomach. I don't either – a snack is fine for me during the day with a good meal in the evening.

C.P. suggested they stay at Beehive and tackle the steep climb up to Ghandruk the next morning and went to find out if there was any available accommodation. Ian would have liked to carry on but thought he should take C.P.'s advice.

While they were resting and enjoying the sunshine, Ian began to speak to an American lady who had just come down from Ghandruk with her porters. He asked her if the climb up was hard. She told him it was steep but comparatively easy and pointed out that those huge stone steps were far easier to climb than descend as some of the stones were really uneven, loose and tipped sideways. You could lose your footing if you were not careful when you stepped down on them, whereas climbing up was far safer. Ian thanked her and wished her good luck, making up his mind to talk to C.P. when he came out of the lodge. After all, it was still only 1.30 p.m. and they had all of the afternoon left.

Poor C.P. he had only just negotiated a price for their overnight accommodation when Ian told him that he intended to climb up to Ghandruk! Bless him, C.P. hardly protested; he realised that Ian was absolutely determined and nothing and no one was going to stop him.

As he wasn't having a meal, Ian told C.P. that he was going to set off immediately so that he could set himself an easy pace and he would wait for them at the top of the hill.

'Enjoy your meals!' he said jubilantly. 'I will be fine – see you in a couple of hours!'

He felt really strong and climbed steadily, so elated that he was moving easily and confidently: at last, he seemed to be regaining all his hiking skills and was glorying in the knowledge. What a lucky man he was!

It was very hot so he paused now and again to have a drink of water, admire the neat houses and fertile terraces and take photos of anything that interested him – he was in his element. The views across the valley were amazing and he could see the path snaking down from Tolka. He hoped their lodge that evening would be as good as the Namaste Guest House – that had been outstanding in every way. He kept looking back down the trail to see if he could spot Rachael or C.P. but he couldn't. He was truly delighted that they were obviously well behind him because he did not even catch a glimpse of them: he'd show them he was fit and raring to go! Near to the top of the hill, the path divided and Ian was unsure which fork to take so he stopped and decided to wait for Rachael, C.P. and Ubick. In fact he was only about two hundred yards from the lodge where they were staying but could not see it due to the curve of the hillside.

A little while later, Rachael appeared puffing as she mounted those steps really quickly.

'Dad, Dad! I really need a drink. Will you please pull my water bottle out of my rucksack pocket and give it to me. I'm desperate!' she gasped.

Of course Ian bent down and pulled the bottle out of the side pocket and handed it to her.

'Thanks, Dad!' she cried holding the bottle up in the air like a trophy. 'I didn't really need a drink but I wanted to beat you to the top and get to Ghandruk first and I will do!'

With that she dashed past him, turned to the right as C.P. had told her and climbed the last steep steps to the summit at 1,960m, nearly 6,500ft. At the entrance to the village, she touched both tall stone columns that supported a brightly painted noticeboard saying,

WELCOME TO OUR BEAUTIFUL VILLAGE – GHANDRUK

She turned round and faced Ian holding her arms up triumphantly with a huge grin on her lovely face and laughed excitedly.

'Ha, Ha! I've beaten you, Dad and everyone else! That was a good joke of mine, wasn't it? Pretending to be really thirsty. And it worked – hurray!'

She was ecstatic! What a competitor she is, Ian thought and he had to admit that she had succeeded in fooling him; she had said she would get her own back for his terrible joke about the log crocodile and sure enough, she had!

C.P. and Ubick soon caught up and they all went to find their accommodation for the night – the Hotel Sakura and German Bakery. They followed the trail round a bend and caught their breath when they had their first view of Ghandruk, the second largest Gurung village in Nepal. It is, indeed, a beautifully ornate village in a magnificent setting. Ringed by lovely trees, it nestles into a bowl-shaped depression near the top of the hill with some lodges and houses cascading down the hillside. The views are utterly outstanding – some of the very best in the Himalaya. They were all entranced and stood there gazing in wonder at the variety of sights and splendours in that vast panorama.

Ghandruk is a well known Gurung village and home to many of the Gurkhas, famed for their courage, loyalty and valiant military service. Some call it a 'model village' as it was the pilot project of ACAP in 1986: The Ghandruk Village Development Scheme. Ghandruk was chosen because of its fabulously scenic location and accessibility, its unique Gurung culture and its rich bio-diversity. There are around three hundred individual households in the village and the whole community ethos is based on responsible eco-tourism: there are generally over 45,000 visitors and trekkers each year. Most of the village houses are very traditional with stone and slate roofs and lovely gardens full of a huge variety of flowers and vegetables. There are more than eight micro-hydroelectricity schemes, which supply ample electricity for everyone and, in addition, most buildings have solar panels. Of course, there are many lodges, hotels and guesthouses to cater for all travellers' needs; in fact most people in the village are employed in the tourist industry: good hospitality and friendliness are their maxims.

They soon found the Hotel Sakura and German Bakery as it is located in what they call the upper street of Ghandruk. It has glorious uninterrupted views of the valley of the Modi Khola and all the fabulous

surrounding mountains. It is a lovely traditional-style two-storeyed lodge set within a beautiful garden and has a fantastic terrace with a 360-degree panoramic vista. They were warmly welcomed and after a refreshing drink, Ubick took their bags up to their room, which was on the second storey and had a lovely balcony. The shower room (with a Western-style toilet) was just around the corner of the balcony, so easily accessible. The view from that balcony was incredible: dominated by the massive bulk of Annapurna 1 and the whole 'fishtail' of that incomparable mountain, Machhapuchhare, clearly visible for the first time.

As soon as she had undone her rucksack and retrieved Patrick Bear, Rachael went for a shower while Ian went down to the terrace and relaxed, gazing at that magical view. He reflected on the day's trek: he was totally exhilarated by his achievements. He had always been a walker and done some very long and challenging hikes like Land's End to John O'Groats in the UK – 1110 miles. He had completed this in a tremendous sixty-four days! He had always considered his greatest achievement (in a single day) was when he finished the Yorkshire Dales Fellsman Hike in twenty-one hours and twenty-six minutes. This hike is probably the hardest one in the UK: sixty-one tough miles

that need to be completed within twenty-four hours. It includes a high traverse over very hard rugged moorland and climbs over 11,000 feet in total height. As much of the challenge is over privately owned land, there are few paths so good navigational skills are vital, as is a high level of fitness and experience. Until this point, Ian had thought this was his greatest triumph, however, considering his recent history of a broken back only ten weeks previous, the difficult and challenging hike he had just done in the Himalaya was a greater accomplishment by far. He had overcome a massive disability with determination and courage and been victorious. He was quietly but justifiably proud.

After Ian had finished his shower, he and Rachael went down to the dining room for a meal. They had dhal bhat, one of their favourites, and the version at the Hotel Sakura was superb. After dinner, Rachael and Ian went out onto the patio and spent a wonderful relaxed evening just chatting to C.P. They had hoped to see a fantastic sunset but unfortunately clouds had descended so the sunset was muted and most of the surrounding peaks were obscured. Hopefully tomorrow morning's sunrise would be spectacular. Although until now Ian had restricted his drinks to still Red Bull, he decided to celebrate the achievements of the day with a beer. When it became quite chilly they went inside the lodge and settled at the bar where they chatted to other trekkers. It was a very friendly and happy evening.

Eventually Rachael and Ian went upstairs to bed. Ian had been drinking his well-earned beer very slowly so he took his still half-full glass up to their bedroom. This turned out to be very fortunate as you will discover!

They undressed quickly and snuggled down in their sleeping bags. As always Rachael had chosen the bed on the left of their room. Suddenly she screamed and leapt out of bed. Ian sat up quickly and asked her what was wrong. Shakily Rachael pointed up to the wall about two feet above her bed; crouched there was an absolutely enormous spider looking as though it would spring down at any minute.

'Dad, Dad!' she cried terrified. 'Please catch it! I'm really scared. It's so big and it's going to fall on me.'

She sat determinedly on Ian's bed, as far away from that spider as she could get! Ever the knight in shining armour, Ian looked for something that he could catch the spider in – there wasn't anything except his beer glass that still had about half a pint of beer in it. Quickly he opened the door and poured his beer away: what a sacrifice! He reached over her bed with the inverted beer glass and trapped the spider against the wall: it seemed to nearly fill the glass! He asked Rachael to find some paper or cardboard quickly so that he could slide that over the top of the glass, trap the spider inside and put it outside on the patio. Rachael searched and searched but could not find anything appropriate and when Ian looked up, mysteriously the spider had disappeared from the glass. It hadn't dropped down nor had it climbed up the wall, so where had it gone? That was worrying!

They looked carefully everywhere but there was no sign of the spider. Eventually Ian managed to persuade Rachael to go back to her bed. Apprehensively she snuggled deep inside her sleeping bag but kept her eyes firmly fixed on a crack in the wall above her head. That was where she had first seen the huge spider. Ian wisely kept the light on.

He was just about to fall asleep when there was another horrific scream and Rachael, still in her sleeping bag, jumped out of her bed clutching Patrick Bear. She vaulted over Ian and squeezed into the tiny space between him and the wall of the bedroom. Momentarily speechless, she pointed up to the wall above her bed. Out of the crack, the long hairy leg of a spider protruded. They both looked at it for some time and it did not move.

'I am **not** sleeping in that bed tonight!' Rachael stated adamantly. 'You can sleep near that creature – I am *not* moving!'

An amusing and lengthy conversation ensued. This is the gist of it:

'But this is *my* bed!' protested Ian. 'You chose the one on the left-hand side as you always do. Go back to your own bed!'

'No way!' responded Rachael with determination. 'I didn't know there was going to be a massive spider hiding over my head, did I? I am *not* sleeping there! It could drop down and grab me any minute!'

'It won't hurt you, honestly,' Ian replied.

'Well, *you* go and sleep there, then. I am not and that is that!' was Rachael's quick reply.

Ian tried repeatedly to persuade her to move (with no luck whatsoever), pointing out that they would be squashed.

'I don't care!' Rachael cried emphatically, adding, 'Anyway you are the adult and my dad. I am the child and your daughter. You are supposed to protect me, aren't you?'

A brilliant response and a masterstroke! There really wasn't anything Ian could do (only accept it). Once again, he had been out-manoeuvred by an expert!

With a sigh of resignation, he replied, 'Okay then, darling. Stay here and we'll manage somehow.'

Rachael did not say a word, but firmly turned her back on Ian, snuggled right down in her sleeping bag and pretended to be fast asleep, adding a few theatrical snores to emphasise the fact. Ian may have been victorious on his hike that day but he'd been defeated by a spider and one determined daughter.

In fairness, I must confess that I am the world's

worst coward when confronted by spiders of any size. Over the years, I have been rescued many times by Ian using his glass and paper technique, which, until this episode, had been perfect. I can only assume that the spider at Ghandruk was of tarantula proportions and very clever at avoiding capture. Neither of our 'brave' pair slept soundly that night: at different intervals, they both kept their eyes on that hairy leg protruding from the crack in the wall. Thankfully it did not move and neither did they.

Their mood was lightened a little by overhearing what was happening in next door's room, which was occupied by a Dutch couple. The walls in Nepalese lodges are really thin so noise and voices carry very easily. Apparently the gentleman had eaten something that had disagreed with him and was consequently suffering with excessive amounts of wind, which he was expelling loudly – particularly from his nether regions! His wife complained bitterly and continually about the smell and the noise (which was considerable – both Rachael and Ian could hear each time he 'trumpeted'!) It was rather like trying to sleep next to a brass band. Rachael and Ian felt really sorry for his wife – poor woman! Nevertheless, like two naughty schoolchildren, they giggled together each time they heard him.

'There he goes again!' was their frequent comment. Rachael speculated at intervals that the man was doing it deliberately to keep the spider from going through to their room. Eventually peace was restored so Rachael and Ian should have been able to sleep, however although they managed to doze a little, they never completely relaxed as they kept watch over that spider's hairy leg. They could not wait for the dawn to break.

GHANDRUK TO BIRETHANTI

Eager to see what they hoped would be a fabulous sunrise, both Rachael and Ian were up early. As the spider's hairy leg was still poking out of the wall above Rachael's bed, they dressed quickly (over in Ian's side of the bedroom), picked up their cameras and were soon downstairs on the flower-bedecked front terrace. There was a little haunting mist drifting along the valley floor but the dark sky was clear and cloudless with the last few brilliant stars being overtaken by the first glimmers of the promised sunrise. Grey turned to purple drifts and then warm red and orange as the nascent glow of the sun crept across the dark sky gradually illuminating the whole wonderful scene: just like a spotlight irradiating the grandest stage you could ever imagine. As the sun soared higher in the ever-brightening sky, it crowned the surrounding snow-capped peaks with a golden glow that made them glisten and sparkle like immense jewels. It highlighted the iconic fishtail peak of sacred Machhapuchhare standing like a huge holy sentinel guarding the deep, Stygian depths of the gorge leading to Base Camp. Further to the north-west, the massive, majestic bulk of Annapurna 1 dominated the Annapurna Sanctuary and Base Camp.

C.P. joined them and pointed out some more of the magnificent peaks encircling Base Camp: He began with the mountains to the northeast, namely Annapurna 2 and 4 hiding behind Machhapuchhare. Then towards the north, superb Annapurna 3 and glorious Gangapurna, Tent Peak, Fluted Peak and Fang, aptly named as it rears up between Annapurna 1 and bulky Annapurna South like an awesome sharp tooth. In front of Annapurna South, they could see the smaller but still beautiful peak of Hiunchuli and further to the west a glimpse of the daunting, sheer face of majestic, forbidding Dhaulagiri, one of my favourite mountains. What an awe-inspiring vista!

Around and below them, the whole valley was bathed in golden sunshine. The water droplets in the last tendrils of mist that drifted lazily up the hillsides, glistened like wondrous diamond necklaces reflecting all the colours of the rainbow. Rachael, Ian and everyone watching from the terrace of the Hotel Sakura were engulfed in a maelstrom of colours: they were totally spellbound. For a while no one spoke: the experience was so overwhelming, the only sound was that of many cameras clicking, trying to capture the whole of that life-enhancing scene.

Eventually Rachael and Ian came down to earth and went upstairs to pack before breakfast so that Ubick could strap their bags into a stable load. As they had expected, that menacing spider's leg was still protruding from the crack so Ian endeavoured to bring some lightness and humour to the situation. He reminded Rachael about Mr. Tinselhead, a large black, fluffy, tarantula-style toy spider that Rachael and Catherine had been given as a present. He crouches alongside some teddies on the exposed beam supporting the ceiling in their cottage home at Old Water View. To brighten him up one Christmas, they had decorated him with some sparkling tinsel, hence his name, Mr. Tinselhead.

'Perhaps someone will decorate that spider when it comes out again!' joked Ian.

'Well it won't be me!' declared Rachael emphatically, adding with a laugh and a wicked grin, 'I wonder if it will pounce down on the next guests in that room because we escaped it. I *do* feel sorry for them!'

Ian raised his eyebrows: he was not convinced that she was being truly sympathetic but at least she was laughing again. Later this incident became a family joke when it was retold and, of course, embellished.

They had breakfast on the lovely terrace surrounded by pots of bright, fragrant, multi-coloured roses, scarlet

Mr. Tinselhead.

geraniums, statuesque lilies and orchids and endless brilliant orange marigolds – one of the national flowers of Nepal. Ian had his usual black coffee but Rachael indulged herself with a mound of delicious scrambled egg on several slices of toast and her usual hot chocolate. In spite of their interrupted night's sleep, they both felt very upbeat and happy as they surveyed the magnificent panoramic view. They tried very hard not to snigger when the Dutch couple chose a table on the terrace close to theirs, especially as the Dutch lady looked extremely tired. Her poor husband quietly settled down to tea and toast!

After breakfast, Rachael, Ian, C.P. and Ubick set off in lovely warm sunshine to explore the village of Ghandruk. Their walk that day was not a demanding one as it was mainly downhill so they had plenty of time to learn more about the culture and lifestyle of this beautiful, traditional Gurung village. C.P. directed their gaze towards particular points of interest. Unlike a lot of scattered villages, all the lovely stone houses with their neat slate or stone roofs were arranged in a reasonably orderly fashion along two main streets – one above the other – and all were very well conserved. Each one seemed to have a productive garden enhanced by a myriad of lovely flowers and decked with creepers hanging from the roof and posts. Bunches of golden corn hung from the eaves drying in the sun and many houses had beehives; all Nepalese people appear to love honey for its unique flavour and sweetness but also for its health-giving properties. The group also saw large beehive-shaped stores of corn and a large variety of vegetables. Further down the hill, in a complicated network of terraces, wheat, barley and rice were growing. All the buildings seemed to have an electricity supply and some of them, especially the lodges, had supplementary solar panels. Everywhere, standpipes supplied clean water.

C.P. showed them where the helipad was situated at near the top of the mountain and above that was an ornate temple. They decided however not to climb up there as they wanted to visit the Education Centre and the Traditional Gurung Museum.

At the Education Centre there was a classroom and an exhibition explaining the development of the village since ACAP chose it to be an example of how eco-tourism can be introduced and extended responsibly without destroying the unique and traditional aspects of a village community. They had to pay a small entrance fee at the Gurung Museum which was a true working museum with fascinating displays of traditional crafts such as wicker-basket making, pottery of all shapes and sizes and cooking utensils. In addition there was a local artisan plough, invaluable when tilling those narrow terraces, and illustrations of the skills needed to operate it successfully. There were also examples of intricate, brilliant weaving and traditional costumes, some of which could be bought from the factory in upper Ghandruk. Outside there was a beautiful wicker baby's crib suspended from the overhanging roof.

They slowly wended their way back towards the Hotel Sakura where they had some refreshments and relaxed while Rachael just wandered around in a little world of her own. She kept pausing to taking close-up photos of butterflies, bees and insects, flowers, leaves and anything that interested her – even patches of moss and lichen on the stone walls. She was totally oblivious to anyone around her, enthralled to be in such an interesting and peaceful place.

Eventually of course, they had to collect their rucksacks and Ubick hoisted the large pack on his back which he supported by the namlo around his forehead. As always he was smiling and really happy to find he could cope very well with the demands of being a porter. Ian and Rachael thanked their hosts and as they left that lovely terrace to begin their downhill walk, Rachael waved upwards towards their bedroom.

'Goodbye Mr. Spider!'

As they began to descend the steep stone steps leading down towards the gorge of the Modi Khola river far below, she asked Ian a question.

'Dad, do you think the spider will drop down and grab the next people to sleep in that room? Well good luck to them. I really mean that!'

The Sakura spider had made a huge impression.

They deliberately ignored the access road from Nayapul to Ghandruk that had been built since I was there in 2006: none of us likes walking on roads, if they can be avoided. Instead when the stone steps ended, they continued on the old well-worn trail to Nayapul: the one that had been used by trekkers for centuries.

Eventually they had to cross the new road but quickly re-joined the trail and continued downwards traversing the hillsides on the rough stone and earth path, which was stepped intermittently where the descents steepened. Initially, the neatly terraced hillsides were full of rice, wheat and barley with the occasional patch of vegetables and some were being ploughed by skilful farmers using traditional ploughs. Here and there were scattered trees and bushes and several sparkling streams

tumbled across the undulating trail, plunging over sparkling waterfalls on their way down to the Modi Khola. The view across the valley to Landruk and Tolka was superb and brought back lovely memories of that part of their trek.

Just before they reached the hamlet of Chane, their trail crossed what had previously been the scene of various landslides. Happily for our travellers, there was now no sign of these disasters as small trees and bushes covered the hillside hiding the scars and usefully consolidating the earth, thus making it less vulnerable to landslip of any kind. Several times they had to stop on the uphill side of the trail to allow strings of laden ponies to pass safely. Often these ponies, especially the leading ones, have brightly coloured and decorated harnesses and high, trailing red head-dresses. In addition the leader usually carries a bell, which he rings loudly as he plods along, warning travellers of their approach and allowing them to employ avoidance tactics.

Never once did anyone in the group wish they had arranged a lift to their destination at Birethanti, nor indeed think they should take the easier and more direct road route. They were dedicated trekkers, and trekkers rely on their feet, not mechanical assistance and they walk on quiet, scenic paths whenever possible. Rachael, in particular, was adamant they would walk on the old trail right to the end.

It wasn't too long before they reached the village of Kimche at 1,640m (around 5,380ft.) Already they had descended almost a thousand feet overall from Ghandruk but of course, the trail had involved some brief climbs as well: that it is an undulating trail is an understatement. Kimche is actually where the trail briefly joins the new road and is the terminus for buses and large vehicles heading for Ghandruk. From Kimche, passengers – some of whom will have come all the way from Pokhara – have to change to 4x4 transport to reach Ghandruk.

By now it was really hot, so C.P. suggested they stop at the Binishka Guest House for drinks and a snack: they all readily agreed. Apparently this lodge had developed a well-earned reputation for brewing great sake – rice wine and rakshi –

a particularly potent brew of the local whisky. Fortunately our trekkers did not sample these but settled for cola and snacks. They relaxed in the sunshine but didn't particularly enjoy the crowds milling round the village. Most were bus passengers seeking refreshments before they continued the journey by 4x4 vehicles, which were parked nearby. You can imagine what Rachael's opinion was:

'They are all cheating, Dad!'

Ian had to smile: she was totally uncompromising about her belief that undertaking a trek or hike meant that you should walk *all* the way!

The new road had obviously brought a degree of prosperity to Kimche hence the new buildings like the Binishka Guest House and several shops to cope with the needs of passengers and travellers. However, as Rachael and Ian were soon to discover, from Kimche through to Nayapul, many of the lovely stone houses, little shops and attractive lodges on the old trail were very run down and some of them derelict with their owners struggling to make a living. Nearly all their potential guests just whizzed past on the new road above the trail and no one wanted to stay or have a meal and a drink anymore. They had lost their income. Ian told me that, sadly, the trail I loved and had trekked up and down several times had become a 'ghost trail'. Their sombre mood was lightened by several episodes where they had to squash into the hillside to allow herds of unruly goats to pass them. The angry shouts and endless waving of sticks by the inexperienced drovers only seemed to confuse the goats and so for a while chaos reigned.

As our trekkers began to descend more steeply towards the turbulent Modi Khola, they witnessed the effect of the new road on the surrounding countryside. Many of the once well-maintained and fertile terraces were empty of produce; many of the formerly beautiful retaining walls were broken with stones scattered. The local farmers, shopkeepers and lodge owners had abandoned them when tragically a lack of work opportunities meant they had to leave their homes: a sad end to a scattered but friendly and welcoming community.

At last they reached the huge bend in the trail that leads down to the verdant valley bottom and turned southwest across a well-constructed bridge built by the Gurkhas over the cascading Thado Khola, a tributary of the snow-fed Modi Khola. They looked up the valley towards Machhapuchhare and, in the distance, saw the splendid high steel suspension bridge built by the Swiss, spanning this tumultuous river that thunders, swirls and plunges over the many rocks in its deep gorge. In fact this huge bridge was so admired by the local people that as soon as it was built, they renamed the small settlement of Himalkyo, on the opposite bank of the Modi Khola, 'New Bridge'. Trekkers, too, are very grateful for its construction because it provides a safer and more direct route to the Annapurna Sanctuary and Base Camp.

The trail now continued on a large rough yet lush embankment above the Modi Khola. Although far from flat, the walking was much easier – very welcome as the day was really hot. They would follow this spectacular, angry river all the way to their destination for the night: the Moonlight Hotel at Birethanti. Above and below them the banks and steep hillsides were covered with large boulders, around which grew thick shady trees and a great variety of multi-coloured bushes and bright wild flowers. Across the river rugged cliffs bordered the banks, above which the steep slopes were thickly forested. By mid-afternoon, the valley began to widen out slightly on their side of the river and they reached Syauli Bazar, a once prosperous village, surrounded by fields of rice and banana trees. C.P. suggested they stay here for lunch, as it was still quite a way to Birethanti.

There were several lodges, small shops and houses but all showed some degree of neglect as few trekkers or visitors ever stopped there now. The new road had been constructed high above the village to avoid possible flooding so it bypassed

Syauli Bazar turning it into a ghost village. I remember it as a bustling place with happy welcoming people and lots of trekkers eager for food; it had been a hive of activity. However when Rachael, Ian, C.P. and Ubick arrived for lunch, they discovered they were the only guests. Nevertheless the welcome they received at the lodge was warm and friendly and they soon settled down at some tables amongst the pots of bright orange marigolds, geraniums and roses. Extremely noisy cicadas filled the bushes and birch trees, their cacophony adding to the background of angry murmuring from the Modi Khola below. Their lady host suggested that they might like her special vegetable curry. They all quickly agreed, so she went out into the garden, picked a variety of fresh vegetables and put some fresh rice on to cook.

While they were waiting, C.P. described to Rachael and Ian what the village used to be like. He added that the same had happened in the popular Kali Gandaki river valley that led up to Muktinath, a holy centre of worship and pilgrimage for both Hindus and Buddhists at the bottom of the high Thorung La pass. A road had been built up the wide river valley to take visitors as near to the temple complex as possible but all the beautiful little villages on the way were now not patronised, including my own special favourite, the glorious white-washed village of Marpha: a little gem. 'Progress' can bring welcome prosperity for some but also tremendous hardship for others.

The special vegetable curry was superb as it contained many different fresh vegetables, all beautifully spiced, and the rice was hot and fragrant. They all enjoyed a Pepsi each and relaxed for a while before setting out once more on the path above the rushing Modi Khola.

Although their view was not as expansive as it had been when they were higher up, the scenery was still stunning with cliffs to their left and rich forest towering above them. The rock-strewn Modi Khola below them foamed and swirled while on their side of the river the trail wound its way through scrub and boulders with occasional glistening waterfalls tumbling down the tree-covered hillside. Finally the trail took them through a beautiful birch forest. Rachael skipped ahead completely happy and carefree. The weather was hot and the scenery stunning with lots of opportunities for taking photos. Above all, she was walking with her dad and two great friends: C.P. and Ubick.

They reached the outskirts of Birethanti in the early evening. It had obviously once been a prosperous little town with lots of brightly painted lodges, well-stocked shops and attractive houses. However, just like most of the villages along the bottom of the valley, it was beginning to look rather run down – very few visitors now stayed there since the new road was built. Its inhabitants were beginning to leave and seek employment elsewhere. The Hotel Moonlight had clearly seen better days: it must once have been very attractive and well-decorated but now was becoming shabby. The owners were likely not earning enough to keep it maintained, as they would have wished.

Nevertheless our trekkers were welcomed heartily. Ian and Rachael's room was upstairs along a balcony on the side of the hotel while C.P. and Ubick shared a room downstairs. They soon discovered that they were the only guests in what was quite a large hotel. Unfortunately the electricity supply had failed so there was no light in Rachael and Ian's bedroom or in the washroom at the end of the balcony. There was however a Western-style toilet. Bliss! They didn't mind at all having a quick cold shower as they were still very hot from the day's walk and the evening hadn't yet cooled down. Their head-torches proved to be very useful in the bedroom, which although a little dilapidated was immaculately clean with no spiders. A definite bonus!

After their showers, Ian and Rachael went downstairs and were directed to the hotel restaurant in a separate building and found C.P. was already there, waiting for them. Ian bought C.P. a bottle of Everest beer and had one himself to celebrate the end of their fantastic trek while Rachael had a Coke. They all ordered dhal bhat, thinking it would be quicker and easier for the owner if they chose the same meal: although there was lighting in the dining room, they assumed the owner must be using a costly generator.

Ubick soon joined them so Ian bought him a beer to thank him for being such a fabulous porter. He beamed with happiness!

He explained that he had been washing some of his laundry and had hung it outside on the washing line to dry; he would not have time to do it at Pokhara as he would be travelling back to Kathmandu on the bus. He hoped it would not rain. It didn't ... at least not in the evening! Ubick went to check if it was dry before he went to bed but as it was still quite wet, he decided to leave it on the line. This was to prove an unfortunate decision ...

Soon their meal was ready and served with a smile: the dhal bhat was excellent[1] – really hot and tasty and their plates were replenished as soon as they were empty, until even C.P. and Ubick were absolutely full. They all chatted happily about their trek together and looked at some of the fabulous photos Rachael had taken. She had become very skilful, grasping exactly how to frame a photo; the detail some of her close-ups was wonderful.

Shortly afterwards, Ian and Rachael went upstairs to bed and snuggled down in their sleeping bags. It had been a very busy day.

'I'm a bit sad that we have finished trekking, Dad,' said Rachael. 'But I'm excited about going back to Pokhara. I wonder what we are going to do.'

'You'll just have to wait and see, won't you? Goodnight, darling and thank you for being such a wonderful walking partner,' Ian responded.

'That's okay, Dad,' she replied. 'You know I love walking with you. Goodnight.'

Ian could tell that she fell asleep almost immediately by her even breathing and gentle snores. He hadn't said anything to Rachael but, as you know, he had decided that, if the weather was clear, he would book a paragliding trip as an extra treat for her while they were at Pokhara. Wisely, rather than build her hopes up, he thought it was better to surprise her the next day as it all depended on clear skies and no wind. He would keep his fingers crossed and hope for suitable conditions so he could fulfil another of her dreams.

---

1 It wasn't until the next morning they realised that lovely meal had been cooked over an open fire outside at the back of the hotel.

BIRETHANTI TO POKHARA

Next morning Rachael and Ian were up fairly early and were soon fully packed. C.P. had told them that their transport to Pokhara would arrive around 9 a.m. Ian hoped he would be able to cope with the long and bumpy ride as he had really pushed it with his back throughout their trek.

When they opened their curtains, they spotted poor Ubick sheepishly trying to wring out his soaking laundry without anyone noticing. Unfortunately it had rained heavily overnight so his washing was wetter than it had been before he pegged it out to dry! When he realised that Ian and Rachael had seen him, he was clearly embarrassed. They smiled and waved to him but this only seemed to embarrass him even more. This is where Nepalese and English cultures differ: when you smile or laugh sympathetically if a Nepalese person has a minor problem or makes a mistake, they tend to think that you are laughing *at* them not, as we intend, laughing *with* them. This is a concept they don't seem to understand. Ian and Rachael turned away from the window while Ubick quickly stuffed all his wet clothing into a large plastic bag before anyone else saw him!

The pair did a quick check round their bedroom to make sure they hadn't left anything behind and then went across to the restaurant for breakfast. For once Ian had some gurung bread (rather like chapattis) as well as his usual black coffee. Rachael had a substantial breakfast of fried potatoes, egg and gurung bread with her favourite hot chocolate. Afterwards they thanked their kind host warmly for all his help and went back into the main hotel to wait for their transport to Pokhara. They both agreed that although the Hotel Moonlight was a little run down now, once it must have been great. In spite of the conditions, they had truly enjoyed their stay and their host had been fantastic; helpful, kind and a very good cook too. He had tried his very best to make their stay as comfortable as possible in spite of all his problems. He thoroughly deserved their admiration.

Just after 9 a.m. a large jeep-type vehicle drew up outside with several people, who looked like porters, already inside. C.P. made sure that Ian had a comfortable supportive seat, explained to the driver about Ian's injured back and politely asked him to drive slowly. Ian was naturally a little apprehensive, especially as the rough road up to Nayapul was bumpy and the first part of the main road back to Pokhara was very uneven. He was thrown about quite a bit as the road switched backwards and forwards up the hill in steep loops and hazardous bends. He was just wondering how much of this he could stand, when the road surface at the top of the hill suddenly improved as it became tarmac. Inevitably, as this was Nepal, there were many potholes and places where there had been landslides, so rubble was strewn on the road and, at times, streams cascaded across it. However the driver seemed very skilled and so familiar with the road conditions that he managed to keep the ride as smooth as possible. Ian was very grateful.

Rachael and he chatted cheerfully about their trek and the interesting scenery and unusual traffic kept them both occupied. They were particularly amazed by the highly decorated lorries that were painted all over with brilliant intricate designs – some even had charms hanging down and silky window curtains. The time passed quickly so when they arrived at the Hotel Tulsi it really did not seem to have been a journey of around two hours. Ian thanked the driver for his care and consideration. As their rooms were not yet ready, Ubick took their luggage and rucksacks into the reception area of the hotel where they would be safe before he went to catch his bus back to Kathmandu.

Meanwhile C.P. went to look for a taxi to take Ian and Rachael up to that magnificent brilliant-white World Peace Pagoda – an important Buddhist stupa and shrine situated on the narrow ridge high above the south shore of Fewa Lake. Ian had informed C. P. earlier that morning about his plans to treat Rachael to a paragliding trip but when they arrived at Pokhara, the weather was dull and cloudy: all the beautiful mountains were completely hidden. Obviously it was not suitable weather for paragliding so Ian was very pleased that he had not mentioned anything to Rachael.

He knew they were planning to return in 2016 so he would be able to treat her then; that was a promise he would keep. C.P. had suggested a visit to the Shanti Stupa, the local name for the World Peace Pagoda, because Rachael had admired it so much on her boat trip around Fewa Lake and had wanted to climb up to it. As their time was restricted, going by taxi was a good compromise.

The Shanti Stupa is a massive Buddhist stupa, built as a monument to inspire peace and designed to provide a focus for people of all races and creeds to unite in seeking world peace. It is one of the many World Peace Pagodas built all over the world under the guidance of a monk, Nichidatsu Fujii, who founded a Japanese Buddhist order. Earlier in his life, he had been greatly influenced by a meeting with

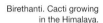
Birethanti. Cacti growing in the Himalaya.

Mahatma Gandhi and had decided to devote his life to promoting non-violence. In 1947, he began constructing Peace Pagodas all over the world as shrines to World Peace. Significantly some were built as a symbol of peace in Japanese cities including Hiroshima and Nagasaki, where the atomic bombs took the lives of thousands of people. By the year 2000, eighty Peace Pagodas had been built in Europe, Asia and the USA.

It wasn't long before their Suzuki taxi arrived to take them up to the impressive Shanti Stupa. The building was magnificent; pristine white and glowing in the watery sunshine that was just beginning to brighten the sky. As Rachael and Ian stepped out of the taxi, they were overwhelmed by the sense of peace and tranquillity that surrounded this serene haven. They gazed at the stupa in awe. Its huge gleaming white dome rested on high white circular walls in which there were four deep golden recesses like closed doorways. Fabulously carved golden columns surmounted by wonderful gold arches surrounded each recess, in which rested beautiful shining gold statues depicting Buddha in the posture he assumed when he was born. This central building in turn rested on two tiers of white circular platforms surrounded by white fence-like walls, through which a flight of stairs gave access to the 'door-ways'. Above the dome a square white platform supported a red and gold circular column and above this a spire of decreasing golden spheres reached up towards the heavens. Lines of multi-coloured prayer flags fluttered from the four corners of the upper platform carrying their messages of peace and love around the world. It was really inspiring.

Its position on that high narrow ridge and cliff added to the stupa's majesty, as did the spectacular panoramic view. The weather had improved considerably: the sky was now broken by splinters of brilliant golden sunlight that dazzled on the pristine snow of the mountain peaks, dappled the lush green hills and glistened on the surface of Fewa Lake. Rachael and Ian could see the whole of that gleaming lake, Pokhara city far below them and the entire Annapurna Range stretching into the hazy distance with magical Machhapuchhare appearing like a huge elegant peak dominating the immediate skyline to the north. On the walls around the complex were several noticeboards with instructions for visitors and pilgrims alike: 'Take your shoes off', for example. But the most amusing was the sign on the wall above the sheer drop to Fewa Lake. It read, 'Stay Calm and Don't Jump' and was accompanied by a picture of a falling figure with outstretched arms.

I think they mean Knockout View!

Sign on the temple wall.

'I'm certainly not going to jump, Dad,' said Rachael with a wicked grin, 'so don't worry!'

She was definitely developing the same strange sense of humour as Ian.

There was a small café near the stupa, which had really funny name: 'Not Out View.' They both burst out laughing. Ian worked out that, as many Nepalese people have a penchant for corrupting English expressions, the 'Not Out View' should really have been 'Knockout View' because the view from the café was, indeed, a knockout one![2]

The taxi took them back to the main street in Pokhara because by now they were all feeling rather hungry. They went to the lovely vegetarian restaurant they had visited before their trek. Rachael and Ian had super pizzas while C.P. had his usual dhal bhat; they thoroughly enjoyed their tasty meals. Then they walked back to the Hotel Tulsi for a shower and a well-deserved rest. Before Ian and Rachael went up to their comfortable bedroom, which had a lovely en suite, they arranged to meet C.P. later so they could all go out for an evening meal at the Fewa Paradise Restaurant that Rachael loved so much.

As always Rachael was first in the shower and delighted that the water was consistently hot but easily controllable so she spent some considerable time under the shower indulging herself, knowing there would be plenty of hot water left for her dad. Ian stretched out on his bed relaxing his back. Amazingly, it did not ache very much in spite of all the pressure he had put on it that day and he appreciated just how lucky he had been throughout this adventure.[3]

After Ian had showered and dressed, he and Rachael went downstairs and found C.P. waiting for them in reception. Together they walked down to the Fewa Paradise Restaurant with its beautiful multi-coloured lights and haunting music. Rachael was very happy to see that the stage was already lit up so she knew that soon the traditional Nepali dancing would start. This time she was going to join in! It was a lovely evening: stars were already beginning to shine in the darkening sky and although the temperature had dropped, it was still quite warm. It was ideal weather for sitting outside around one of the many tables facing the stage.

They ordered some food and drinks – Everest beer for Ian and C.P. and a special non-alcoholic fruit cocktail for Rachael: she felt really grown-up and sipped it elegantly. Their dhal bhat soon arrived and they all tucked in enthusiastically. Although C.P. always had a good appetite, Ian and Rachael were amazed to find that they were hungry too.

It wasn't long before the dancing started: at first both men and women in traditional dress performed an elaborate dance with many poses and intricate hand movements. A variety of individual dances followed

2 All over Nepal the word 'welcome' is generally split into two words – you will often see 'Well Come' or 'Wel Come'. **3** Lucky – yes – but I would add brave, stubborn and determined. His welcome relief from pain was well deserved.

Hotel Tulsi.

and then some in pairs and groups, each accompanied by contrasting music and singing. All the dances told a traditional story and C.P. tried hard to explain to Rachael what all the movements meant and how every small hand and head alignment and facial expression was significant. Rachael was very eager to try to copy them.

It wasn't long before she had her chance as several of the female dancers beckoned members of the audience to join them on the stage. Ian and C.P. were surprised just how uninhibited, natural and supple Rachael was, she was obviously thoroughly enjoying herself and interpreted the music and rhythm wonderfully. Some of the smiling dancers helped her to use her hands expressively and demonstrated what each tiny gesture meant. She was totally in her element, completely unaware of people watching and admiring her

dancing – she was simply living and loving the experience. In her long-sleeved purple 'Rachael Explore' T-shirt, she blended in with the dancers and lithely matched their sinuous movements. Ian was so pleased he had taken his camera and proudly took many photos of her performance.

Eventually Rachael became a little tired so after they had all celebrated with another drink, they said 'Namaste' to the dancers and made their way back to the Hotel Tulsi. By now both Ian and Rachael were feeling rather tired so they went straight to bed. It had been a long, interesting and busy day.

'Goodnight, Dad,' Rachael murmured drowsily. 'I really loved that dancing. Did I look okay?'

'You were truly amazing and I am very proud of you!' Ian affirmed. 'Goodnight darling. I love you lots.'

'Love you too,' came her sleepy reply.

RACHAEL'S LAST DAY IN POKHARA

Unfortunately it rained again overnight, so when Rachael and Ian woke up the sky was dull and the clouds were low: not a day for paragliding. Ian realised that particular treat would have to wait until Rachael and he returned to Nepal in 2016. He was very thankful that he had decided not to say anything in advance to Rachael.

At breakfast they made plans for their next trip, which was going to be a cultural one. Rachael wanted so badly to discover all she could about the customs, culture, faiths and lifestyle of the Nepalese people. It would be a wonderful learning experience for her. Obviously Rachael said that she would love to see Khushi and Pari again but surprised Ian by asking him if she would be able to go to Khushi's school with her – for a day at least – to see how different education was in Nepal. (School had never been Rachael's favourite place, hence Ian's surprise!)

She also expressed a desire to find out more about the orphanages and children's homes in Nepal, like Milan and Namita's Surya Children's Home, which she had visited on her first trip. As you know, childcare for vulnerable children was a subject very close to Ian's heart, so he was thrilled. Sensibly, Rachael pointed out that all this would be very difficult to achieve in the short half-term school holidays. Ian agreed but promised that when they returned home, he would visit Rachael's school and discuss with her head teacher how her October 2016 holidays could be extended officially. He explained that he would have to think carefully about the right approach but promised he would try his best. Rachael was absolutely delighted.

When they met C.P. in reception, he suggested a walk around the northern shore of Fewa Lake; it would take three to four hours. Ian and Rachael thought this was an excellent idea so they made their way down to the furthest eastern point of the lakeshore. The conditions were quite muggy but the sun was making a real effort to break through the clouds and light breezes drifted from the lake, so walking conditions were fine. They did not need to hurry because, unlike on their trekking days, there was no time limit or specific distance to cover. They just sauntered along chatting and enjoying the lovely scenery of green verdant hills and colourful buildings reflected in the calm waters of the lake. Already there were many rowing and sailing boats out on the lake and the happy voices of their occupants drifted across to our walkers. In spite of the numbers of local Nepalese and tourists it was a peaceful and relaxing place.

Soon the determined sun burnt the clouds away and distant snow-capped peaks of the mountains pierced the cerulean sky: it was pure magic. They continued along the easy lakeside footpath until they reached some revolving gates, built to prevent animals and cyclists from invading the area. Ian went through first, then Rachael, who was amazed to find herself in the midst of a happy, chattering group of Chinese tourists all eager to take her photo and selfies of themselves with Rachael. They were all totally delighted and enraptured. They all thanked Rachael profusely, bowed to her and went on their way chattering noisily. Ian could see that Rachael had enjoyed the attention but was completely bewildered.

'Why did they want to take my photo so many times?' she asked.

Ian said he thought it was possible they were happy to see a beautiful, blonde-haired white girl.

'Really? They're silly!' Rachael replied, but she did have a smile on her face.

Rachael especially loved the part of their walk when they left the tourist part of Pokhara behind and were passing by the ordinary houses of local people. This was what really interested her – seeing ordinary Nepalese people carrying out everyday tasks like cooking, washing and gardening. Ian smiled thoughtfully: Rachael was going to gain so much from their planned 2016 tour.

Eventually they reached the western end of Fewa Lake so after a pause to admire the scenery – particularly the uninterrupted sight of the whole of the Annapurna Range, so clear from this viewpoint – they turned round and walked back towards Pokhara city.

They walked back along the lakeside path until a road to the left took them to the beginning of the Lakeside tourist area. Rachael wanted to buy some presents for her family and friends, so a shopping trip was becoming urgent. However, as it was well past lunchtime, they decided to eat first at their favourite vegetarian restaurant on the main street.

After their meal, while Ian and C.P. were enjoying a beer, Rachael asked if she could go to the co-operative shop directly opposite the restaurant. It was run solely by and for Nepalese teenagers and ladies who had fallen on hard times, who used the premises as a workshop to make their traditional goods such as clothes, woven goods and handbags, which they sold to tourists. C.P. explained that it operated on a fixed-price basis so there was no bartering.

Ian said, 'Yes, of course you can, Rachael,' and asked if she needed any help.

'No thanks, Dad. I'm sure I can manage on my own,' she replied confidently and skipped across the road.

C.P. and Ian watched with admiration as Rachael managed to make one of the Nepalese young ladies understand exactly what she wanted, although she did not speak Nepali and the girl serving her spoke little English. There was a lot of smiling and laughing and loads of hand gestures: clearly all the negotiations were being conducted in a very friendly manner. After a while, with a huge beam on her face, Rachael came back to C.P. and Ian with a large bag containing four handbags, one for her mum, one for each of her sisters, Catherine and Emily and one for herself. Ian was so proud of her; without doubt his young daughter was growing into a confident young lady. Rachael had definitely made excellent choices because to this day, her mum and Emily use their handbags as their main ones and Catherine uses hers as a bag for her knitting.

Now Rachael had bought presents for her family, she needed to buy little gifts for her friends. She told C.P. that she would like to buy some 'friendship-style bracelets'. C.P. knew exactly what she needed and where they could be purchased. He took her to a shop that he knew very well and said he would help her negotiate a good price. The shopkeeper brought out a tray full of woven and plaited cotton bracelets, which were very bright and intricately made. Rachael was delighted – they were ideal so she carefully selected twenty of them. Then came the bartering, encouraged by C.P. Rachael soon became really good at bargaining; she shook her head several times at suggested prices and kept giving the shopkeeper a lovely pleading smile!

'Poor man,' thought Ian. 'He doesn't stand a chance!'

He knew that over the years Rachael had perfected this technique; after all she had often used it on Ian when she really wanted something!

Eventually the deal was done: Rachael and C.P. said 'Namaste' with their hands together and left the shop wreathed in smiles. Rachael had only paid the equivalent of twenty pence for each bracelet!

Their next purchase was a CD of traditional Nepalese music and songs. Both Ian and Rachael had grown to love the lovely, haunting tunes and the expressive lyrics. Eventually Ian bought one that he loved, which is still a favourite of his. He often plays it in his car to brighten up the necessary journeys he makes most days to buy provisions for his busy B&B. They looked briefly at several other shops then walked back to the Hotel Tulsi. C.P. suggested that they should all return to the Fewa Paradise Restaurant in the evening so that Rachael could join in the dancing again.

'Cool!' was her response so that was that – decision made. The weather had been very hot so Rachael and Ian enjoyed long cool showers then rested for a while on their beds, looked at their photos and talked about Rachael's buying and bartering skills.

'You didn't barter as well as I did!' she told Ian proudly.

Ian agreed she was much better at it but pointed out that she had definite advantages: namely that she was a young beautiful blonde with a winning smile! Rachael just beamed lovingly back at him.

As the daylight began to fade, they walked down once more to their favourite restaurant by the lake and sat down in front of the stage. Of course, Ian and C.P. had beers but Rachael decided to have a thirst-quenching Sprite. Inevitably C.P. ordered dhal bhat but Ian and Rachael selected spicy vegetable momos and pakoras – the small crispy, crunchy fritter-like parcels filled with vegetables – like the ones Rajendra, C.P.'s brother, had cooked for me and my friends when we were at Tolka. They were delicious!

While they were eating, Ian told C.P. about their plans for returning the next year to do a cultural tour, which would give Rachael an invaluable learning experience. C.P. explained that he would probably be away as it was the trekking season and he would be required to lead treks for Mountain Monarch. However, he suggested they use his home as a base: they would be very welcome because Pari, Khushi and he thought of Rachael and Ian as part of their family. Both Rachael and Ian were overjoyed.

'Thank you, thank you, dear C.P.!' cried Rachael. 'You really are a wonderful older brother!'

C.P.'s pleasant face lit up with joy.

'You are most welcome,' he said with a lovely smile.

As you may imagine, it wasn't long before Rachael was invited to join the beautiful female dancers on stage. They remembered her from the previous evening and welcomed her warmly. She joined in enthusiastically with growing skill and the way her face glowed showed just how much she was enjoying herself. She is always so open to new experiences that she really does get the very best out of life. Ian and C.P. watched with approval and affection.

When Rachael and Ian were in their beds that night Rachael chatted excitedly about their busy day.

'I'm so pleased that we finished our trek early, Dad,' she enthused, 'because we got to spend an extra day in Pokhara and I love it here!'

There was a little pause before she added, 'And tomorrow I'm going to meet Khushi and Pari again. Fab!'

Ian smiled indulgently: his lovely young companion always ended a day by looking forward to the next adventure.

Looking forward!

BACK TO KATHMANDU

Rachael and Ian were up quite early as they had packing to do before breakfast and they needed to be at Pokhara Airport by 9 a.m. C.P. had already arranged a taxi so when they had thanked the staff at the Hotel Tulsi, C.P. loaded up all their luggage, only leaving day sacks for Ian and Rachael to carry. She laughed when she saw that the name of the airline was Yeti Airways. She had hoped that they might see a yeti while they were trekking but there hadn't been a single sign. C.P. had told her that many Nepalese villagers genuinely believe that yetis do exist and often blamed them for attacks on the villagers' cattle, sheep and goats.

As she had a window seat on the left-hand side of the plane, Rachael spent most of the flight taking photos of the mountains, which looked totally different when seen from that direction. The sky was a beautiful clear blue and the sunlight illuminated all those fabulous peaks: she photographed some wonderful views.

An hour or so later they were choosing a taxi to take them back to C.P.'s house. Pari and Ubick were absolutely delighted to see them again and quickly beckoned them inside. Pari had already prepared some snacks for them. They all had a lovely, friendly time just chatting and relaxing: the bond between them all was warm and loving. Rachael showed Pari and Ubick some of her fantastic photos and described exactly when and where each one had been taken: she has an excellent memory. She described some of the highlights of their trek and, of course, the story of the gigantic spider at Ghandruk was told with a few embellishments.

The time passed so quickly that they were surprised when Khushi appeared. She was overjoyed and rushed across the room to give Rachael a hug. Then Pari mysteriously disappeared into the bedroom and emerged with a beaming smile. She had planned a lovely surprise for Rachael and Khushi: she was carrying two fantastic traditional Nepalese costumes that she had hired for them to wear to celebrate Rachael and Ian's last evening in Kathmandu. The girls could hardly wait to try them on; they were ecstatic! Pari took them both into the bedroom and helped them to dress, arranging their hair in a special style. Then she used traditional make-up to highlight their eyes and features and added the traditional 'tika' emblem on their foreheads. When she had finished, they both looked very beautiful and were thrilled and proud when they looked in the mirror. The girls hugged Pari gratefully. C.P. Ubick and Ian gasped in admiration when the girls emerged and posed in those lovely bright authentic clothes: one beautiful Nepalese girl with shining black hair and one tall English girl with gorgeous blonde hair – two 'sisters' from very different cultures but above all, close, loving friends.

As the early evening was really warm, they all went up to the roof terrace of C.P.'s house where the girls began dancing with Pari. Ubick had taken a CD player up with him and played some wonderful traditional music that was memorable, haunting and rhythmic. The 'ladies' were really graceful and the men watched with joy while they discussed aspects of Ian and Rachael's 2016 trip. C.P. suggested they visit Chitwan Nature Reserve and Safari Park and said he would arrange for Rachael to go to school with Khushi, if that was what she still wanted to do when they returned.

Before they all went back downstairs, C.P. pointed down from the rooftop to a small patch of wasteland next their current rented property, on which rice was growing. He told Ian and Rachael with pride that he was going to build a house there for himself; Pari, Khushi and he all hoped that it would be finished before they came again next year.

Rachael and Khushi went into the bedroom and did girly things like experimenting with make-up and fashioning hair designs before watching several Disney DVDs with Indian subtitles. Pari, Ubick, Ian and C.P. all relaxed and had a lovely evening just talking and laughing. The house was filled with a loving family atmosphere. Ian gave Ubick his baseball cap because he knew Ubick had admired it while they were trekking. The teenager was delighted and gave Ian a warm and grateful hug. Ian told me later that he thought Ubick was one of the nicest young men he had ever met: he was so polite, genuinely caring and always so full of happiness that it was a true joy to be in his company.

Next morning they were all up quite early: Ian and Rachael made sure they had packed everything and Khushi got ready for school. Subash soon arrived with one of Mountain Monarch's cars to take them to the airport and presented Rachael and Ian with kata scarves to wish them a safe journey and a quick return. There were tears in Pari, Khushi and Ian's eyes as they said goodbye and 'Namaste' – they had all formed such a strong bond that it was a sad parting.

Just after their aircraft took off, Rachael looked down as they flew over Pashupatinath, the holy Hindu Temple complex. Ian had explained to Rachael about the Hindu burial customs and said that she needed to be older before they went to visit that temple.

'When we come back next year, Dad, I think I shall be able to cope with visiting there and I would like to do that,' Rachael said.

'We'll see when we come back, darling,' replied Ian.

Rachael smiled at him: she knew Ian would make a wise and suitable decision when the time came.

A little later the glorious Annapurna Range and magical Machhapuchhare appeared below them. Rachael looked towards them longingly and then at her dad.

'Dad, I am really, really looking forward to our adventures together next year. There is so much I want to learn about and explore. I just can't wait!'

ABOVE: Dancing with Khushi.
BELOW: Pari, Rachael and Khushi.

CHAPTER

NEPAL 3: CHITWAN, POKHARA AND KATHMANDU – 2016
AGED 12 YEARS
6 MONTHS

Before Rachael started Year 7 at secondary school in 2015, Ian had been to see her new head teacher and informed him about Rachael's walking achievements. He explained that although she had tried hard throughout primary school (a superb local school), she had such a love of the outdoors and walking that she had always found the walls of school a little confining; her heart was among the fells and mountains. Mrs. Stewart, her lovely, understanding primary school head teacher had once told Ian that she always knew when Rachael's concentration was slipping because she would have a faraway look on her face.

'Then I realised that Rachael was back in the mountains on Place Fell or Helvellyn and not in my classroom, no matter what subject I was teaching!'

To thank her for all her help and kindness, Ian had given Mrs. Stewart a copy of the first book about Rachael – *Rachael: A Remarkable Record Breaker* – which as you know was the story of her three record-breaking C2C walks by her ninth birthday. So on his first visit to her new head teacher, Mr. Pattinson, Ian had given him a copy of the book too because it clearly showed what a brave, determined girl Rachael really was and what her overwhelming interests were; her motivation and achievements.

Soon after Ian and Rachael had returned from Nepal in November 2015, as promised, Ian went to see Mr. Pattinson again to ask for official permission for Rachael to have an extension to her October half-term holidays in 2016. He explained that Rachael and he had already done two treks in Nepal, but next year they hoped to undertake a longer cultural tour so that Rachael could experience the lifestyle, culture, religious commitments and educational standards of Nepalese adults and children. He added that he had lots of contacts in Nepal, particularly in Kathmandu as being a Rotarian he had strong links with Kathmandu Metro Rotary Club as well as with people who ran orphanages and schools there. Of course, he emphasised that they also had a 'family home' there with C.P., Pari and Khushi. Mr. Pattinson was obviously impressed and very supportive. He responded to Ian's earnest request.

'That is incredible! I know it would be the most marvellous learning experience for Rachael so how can I not support her? I am willing to give her this wonderful opportunity with this one caveat … '

He paused and then added, 'Rachael must continue working really well at school: as long as she tries very hard with all her studies and puts in her greatest effort, I will support your application for additional leave in October 2016.'

He shook Ian's hand enthusiastically and told him to return in July 2016 when they would review Rachael's progress and, if it were satisfactory, all Ian would have to do would be to fill in an application form, which he would endorse.

Later that day, when Rachael came home from school, Ian told her about his interview with her head teacher and how she could earn permission for her much-desired cultural tour by working really hard at school and showing that she really deserved to be given that wonderful opportunity.

'Of course, I will, Dad!' Rachael fervently promised. 'I will try my hardest, I really will. Just you wait and see!'

From that day onwards, she approached her schoolwork with renewed enthusiasm: our determined young lady had a target and purpose now. Rachael was absolutely determined to earn the right to go back to Nepal on that cultural tour with her dad in October 2016.

When Ian met Rachael's head teacher again in July 2016, he was very happy to see that Mr. Pattinson was smiling. In front of him on his desk was Rachael's new school report that all her teachers had just completed, along with his comments, which were as follows:

School Report 2015–2016 for Rachael Jennifer Moseley:

This is a report to be proud of at the end of this critical year in secondary school. Rachael has clearly impressed her teachers with her enthusiasm for her studies and her purposeful attitude towards learning. She is already exceeding her expected grades and can look forward to outstanding results here over the next few years if she keeps this up.

Signed: **N. H. Pattinson**
Head Teacher.

Ian was so proud that he could scarcely speak. Rachael had truly earned her chance to go back to Nepal on an extended visit. What a star!

With a smile, Mr Pattinson gave Ian the necessary application form that he needed to complete.

'Just fill this in, please,' he instructed, 'and return it to my office and I will approve it. Rachael really deserves to be given this opportunity to extend her knowledge. She has earned it by working so hard at her studies and has a good attendance record. She has set an excellent example to the school and I'm sure will continue to do so.'

Ian drove home supremely happy: Rachael had overcome another challenge. He could hardly wait to congratulate her!

At this point Ian would like to say a heartfelt thank you to Mr Pattinson, who, at the time of writing this book, was due to retire at the end of the school year. Without his understanding, encouragement and support, Rachael would not have had the chance of being involved in the marvellous learning experiences and exciting adventures that follow in this chapter.

HEATHROW, LONDON TO KATHMANDU VIA DELHI

Before the end of the summer term, Ian received the eagerly awaited confirmation from Mr. Pattinson that Rachael had been granted an official extension of leave at the autumn half-term break starting in October 2016. Immediately he began to look for flights as October is the beginning of the trekking season in the Himalaya and so finding a suitable flight was not going to be easy. Ian decided that, if possible, he would try to arrange to fly on a different route from Rachael's two previous journeys via Abu Dhabi in the Gulf. It would be good for her to have a different experience so he was delighted when he managed to book a through-flight to Delhi with Jet Airways and thence a short flight on a local plane to Tribhuvan Airport, Kathmandu. Their departure date was to be October 7th 2016 from Heathrow Airport, London and they would return there on November 1st 2016.

Over the following weeks, although it was Rachael's summer school holidays and Ian's busiest season at his popular B&B, they managed to discuss what they both thought should be included in Rachael's cultural tour. There was very little disagreement as their close family understanding; their strong father and daughter bond and their enduring love of the country and people of Nepal were truly complementary. Eventually they compiled an interesting list of activities, visits and learning experiences for Rachael to explore and gain the invaluable knowledge and awareness she craved: it was a true meeting of minds. Her excitement and eager anticipation were growing all the time; she was just buzzing!

Amazingly, both Ian and Rachael came to realise that their ultimate plan for exploring all that Nepal had to offer was to have no fixed plan! It would be impossible to organise an itinerary until they were actually in Kathmandu and had met or contacted all their friends and 'family' there. Through a professional contact he had in Kathmandu, Ian arranged for them to be met at Tribhuvan Airport and taken to their hotel in Thamel, which he booked for one night with the option of extending their stay if necessary. Beyond that, nothing else had been specifically organised although, obviously, Ian had been in touch with his wide circle of Nepalese friends, 'family' and Rotarians and told them the purpose of their long and exciting visit.

To readers, this may sound a little irresponsible on Ian's behalf. After all he was taking his twelve-year-old daughter to Nepal for over three weeks with little booked or planned in detail. But Rachael had already trekked in Nepal twice and Ian four times and he was a very seasoned and capable traveller. He had a comprehensive knowledge of Kathmandu, Pokhara and Bhaktapur, a Nepalese 'family' and a huge supportive network of professional contacts and friends. He was absolutely positive he could keep his adventurous daughter safe and happy at all times; her safety, as always, was his priority. He was also very aware that over the last few years, Rachael's confidence had grown massively and she had the calm ability to deal with any situation. Readers only have to think back to the way she took over and cared for Ian when he broke his back in Iceland. He knew they would be fine. Rachael was totally unconcerned as was I; we trusted Ian completely.

They were in total unison about one aspect of their cultural tour: both Ian and Rachael agreed that to gain as much genuine experience as they could, they would 'go native', in terms of using ordinary hotels, lodges and public transport and eating local Nepalese food. For health reasons, always drinking sterilised water would be their only compromise.

DAY 1 – OCTOBER 7TH 2016

A few days before their departure, I went up to take over from Ian and, with the help of his lovely staff, run Old Water View. I had bought a large notebook for Rachael; significantly on the cover was a view of a forest and mountains with the title *Let's go on an Adventure*. She was delighted with my gift because on this trip she had decided she was going to keep a detailed record of all her wonderful experiences each day. In fact her daily journal has been an immense help in writing this chapter so, thank you Rachael for your meticulous notes!

In Rachael's words, *'After saying goodbye and thank you to Grandma Joyce, we left home at 10:20 to catch the 10:30 bus to Penrith. Then we caught the one o'clock train from Penrith Station to Euston Station in London.'*

Apparently at Euston, they met a charming Nepalese man who was looking very puzzled. Ian asked him if he needed any help. The grateful gentleman introduced himself as Gobinda Neupane and explained that he was unsure which tube train to catch to Heathrow as he was flying later to Kathmandu to celebrate the Festival of Dashain with his family. Of course Ian told him immediately that he and Rachael were flying to Kathmandu from Heathrow so suggested Gobinda travel with them. He accepted Ian's offer thankfully and they all chatted happily during the short journey. Gobinda told them that his real home was in Kathmandu but he worked in England. Rachael was really impressed by how kind and polite he was so when Gobinda proposed that they should all meet up again in Kathmandu (he was booked on a different flight from theirs), both Ian and Rachael readily agreed. They exchanged phone numbers but sadly never managed to meet as Ian had problems with his phone and did not seem to be able to contact Gobinda, no matter how many times he tried. According to Rachael, their Jet Airways flight to Delhi *'took off at 20:45 and was a very, very long one but we had some great spicy food and slept a lot!'*

DAY 2 – OCTOBER 8TH

A rather amusing incident happened at Delhi Airport. As they were going through the scanners, Ian was pulled out of the line and asked to open his daypack. When the officials discovered that he had one hundred 'Rachael Explore' pens in a large plastic bag inside, they looked at him in a very suspicious way. One of the uniformed officials dug deep into the bottom of the plastic bag and held up two of the pens.

'What are these, sir?' he enquired.

Patiently and politely, Ian explained they were presents for the schoolchildren his daughter Rachael was going meet when she attended her Nepalese friend,

Khushi Rai's school. Ian's heart was in his mouth – clearly the officials thought he was trying to smuggle something illegal! They unscrewed each pen and examined the tube of ink inside and then put them back together, making sure they really were pens by writing on the backs of their hands. After testing them thoroughly, they smiled.

'Okay sir, you can go through now.'

Gratefully Ian thanked them and offered them some pens, which they declined, waving Ian and Rachael onwards.

Obviously those officials did not have the sense of humour of the polite and humorous official I met at Delhi passport control some years before. I had a little bear wearing a red jumper, called 'Workington' tied to my small rucksack. He was the mascot Ian and the girls bought to wish me good luck on my difficult Langtang, Gosainkunda and Helambu Circuit trek. The beaming official asked me what the bear's name was and what we both planned to do in Nepal. When I explained the details of my planned trek and that Workington was my mascot bought by my 'grandchildren', he smiled broadly and said that my bear was entitled to a special security pass. He tied a red circular cardboard disc around Workington's neck. On one side were the words, 'Security Check I.G.I. Airport, New Delhi' and on the other 'Executive Class – Air India.' I thanked him profusely but pointed out that I was only travelling in Economy Class, to which he replied laughingly, 'Well madam, I think your brave little bear deserves an upgrade. Good luck to you both!' What an amazing man – and what a heart-warming gesture and welcome to India; I was delighted!

Eventually Rachael and Ian arrived at Tribhuvan Airport, Kathmandu at 2 p.m. When they had cleared passport control and collected their luggage, they went outside and were pleased to find a Nepalese taxi driver holding a board aloft on which their names were written: 'IAN and RACHAEL.' Thankfully, Ian's arrangements seemed to be working.

They were driven to their accommodation, which was supposed to be The Hotel Pomero in Thamel.

Ian paid the fare and the taxi driver unloaded their luggage, just dumping it in front of the hotel. Then he drove off quickly without a word. Ian and Rachael were puzzled by his behaviour but assumed that he had another fare booked. Then the fun began.

Ian began to suspect they were possibly not at the right hotel because they did not appear to be in the familiar Thamel district but in the next one a little to the south: Chetrapati. His suspicions were reinforced when they entered reception and saw the name 'Hotel Pomelo House' on a small notice standing on the reception desk. However, conscious that he may have mixed up the names himself, Ian approached the desk and informed the owner that they had accommodation booked for the night. The owner was very welcoming but clearly had not been expecting them, although he made an excellent attempt at pretending they were booked in. He conducted them upstairs to a very pleasant twin-bedded room, which, although in need of a little refurbishment, was immaculately clean with beautiful new crisp sheets and a nice en suite.

Rachael and Ian were completely satisfied with their accommodation so decided to stay there anyway. After all, they had just completed a very long journey and definitely did not want to start looking for alternative rooms, especially as their taxi driver had already gone. The charge for their rooms and breakfast was extremely reasonable: the equivalent of £5 per person per night. Unbelievable!

When they had unpacked all their necessary gear and toiletries, Rachael settled down on her bed to play on her iPad while Ian decided he would go for a walk to explore the district. He made sure that Rachael was okay and didn't want to accompany him and told her that he would be about two hours. He reminded her that they both had phones so she could contact him immediately if she had any worries.

'I'll be fine, Dad, honestly!' Rachael responded. 'I'll really enjoy just chilling out on my own. You go ahead. It will be good to know exactly where we are and I have some water left and snacks and loads to do. I haven't filled my journal in yet and I've got my iPad so don't worry about me. I may even have a shower as well while you are away.'

Ian gave Rachael their room key, and instructed her to lock the door as soon as he left. Ian demonstrated a special knock that he would use when he returned and told Rachael only to open that door when she heard his knock and voice. Satisfied that Rachael would be safe, he waited until he heard the key turn in the door before going downstairs.

Ian walked around for some time familiarising himself with the area, looking at shops and cafés and other hotels many of which seemed to be closed. Perhaps this was because the Festival of Dashain had already started, he thought. However when he decided to return to their hotel, he realised that he was lost; he did not recognise anything. He searched and searched with no success. He became very concerned for Rachael who, by then, had been on her own for two hours. He decided that the best action he could take was to flag down a taxi and ask to be taken back to the Hotel Pomelo House.

Fortunately the taxi he selected was that of a wonderfully helpful Nepalese driver called Gobinda Shrestha. (Gobinda was obviously a common first name!) The driver admitted he did not know exactly where the Hotel Pomelo House was but said he would drive to the nearby taxi rank and ask the other drivers for directions. He did so, but regrettably none of them knew where the hotel was, in fact they had never heard of it despite having lived in that district all of their lives. Gobinda urged Ian not to be upset and said that he would drive all around Thamel and Chetrapati until he found the hotel. He drove carefully for over forty minutes occasionally pausing to ask people if they knew where the Hotel Pomelo House was but no one appeared to know. Finally Ian spotted it: it was down a tiny side street not far from an intersection of some of the main roads he had walked down. He was elated and thanked Gobinda enthusiastically for all his help. Disaster averted!

Ian dashed inside the hotel, followed by Gobinda, and hurried up to their room and knocked on the door using their special knock. Rachael opened the door quickly and smiled at him.

'I'm so glad you're back, Dad, 'she said 'I was beginning to get a bit bored. Where have you been?'

Gobinda was just as delighted as Ian that Rachael was safe. What a kind and caring person he had proved to be.

'How much do I owe you, Gobinda?' Ian asked.

He replied, 'Just five hundred rupees, Ian. That is what I agreed with you when you first hired me and I always keep my word.'

Five hundred rupees was less then £5. Ian absolutely refused to pay so little for such care and devotion, pointing out that by now Gobinda had spent over an hour helping him. Eventually he persuaded Gobinda to accept one thousand rupees – roughly £10. Ian was truly grateful and knew that he could trust Gobinda so he asked him if he would return the next morning and take them on a tour around the temples in Kathmandu. He explained that they would like to check if there was still any earthquake damage. Gobinda happily agreed and gave Ian his card with

his personal number on it. Before he drove away, he wished Ian a good evening and said that he was so pleased his daughter was okay, adding that he would be back in the morning.

As you can imagine, Ian was immensely relieved to find that Rachael had been totally unconcerned and had just enjoyed chilling out and playing on her iPad. She said she hadn't worried because she knew Ian would soon be back: he had promised her and she knew that her dad always kept his promises. Ian was so proud and relieved with the way Rachael had dealt so calmly with the situation and gave her a huge hug. He went on to explain exactly what had happened; how he had been rescued by a 'Good Samaritan' – their new taxi driver, Gobinda Shrestha. He went on to tell Rachael that he had arranged for Gobinda to pick them up in the morning so they could do a tour by taxi around all the temples to see the earthquake damage and the repair work that would be going on.

Rachael was thrilled because she had been very concerned about all the damage done by the terrible earthquake Nepal had suffered the previous year. She had avidly watched all the programmes about it on television; now she would be able to see for herself how the renovation work was progressing.

It had been a long exhausting day, so very soon Rachael and Ian snuggled down in their beds.

'Goodnight, Dad, I love you' murmured Rachael sleepily, 'I'm so happy to be back in Kathmandu. I really, really love it here!'

'Goodnight, darling!' replied Ian, wondering what surprises the next day may bring.

Whatever happened, Ian knew that together they could and would cope. Rachael had just proved what a confident and responsible traveller she had become and that beyond any doubt, she trusted him completely. What a super team they made!

DAY 3 – OCTOBER 9TH

Rachael and Ian had breakfast on the lovely little patio of the Hotel Pomelo House. It was very pretty with deep-red tiled floors and semi-circular low walls built of red brick, on which rested numerous pots of marigolds, geraniums and many other sweet-scented flowers. There were shady trees and tall poinsettia trees and creepers covered with bright red flowers, which reminded Ian of Christmas. They talked about the unusual happenings yesterday and laughed about them. Ian had discovered from the young manager that the Hotel Pomelo House had only just re-opened. It had been closed for some time but the new owners were determined to make the hotel successful and had begun a comprehensive refurbishment. He confessed that he had only been working there for one day and informed Ian that the owners had given the hotel a new name in order to promote its new image.

That explained why none of the taxi drivers knew where the Hotel Pomelo House was because they had known it by its previous name. One mystery solved. Also Ian and Rachael wondered if the taxi driver who picked them up from the airport the previous afternoon had been confused too, realising too late that he had made a mistake in taking them to the wrong hotel. That would explain why he disappeared so quickly. They also discovered that there really was a Hotel Pomero in Thamel and that was where Ian and Rachael's accommodation had been booked. They were not worried at all as they both thought the Hotel Pomelo House was great, the staff were extremely helpful and, judging by their tasty breakfast, the food was excellent too. They decided to stay another night so they could explore Kathmandu at leisure and see the earthquake damage with the help of Gobinda.

Rachael reminded Ian that it was the time of one of the most important festivals of the Nepalese culture: Dashain. They had planned to be in Kathmandu at this time so that they could experience how the Nepalese celebrated this primary religious festival. Dashain holds the same prominence and distinction as Christmas in Christian culture and as you will discover, it often extends into and merges with the main Festival of Diwali: the Festival of Light. Dashain is the one festival when all Nepalese try to return home to celebrate with their families, just as Gobinda Neupane was doing. It lasts for fifteen days from the 'bright moon' until the 'full moon'. On our Gregorian calendar, the festival falls either in September or at the beginning of October, varying from year to year due to the differences between a lunar and solar-based time-keeping system. It also varies in length and specific customs according to which region in Nepal it is celebrated and, indeed, all over the world. Mainly it celebrates the ancient victory of Good over Evil when the righteous Hindu Gods defeated the evil demon Mahishasura who appeared in the form of a raging water buffalo. One goddess pivotal in this victory was the Goddess Durga, so garlanded statues and pictures of her seated on a tiger are everywhere. Worshippers kneel in front of her, pray and leave offerings of precious objects, food and money. All Nepalese clean their homes thoroughly and decorate them ornately so the Goddess will visit and bless their homes and bring them good luck for the following year. They also prepare special delicious dishes to welcome their families and friends and they buy new clothes and proudly wear them throughout the festival. You often see colourful kites flying high in the blue sky and even adults swing vigorously on immensely high swings – some up to twenty feet high – to drive away the rain and celebrate the end of the monsoon season. Although originally one of the most important Hindu festivals, Dashain is also celebrated by Buddhists and many other faiths, castes and creeds as all rejoice in the triumph of good over evil in their own way. It is a time of celebration, goodwill and tolerance.

Ian deliberately chose this time to begin their cultural tour of Nepal because he knew that most tourists and trekkers avoid the cities during Dashain; accommodation, shops, cafes and other facilities and services are often closed down. This was just what he and Rachael wanted: the streets, squares, homes and temples to be full of happy Nepalese people worshipping and celebrating together, rather than packed with tourists.[1]

One aspect of Dashain Ian was determined to avoid was the day of the ritual sacrifice of animals. He was completely aware of just how fond Rachael was of all animals so knew that this was one cultural practice Rachael did not need to see at her age. The Hindus profoundly believed that the ritual slaughter and sacrifice of thousands of animals: buffalo, sheep, goats, chickens and ducks was necessary to appease the gods and goddesses. All the statues, especially of Durga, were soon dripping with blood, which was frequently renewed. Ian had made sure that they would be in Chitwan Safari Park on the day this happened. He too did not want to witness the lengthy blood sacrifices.

As soon as Rachael and Ian finished breakfast, they retrieved their daypacks and went to the front of the hotel to meet Gobinda. He was delighted to meet them again and had been waiting for over fifteen minutes so had begun to fear his services were not needed. Ian shook his hand gratefully and Rachael greeted him with a smile.

'Namaste, Gobinda! It is lovely to meet you properly and thanks for rescuing my dad!'

Gobinda was obviously delighted.

Ian reminded Gobinda that they wanted to revisit some of the superb temples they had already seen but did not need to spend much time there. Mainly they were interested to see the extent of the earthquake damage and how far the renovations had progressed. They knew that many countries worldwide had contributed to the rebuilding in Nepal and they were looking forward to reading the commemoration plaques. Also Ian asked if they could visit Patan and view the temples there and see the Pashupatinath Temple complex that Rachael had not yet seen. (On previous visits Ian had considered her too young to cope with the Hindu burial rites.) Gobinda was happy to oblige and suggested that they took a circular route visiting the Swayambhunath Stupa – the Monkey Temple first, then down to Patan and back to Kathmandu Durbar Square and the Boudnath Stupa. Then, if there was sufficient time, they could drive over to revisit Bhaktapur, the city that had suffered the most damage in the recent earthquake.

Just before they set off Gobinda handed Ian and Rachael some photos showing what had happened to his home in the earthquake. The roof had collapsed, there were numerous large cracks in the walls and one wall was completely missing. You could see the entire interior including the furniture and fittings. He explained that he, his wife and children were still living there in those awful conditions because they could not afford alternative accommodation. In the centre of Kathmandu, many residents had been 'rehoused' in tents however people, like Gobinda, living on the outskirts, did not have that option: no tents were available. To add to their problems, his wife had been knocked off their motorbike and broken her leg. They had just enough money to pay for her to have her leg set in plaster at a local hospital and buy painkillers but they could not afford further treatment so, at the moment, she could not work. Unbelievably, he was still very cheerful.

'We are all alive and safe, that is all that matters,' he said thankfully. 'We have each other, and houses can be rebuilt – people can't!'

---

[1] By this time, Ian realised that the lack of usual services was probably the reason why his phone could not connect to the Nepalese network – hence his inability to contact Gobinda Neupane.

I have always found that Nepalese people are amazingly resilient: they seem to face all problems with a positive, joyous attitude and an understanding of the really important values in life.

Rachael and Ian could hardly believe their eyes when they saw the magnificent Monkey Temple again, sitting atop its beautiful green hill. It looked exactly the same as it had on their first visit. There was no scaffolding and no visible damage; all repairs seemed to have been completed. From its commanding position over-looking the Kathmandu Valley, it stood proudly as a monument to the all-encom-passing faith, commitment and hard work of the Nepalese people, determined to restore this symbol of their culture, religion and national pride. A wonderful sense of peace, serenity and spirituality pervaded the whole complex. As they mounted the seemingly unending steps accompanied by scampering, chattering monkeys, they saw a small temple building near the top of the hill that they had not noticed before. Inside were lots of Nepalese mothers nursing their sick children and babies. Clearly they were desperately hoping that some miracle would occur at this impor-tant time of worship and that the gods would help them.

Some of the children were obviously very ill; terminally ill in some cases and others were crippled. A monk was blessing the sick infants and anointing them in a calm, caring way while others were praying earnestly. Gobinda explained that this was a special ritual that few tourists ever see as Dashain was a time of the year they avoided because of the general 'shut-down'. Rachael and Ian realised they were very privileged to witness this private holy custom and felt truly humbled. It added greatly to their understanding and made them feel part of Nepal's culture and traditions – not mere visitors or observers.

Both Rachael and Ian were quiet for some time while Gobinda drove in a south-easterly direction down towards Patan Durbar Square situated in the centre of the city of Lalitpur. As they discovered later that evening when discussing the events of the day, they had both been thinking about how lucky we are in the UK to have the National Health Service which provides free medical care. In Nepal all treatment, necessary medication, operations and hospitalisation for critical illness and disease has to be paid for; this is often beyond the means of poor people. Also fees are charged for all education from primary through to university so many poor Nepalese simply cannot afford to give their children a really good education.

Gobinda parked on the outskirts of Patan Durbar Square, which is in the cen-tre of Lalitpur City. The square is tiled throughout with beautiful red bricks – just like the ones on the patio at the Hotel Pomelo House. Lalitpur is one of the three Royal cities of the Kathmandu Valley, Kathmandu and Bhaktapur being the other two. The name Lalitpur means 'City of Beauty' – an accurate description before the devastating 2015 earthquake.

Gobinda led Ian and Rachael to one of the kiosks where they each had to purchase a plastic-covered 'Patan Tourist Entrance Pass'. These were on gold silky string and had to be worn around the neck while they explored the area. There was an additional small entrance fee for most of the temples but Gobinda, a local resident,

27.05.2007

Earthquake repairs.

did not have to pay at all and accompanied them on their tour. Sometimes the temples, museums and public buildings were quite a distance apart so on these occasions, Gobinda drove them.

Patan Durbar Square is a UNESCO World Heritage Site full of temples, stupas and idols and is the centre of Buddhism and Hinduism. It is famous for its handicrafts, carvings and magnificent art works. One of its main attractions is the ancient Royal Palace of the Malla kings, which Rachael and Ian visited and were dumbfounded by its sumptuous decoration and magnificent interior. All the intricately carved temples built originally by the wonderfully skilled Newar craftsmen are aligned to face the east where the Royal Palace is situated. Many of the fifty-five major temples were severely damaged in the earthquake, as were public and commercial buildings and old Newari residential homes: some were reduced to piles of rubble. The pagoda-style construction and delicate carving and tracery of the temples made them particularly vulnerable to earthquake devastation.

Rachael and Ian were thrilled to see the vast amount of renovation work that had already taken place: the progress was remarkable. Behind the surrounding scaffolding and barriers, the temples and buildings were rising like phoenixes from the ashes. Everywhere skilled builders, workmen and craftsmen laboured devotedly in the hot sun. The quality and standard of their workmanship was astounding. On the barriers were plaques indicating the main sponsors of the reconstruction work; it was amazing to see just how many countries, governments, organisations and businesses had contributed towards restoring this centre of Nepalese culture, religion and commerce.

Ian and Rachael paid to go inside some of the temples; one that particularly attracted them was the shining three-storeyed Golden Temple (the Hiranya Varna Mahavihar). Situated to the north of Durbar Square, it had not suffered massive damage but was encased in scaffolding masking part of it. Originally built in the 12th century, it is a pagoda-style Buddhist monastery adorned with a façade of sparkling gold and has four gateways, a clock tower and two huge lion statues: it is breathtaking. Rachael and Ian went inside to see the gold images of Buddhas, beautiful wall carvings, artwork and a large prayer wheel.

While they were in Patan, Rachael and Ian were very careful to only drink the clean bottled water they had taken with them. Water in Patan is very polluted as the city is a long way from the fresh water supply in the hills. The water is stored in huge tanks, which get really hot in the sun and bacteria grow quickly inside them. This can cause outbreaks of severe gastro-enteritis and, more seriously, cholera and dysentery. Locals generally develop immunity but many unwary tourists can become very ill if they ignore health advice and drink the local water.

Eventually they made their way back to Gobinda's taxi and he drove north to revisit Boudnath and its fabulous Stupa. They were all delighted to see that the top part of the structure above the dome including the all-seeing, all-knowing eyes of Buddha, the gilded tower and golden canopy with its beautiful gold spire had been repaired and hoisted back onto the platform on top of the dome. The bright multi-coloured prayer flags were fluttering again in the breeze carrying their messages of peace and goodwill around the world. Huge cracks in the dome itself had been filled and were being painted as they watched, so that soon the yellow semi-circular lotus petals could be added. The restoration of this magnificent monument was almost complete.

As they walked towards their next destination, Ian and Rachael noticed a lovely young Nepalese girl who was an itinerant street artist. She was sitting on one of the high steps that bordered the street and a lady tourist was sitting beside her. The girl artist said her name was Beka and she was an expert at drawing henna decorations. She had a canvas bag in which were several henna pens and she was busy finishing the last curlicue of a wonderful design on the tourist's right hand. The lady was obviously delighted and showed Rachael and Ian the exquisite artwork; clearly Beka was very talented. Ian asked Rachael if she would like a henna decoration on her hand and, of course, she was very eager to have one.

'Please, Dad,' she said quickly, 'I would love one and then I will feel like a proper Nepalese lady!'

Beka worked quickly and expertly and soon Rachael was excitedly showing Gobinda the beautiful design in different shades of henna from golden brown to deep brown tints stretching up her right forearm. Beka had drawn intricate patterns of swirls, curlicues and leaf-like shapes and had cleverly incorporated Rachael's name. It cost Ian a thousand rupees (about £10) but was well worth it for it was a masterpiece! Beka told them that the decoration would last about two weeks, after which it would fade and have to be renewed and she gave Ian her card. Throughout that day, Rachael kept looking proudly at her wonderful henna design. It was truly gorgeous!

They soon reached the ruins of the unique Dharahara Tower in Sundhara, Kathmandu which, sadly, Rachael had not seen on her previous visits when it had stood 203-feet high (nearly sixty-two metres – ten metres higher than the famous Nelson's

Column in Trafalgar Square, London). Like Boudnath it is a UNESCO World Heritage Site and was the highest building in Nepal. It had originally been built as a nine-storeyed military watchtower in 1832 as, from the circular balcony on the eighth floor, the whole of the Kathmandu Valley could be seen. When incidents of national importance occurred, bugles were blown from the top of the tower as a signal for the soldiers to assemble. The tradition of bugle playing continued until the collapse of the tower in the 2015 earthquake. It used to have a spiral staircase of 213 steps and a seventeen-foot-tall bronze mast on the top. It was a popular tourist attraction for visitors from many countries as well as locals for its fabulous panoramic view from that eighth floor balcony.

Most of the tower had completely disintegrated during the earthquake leaving just a stump of the base about thirty-three feet high. Unfortunately over two hundred people were in the tower when it collapsed and when the rubble was cleared, sixty bodies were found. Although the tower had been reconstructed after an earthquake in 1934, most local Nepalese, including Gobinda, believed that this time the tower would not be rebuilt but instead, the base left as a memorial to all those who had perished.

However in February 2016, a decision was made by the Nepalese Government to rebuild the tower and a foundation stone is said to have been laid down in April 2016. Rachael and Ian could not go up to the rubble but had to view the ruins from behind the surrounding wall, as the site was considered dangerous. The base of the tower was completely surrounded by shutters and barriers so they could not see whether or not that foundation stone had actually been put in position. Apparently the civil engineer in charge of the National Reconstruction Agency, Sushil Gyawali, is confident that the new tower will be earthquake resistant. The reconstruction of the tower is planned to begin in November 2017.

'Wow, Dad!' Rachael exclaimed, 'I hope that when the tower is rebuilt, we can climb right to the top and see all over the Kathmandu Valley: that would be really cool.'

Clearly she was thinking about another visit to Nepal. Wisely Ian did not comment! He was hoping that Rachael would find their next destination, the largest temple complex, Pashupatinath just as fascinating and would be able to cope with the Hindu burial rites and cremations, which are not for the faint-hearted. However he knew that he could allow Rachael to gain knowledge from the experience, while protecting her from some of the more upsetting details.

Pashupatinath Temple is a famous, sacred Hindu temple dedicated to Lord Shiva and is one of the four most important religious sites in Asia for devotees of Shiva. It is said to have been built in the 5th century and later renovated by the Malla kings. Obviously it is yet another UNESCO World Heritage Site. The whole complex is huge and stretches both sides of the Bagmati River, which is considered to be holy as it is a tributary of the sacred River Ganges. The main pagoda-style temple has a gilded roof that shines magnificently in the sunshine, four sides are covered in fantastic contrasting silver and the intricate wood carvings and stone sculptures are of the finest quality. The inner sanctum has an immense Shiva lingam (erect phallus) and just outside the entrance sits the largest statue of Nandi the Bull, the frightening manifestation of Shiva.

Temples dedicated to other Hindu and Buddhist deities surround the main temple so it has become a spiritual and religious centre for many faiths and cultures. Amazingly the complex includes over four hundred temples of various sizes, fifteen shrines dedicated to Lord Shiva and twelve large phallic shrines as well as hundreds of Shiva lingam scattered throughout the site. The latter are often visited by Nepali ladies wishing to become pregnant! Only Hindus are allowed inside the gates to the north of the temple and access for all other faiths and visitors is generally limited to the south bank of the Bagmati River.

After Gobinda had parked his taxi, he decided to stay with it, so Ian and Rachael walked past two armed guards towards the main temple, as Ian was interested to see what was inside. He had no intention of trying to gain access to the interior and was definitely not showing any disrespect for the Hindu religion, he was merely curious. I am amazed that he and Rachael were even allowed *near* the entrance gates as whenever I have been to Pashupatinath, visitors have been strongly directed by soldiers with rifles over the bridge spanning the Bagmati to its south bank. Soon Ian and Rachael were spotted by a guard – a soldier in blue camouflage uniform – who was firmly holding a Kalashnikov rifle! The guard indicated strongly that they should turn round and cross the bridge. Wisely, Ian did not argue but apologised profusely and he and Rachael crossed the Bagmati bridge to join the other visitors.

Almost immediately they were accosted by a very persistent 'guide'. He told Ian that he needed the services of a guide, as he had been lost; he said he was the best and only charged one hundred rupees (£1). It took some time for Ian to convince the guide that his services were not needed. Initially, he conveyed this politely but then had to employ much firmer tactics. This is a major problem at Pashupatinath: the number of 'guides', sellers of trinkets and beggars who pester tourists and spoil what would otherwise be a fascinating and unique experience.

Ian pointed out the sadhus to Rachael. (They are basically wandering Hindu 'holy' men who have given up their entire lives to worship, prayer and meditation although some do seem to stay permanently in the caves at Pashupatinath). Some of them had painted their bodies with a mixture of white powder and they were all barefoot and meagrely dressed. Many of these sadhus explain to visitors that they have not eaten for days as they are fasting but they welcome donations.

When I visited some years previously, one remarkably healthy-looking sadhu told me he had not eaten for twenty years but lived only on milk! The displays they put on for tourists are astonishing and, when the audience seems appropriate, some put on very invigorating performances, especially for female tourists whose cameras suddenly become very busy!

Many years ago when I first went to Nepal and was doing the usual cultural day tour, which included a visit to Pashupatinath, I witnessed an extraordinary act by one of the sadhus: on the floor, he spread out a length of white cotton, onto which he proceeded to load a number of heavy-looking stones. A supreme actor and performer, he invited some of the watchers in his captive audience to test the weight of the stones; with their considerable weight verified, he tied the ends of the white cloth together to form a sling and struggled impressively to lift it. Then he bent down, raised his 'skirt' and placed the sling containing the stones over the stem of his now erect penis and stood up with outstretched arms – 'hands free' so to speak! The tourists' cameras clicked and clicked! There were looks of disbelief and envy from the male observers and gasps of awe from the ladies. One large American lady, poor soul, fainted and had to be revived by her companions. The first thing she asked when she had recovered was, 'Ya sure ya got some snaps, didn't ya?' They assured her that they had taken a lot!

When the performance was over, the 'artistic' sadhu held out his begging bowl and gratefully received generous donations from his audience. I am ashamed to say that I had a fit of giggles; it had been a very enlightening and memorable experience!

Gobinda and Rachael.

Thankfully, as it was Dashain there were very few tourists when Ian and Rachael were there, so there were no such performances. Ian did not have to shield Rachael from any potentially embarrassing and inappropriate exhibitions and she did not seem to realise the significance of the many lingams.

As you might expect, Rachael was totally amazed by the cremation rituals of the Hindu burial rites and watched in fascination. Fortunately as Ian and Rachael were some distance away on the opposite bank of the Bagmati, Rachael was unable to see all the detailed rituals and Ian was able to redirect her attention whenever necessary. The whole cremation ritual is a truly interesting and amazing experience. Many terminally ill Hindus go to Pashupatinath to spend the last weeks of their lives in special accommodation there. They believe that anyone who dies in or near the Great Temple is reborn as a human, not a creature, regardless of any misconduct and their good karma is preserved. When they die, their body is wrapped in a shroud and placed on a wooden pyre on one of the numerous ghats – stone platform-like structures built into steps that lead down the northern riverbank and into the Bagmati. The wood is set on fire and the body cremated in the open air. The smoke, Hindus believe, carries the spirits of the dead up into the air. There is no offensive smell as the bodies are anointed with spices and oils, which help to hasten the process. After the body had been reduced to ashes, temple servants brush the ashes into the Bagmati River, which carries them down to the holy Mother Ganges. It is a humbling spiritual experience to witness.

As you may imagine, after the horrific loss of life in the 2015 earthquake, the funeral pyres burned ceaselessly, day and night, for many weeks. Unbelievably, in October 2016, the Pashupatinath complex showed hardly any signs of earthquake damage. Perhaps as it is on the eastern edge of Kathmandu, and therefore further away from the epicentre of the earthquake, it had not been subject to so many violent shocks.

What is slightly disconcerting to our culture is to see the number of people bathing in the heavily polluted water and local women washing clothes downstream of the cremations (the amount of fat in the water helps to cleanse the linen). Understandably Rachael was a little subdued but seemed very aware that all the cremations were part of Hindu culture and very important rituals to them. She told Ian that she was glad they had visited Pashupatinath especially as Khushi, Pari and C.P. were Hindus and it was interesting to be aware of the customs of their religion, but she wasn't sure that she would want to return. Ian confirmed that this visit would be the only time he ever came here.

As they walked back to Gobinda's taxi, Rachael had a very thoughtful look on her lovely face.

'You know, Dad, Hindus probably think that some of our customs and religious celebrations are very strange – like Christmas and Easter. Don't you think?'

Ian readily agreed; it was obvious that Rachael had been thinking deeply about her experiences at Pashupatinath and was gaining an invaluable awareness and tolerance of different cultures and religions. This was exactly what he had wanted to happen and he was so proud of the way his daughter was growing in understanding.

Gobinda was delighted to see them again and very happy when Ian decided they had sufficient time to revisit Bhaktapur, so soon they were speeding towards that wonderful city. It is the third of the royal cities in the Kathmandu Valley and a living museum. Naturally the whole of the city is a UNESCO World Heritage Site. They were eager to see how the restoration was progressing, as they knew the city had sustained devastating damage in the earthquake. Like many buildings in Patan, much of the architecture was of delicate Newar construction, terracotta tiles and intricate carvings, and so prone to the massive destruction caused by earthquakes.

Rachael, Ian and Gobinda were delighted to see that a vast amount of renovation had already taken place. There were probably still years of work ahead to completely restore the city, but like everywhere in Nepal, enormous amounts of energy and dedication had enabled the reconstruction to progress at an admirable pace. Many buildings were still shrouded in scaffolding and surrounded by barriers but there was a wonderful spirit of hope and determination throughout the city. The more modern commercial buildings seemed to have survived almost intact. Ian told Rachael and Gobinda that although he realised the ancient buildings must be preserved and rebuilt in their old traditional style, he hoped that modern building techniques would be incorporated to make them more resistant to earthquakes. Rachael and Gobinda fervently agreed and Rachael added that when she returned to Nepal, she would like to revisit Bhaktapur to see it once all the rebuilding was finished.

'I just love this city so much, Dad! I never liked history much at school but here it is all around you and it's so interesting. Can we come back one day, please?' she begged with one of her winning smiles.

'We'll see, darling,' Ian replied.

Gobinda drove Ian and Rachael safely back to the Hotel Pomelo House. He said that he had really enjoyed their day and hoped he would be able to drive them again someday when they were back in Kathmandu.

Ian promised that he would never use another taxi driver but would always contact Gobinda. Ian went on to tell him that both he and Rachael felt Gobinda was part of their team and they both really liked and admired him. He asked Gobinda how much they owed him for the whole day tour and when he was told one thousand rupees, Ian gave him an additional thousand rupees tip. With a warm smile, Ian said Gobinda had earned that amount for all his kind, cheerful company and emphasised that he was their number one taxi driver. Rachael enthusiastically agreed. Gobinda was almost overcome with emotion and gratitude.

'Namaste, Rachael and Ian! Thank you – thank you so much and very good luck to you both. I will always remember you.'

With that, he climbed into his taxi and drove away. Rachael waved goodbye to him enthusiastically and turned to Ian.

'I *do* hope we meet Gobinda again, Dad!'

They went upstairs to their room to freshen up. Ian needed to go and book their Chitwan Safari with the nearby travel agent so he asked Rachael if she wanted to accompany him. She said she needed to write up her journal while she could remember all the wonderful things they had done, so Ian told her to lock the door as before and wait for his special knock before she opened it. He knew he would not be long.

He went into the travel agency – Rainbow Safari Tours to make the arrangements and was thrilled to find that the agent owned The Safari Resort Hotel in Chitwan National Park so he booked to stay there for two nights with the option of extending their visit. He also arranged for Rachael to have a ride on the back of an elephant.

The agent told him that one of the best and exciting ways to get to Chitwan was on a local bus that left at 7 a.m. – the journey took between six and seven hours. He told Ian that he would book specific seats on the bus and, if Ian and Rachael came to the agency next morning, he would meet them and take them to the correct local bus. He explained it might be difficult to find as the local and tourist buses parked on a road called Kantipath – not at a bus station or terminus as in the UK. Also, he wanted to ensure that Ian and

Rachael had the comfortable seats he had booked for them and that the driver would not ask them to move! He added that this was important because the journey of approximately eighty-five miles could be a little difficult and uncomfortable at times. Since breaking his back the year before and having had to fly to Pokhara instead of going by bus, Ian had desperately wanted to take a 'native' bus ride like all the local people and now he had the chance. Great!

He rushed back to the Hotel Pomelo House, climbed the stairs swiftly and knocked on the door of their room in his special way. He could hardly wait to tell Rachael what he had booked for them. She was ecstatic and gave him a huge hug.

'I'm going on an elephant ride, hurray!' she sang joyfully.

Ian was excited too: it would be a new adventure for him. They packed one rucksack with the few clothes and the equipment necessary for the next two days on safari and stuffed all their spare gear and toiletries into their other rucksack. Ian had arranged with the hotel owner that this bag would be stored safely until they returned. He had to trust that it

would be waiting for them when they came back but he was not entirely confident; the hotel did not have a proper secure room and their rucksack would be hidden behind the desk in reception!

It was not long before they were both snuggled down in their beds; it had been a very long and busy day. Ian could hardly believe how much they had done. Rachael fell asleep almost immediately but Ian lay awake for a while with a secret smile on his face. He was thinking of the exciting surprise he had planned for Rachael. She had been over the moon when she heard she was to have a traditional elephant ride but she did not know that Ian had also booked an extra treat for her: an elephant bathing and washing activity. She would help make sure her elephant had a proper bath and a thorough wash in the river, which meant she would be able to climb onto its back, pose and ride it up and down in the shallows. There were going to be a lot of laughs and shrieks and Ian just knew Rachael would be soaked as well as her elephant and would glory in every minute! He would certainly have his camera ready; there would be some memorable photos to treasure.

DAY 4 – OCTOBER 10TH

Rachael and Ian were up and dressed quite early: Rachael was buzzing with excitement. Ian checked their rucksack and added bottles of sterilised water to the snacks already packed. They had decided the previous evening that they would not have any breakfast because they did not know just how bumpy the bus ride may be and they did not want to be sick. Ian had already settled the bill when he took their spare rucksack for storage so soon they were leaving the Hotel Pomelo House and heading to the office of the Rainbow Travel Agency.

Just as he had promised, the owner was waiting for them and together they walked through the almost deserted streets of Chetrapati towards their bus on Kantipath.

Although it was too early for the streets to be bustling with people, they were certainly full of dogs happily tackling bowls of food and other treats that had been put out for them. Bizarrely, they all had garlands of marigolds around their necks! Rachael and Ian were puzzled until their companion explained it was 'Dogs Gift Day': the day every year during Dashain when Nepali people reward their dogs for their faithful companionship and protection. Rachael thought that was a wonderful custom!

When they reached their bus, it was ready for departure so Ian and Rachael climbed aboard and settled down in their reserved seats over one of the back wheels. Apparently this is by far the most comfortable place to be, as you are not thrown about as much as you would be in other seats – especially those right at the back of the bus. All the locals try to avoid sitting on the back seats of buses as it is just a long elevated bench – there is nothing you can grab or brace yourself against. Inevitably, as the bus swerves round the numerous corners and jumps over bumps and stones in the road, you are thrown around and shaken. Many backseat passengers are sick. In addition, (I can confirm, from several hair-raising experiences), if you sit next to the open windows, because you are higher up, it is just like sitting in an open doorway; each time the bus swerves, you are in danger of being catapulted out the window!

They left Kathmandu and headed westwards initially on the scenic Pritivi Highway through the outskirts of the city where the Nepalese people were beginning another day of Dashain celebrations. Further on, the road narrowed a little and turned to the southwest as it approached a mountainous area. Before long, it started descending towards the lowlands of the Terai where Chitwan National Park is situated. Gradually it became increasingly rough with frequent potholes and sharp bends but this did not concern Rachael who was completely engrossed in the scenery and the scattering of village houses.

Further on, the road narrowed even more and began to descend steeply in switchback bends. Rock falls and streams raced across the road and, to their right, lay a huge drop to the valley below. They were on a cliff edge. In Nepal, as many nervous travellers will confirm, few of these roads have any safety barriers so your heart is in your mouth constantly!

Although Rachael and Ian were sitting on the side of the bus away from the cliff edge, they could see ahead down the ravine and realised with astonishment that the bottom was littered with smashed buses, lorries, cars and many other forms of transport. It was like a huge breaker's yard! I'm sure all the passengers in the bus were grateful to have a very skilled driver but some of the tourists looked terrified and several had their hands covering their eyes! (I know I would have done the same.) However, Rachael and Ian found it exhilarating: they thought it was like riding a gigantic, hazardous rollercoaster. It was terrific! That mad pair clearly like being challenged. When Ian told me later that he had 'absolutely loved it' – it had been one of the best journeys of his life, I told him he was crazy!

At last the terrain became flatter and the road not quite as terrifying or bumpy but then the engine of the bus started to sound really unhealthy and finally ground to a halt. Although they were near a small village, there did not seem be any repair facilities in this part of the Terai. As Rachael wrote later in her journal, *After three hours we broke down in the middle of nowhere!'* They all climbed out of the bus and went to sit in the shade of some roadside trees. The bus driver tried repeatedly to restart the engine but had no success. One of the passengers, an American gentleman named Matt, tried to help the driver by explaining that the engine had probably overheated and all he needed to do was to let it cool down. Matt kept begging him not to keep trying to restart the engine as all he was doing was flooding it with petrol. However Matt did not speak Nepali and the driver did not understand English so little progress was made. Sadly there was a complete breakdown of communication, which was frustrating for both of them.

The driver took out his phone and started to talk loudly and excitedly, presumably arranging for another bus to come and pick up the passengers. Eventually with many gestures, he managed to make the group understand that another bus was coming. It was quite pleasant in the shade so no one complained but just accepted that this was typical of bus journeys in Nepal; each one was an adventure of some sort!

Fortunately it wasn't too long before a replacement bus appeared. The drivers and passengers took all the luggage off the roof of the broken-down bus and reloaded it onto their new bus, where the drivers tied it down securely to the roof racks.

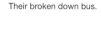

Their broken down bus.

This all took some time so everyone cheered when at last all the passengers and their luggage were safely aboard their new transport. Before they actually departed, the driver tried to start the engine of the old bus and, guess what … yes, it fired-up immediately! Matt had been right – clever man.

Their journey now was through a shady, lush, sub-tropical forest of broadleaf trees interspersed with numerous stands of sal: a kind of Indian teakwood tree. Grey downy balsam hung down from many of the trees making them look as though they were bearded, and lots of colourful creepers wound around their trunks. The dense undergrowth of bushes, shrubs and grasses undoubtedly offered shelter and was home to a great variety of animals but sadly, none could be seen from the bus.

Eventually the road was surrounded on both sides by enormously tall elephant grass and although Rachael could see movements within it, she was disappointed not to see any animals. Ian assured her that when they reached their destination, she would be able to see lots and lots of wildlife.

After four hours or so they arrived at their wonderful hotel – The Rainbow Safari Resort in the tourist town of Sauraha in Chitwan National Park. They were both astonished – they had not expected such luxury in the middle of a jungle. It was unbelievable! Originally built in 1999, the resort has been extended several times and completely renovated in 2011. Now there were twenty-four spacious rooms, each with an en suite and containing a double and a single bed. They were all beautifully furnished and decorated with painted panels depicting Nepalese

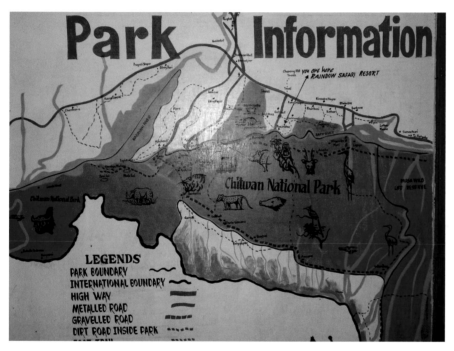

people and activities. Over the beds hung mosquito nets and there were lots of other amenities including fans, air conditioning and laundry services. Wide shady balconies surrounded each storey of the hotel and the whole complex was set in magnificent gardens full of an amazing range of trees, shrubs and brilliant flowers. It was a true jungle haven.

Ian and Rachael were delighted to find that their room was actually one of the new chalets built around the garden: their own little house! Once inside, Rachael quickly chose the double bed leaving Ian with the single but even that was a generous size and very comfortable. He rested on the bed while Rachael went for a welcome shower. Almost immediately, wrapped in a large fluffy towel, she poked her head round the bathroom door.

'Wow, Dad! This bathroom is fab and the towels are so soft and lovely. And look what I found: amazing bathroom slippers and there's some for you too!'

'That's good,' replied Ian, 'but please don't be too long because I need a shower too and I think we should go and explore a bit before we have dinner.'

'I promise I'll be quick, don't worry, Dad,' she replied and true to her word, less than five minutes later, she emerged wrapped up like a woolly white cocoon with a bright, shining, rather red face. Obviously the water was hot and continuous, just as the hotel brochure had promised, so Ian indulged in a long hot shower to ease his back, which although not painful had become rather stiff.

The only disappointment for Rachael was that WiFi was not available in their room – only downstairs in the main hotel building. Like all girls her age, she did

Chilling at Chitwan.

love her iPad! Ian reminded her somewhat caustically that they were in the middle of a jungle – what did she expect? It was a miracle that they had WiFi anywhere. They were on a safari to enjoy the scenery and the wildlife; iPads were for city life. Rachael smiled happily.

'Of course – you're right, Dad. I'm being silly! Come on, let's go for a walk.'

Immediately in front of the hotel gates was the National Park Office where visitors not part of an organised safari could purchase their obligatory tickets. In Chitwan, as in all Nepal's National Parks, safaris and treks are not allowed without a pass. Formerly Royal Chitwan National Park, in 1973 it became Nepal's first national park and was granted World Heritage Site status in 1984, dedicated to the preservation and conservation of all wildlife and their habitats. From the 19th century, it was used as a favourite hunting ground for Nepal's ruling classes during the cooler seasons. Comfortable camps were set up for wealthy, feudal big-game hunters and their entourage. They would stay for a couple of months, shooting hundreds of tigers, rhinoceros, leopards and sloth bears. Yet in spite of this, there were still around 800 rhinoceros in 1950.

When the poor Nepali hill farmers moved into the Chitwan Valley in search of arable land, the area subsequently became open for settlement. This was when the widespread poaching of wildlife became rampant, particularly that of rhino, whose horns fetched colossal prices on the Far Eastern market. There, it is still highly prized for its supposedly valuable medical properties and enhancement of sexual prowess.

By the end of the 1960s, only ninety-five rhinos were left. The Nepalese Government realised that something had to be done to prevent the rhino and other species from being hunted and poached to extinction, hence the birth of the Chitwan National Park. The Gaida Gasti, a government reconnaissance patrol of 130 armed men, was established and guard posts were built all over Chitwan. Due to their vigilance, the numbers of all species have risen remarkably, and now Chitwan boasts the largest population of the Indian one-horned rhinoceros in Nepal, estimated at 605 individuals out of 645 in the whole country. It has become one of Nepal's most popular tourist destinations with up to 100,000 visitors every year.

Sauraha, where Rachael and Ian stayed, is well known as the prime spot for safari package tourists and offers a choice of hundreds of hotels, lodges, restaurants and agencies. However, scattered throughout the park are village homes offering accommodation, budget guesthouses and several jungle lodges. Chitwan National Park is thriving: it not only provides fantastic experiences for tourists but invaluable employment for many Nepalese.

As soon as Rachael and Ian left the beautiful hotel garden behind, they saw a group of elephants of various sizes and paused to watch them. Rachael was enthralled; she had never seen elephants in the wild before. Clearly these elephants were pretty tame as they ignored all the visitors and carried on eating. Then Rachael and Ian walked down towards the river and to their surprise found that near the bank was a super

bar stocked with all kinds of drinks. Three of the people who had been on their bus beckoned them over and reminded our adventurous pair that the first drink was a welcome one and free. Great! After Ian had chosen a beer and Rachael a Coke, they introduced themselves and found the older lady was called Sally and her daughter Lucy was with her partner, Wayne. They chatted about their experiences in Nepal, and were amazed when they discovered just how much walking, trekking and touring Rachael had done with her dad and what was planned for the present trip. They were full of admiration and fervently wished Rachael and Ian every success in their future adventures together.

Gradually a wonderful fiery orange and deep-red glow illuminated the cloudless sky above them as the glorious sun began to set. The reflections in the river were fabulous: the darkening colours seemed to chase each other across its rippling surface. It was so beautiful they wished they could stay a little longer but it was time for dinner. Suddenly they all realised they were very hungry.

They walked back together to the large indoor dining room where a long table was set up with sparkling glasses, shining cutlery and immaculate table linen: an attractive candlelit setting. The five of them sat at one end of the table and waited for the other three members of their group. (Each safari group is usually made up of twelve people as that is the number of seats in the safari jeeps but Ian and Rachael's group only numbered eight.)

As soon as the group was complete, the leading guide introduced himself and requested they do the same, one by one, saying where they had come from. Sally, Lucy and Wayne, whom Rachael and Ian had already met, were from Stanthorpe, Queensland, Australia; Matthew (the mechanical expert) was from the USA and Jill and Kim were from Canada. And so their small group consisted of people from four different countries – fantastic!

The guide then briefly outlined their activities for the next day's safari and wished them good luck. He explained that even with their expertly planned programme, luck played a huge part in just how many varieties of animals they might see:

'People can be programmed but animals can't!'

The meal that evening was superb – completely beyond what Ian had expected in 'the middle of a jungle' in terms of both variety and quality. As Rachael recorded in her journal, 'The veggie-burgers I chose for dinner were the best I have ever had – they were absolutely fab!'

The hotel website had stated that the menu was comprehensive:

'We have a multi-cuisine restaurant which offers à la carte and buffet options to its guests and we serve only organic vegetables.'

In fact, the website had completely undersold the superiority of their food. The portions were very generous, beautifully plated and served with friendly efficiency. A warm friendly atmosphere pervaded, helped by the wide range of drinks available for all the guests. There was much laughter, joking and happy expectation: the whole gang seemed to gel very well, which delighted Ian as he had wanted Rachael to enjoy the experience of exploring new activities with different companions in a larger multi-national group. As they strolled back to their lovely chalet, Ian and Rachael chatted happily about their tiring, unusual but totally exhilarating day: Up at six in the morning, a hair-raising rollercoaster of a bus ride, a breakdown, a Nepalese luxury hotel and a fantastic dinner with drinks in the middle of a jungle! What would happen tomorrow? They couldn't wait to find out!

DAY 5 – OCTOBER 11TH

The next morning was bright and sunny, ideal for a two-hour bird-walking safari. However the leading ranger asked Ian to change his red T-shirt for one in a more muted colour, as in the jungle the colour red apparently encourages insects and animals to attack! With Ian appropriately dressed, our group of eight adventurers set off at a steady pace through the lush jungle, which teemed with birdlife of every kind. They were surrounded by a cacophony of birdsong and calls: a true surround-sound experience. The brilliantly coloured parakeets were especially noisy and squawked incessantly but they were only part of the orchestra of melodious singing, warbling, whistling and chirping interrupted by intermittent screeches, piercing calls and the tap-tapping of woodpeckers.

As you may imagine, Chitwan National Park is host every year to numerous dedicated birdwatchers and conservationists, as it is recorded to have at least 543 different species and about two thirds of Nepal's globally threatened creatures – much more than any other protected area in Nepal. Before coming to the park, Ian had done a lot of research about Chitwan fauna so he and Rachael were able to identify quite a lot of the birds including flycatchers, warblers, pheasants, horn-bills and woodpeckers. Peafowl and jungle fowl were scratching their living on the forest floor among the grasses and leaf litter. The two Nepalese guides were very knowledgeable and directed the group's gaze to rare species like a pair of stunning sunbirds and a male paradise flycatcher. Both of these dedicated guides were armed

They saw a real one too …

… but they didn't see one of these!

with four-foot wooden staves supposedly to protect the group from tiger attacks. (Ian fervently hoped any Bengal tigers in Chitwan were genuinely deterred by sticks!)

In wetter areas, especially around the lakes, there were endless varieties of ducks like Brahminy and goosanders, while egrets, stately storks and beautiful white-throated kingfishers patiently watched for movements in the water below them that signified a dining opportunity.

Although it was mainly a bird-watching safari walk, to their joy Rachael and Ian spotted a one-horned rhinoceros in the distance, quite a few different types of deer like sambar and red muntjac and inevitably lots of monkeys that chattered noisily in the trees above them.

Before they reached the river, the guides pointed out two species of fearsome-looking crocodiles: apparently one was 'harmless' as it only ate fish but the other was a meat-eater and our intrepid group were just about to embark on a boat ride!

However, the biggest problem by far, was the massive amount of leeches that infested the ground. They were like long worms that reared up, waving their heads backwards and forwards and attaching themselves to any bit of exposed flesh. Not only did they crawl into shoes and boots and up the walkers' legs but they dropped from trees onto their arms and backs. Poor Rachael was bitten four times!

'Urgh! Dad! These leeches are disgusting!' she cried.

The guides just laughed cheerily and plucked the leeches off everyone's skin with their fingers. Unfortunately the leeches inject their hosts with a substance that inhibits blood clotting, so our walkers had some small bleeding wounds for a while: not a pleasant experience but a normal jungle one.

It was a welcome escape from those bloodsucking pests when, at last, they found their boat waiting by the riverbank. It was made from a long hollowed-out tree trunk so they all had to sit one behind the other. Worryingly, the boat seemed to float quite near to the surface of the river especially when they had all climbed in. The guides skilfully poled the boat away from the bank and soon they were moving silently downstream with the current. As Rachael recorded later in her journal, *'We went for a boat ride in a hollow tree trunk on a crocodile- and rhino-infested river! We were only just above the water and we saw lots of rhino in the shallows near the banks of the river, four man-eating crocodiles and one fish-eating one! It was a bit scary but exciting!'*

Ian told me that it was a wonderfully peaceful journey of around an hour. The sun was shining down from a cloudless blue sky, gleaming off the surface of the rippling water in a myriad of sparkling rays and tiny shafts of light. Everyone seemed mesmerised; they looked left and right but did not speak. There was no sound except the gentle lapping of the water and the faint caressing breeze off the river; it was entrancing and serene.

As they neared the place they were to disembark, a Chinese gentleman in a similar boat behind them broke that tranquillity by answering his phone, which had an annoyingly loud ringtone. Our gang were very pleased that incident had not happened in their boat: phones and chatting seemed to be completely out of place in this natural primitive setting.

Both boatloads of people then joined together as one group and set off to walk for approximately two hours back to the Rainbow Safari Resort Hotel for lunch. The guides explained that uniting the groups was necessary for their safety against tiger or rhino attacks, although many of the walkers were sceptical. The tree-trunk boats had to be poled back to the starting point by only one poor Nepali boatman per boat; this must have been very difficult as the men would be poling against the current!

The feared tiger/rhino attacks never happened, just as our walkers had thought. In fact the only creatures they saw were several varieties of deer, a few hares and those endless blood-sucking leeches. The group was also pursued by clouds of biting mosquitoes – many walkers in the group were quite severely bitten. Ian was very pleased that he was wearing long trousers but poor Rachael was wearing shorts.

Before she had set out on the jungle safari, like Ian, she had put lots of insect-repellent on her face and arms but obviously had not put enough on her legs because she sustained some very angry, itchy bites all over her lower legs.

Eventually they arrived back at their lovely hotel where a splendid lunch was set up for them in the dining room. There was a fabulous outside eating area underneath the large shady veranda but as it was open to the invading mosquitoes, everyone wisely opted to eat inside.

While they were eating, Ian told Rachael about the extra surprise he had booked for her the next day: an elephant bathing and washing activity. She was absolutely ecstatic and gave him a huge hug.

'I do so hope that we can stay that extra day, Dad!' She said anxiously.

Ian promised that as soon as they returned from the elephant safari, he would check and book an extra day because at the moment reception was closed.

'I'll keep my fingers crossed then,' she replied quickly.

After an hour or so, it was time for the much-anticipated group elephant safari. As always, there would be four people on each elephant sitting on a howdah. This is a kind of platform suspended across the elephant's back with a handrail that you can grasp as the ride is very bumpy. One person sits at each corner for balance, with their legs hanging down the elephant's sides. The mahout, who controls the elephant, sits on its neck just behind its ears and guides it with his voice and with the pressure of his legs. Although it is a marvellous experience which Ian would have loved, sensibly he decided not join in because he was aware that such a ride

could be potentially injurious to his recently broken back. He and Rachael still had lots of wonderful adventures and experiences planned for this trip so he could not risk any accidents at such an early stage of their explorations. He explained all this to Rachael who understood completely. Although she would have loved her dad to be with her, she had been concerned that he could be hurt. Ian promised he would walk with her to the edge of the jungle where the elephant safari began and wait there for her to return. He added that he was sure she would be fine as she would be sitting on the howdah with Sally, Lucy and Wayne.

They walked to the area at the edge of the jungle where the elephants with their mahouts were waiting. Astonishingly there were about forty immensely strong-looking elephants gathered together, each with its colourful howdah on its back ready for our intrepid riders. Ian watched Rachael climb nimbly up the ladder to join Wayne, Lucy and Sally and with a gentle command and pressure from his legs, their mahout urged the elephant forwards. Ian waited until they had disappeared into the jungle before he went to join the group of Nepalese guides playing cards in a large shelter. He spent a very pleasant, friendly hour relaxing and watching them play. Wisely he did not join in as he assumed he would likely be the one to lose! However he accepted a beer and thoroughly enjoyed the laughing and joking antics that accompanied the card game.

Afterwards he went for a short exploratory walk through a small local village. He was amazed to see that all the houses, no matter what size they were, had compounds and facilities for keeping at least one elephant. Each one was full of food, elephant dung and restraining chains and every compound was surrounded by a high elephant-proof fence. These were necessary, one of the mahouts explained, to keep out the testosterone-fuelled wild bull elephants that roamed the park and tried to get access to any of the village female elephants. He added with a smile, that occasionally these female elephants (when in season) were overcome by the urge to procreate and tried to break out to 'visit' wild elephants in the vicinity!

Ian made his way back to the start of the elephant safari and it wasn't long before Rachael and her three companions, perched somewhat precariously on the back of their elephant, emerged from the jungle. Rachael climbed down rather slowly rubbing her bottom and legs but her face was glowing with delight.

'That was so cool, Dad!' she exclaimed. 'It was fantastic but very, *very* jolty. My back, legs and bottom are really sore but it was worth every bump and bruise!'

Ian had obviously made a wise decision not to accompany her. She then proceeded to tell him about all the highlights of her exciting elephant safari:

'We crossed two big rivers and saw lots of crocodiles and rhinos. In the jungle we saw loads of deer and monkeys that grumbled at us and threw things and birds were flying around us all the time and those awful mosquitoes had me for lunch – my bites really hurt! I was a bit scared when our elephant got too near another one, which turned round and was about to charge us. Luckily our mahout knew what to do: he took action, stopped her and drove her away. He was great! I really, really loved every minute, Dad! Thank you so much!'

She was so exhilarated that she seemed to be bursting with joy.

'What on earth will she think of the elephant bathing and washing tomorrow?' Ian wondered.

Before they left this group of elephants, Rachael reached up to pat the trunk of their particular elephant. It quickly wound its trunk affectionately around her arm and squeezed it. Going by the expression on Rachael's face, this must have been a little painful. Then it sneezed violently and deposited a huge glob of snot on her arm.

'Urrgh! That is totally gross!' Rachael cried, holding up her arm in disgust, but when everyone in the group laughed and giggled out loud, she soon joined in. Nothing ever upsets Rachael for long. Luckily Ian had some wet wipes and tissues in his rucksack so he cleaned her up quickly.

They all sauntered back to the hotel and while Rachael had a very welcome and very necessary hot shower, Ian went into the main hotel. He wanted to book that extra night so they could visit the local village, take part in a jeep safari and, more importantly, Rachael could have that entertaining and exciting treat: the elephant bath in the river. Happily he soon discovered this was possible providing they were willing to move into another room within the main hotel – their chalet had already been booked. This was no problem and would completely satisfy Rachael so he readily agreed.

When he returned to their chalet, Rachael was already out of the shower, her newly shampooed hair shone like gold and her face glowed. When Ian told her that he had managed to book the extra night and explained that they had to move into the main building, she squealed with delight.

'That's no problem, Dad! I'll help you to move our gear. We'll be fine!'

Ian had to smile: Rachael was adopting a lot of his expressions and making them her own. He was so proud of his jubilant and indefatigable daughter.

Rachael even managed to have her favourite Nepali meal at dinner – tasty dhal bhat, fluffy white rice and fresh fried vegetables. Over dinner when they were all discussing their exciting day, she made an announcement to their group:

'Dad and I are staying another night so we can have a jeep safari and I can have my special treat: an elephant wash and bath in the river that Dad has booked for me. Aren't I lucky?'

She was really pleased to find that the remainder of the group were staying an extra night too so they would be able to do the jeep safari together.

After dinner, they all walked to the nearby village where a cultural evening display of singing and dancing had been organised for the tourists. Although it was pleasant, it lacked the grace, beauty and artistry that had delighted Ian and Rachael at the Fewa Lake Restaurant in Pokhara. Also tourists were not invited to join in, which was disappointing. However the dancer dressed up in a heavy peacock costume was fantastic: very expressive and agile. In fact, Rachael wrote in her journal later that night: *The dancing wasn't as good as Pokhara and I wasn't allowed to join in. But that man in the peacock costume was fab. He deserves a medal!'*

Ian and Rachael stayed until most of the performance was over and then made their way back to their chalet. By now Rachael's mosquito bites were quite angry so Ian knew that the next morning they would need to find a pharmacy. Luckily she was really tired so she dropped off to sleep reasonably easily but not before she had murmured with a yawn, 'I have had a fab day Dad and I can't wait for tomorrow and that elephant bath!'

Ian couldn't either: there would be some more memorable photos to take that they could cherish forever.

DAY 6 – OCTOBER 12TH

Next morning, as soon as breakfast was over, Ian and Rachael moved their gear into their new room in the main hotel. It was very nicely decorated, beautifully clean and had a well-equipped bathroom just like their chalet room. Again there was a double bed and a single one, both with mosquito nets and I bet you can guess which bed Rachael bagged! Then, because her bites still looked very angry and were really itchy, she and Ian walked to the local village pharmacy to buy some medication that they hoped would relieve her symptoms. The pharmacist recommended some cream that proved to be very effective.

Just opposite the pharmacy, Rachael noticed a rather attractive-looking village clothes shop: it had real glass windows and displayed a wide range of goods. After asking Ian's permission, she went in on her own to have a look around. She soon emerged and described to Ian a dress that she would love to try on. It was a long dress made of cool T-shirt material and had grey and light brown prints of different elephants on a white background. Ian told her to go and try it on and, if it fitted perfectly, he would buy if for her as a memento of their Chitwan Safari. Rachael was overjoyed but asked that, if the dress fitted, could she negotiate the deal herself? She did just that and in no time at all, she rushed out of that shop proudly clutching a bag containing her souvenir dress. It had cost the equivalent of £8!

'I'm getting really good at bartering, aren't I, Dad?' she asked.

Indeed she was!

When they returned, the remainder of their group were still in the hotel having enjoyed a relaxing, prolonged breakfast. So after Rachael had taken her present upstairs to their room, put some more healing cream on her bites and added a plenty of mosquito repellent, they all headed towards the area of the river where the elephant bathing took place. It was only about a ten-minute walk. Matt had also booked an elephant bath and wash but the other members of the gang were just going along to observe all the antics and hopefully take some amusing photos.

Soon they could hear the excited shouts of tourists already having lots of fun. A group of elephants was standing waiting patiently in the shallows. One of the mahouts beckoned Rachael and helped her to climb up on a medium-sized female. She waved excitedly to Ian who, of course, had his camera ready to take lots of photos. Matt said he would wait until Rachael's session was over so he could take a video of everything that happened on her phone. What a kind young man! Even for the tourists watching from the riverbank, seeing the elephants and people playing together just like a group of oversized children, it was a happy and unforgettable experience. There were hoots of laughter at the ridiculous antics and cameras were constantly clicking!

Rachael's elephant bent its head down and filled up its trunk with water, lifted it up and squirted it all over her; an elephant shower – magic! She squealed with happiness, which only encouraged her elephant to repeat the process. What a treat! Rachael was completely soaked but elated – her face and hair were streaming with water and not one single piece of clothing was dry! Her mahout guided them

further into the river where her elephant could partially immerse itself and have a proper bath and then they rode up and down in the river shallows. When they were a little deeper, at a signal, Rachael's elephant tipped her off its back into the river and she had to swim to the shore. Bubbling with laughter, she rushed to Ian with arms outstretched and he enveloped her in the huge towel he had taken from his rucksack. She was blissfully happy; soaking, grubby, bruised and bitten to death – she just radiated a total joy of life. Ian had tears in his eyes.

After watching Matt's escapades, the group made their way back to the hotel for lunch. Rachael skipped with delight most of the way. At least two of the gang badly needed a hot shower and some clean, dry clothes before they could eat.

After lunch, they all climbed into their safari jeep that was parked outside the hotel, eager to see how many more creatures they could spot on their tour. This time Rachael was wearing some sensible long trekking trousers and a long-sleeved T-shirt. In spite of using liberal amounts of soothing cream and layers of insect repellent, she was not going to give those bloodthirsty mosquitoes the chance to have her for dinner again!

As the jungle track taken by the jeeps was a different one from the elephant safari, they hoped that perhaps they might catch a glimpse of an elusive Bengal tiger and perhaps closer views of the one-horned rhinos

from the relative safety of the jeep. Like Ian, they all knew that civets, Bengal foxes and honey badgers were supposed to be plentiful and that leopards could occasionally be seen too. Also Chitwan was reputed to have the highest population density of sloth bears at over two hundred individuals. For around an hour they drove slowly on a variety of muddy, bumpy dirt tracks deeper into the jungle with everyone watching intently for signs of animal life on either side of the track. Did they see lots of animals? No! They had no success whatsoever! Except for one very brief sighting of a spotted eagle, even the birds seemed to have flown away. Perhaps they were disturbed by the noise of the jeep's engine. The only slight excitement on the whole of the outward drive was when the jeep got stuck twice. The inexpert endeavours of the driver and guide as they tried to extract the jeep from two deep, squelchy holes were highly amusing!

Before making the return drive, they climbed out of the jeep to stretch their legs. There was a scream from one of the ladies as she pointed to a large spider flexing its legs as it sat in the bottom of the jeep! As you may imagine, it brought back memories of that persistent spider at Ghandruk to both Ian and Rachael so neither of them volunteered to remove it! The jeep driver scooped it up and deposited it unceremoniously in the undergrowth: excitement over. Ian speculated that it must have been hidden in the jeep all the time as it could not have climbed up while

the jeep was moving and it certainly hadn't dropped down on anyone. They had been riding with a stowaway!

The return journey was equally unrewarding, enlightened only by the combined determination of the group to enjoy themselves by telling jokes that grew progressively worse. Ian's contribution made Rachael cringe and earned him that special disparaging look all parents recognise when they have done or said something embarrassing. He had adopted a totally innocent expression:

'You know, Rachael, I reckon that spider in the jeep is the same one you were scared of in Ghandruk. I bet it's been hiding in your rucksack all this time!'

Everyone, except Rachael of course, had laughed! When they eventually reached the hotel, they all headed for the bar as they agreed they had earned a drink. They had endured a long, hot and very uncomfortable jeep safari and all they had seen was one bird and a spider that had probably hitched a ride with them for half of the tour. What a disaster! They all laughed uproariously and agreed to meet for dinner.

As soon as Ian and Rachael were back in their room, she asked Ian in a very concerned tone, 'Are you okay, Dad? We were thrown about a lot in that jeep, especially when we went over those huge bumps. I'm worried that you may have injured your back.'

Ian assured her that he was fine and, naturally, asked her if she was all right.

'Not really, Dad!' She replied. 'All that shaking has made my tinnitus much worse.'

Rachael has always had slight problems with her hearing in her right ear. In certain circumstances, the ringing grows much worse for a while. When he asked her how much she could hear on a scale of one to ten, she replied sadly, 'only about three at the moment but I'm sure it will get better soon.'

She is not a girl who complains about little problems and is always optimistic.

They both showered and changed for dinner: Rachael decided to wear her lovely, newly acquired elephant-print dress. Everyone in their group really admired it and said she looked stunning and so she did. A superb meal had been prepared and the friendly, expert service and wide range of drinks added to the wonderful ambience of that lovely hotel. It was a great way to end their safari adventure. The splendid, convivial evening just sped by as they all relaxed and chatted about their adventures, their highlights, minor and major 'disasters' and how lucky they all were to have been so compatible. That, they all agreed, was what had made the whole safari so enjoyable and memorable – not just the activities but the warm companionship and understanding. Rachael was thrilled with the video Matt had made of her and the elephant during that exciting elephant bath and Ian promised everyone he would download it on her website when they arrived home.

Inevitably they discussed what everyone was going to do the following day; only Ian and Rachael were going on to Pokhara by local bus – the other six were travelling back to Kathmandu by tourist bus. There were many wishes expressed for safe journeys, and joyful hugs as they reluctantly parted.

'I'm really sad that, after breakfast tomorrow morning, I won't see them again,'

Rachael told Ian with a mournful expression, but then she cheered up.

'But I am really, *really* looking forward to our rollercoaster ride on that bus to Pokhara tomorrow. Aren't you?'

Ian agreed and gave her a hug.

DAY 7 – OCTOBER 13TH

Rachael and Ian were up next morning by 6 a.m. because the jeep that was taking them all to the bus station was booked for 7 a.m. They went to have breakfast with their group but were surprised to see Sally, Lucy and Wayne sitting on a smaller table away from the main one. Strange. Ian wondered if somehow they had been offended by something that had been said on the previous evening so he went over to Sally to ask what was wrong. She seemed very quiet and just said that it was better if she did not join them. How puzzling! However, a few moments later, Lucy came to the main table and explained to Ian that her mum, Sally, had been ill all night having picked up some sort of bug and did not want to pass it on to anyone in the group. She gave Ian Sally's email address and said that her mum wanted Rachael and Ian to keep in touch. They promised that they would email her when they were back at Old Water View.

It was about half an hour's drive to the bus station. The six people going to Kathmandu were taken quickly to the line of tourist buses and shown which one had been booked for them. They waved goodbye to Rachael and Ian and climbed on board. Our adventurous pair just sat in the shade and relaxed, watching all the tourists and locals loading the luggage, and listening to all the loud instructions and disagreements in Nepali: it was chaos but very amusing.

It was around 9 a.m. before all the tourist buses had departed and the rickety local bus that was Ian and Rachael's drew up. Luggage was securely fastened on the roof and sacks of what looked like vegetables were deposited on the floor of the bus. Only a few locals boarded initially so Ian and Rachael were able to choose the more comfortable seats over the back wheels. However, this time, knowing that they were

travelling back up the same steep mountain road that they had descended on the way to Chitwan, they deliberately chose to sit on the side of the bus that would be hanging over that cliff edge. Mad fools! They would be looking down that deep ravine directly at the 'breaker's yard' below! Ominously, as before, the driver gave every passenger who got on the bus a sick bag!

In spite of all this, Rachael and Ian could hardly wait to start their rollercoaster ride and absolutely loved it when the bus careered around all the switchbacks. Although the bus had certainly seen better days, the driver was very skilful and manoeuvred his way round the stones, rocks, streams and deposits of mud like a professional rally driver. About halfway up that mountain dirt road, they had to stop for around one and a half hours as the road was blocked by a crash and one car had been catapulted down the mountainside into the ravine. As soon as the road was clear, they carried on. No one seemed to be particularly upset probably because they knew this happened quite frequently on this stretch of cliff edge and miraculously people often survived.

The bus had to stop frequently for locals to get on; it was almost the end of Dashain so they were all returning to work in Pokhara. Most of the stops were quite lengthy as the locals had lots of luggage and sacks of possessions and vegetables that needed to be distributed inside the bus or lifted up onto the roof and tied securely. At one stop, a passenger brought a wicker basket full of chickens into the bus and at another it took ages for several locals to find a way of hoisting a motorbike up onto the roof … and then they had the problem of making sure it didn't fall off! Everyone seemed to have a different opinion of how this should be done resulting in absolute chaos. Rachael and Ian thoroughly enjoyed watching them; it was really entertaining and interesting. They had wanted so badly to share the experience of riding on a local bus with local people and found it exhilarating.

One memorable episode occurred when a young Nepali boy, around three years old, and his mum sat in the seats across the aisle from Ian and Rachael. It wasn't long before the boy began to look very white and started heaving. Obviously the rolling, bumpy motion of the bus was making him feel sick. Poor little lad! He was violently sick, filling his sick bag and most of his mum's! Ever the knight in shining armour Ian leaned across the aisle and gave the boy his hat as a much needed extra receptacle. Bless him, the little boy was sick in that too! Ian passed some tissues to his mum and soon the little lad was cleaned up and more comfortable. His mum thanked Ian profusely in very good English so they all chatted during the journey with Ian amusing her son with some of his jokes and tricks.

Eventually, tired, dusty and very grubby, they arrived at Pokhara. As soon as they stepped out of the bus and retrieved their luggage, Ian and Rachael were surrounded by taxi drivers offering their services.

'I take you to Hotel Tulsi. Too far to walk!'

What they did not realise, of course, was that Ian and Rachael were not normal tourists. They knew Pokhara almost as well as the taxi drivers! The Hotel Tulsi was only a twenty-minute walk from the bus station so they politely refused a lift and set off at a brisk pace. Before long they were installed in a comfortable twin-bedded room and Rachael, as always, had bagged the first shower.

By now they were both very hungry, so as soon as Ian had showered and changed, they went to a lovely vegetarian restaurant on the main road that Rachael chose: The Lemon Tree. She was very disappointed to find that the lovely co-operative shop where she had bought those fantastic handbags had closed down. She had been looking forward to meeting the friendly ladies there and bartering for some presents and souvenirs. They took their time over the meal and just enjoyed watching the world go by. They had earned a quiet time of relaxation after their exhilarating but tiring bus ride from Chitwan; that had been some experience and a tick off on Ian's bucket list!

They strolled around for a while but then wended their way back to the Hotel Tulsi for a welcome rest as they had been up since 6 a.m. They were both buzzing so it was a time for reminiscing rather than snoozing. They had lots of wonderful memories to share.

Later on they walked down to Rachael's favourite eating place in the whole of Nepal: the Fewa Paradise Restaurant. Originally The Rum Doodle had held that accolade, however, it had suffered extensive damage in the earthquake and had closed. There was the usual lovely, haunting Nepali music and a display of highly artistic dancing but, for once, Rachael was too exhausted to join in and she and Ian just chatted about their amazing experiences to date and what they were hoping to do in the next few weeks. Ian smiled as he told her he had another treat planned for her while they were in Pokhara. It *was* a surprise, he said, so he wasn't going to tell her what it was – not that evening anyway.

'Really, Dad!' Rachael protested. 'As Grandma Joyce always says, it's a good job I love you because you love teasing me and making me wait and wonder!'

Ian just looked very smug and smiled enigmatically. Rachael was not going to find out yet and neither are you, dear readers. You will have to read on to find out!

A rickety eight-hour bus ride.

DAY 8 – OCTOBER 14TH

At breakfast the following morning, Ian remarked with a knowing smile that it was a beautiful morning: a clear blue sky and bright sunshine.

'Ideal weather, Rachael,' he added, 'for paragliding.'

She was absolutely speechless. Ian went on to explain that while she was playing on her iPad the previous evening and he had gone for a little stroll, he had actually gone into Sunrise Paragliding in Lakeside and booked a one-hour tandem paragliding flight for her. He had also arranged for a video to be made of it so she did not have to worry about taking her camera. Rachael squealed and flung her arms around Ian.

'Oh Dad! Thank you – thank you! I am so lucky to have you for my dad! When exactly is it?'

Ian replied that they had to be at the Sunshine Paragliding Agency by 10 a.m. because her flight was booked for eleven o'clock and she would be taken in a 4WD jeep up to Sangarkot on a mountainside high above the Pokhara Valley. He made sure that she understood he would not be able to go up to Sangarkot as lots of paragliding flights had been booked that morning and there wouldn't be any room for him in the jeep. Instead he planned to walk to the landing zone at the western end of Fewa Lake and wait for her there.

'Rachael, are you really sure that you will be okay on your own?' he asked.

After all, his brave daughter was only twelve years old. She just gave him a hug and smiled.

'Of course I will Dad. I'll be fine. I am so up for another exciting adventure!'

Apparently, the government of Nepal has no system in place for regulating paragliding. Out of over a hundred Nepali paragliding pilots in Nepal, not a single one holds a paragliding licence because there isn't one! However, all pilots have to be internationally certified which means they have undergone training and passed. This means that they are certified to fly anywhere in the world on their own. It takes an additional two years of experience before they can become a registered tandem paragliding pilot. During this period they have to prove their competence by paragliding successfully in many different locations and weather conditions. They must have a thorough understanding of how and when to use their safety reserve parachute. Then they have to pass a tandem exam with an APPI instructor. Nevertheless paragliding is generally safer than crossing the main road in Pokhara and each pilot has a reserve safety parachute and if necessary they can use Fewa Lake as a soft landing area. However paragliding is an extreme sport so there are risks and it is absolutely essential that you employ a well-known and reliable agency. Ian knew all about this and had deliberately chosen Sunrise Paragliding as they were the oldest, well-established family business in Pokhara with an excellent reputation for safety and professionalism. They were also well insured so Ian felt that he had done everything he could to give Rachael a fabulous experience whilst ensuring her safety.

Before they set out to walk to the Sunshine Paragliding Agency, Ian made sure that Rachael was wearing her thickest leggings and had her wind and waterproof

they reached Sangarkot. Rachael was given a pair of safety sunglasses and a blue helmet before she hopped on board the jeep for the thirty-minute drive up the mountainside to the take-off zone. She enthusiastically waved goodbye to Ian and yelled, 'See you soon, Dad!'

Ian felt the same emotions all parents do when they let their children go on an adventure holiday or embark on a difficult challenge. He was so happy to be able to give Rachael this wonderful opportunity, but had a sinking feeling in his chest as he watched his young daughter disappear into the distance. He had fervently hoped he would be able to share the paragliding experience with Rachael but he dare not risk damaging his fragile back. He prayed earnestly for Rachael's wellbeing and safety and was filled with mixed feelings of overwhelming pride, relief and envy. His daughter was a true explorer and an absolute star.

Ignoring the persistent offers of taxi drivers to take him the end of Fewa Lake, Ian made his way to the beginning of the lakeside path and began to walk along the lovely shore. It would take him at least an hour to reach the far western point of the lake: the landing zone for the paragliders. Even then he would probably arrive before Rachael made her final descent.

pink and purple jacket with her. He knew that although the morning was really warm and sunny, it was going to be cold at the high altitudes at which Rachael and her pilot, Robin would be flying. She was so excited; she skipped most of the way with a broad happy grin on her face. It was going to be magic!

When they arrived, the manager told them that Rachael's 11 a.m. flight may be a little delayed as everyone had to wait until the ground was thoroughly heated up and the vital thermals were really active. They would be given their specific flight times once

Meanwhile Rachael was buzzing with elation and grinned so widely that her cheeks ached. During the journey, she sent her mum a text knowing that with the difference in time between Nepal and the UK, her mum would still be in bed.

'I'm just about to jump off a mountain, Mum!'

She could not help teasing her mum who had never understood Rachael's innate thirst for adventure and challenges of every kind.

When they reached Sangarkot, Robin, her pilot, introduced himself and gave Rachael instructions on how to use her hands and feet to help steer the paragliding wing and how she must draw her feet up as they came in to land. He told her not to worry because he would be talking to her all the time and reminding her of the things she should do. He promised that he would point out some of the fantastic features of the landscape as they flew together like a huge bird. Rachael was really pleased that Robin was so cheerful and friendly … and handsome too! He had a moustache and a tiny goatee beard – very cool!

He made sure that she was harnessed securely in the tubular frame of the paraglider, sitting on a sort of black padded bucket seat with strong supports strapped around her chest, shoulders and waist and between her legs. Then he fastened her tightly to his harness and told her that he would be immediately behind her. When they were flying, she would virtually be sitting in his lap and he would have his legs either side of her. He would protect her completely.

'I will not let you fall, Rachael,' he emphasised. 'You are perfectly safe with me. I have done hundreds of these flights, so enjoy yourself!'

She was thrilled to find that their paragliding wing was of a brilliant luminous yellow and noted just how strong all the ribs and padded cables were. Nevertheless it was reassuring to be told that Robin had a safety reserve parachute strapped to his back in case of emergencies. She told Robin that she felt absolutely safe and couldn't wait to take off. Robin told her that they were the second flight so as soon as the first one took off, he would ask her to run as fast as she could and leap off the mountainside. She was more than ready and did exactly as he had told her. Soon they were soaring like an eagle over the verdant hillsides and forests. As they glided, swooped and climbed in the clear azure sky, Robin showed her how to angle her arms and legs to manoeuvre the paraglider; how to bank and swerve. Rachael was ecstatic and completely without fear; she never lost her beaming smile. She was in heaven!

Far below them, the roads and paths wound like yellow and brown snakes through the terraced fields and forests of myriad greens, climbing up and over the rugged foothills of the Himalaya. The rivers and streams glistened in the beautiful sunshine just like silvery threads in a magnificent tapestry of nature. Realising that Rachael was very brave, Robin took them up even higher so she could see the wonderful snow-capped peaks of the high Himalaya. These included most of the Annapurna Range and the magnificent peak of Machhpuchhare, guarding the city of Pokhara and the villages and settlements of the valley. All the buildings and cottages looked like dolls' houses and the gardens, plots, pools and ploughed fields like pieces of a giant jigsaw. Fewa Lake gleamed like a mirror in the sunshine.

They spiralled downwards and sideways and performed lots of tricks. Rachael was enthralled and told Robin that she felt like an eagle soaring and swooping over her territory. Robin told her that had she come about a month later when the eagles and vultures had come down from the high Himalaya, she would have been able to wear a special glove and hold pieces of meat which they would take gently from her hand.

'Wow!' she exclaimed, I would have loved that! Next time, I shall have to come a month later so I can feed the eagles. That would be fab!'

Inevitably, the time came to land. They been gliding for over an hour but the time had flown past swiftly as though on wings. Robin headed towards the western end of Fewa Lake and guided the paraglider downwards.

'Shall we play a trick on your dad, Rachael?' Robin asked with a mischievous grin on his face. 'Are you up for it?'

Of course she was! Robin explained what they were

going to do and emphasised that she would be perfectly safe.

'I know I will be,' Rachael responded confidently, 'Come on, Robin. Let's do it! I can't wait to see Dad's face!'

Ian was waiting in the landing zone and noted with relief that a tandem pair had already descended safely. The pilot directed Ian's gaze upwards to the luminous yellow paragliding wing that was ready to begin its descent and told him that was Rachael and Robin. Suddenly the wing started plummeting downwards in a corkscrew spin as though completely out of control. (Of course, this was the trick: one of Robin's steep but completely safe spirals.) Ian was briefly panic-stricken: his little girl was going to crash!

'What the f***!' he shouted.

The pilot, who had just landed, smiled and told Ian not to worry – that was one of Robin's favourite tricks and he was a master pilot. Sure enough Robin controlled the spin and soon Rachael and he landed gently and safely. Rachael climbed out of the harness and rushed towards Ian with arms outstretched.

'Dad, Dad! I've been on top of the world and it was magic!'

Ian was so relieved, he completely forgot to tell them off and thanked Robin profusely. Robin told Ian that he had a very brave and adventurous daughter.

'I know. I'm so proud of her but sometimes, I must admit, she frightens me!' Ian said.

Ian and Rachael walked back slowly along the lakeside path towards Pokhara. Rachael told him every detail about her marvellous flight; she was so exhilarated that she bounced with joy.

'I'm sorry if we scared you at the end, Dad. But when Robin asked if I was up for it, I really couldn't resist playing a trick on you,' Rachael explained with a loving look.

'I wasn't scared,' replied Ian quickly.

'Really?' Rachael responded. She remembered the look on Ian's face when they landed, but wisely didn't say anything.

When they reached the village homes on the outskirts of the city, Rachael noticed a group of Nepali ladies dressed in beautiful traditional costumes. The colours were really vibrant and the embroidery and intricate bead work exquisite. Rachael looked at them with admiration and longing.

'Oh, Dad,' she whispered, 'don't those ladies look fantastic? I do so wish that I could wear a sari like those. Our clothes in the UK are dead boring.'

Ian agreed that the ladies looked really lovely and smiled as they walked along the streets. Rachael's remarks had planted the seed of an idea in his head, which he knew he could revisit later. They stopped for a quick meal at their favourite vegetarian restaurant and then made their way to the offices of the Sunshine Paragliding Agency to pick up the DVD of Rachael's fabulous flight.

They decided after having relaxing showers, they would just chill out in their room that evening at the Hotel Tulsi. It had been such an exhilarating and hectic day for Rachael and a stressful but proud day for Ian that they both craved some down time. Unfortunately neither Rachael nor Ian had the equipment to watch the DVD but that did not stop them from reliving every minute. Ian watched how Rachael's face was illuminated with joy as she related some of her paragliding antics with Robin. Her whole being was just bursting with the glory of her experience and she found it difficult to find the words to fully express her feelings. Of course Ian understood completely.

Rachael snuggled down in her bed still playing on her iPad but to Ian's amazement she fell asleep quite quickly. She had a wonderful smile on her face. Ian reflected on the day's events and marvelled how well Rachael had coped with every challenge.

'How many twelve-year-old girls would ever experience such a day – paragliding in the Himalaya? Very few,' he thought.

Ian settled down in his bed and, mulling over the idea he'd had when he noted Rachael's reaction to the beautiful saris, he worked out a plan.

DAY 9 – OCTOBER 15TH

As soon as Rachael woke up next morning, Ian told her what he had been planning while she was asleep.

'Yesterday was absolutely fabulous, wasn't it darling?' he asked, 'but just wait to hear what I have planned for today.'

Rachael readily agreed that the paragliding had been one of her most exciting adventures but naturally she was full of curiosity as to what her dad had in mind for their last day in Pokhara. She knew that it would be something extraordinary.

'Dad, Dad!' she exclaimed. 'Come on – please tell me what we are going to do. *Please!*'

Her eyes sparkled and her face was aglow with anticipation. Ian went on to explain that on the previous day, as they were walking back to their hotel, he had noticed her longing expression when she had looked at the Nepalese ladies wearing those beautiful traditional saris and had heard her fervent wish that she too could wear one. So he had decided that after breakfast, they would go into Pokhara and find a shop where he could buy a sari for her.

'Then you will always have a fantastic reminder of all your adventures in Nepal,' he added, 'and you will be able to wear your sari when we go to the Fewa Paradise Restaurant this evening and dance on their stage. Won't that be great?' For once, Rachael was speechless as she struggled to realise what her dad had just said. Bubbling with excitement, she finally managed to respond.

'Wow Dad! Thank you! I am such a lucky girl! What a wonderful surprise! I do so love you!'

As you may imagine, Rachael washed and dressed in record speed and consumed her breakfast with equal urgency. So it was not long before they were looking in the shops on the main street. They searched and searched but could not find one single shop that sold saris. They extended their search to the side streets but had no luck there either and were both becoming quite despondent. Ian decided to return to the main street so he could ask the next Nepalese lady they saw wearing a sari where they could buy one for Rachael. Eventually two Nepalese ladies wearing traditional dress came towards them. Ian complimented them on their lovely saris and asked where they had bought such beautiful outfits. The ladies were really happy to help and explained that saris were not sold in the tourist area at this end of Pokhara but in the market at Mahendra Chowk, on the outskirts of the city. They advised Ian and Rachael to hire a taxi as it was too far to walk and told him that the fare should not be more than 400 rupees.

After thanking those lovely ladies, Ian flagged down a passing taxi. The driver, whose name was Rajen, was really friendly and proved to be wonderfully helpful: a real saviour – their Good Samaritan in fact.

When they arrived at Mahendra Chowk (Market Street), Rachael and Ian were delighted to discover that it did indeed live up to its name because it was a long street lined on both sides with a huge variety of little shops, some with proper shop windows, others just open at the front. Down the middle of the street were lots of stalls selling goods of every description; clearly Mahendra Chowk was where all the locals shopped. Rajen asked Ian how long he and Rachael were going to be and enquired if he should wait for them – this would only cost 200 rupees an hour. When Ian explained that he was looking for a shop that sold saris so that he could buy one for Rachael, Rajen suggested that he could help by showing them the best places for saris. Also he could translate for them and explain exactly what they wanted as quite a few of the local shopkeepers did not speak much English. He was willing to stay for as long as they needed him and when Rachael had decided which sari she liked best, he would drive them back to the Hotel Tulsi. Obviously this was a brilliant solution and when Ian asked how much that would cost, he was astounded when Rajen replied with a smile that the complete fare would be only 1000 rupees (around £10) – an absolute bargain!

Rajen's advice proved to be invaluable: he took Rachael and Ian to several places that sold the most exquisitely embroidered saris, which were draped gracefully on models and hangers. Rachael was ecstatic: she was sure that she would find the sari of her dreams. However it soon became apparent that Rachael was too tall for a ready-made sari; Nepalese ladies tend to be quite small and all those fabulous saris were far too short for her. Understandably, she was really disappointed.

Resourceful Rajen quickly came to their rescue by advising them to buy some suitable lengths of material and have a sari tailor-made to fit Rachael. She could choose the colour, silk and style of embroidery and the bead-encrusted borders she liked best; then her sari would be very special. Rachael was elated – this was certainly a step in the right direction. Ian was a little doubtful whether a sari could be made in time for Rachael to wear that evening at the restaurant. He explained to Rajen that he had reserved a special table at the side of the restaurant stage for seven o'clock and it was already one o'clock. The shopkeepers said that it would only take around six hours, possibly less. However, this would mean that Rachael and Ian would

be late for their celebratory meal. Again Rajen proved to be a knight in shining armour; he proposed that Rachael should select the material and trimmings from this shop and then he would take them to a tailor he knew who could make a beautiful traditional sari in *four* hours. Marvellous!

Rachael chose some shiny embroidered golden material for the bodice; filmy gold, gossamer-like silk for the sleeves and rich brilliant-red silk for her skirt and sari-stole (a long decorative scarf.) She also chose matching linings and beautiful patterned borders intricately and heavily embroidered with gold thread. She was buzzing with excitement and couldn't wait to meet the recommended tailor; soon she was going to be measured for her dream sari!

Rajen rapidly drove Rachael and Ian right across the city of Pokhara. Things seemed to be working out very well … or so they thought! Unfortunately when they found the tailor's shop it was closed and none of the neighbouring shopkeepers knew where the tailor had gone. It was possible he had not yet returned from celebrating Dashain with his distant family. Refusing to be beaten, a determined Rajen drove Rachael and Ian to a small open-fronted shop owned by a long-established Nepalese family of lady tailors that he knew: grandma, mum and daughter, who were all experts. Rachael and Ian were welcomed enthusiastically and assured that the special sari would be finished by 6 p.m. They would all work on it. The ladies took numerous measurements of Rachael very carefully and listened respectfully to her ideas of how she would like her sari designed and where each different type of material could be used. Both Ian and Rachael began to feel much more optimistic; clearly this family of tailors was very efficient and skilful. If anyone could fulfil Rachael's dream, they could! They bid each other 'Namaste', left the shop and went back to Rajen's taxi.

Amazingly Rajen then said that he would take them back to their hotel and pick them up again at 5.50 p.m. so they could collect Rachael's sari. What a genuinely lovely man! As Ian and Rachael enjoyed a relaxing drink and a snack they talked about Rajen's

unbelievable kindness and generosity and how different an attitude he had from most taxi drivers in the UK and other parts of the world.

Just as he had promised, Rajen arrived promptly and took Ian and Rachael to pick up her special sari. That lovely family of tailors was waiting for her with the sari already packed in a bag. They assured Rachael and Ian that they guaranteed the sari would fit perfectly so there was no need to try it on. When they were back in the taxi, Rajen asked them if they would like to go home with him and meet his daughter, wife and mother-in-law. He explained that they would help Rachael to put on her sari correctly and would dress her hair and do her make-up in the traditional Nepalese style. Rachael was so eager to have this done that Ian readily agreed. As soon as they arrived, Rajen's smiling family greeted them warmly and whisked Rachael away into another room to work their magic.

By now it was around 6.30 p.m. and Ian was becoming a little anxious about the time. He need not have worried because less than fifteen minutes later, Rachael emerged looking a million dollars. Ian gasped with incredulity and pride; his daughter truly looked like a film star! Her beautiful sari looked fabulous and fitted perfectly and the ladies had dressed Rachael's lovely blonde hair in an amazing traditional style. Her make-up was superb and included a traditional tika mark on her forehead. They had even given her a collection of brightly coloured bangles to wear on her henna-patterned arms. Ian could see that Rachael was over the moon; she radiated joy. Rajen's wife pointed out that Rachael's trainers were not really suitable to wear with her beautiful sari so she popped back into the bedroom and emerged with a pair of stretchy black slip-on shoes. They were exactly the right size for Rachael and totally complemented her outfit. It was a Cinderella moment! Rajen's wife emphasised that she did not want any money – she was just happy to help a girl like Rachael who clearly loved Nepal and embraced its culture. Ian, however, insisted that she accepted 1000 rupees, tactfully pointing out that it could be used to help her daughter in some way.

Then Rajen drove them to the Fewa Paradise Restaurant and incredibly they were only seven minutes late. When Ian asked how much he owed, Rajen replied that he had quoted 1000 rupees so that was the fare. He was an honourable man and always kept his word. Ian told him that this was not enough for all his loyalty and help and gave Rajen 2000 rupees, insisting that he accepted the money for his wonderful family. Rajen was overjoyed, especially when Rachael told him that he was the nicest Nepalese man she had ever met and he had proved to be a true friend.

As they sat down at their table near the stage, one of the dancers noticed Rachael in her glorious sari and gave her a thumbs-up sign.

'You look beautiful!' she said.

Rachael was incandescent with joy and pride and Ian had tears in his eyes. Over the meal, they talked about Rajen and his unexpected help and dedication. As Rachael wrote later in her diary: *'We met a random taxi driver today who was marvellous and helped us so much. None of our English drivers would do so much for a client and ask for so little reward. He is my hero!'*

After they had eaten, Rachael climbed onto the stage and joined in the dancing gracefully and naturally. She had a huge smile on her face. All the Nepalese dancers admired her and helped her to mimic the intricate hand movements and steps. Ian was incredibly proud and took some amazing photos, although at times he could hardly see through his tears of love and gratitude. It gave him an immense sense of satisfaction to be able to fulfil one of his brave daughter's dreams. He knew that none of this would have been possible without the wonderful care shown by Rajen and his lovely family. They were so typical of all that is the very best of Nepalese culture: honour, helpfulness, dedication and kindness. Rajen, indeed, was a superstar!

DAY 10 – OCTOBER 16TH

Although Ian and Rachael had packed the previous evening, they were up by 6 a.m. so they could have a drink and a snack before walking to the bus station to catch their 8 a.m. local service bus to Kathmandu. Ian had already reserved their seats when they arrived in Pokhara from Chitwan. As usual, the booking clerk had tried to persuade Ian to buy tickets for the much more luxurious tourist bus but both Ian and Rachael were adamant that they wanted to travel with all the local people. Undoubtedly it was a much less comfortable journey but far more interesting with numerous stops for locals getting on and off often in the middle of nowhere with a wide variety of 'luggage'. This could be live animals like chickens or bags of vegetables deposited inside in the aisle; or furniture, motorbikes, huge cases and bags stashed on the roof – all of which had to be secured often with hilarious, noisy inefficiency. (On one journey I made by local bus, there were three goats tethered to the roof and an upside-down table! Such journeys are never dull.)

The 8 a.m. service bus actually left Pokhara at 9 a.m. so Ian was pleased he had already arranged for a twin-bedded room for the pair of them back at the Hotel Pomelo House in Kathmandu where, you will remember, they had left their spare luggage. He fervently hoped that their big rucksack would still be there underneath the counter in reception!

Not long after Rachael and Ian sat down, Ian realised that his trousers had split right down the back seam and every time the bus swerved or he moved slightly, the seam continued to give way until it opened past the crotch of his trousers and began to descend down his leg. He had decided to wear his old hiking trousers for the ten-hour bus ride because they were the lightest and most comfortable: a decision he now regretted! When Rachael realised what had happened she started giggling and found it hard to stop. Fortunately they had taken a large carrier bag full of sweets on board with them, so Ian clutched this in his lap and initially managed to hide his embarrassing wardrobe malfunction. But at some point, when they stopped for a 'comfort break', he would have to get up and this would require some forethought and ingenuity!

Road conditions in Nepal ensure that no journey is dull especially on the ramshackle local buses. Ian and Rachael found the popular main road from Pokhara to Kathmandu was slightly less hazardous than the one they had experienced from Kathmandu to Chitwan (and the one from Chitwan to Pokhara) and thankfully, their bus driver was really skilful. He had to negotiate his way around numerous broken-down vehicles and through many accident areas and there was the constant problem of huge, highly decorated and slow-moving lorries. Understandably, because of the narrow, switchback nature of the roads in the steep hilly areas, Nepalese lorry drivers tend to stay in the middle of the road and clouds of horrible dense black smoke are emitted from their exhausts as they struggle up the sharp inclines. Clearly the fantastic paintwork is generally maintained far better than their engines! How on earth the bus driver managed to overtake any of the lorries was a miracle but he did so successfully.

Ian and Rachael absolutely loved this hair-raising experience but I must admit I was usually frightened – as I am sure many of our readers would be. The roads do not have any proper edges or safety barriers, even when they snake up and down the steep hillsides. Often when you look out of the windows the precipitous drops to the rivers or land below are truly alarming. In addition, streams often tumble across the roads and there are always rough rocky surfaces as a result of landslides. Amazingly, although there are quite a few accidents and spectacular crashes, generally none of them are serious and there are few fatalities on Nepalese roads. In spite of their driver's excellent road handling, the inevitable bumping up and down of the bus did not help the situation with Ian's fragile trousers!

The views to their left across the valley towards the snow-capped Himalayan ranges were spectacular and even when they descended to the valley bottom, these mountains watched over them like benevolent guardians. The road here was wider and so they made good progress past fields, villages and isolated houses. Some of these were brightly decorated but, inevitably, many were in sad states of disrepair. The constantly changing scenery made their long, somewhat arduous journey really fascinating.

Eventually they had to stop for a 'comfort break' but by now Ian had worked out a way of hiding the increasing split in his trousers. He let all the other passengers get off the bus first then, as all trekkers do, he fastened his fleece around his waist by its sleeves. The bulk of it covered his back, hiding the split in the seat of his pants while the sleeves dangled down the front obscuring the embarrassing holes there. He hoped his trousers would not disintegrate further before the end of their journey. (Though secretly, as you may imagine, Rachael was hoping for a disaster!) Thankfully this did not happen even when, exhausted and grubby, they managed to climb off the bus at the roadside bus station in Kathmandu much later that evening.

With the fleece firmly tied around his waist, Ian guided Rachael back to the Hotel Pomelo House where, to their delight, they retrieved Ian's large rucksack from under the reception counter before heading upstairs to their lovely twin-bedded room. Neither of them could wait to have a refreshing shower, though as you will have guessed, Rachael managed to nip in first after selecting one of the twin beds. Ian was content just to relax on his bed and wait. He was so relieved that he had avoided making a spectacle of himself. Later those offending trousers were firmly consigned to the rubbish bin!

DAY 11 – OCTOBER 17TH

Ian and Rachael had a late, relaxed breakfast on the sheltered terrace of the Hotel Pomelo House the next morning and discussed all the exciting adventures and encounters they'd had since the last time they were there. Before they had gone to bed the previous evening, they had both agreed that they needed to have a 'chill-out' day before Rachael began the next part of her educational and cultural learning experience. This was to involve attending a Nepalese school, visiting orphanages and prisons and representing Grandma Joyce's Rotary Club of Bakewell (as a Young Ambassador) at a meeting of Kathmandu Metro Rotary Club. These were all serious commitments and responsibilities for a twelve-and-a-half-year-old girl!

For the next day or so, they decided that they needed to be nearer the centre of Thamel so Ian phoned the manager at the familiar Hotel Shakti and booked a twin-bedded room for them. Ian and Rachael packed quickly and Ian went to pay their bill while Rachael checked they had not left anything behind. They both thanked the manager for his care and wished him every success in his new enterprise: re-launching the Hotel Pomelo House. Ian affirmed that they had thoroughly enjoyed their stay and thought the manager was definitely on the right lines.

They took their time and enjoyed sauntering through the vibrant bustling streets towards the Hotel Shakti. When they arrived they received a very warm welcome and were shown to their room upstairs.

After depositing their rucksacks and sorting out some clothes, Ian suggested that they went for a walk around Thamel. They could look at the shops, perhaps have a meal at a café and hopefully they might see Beka so that Rachael could have the henna decoration on her arm renewed. Rachael thought this was an excellent idea; she had been longing to have that henna design done again so that she could show Khushi, Pari and C.P. when she met them the next day. It would be especially nice to have an authentic henna decoration when she danced with Pari and Khushi wearing her own sari.

Ian realised that he needed some money so their first point of call was at a local cash machine. However, when Ian inserted his credit card, the machine swallowed it. He was astonished and very annoyed; he had used that card several times in Kathmandu, Chitwan and Pokhara with no problem whatsoever. Immediately he rang the bank but his contact was most unhelpful. He refused to send Ian another credit card as he was in Nepal and also refused to make arrangements for Ian to withdraw money from one of the many banks in Kathmandu. Ian explained that he was staying in Nepal for at least another two weeks and that he had his twelve-year-old daughter with him. He desperately needed access to some money to ensure his daughter's comfort and safety. Incredibly, the contact (whose job it was to provide assistance to customers) again declined to help Ian and Rachael and could not be persuaded to do so. It was as if he couldn't have cared less: he did not seem in the least bothered that he was essentially abandoning a child and her father in a Third World country without any means of supporting themselves. Ian was furious! The phonecall to the bank had cost him £16 so he was determined to report that horrible unsympathetic man when he got back to the UK. But none of this helped him now – what should he do?

He did have an alternative credit card with him but understandably was reluctant to use it in case that card was eaten too. But he had no choice, so with his heart in his mouth he inserted his other credit card into the cash machine. To his great relief, there was no

problem, and Ian was able to withdraw the amount he needed. Nevertheless, throughout their stay, whenever Ian needed to use that card, he was very nervous indeed.

Disaster averted, they stopped at the nearby Pumpernickel Bakery: a superb café that was rapidly becoming an institution in Kathmandu, much as the Rum Doodle Restaurant used to be before it closed. The pair badly needed some refreshments and a drink after all the stress they'd endured. While they were eating some delicious croissants, Rachael spotted that the café had WiFi – a must for all young people and Rachael was no exception! Fortified, they continued wandering around Thamel, enjoying dodging the traffic, pedestrians and cows. Ian smiled as he reminded Rachael how much she had hated her first walk in the streets of Kathmandu. Rachael just laughed and retorted with the superior wisdom of a twelve-year-old:

'Well, Dad, I was much younger then and it was a bit of a shock!'

To their joy, they soon spotted Beka walking towards them with an older lady – Beka's mother. Rachael was ecstatic; how lucky was that! They soon found a place where Rachael could have her henna decoration redone but this time Beka's mum drew it. It was fabulous; obviously Beka had inherited her artistry from her mother. After Ian had paid for Rachael's exquisite henna design, they bid the two clever ladies, 'Namaste' and slowly made their way back to the Hotel Shakti.

That evening they were surprised to find Pradip, the managing director of Mountain Monarch Adventures, and a trekking group in the reception area of the hotel. Pradip was briefing the group about their trek to Everest Base Camp the following day. Rachael felt really envious and curious at the same time. Base Camp was the one trek she was desperate to do at some stage so she listened avidly to all his instructions. Then Pradip introduced her to the group and she showed them her lovely henna decoration. Some of the ladies decided that when they returned to Kathmandu, they would like to have a similar one and would try to find Beka and her mother.

When the group had dispersed, Pradip told Rachael that he had brought a special present for her. He handed her a glossy book about Everest that he had signed especially for her on the title page. It was a superb, beautifully illustrated book called, *In the Shadow of Everest* and was written by Robert Weiss, with many of the diagrams and photographs taken by his family. Inside Pradip had written: 'Rachael – Another destination for you. Sure you can do it!' and he had signed it.

Rachael's face lit up as she read his dedication carefully and proudly showed it to Ian. He agreed that it was a great present and pointed out that all the royalties from the sale of that marvellous book were being donated to the Sherpa and Porter Children's Education Charity Programme. Both Ian and Rachael had always been very concerned about the conditions under which some Sherpas and porters were employed. They had no security nor suitable clothing or footwear. I have seen porters wearing flip-flops when walking over snowy and rocky terrain. Few of the porters' families ever received compensation if their husbands had an accident that rendered them unable to work or, indeed, died undertaking their duties. There was little provision made for their wives and children who struggled merely to survive and so there was no money for their children's education.

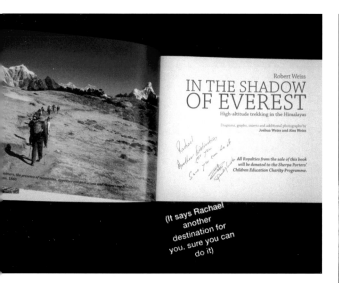

Robert Weiss

IN THE SHADOW
OF EVEREST

High-altitude trekking in the Himalayas

Diagrams, graphs, inserts and additional photographs by
Joshua Weiss and Alex Weiss

All Royalties from the sale of this book
will be donated to the Sherpa Porters'
Children Education Charity Programme.

(It says Rachael
another
destination for
you. sure you can
do it)

Mountain Monarch Adventures – Pradip's company – is very different. They make sure that everyone who works for them has appropriate clothing and boots and is covered by a generous insurance scheme. Should they become ill or injured and cannot work or worse still if they die, as well as the insurance money, Pradip always continues to support their families for as long as they need help. He truly is one of the good guys and takes wonderful care of his Nepalese countrymen. Not all climbing and trekking companies follow his good example, especially some of the international ones.

Rachael thanked Pradip enthusiastically and said that when she and her dad trekked to Everest Base Camp, they would most certainly be going with Mountain Monarch Adventures and hopefully their leader would be our wonderful C.P. Ian just smiled; that would be another challenging adventure for the future!

When they were in their beds much later that evening, Ian was pleased to see that, for once, Rachael was not playing on her iPad but was earnestly looking at all of the photos in her Everest book and reading the captions. Her face glowed with joyous anticipation.

DAY 12 – OCTOBER 18TH

Next day Ian and Rachael did not have a specific schedule other than to be back at the Hotel Shakti before 4 p.m. That was when Ian had booked their kind reliable taxi driver Gobinda to pick them up and take them to C.P.'s new house so that Rachael could go to school with Khushi the following day.

They decided that they would go out for breakfast and Ian let Rachael choose the café so it was no surprise when she said she would love to go to the Pumpernickel Bakery again. It had a fantastic variety of breads, croissants, cakes and pastries but the deciding factor for Rachael, of course, was that it had WiFi! Actually Ian and Rachael went there for breakfast every morning when they were in Kathmandu and it was always very busy: the first choice for trekkers and many locals. Although the big attraction for Rachael was the WiFi, she adored their chocolate croissants and thoroughly enjoyed many huge slices of their famous chocolate cake. Ian was amazed that she managed to eat every single crumb every time because the portions were so large!

The Pumpernickel Bakery is owned and run by a charming Nepalese couple, Norvel and his wife. Initially he just had a very small building and one oven and made everything by hand. However when he was invited by a friend to visit him in Montana, USA, Norvel discovered how to bake cakes and a huge range of bread using machinery. His favourite bread was pumpernickel: the delicious wholemeal rye bread that originated in Germany. The flour is made from roughly ground whole rye berries and their outer endosperm, which gives the bread its rich dark colour. Although the bread is very nutritious and provides valuable roughage, it tends to be rather indigestible. This is possibly where the name pumpernickel originated: 'pumpern' is the German word for flatulence or passing wind and 'Nickel' is a form of Nicholas, a name associated with goblins and Satan, the devil or 'Old Nick'. So, amusingly, pumpernickel means 'devil's fart!' Ian knew this because he had spent quite a long time in Germany as a child – that is the kind of information a child does not forget! When he explained this to Rachael, who had been curious about the name of the bakery, she had thought it hilarious and promised not to 'pump' when they were in the café. Ian wasn't entirely sure that he believed her especially as she was unable to disguise the wicked little grin on her face!

When Norvel went back to Kathmandu, he and his wife decided to extend their business and premises and installed similar machinery to that he had used in Montana. Over some years they worked incredibly hard and built up the Pumpernickel Bakery into the wonderful café they own today. The ambience is superb: beautiful tables, lovely linen and a shady courtyard with a statuesque tree. It is a peaceful haven for weary travellers in the midst of the bustling city and in addition serves delicious food – small wonder that it has become such an iconic place.

When Rachael and Ian arrived there that morning for breakfast, there were no empty tables so they had to share with a trekker from New Zealand. Naturally, they all began talking. Rachael told him about all her adventures in Nepal and what she and her dad still planned to do. He wished her every success and went on to tell a tragic but inspiring story. Some years before when he had been in Nepal with his friends, they had booked a flight to Pokhara so they could go trekking. However when they reached the airport, they were told that the flight was overbooked. There were only two seats left instead of the three they needed. He had volunteered to wait for the next flight and said he would meet up with them at Pokhara Airport. That was the last time he saw them because tragically the plane had crashed and his two friends were killed. He owed his life to that simple booking error. The parents of his two friends had not wished to benefit from the insurance compensation but had requested a school for 500 Nepalese children be built near the Monkey Temple with the money. He had arranged for this work to be done and had just been back to see the school. He said that he had been given the warmest welcome by the grateful local children and their families when they realised that he represented the loving parents of his friends who had passed away. Ian and Rachael were very impressed at such generosity of spirit and thoughtfulness.

Rachael (12) and Ubick (18).

After what was really a brunch, Ian and Rachael spent some time quietly chatting, looking in the shops and exploring the side streets and bazaars. The New Zealand trekker's story had left them feeling very humble but immensely thankful for such caring people. Eventually they arrived back at the Hotel Shakti and went upstairs to sort out their rucksacks and carrier bags containing Rachael's special sari and the presents for Khushi's family. After paying the bill, Ian and Rachael just relaxed in the garden enjoying a drink while they waited for Gobinda to pick them up in his taxi.

As always, Gobinda arrived promptly so soon Ian and Rachael were on their way to C.P.'s new home. Ian thanked Gobinda, paid him and promised that while they were in Kathmandu, whenever they needed a taxi, they would choose his. Both Ian and Rachael were amazed when they first saw the new home that had been built next door to the house C.P. used to rent for his family. It had been built in less than a year so they had half expected it to be a little rough as many ordinary Nepalese buildings are, but the quality of workmanship was outstanding. It was square shaped and two storeys high with marble steps leading up to a large roof terrace. They were greeted warmly by Pari, who took them inside, where Khushi and Pari's nephew Ubick eagerly awaited them. She told them that C.P. was on his way back from leading a trekking group and sent them his love.

Of course, as soon as Ian and Rachael put their rucksacks and carriers down, a very proud Pari immediately took them on a tour of the new family home. The interior showed the same degree of care and skill as the outside; obviously C.P. and Pari had scrupulously supervised all the building work and installation of the fittings. There were two bedrooms, a lovely lounge and a well-fitted kitchen, which must have delighted Pari who used to work as a chef. As you know, she has a talent for cooking all kinds of delicious food. The part-tiled bathroom had a Western-style toilet, hand basin and a generous shower area. C.P. and his family must have been over the moon. Through all the years that I have known my lovely C.P. his dream had always been to build his own house and provide a good home for Pari and Khushi and now he had achieved that dream. Pari took them up the marble steps to the roof terrace which was full of pots of beautiful bright flowers: brilliant orange marigolds, pink and red geraniums and fragrant roses and orchids – Pari certainly has green fingers. Whenever C.P. and I went trekking, he used to collect specimens for Pari to plant and nourish. C.P. had also built a wonderful Hindu shrine on the terrace so that he and his family could worship up there every day.

Once they were back in the lounge, Rachael gave Khushi her present and then gave one to Pari and asked her to keep the one for C.P. safe. Ian had bought them all a mug and had their photos from the previous year printed on them. Inside Pari and C.P.'s mugs were English teabags and in Khushi's a sachet of Cadbury's hot chocolate. They were so thrilled. Khushi could hardly wait for Pari to make her a lovely hot chocolate drink. She had a beaming smile on her face as she sipped it slowly. Then they all settled down, chatted for a while about Rachael's exciting adventures and looked at her amazing photos. Ubick was especially interested because, as you will remember, the previous year he had been the porter on their trek in the Annapurna Region. It wasn't long before Pari excused herself and went into the kitchen to prepare a meal for all of them. She is a wonderful hostess and like all Nepali people is dedicated to feeding family and guests really well: no one is allowed to go hungry and as soon as you empty your plate, it is quickly replenished. Eventually you do learn to leave a little to avoid this happening. Naturally Ubick cleared his plate very quickly and was soon wading through another one but Ian and Rachael struggled to finish their tasty meals because of the huge quantities Pari had given them. The food was cooked really beautifully and was delicious but they felt as if they would soon burst if they didn't stop eating!

In her diary that evening, Rachael drew a high steaming mountain surrounded by little bowls filled to the brim. She added a note which said, *'This is the huge mountain of fantastic food that Pari gave each of us! We were very sorry that we couldn't quite eat it all. We tried our best because we didn't want to offend her because she is such a good cook. Pari is just so generous and lovely!'*

After dinner, Pari, Ubick and Ian continued to chat and exchanged all their news while Khushi took Rachael into her bedroom where they watched movies together and styled each other's hair: it was just as though they had never been apart. Khushi was so proud of her room because this was the first time she had ever had one of her own. She kept it very clean and tidy and had arranged all her teddies and toys in a neat row and put away all her clothes. Her books were stored in the desk that C.P. had bought her as a reward for working so hard at school. Later that evening when Ian and Rachael were sharing Khushi's room, Ian noted just how neat and well-organised Khushi had made it.

'You could certainly learn some lessons in tidiness from your young Nepalese "sister"!' he observed wryly.

Of course Rachael promptly blamed her sister Catherine for all the mess in their room back at Old Water View!

Before she went to sleep, Rachael told Ian how happy she was to be back with Khushi.

'Dad, I know we have stayed at some fab hotels but being here with Khushi, Ubick and Pari is far better. I feel that we are part of their family and that is cool!'

Ian agreed wholeheartedly. Nepalese people are very kind, caring and hospitable but staying with a family is a real privilege – one to remember and treasure.

DAY 13 – OCTOBER 19TH

Both Khushi and Rachael were up very early next morning because it had been arranged for Rachael to go to school with Khushi. They were both very excited and quickly dressed in their respective school uniforms. (Rachael had brought hers from England!)

After breakfast, they all walked to where Khushi normally caught the school bus. When the bus arrived, it was very different from Rachael's; to say the bus was rickety would be very kind. Ian had thought that Rachael would be apprehensive about attending a school in a Third World country, particularly as she did not speak Nepali. However she felt confident that Khushi would translate for her. With her usual bravery and determination, Rachael was really up for it. To her it was yet another challenge. They all waved the girls off and went back home.

Ready for school.

FAR LEFT: Kopan Monastery.
LEFT: Pari at Kopan Monastery.

While the girls were at school, Pari and Ubick took Ian to the Kopan Monastery in the hills above their new home. It was a very pleasant walk and Ian was astonished when he saw the monastery: although it was small, he thought it was one of the most exquisite buildings he had ever seen. It had intricate and elaborate carvings and brilliant paintings all enhanced with gold. It was like a miniature of the famous Monkey Temple. Pari went to ask for approval for Ian to look inside. Normally Westerners were banned from entering but Ian was granted special permission,

lucky man! Outside the monastery was a large and very curious sign. Ian could not help smiling as he read it, as I'm sure will you! This is what it said:

'While at Kopan Monastery Please Refrain from Killing, Stealing, Lying, Sexual conduct, Intoxicants including Tobacco. Thank you.'

One assumes this was directed at tourists and not the many pilgrims or monks that visited the site!

In the afternoon Ubick asked Ian if he would like to meet his family. It was obvious that Ubick was really keen so Ian readily agreed. However when Ubick suggested Ian rode pillion on the back of his motorbike, Ian sensibly refused: a wise decision! He explained that due to his recently broken back, he dare not risk hurting it with the swerving, stopping sharply and rapid acceleration necessary when driving in the chaos of the Kathmandu traffic.[1]

Ubick went next door and asked the taxi driver (who lived there) to drive them. Unfortunately it wasn't long before they became stuck in a massive traffic jam on the ring road that lasted for ages. They were surrounded by trucks and buses all belching thick, black, poisonous fumes. This made it very difficult to breathe and made Ian's eyes sting. He knew that he could not allow this to go on much longer or he was going to faint. Ian began to feel very ill indeed – he needed to get out of the taxi, and quick. Just as he had decided he could not stand it anymore, the traffic began gradually to clear and it wasn't too long before they arrived at Ubick's home. All his family welcomed Ian as an honoured guest; it was the most wonderful welcome. He was introduced to Ubick's mum and grandma and all of Ubick's siblings. Ian realised just how proud Ubick was to be able to have Ian in his home, but Ian felt very honoured to be there. They were a typical happy, hospitable Nepalese family.

The journey back to Pari's, thankfully, was free of traffic jams. By now Ian was beginning to feel quite faint and nauseous as a result of inhaling all those obnoxious traffic fumes. Nevertheless he was very eager to hear all about Rachael's day with Khushi at her school – Trungram International Academy. Rachael was bubbling: she was so excited about all the experiences she had that day, her words just came tumbling out! She had taken lots of 'Rachael Explore' pens and cards with her and said how all the children wanted her autograph so when she ran out of cards, they had asked her to sign their hands!

'I bet you can't guess what they called me, Dad!' she exclaimed. 'I'll tell you: they called me Barbie because of my long blonde hair – that was real cool!'

Then she settled down and described her amazing day from the very beginning. As was customary, the day had begun with assembly when all the children sang the Nepalese National Anthem. Then Rachael had been introduced to the whole school and had stood up in front of 600 children and their teachers and explained what a 'normal' school day was like back in England. She was asked lots of questions very politely and thoroughly enjoyed the experience. Ian felt so proud; to most children that experience would have been terrifying but Rachael just took

---

1 I only once rode pillion behind C.P. in Kathmandu. Never again! It was a miracle that I survived and was not thrown off or tossed into the back of one of the many trucks that my daredevil of a motorcyclist 'son' C.P. swerved around.

it in her stride. She even recorded it all on her iPhone! After assembly, Rachael joined Khushi's class. They studied different kinds of maths and then English because Rachael was there.

'I felt like an honoured guest,' she said. 'It was great!'

What had surprised her most was the really high standard of the work; Rachael thought Khushi's lessons were much harder than those she had in her secondary school and Khushi and the children in her class were two years younger than Rachael.

'Wow, Dad!' she exclaimed. 'They are so clever – they study really hard and don't mess about at all!'

Obviously Rachael had expected that as Nepal was a Third World country, the standard of education would be lower than that of the UK. At first, Ian was amazed too but then began to look for an explanation. He thought that probably the main reason was because all schooling has to be paid for in Nepal and parents are desperate for their children to have the best education possible – a far better one than they ever had. All their lives Nepalese children are instilled with the importance and value of a good education and high qualifications and so very early in their school lives, they develop strong ethics of hard work to achieve success. They know this is the way forward to securing a bright and prosperous future. This is part of their culture as is compassion, politeness and respect.

When Ian explained this to Rachael she became quite serious.

'I don't think we realise just how lucky we are in our country, Dad,' she said thoughtfully. 'I'm glad I have started to work really hard at my new school – I'm only just beginning to realise how important it is that I try my hardest.'

Ian reminded her that she had been granted extra leave for the full cultural and educational experience she was having now because she had worked hard and earned it.

'I am so proud of you!' he said, 'And I am proud of Khushi too!'

Before their evening meal, Rachael helped Khushi with her maths homework and thought it was most unfair when Khushi told her that in the SAT tests at the Trungram Academy there were only five questions to answer.

'I had to answer loads!' Rachael said. 'It's not fair!'

Ian pointed out that the answers needed were probably quite lengthy and it was difficult to make a judgement until both tests could be compared side by side.

'I don't care!' Rachael responded with a sniff, 'I'd rather take my next exams in Nepal, Dad.'

By now, Ian was deteriorating rapidly, so he asked Pari if it was okay to go to bed because he was feeling really poorly. He described to her just how dense those traffic fumes had been and he was certain that he was suffering from a degree of carbon-monoxide poisoning. He felt really faint and sick and apologised that he would not be able to eat anything that night: he just needed to sleep. Pari, understandably, was very concerned and said she would make sure Khushi, Ubick and Rachael were quiet. She said that she would keep looking in on him to make sure that he wasn't getting worse. What a caring lady!

Ian later told me that evening was one of strangest he had experienced. He remembered lying down on his back with his arms straight down by his sides, trying hard to breathe properly and fall asleep. But strangely, he felt as if he was floating above his body and looking down on himself. He had his eyes closed but was not asleep and no matter how hard he tried, he could not open them. He seemed to have no control of his body at all. He heard Pari come into Khushi's bedroom several times and because his eyes were closed, she clearly thought Ian was asleep but he wasn't – he just could not open his eyes, move or say anything. It was really weird! Eventually he must have fallen asleep properly because the next thing he remembered clearly was Rachael asking him the next morning if he was okay. His nausea seemed to have gone and he could move his limbs and open his eyes and speak. Fantastic! Apparently he had slept off the horrible effects of the carbon-monoxide poisoning – he had been very lucky.

DAY 14 – OCTOBER 20TH

Rachael was absolutely delighted that her dad was feeling better. She had been very worried that their planned cultural visit to the Firefly (Junkiri) Children's Home at Nayabazar founded by Indira Ranamagar would have to be postponed until Ian recovered. Ever since she was a small child, Rachael had been aware of her dad's dedication to caring for vulnerable children, as illustrated by his founding of Miller's Homes for Children in England and, in a worldwide context, through organisations such as his F.I.N.C.H. website. So her greatest desire on this visit to Nepal was to spend some time with Indira and experience what life and conditions are like in the wonderful homes Indira had founded for the children of prisoners and their families: namely Prisoners Assistance Nepal. The aim of PA Nepal is to meet the basic needs of and advocate for prisoners and their families and to continue to help them comprehensively to build worthwhile futures. As their maxim states: 'To give prisoners and their children a better today and a brighter future.'

Indira initially founded three large residential homes with schools attached for the children of prisoners. She expanded by adding the Kumari Home and Safe Children's Home to the PA family, thus providing care and support to children rescued from prison but always maintaining the bond with their parents. Up to now Indira has rescued over a thousand children from damp, dirty prisons and given them warm, loving homes. In addition she provides education and literacy for women in prison and day care centres for children in prison who are too young to leave their mothers. She ensures there is extensive training in handicrafts and farming to aid prisoners and their children to have skills that will help them in the future.

An amazing example of this is the home at Palpa, which both Ian and I have visited. It was built in the Himalayan foothills by teenage boys from Indira's homes under the supervision of their teacher. Obviously by the age of eighteen, teenagers have to leave their children's home but Indira continues to support them with training, employment and a loving home. At Palpa, Jhapa and Balaju Lolang Farm House they practise their farming skills specialising in organic produce and permaculture.

Indira's Children's Home.

Rachael had heard so much about Indira from Ian and me that she was longing to meet her and learn more about her work and beliefs. She knew that Indira had chosen the name 'Firefly' or 'Junkiri' for her children's homes because she firmly believed that just like a firefly has a hidden light, every person has a light inside them and 'we have to find that light inside every child to help them to grow and achieve their potential.' Indira's work had inspired Rachael so much that she was eager to meet her and some of the children in her loving care.

Rachael was delighted when Ian phoned Gobinda and arranged for him to pick up Rachael and himself and take them to the Hotel Shakti from where they could easily walk to the Firefly Children's Home in Nayabazar. Ian arranged with Pari to leave their surplus luggage with her until they returned. So as soon as breakfast was over and Khushi had gone to school, Gobinda arrived with his taxi and, after saying a warm and fond farewell to Pari and Ubick, promising that they would return very soon, Ian and Rachael were driven swiftly to the Hotel Shakti.

After depositing their rucksacks in their twin-bedded room, Ian and Rachael set off to Nayabazar. Rachael was so excited that she skipped most of the way! The Firefly Children's Home was the first that Indira established and although it is home for around thirty children, it is also where Indira, Subani (her beautiful daughter) and her mother live too. As it is in Kathmandu it is also the administrative centre for PA Nepal and is often the first place that newly rescued children are given a temporary loving home until Indira and her co-workers have assessed which of their homes would most suit their particular needs.

Knowing how sensitive Rachael is, Ian wondered if she would feel just as he did the first time he visited this Firefly Children's Home. With all his experience in childcare and protection, as soon as Ian enters a home, he can always sense the level of love and care there. He had told me that when he had stepped over the entrance at Firefly he had experienced a complete atmosphere of devotion: this was a haven where children were loved, cared for and nurtured. When he gazed at Rachael's shining, awestruck face he knew that she felt this too. Magic!

Indira welcomed them warmly and introduced them to her dedicated staff in the office area. Ian was delighted to see that one of teenage boys he had met on a previous visit was now employed by Indira as a kind of security guardian for the children. He was obviously very proud of his role and beamed at Ian and Rachael when they congratulated him. Indira then took them on a guided tour, showing Rachael and Ian the brightly decorated living rooms enhanced by the children's numerous wonderful drawings and paintings and full of toys and games of every description. Next they took in the bedrooms, where each child's bed was covered with brightly knitted throws and each had a small, snuggly comfort blanket. Although everything was well-worn, it was clean and comfortable and spoke of love; small wonder that all the children called Indira 'Aama' meaning 'Mother' for, indeed, she was mother to so many. This is best summed up by the words of Indira's beautiful, brilliant, biological daughter, seventeen-year-old Subani, who was once asked if she was jealous of all the time her mother devoted to caring for vulnerable children:

'No! I am never jealous,' she stated. 'The rescued children feel like my real siblings and I love them all. Of course, I wish that I had more time with my mother, but I understand her work and I am very proud of her. I love playing music for my brothers and sisters and singing to them. We are one big happy family!'

They met about twelve happy children on their tour who greeted them with huge smiles and the traditional 'Namaste!' but obviously more children lived there so naturally Rachael asked where they all were. Indira replied that all the others were at school.

'However,' she said with a huge smile, 'I have two little girls waiting for you to play with them, Rachael. Follow me and I'll show you.'

Rachael's face lit up when she the two tiny, beautifully dressed girls: they were enchanting and eagerly waved their arms and giggled. Rachael squatted down beside them and was soon completely engrossed playing with them, tickling them and singing to them. She was in her element and the two girls obviously adored her and kept touching her long golden hair. Ian and Indira looked on smiling in admiration. Rachael certainly had inherited that caring, loving quality that all children, no matter what their nationality, culture or creed recognise and trust. Later Rachael described the babies and their respective stories in her diary: (I have modified their names slightly to protect their identity.)

'One fantastic pretty little girl with lovely curly black hair was called Bhavaroopa – Bha for short which in Nepali means 'unique'. She is nicknamed Bha-in-a-box because she loves sitting in one (that is when she is not sitting on my knee!) She had been born prematurely during the terrible earthquake in 2015 and although her mother had

died, Bha had been dug out from under the rubble and saved. Indira has 'adopted' her and is bringing her up as her own. She is gorgeous and loves playing with my phone. You can see the results on my website – "This is what happens when you give a Nepalese baby your phone!"

The other baby is called Mirvisha – Mir for short, which in Nepali means 'fighter'. Indeed she is because she was very weak and small at birth but she survived. Many people, especially Indira, have fought to keep her alive. Her mother was only fifteen years old and Mir was the result of her mum being raped. In the Nepalese culture and faith this is considered to be a dreadful sin and the only way to prevent evil, bad fortune and shame from descending on all the family, is for the baby to be killed after it is born. I found this difficult to understand but Dad explained to me that this is the Nepali custom and cultural law that the family feel they must obey. Eventually Indira managed to intercede and persuaded the family to let her have Mir and bring her up at The Firefly Children's Home as her own child. She had explained that by removing Mir from their family, Indira was removing their shame and people would think that she had been taken and killed. They really were a loving family so they agreed and Indira took that tiny sick baby home and nourished her. Mir now is a bundle of joy and mischief and I really love her!'

Rachael and Ian spent the whole day with Indira and those enchanting babies. Ian had never seen Rachael so elated; she was utterly in a world of her own. She was so completely enthralled in entertaining and cuddling those babies that she seemed absolutely unaware of Ian and Indira. Throughout all her adventures and achievements Ian realised that he had never seen his daughter so animated; she was incandescent. It was as though she had found her life's purpose and had that inner glow that comes with knowledge and understanding.

As soon as they left the Firefly Home, Rachael begged Ian to let her return there.

'It has been the best day I have ever had in my whole life!' she said passionately. Her face was shining with joy. 'Please, please Dad, I need to go back. It is the best place and the best thing I have ever done. We have just got to go back!'

Then she asked Ian if they could adopt some of those children and take them back to live at Old Water View.

'We can give them a fantastic life, Dad, can't we?'

Ian had to explain that although that was a wonderful and generous idea, lots of those children had parents in jail who would eventually be released and anyway they had other family members too. They were Nepalese and needed to be brought up in their own culture and faith. Rachael seemed disappointed but clearly understood and settled for a return visit.

On the way back to the Hotel Shakti that evening, they stopped at a lovely restaurant they had never patronised before and had a really tasty meal. They ate on the superb roof terrace, which had wonderful balconies and the whole area was full of beautiful flowers in pots of every description. Pleasant Nepali music drifted up and they were surrounded by twinkling multi-coloured lights. It was like eating in a fairyland: a suitable ending to what had been, for both of them, a truly magical and enchanting day.

DAY 15 – OCTOBER 21ST

When Ian woke up next morning, he was surprised to find that Rachael was still asleep. He decided not to wake her but to let her catch up on some much-needed extra sleep. Clearly she was exhausted from the long, enthralling but very emotional day at Indira's Firefly Children's Home. He reflected on her wonderful inspiring experience with those two enchanting babies, Bha and Mir. He felt that Rachael could have found a future channel for all her energy and determination. She had been in her element and had shown true compassion and caring. He made up his mind that he and Rachael would revisit Indira's Firefly Children's Home several times if possible before they left Nepal so that Rachael could learn from Indira as much as possible about what was involved in caring for vulnerable children in a Third World country.

When at last Rachael woke up, Ian confirmed that they would go back to the home very soon. As you may imagine, Rachael was absolutely thrilled.

'Thank you, thank you, Dad!' she exclaimed joyfully. 'I definitely had the best time ever there and I really, really want to learn all about Indira's work and, of course, see Bha and Mir again!'

Ian smiled at her enthusiasm but said that he thought they should take the opportunity to have something of a 'rest day' and relax before they visited Suntakhan with Santosh early the following morning. He suggested they explore Thamel and find a new café where they could have breakfast, do some shopping and then later that evening, he would help her with the PowerPoint presentation she was planning to do for her school and Kathmandu Metro Rotary Club.

Rachael thought these were excellent ideas and dressed quickly.

'Come on, Dad!' she urged. 'Let's get going!'

Ian smiled: when Rachael wakes up, she really is ready for anything.

Not far from their hotel, they found an attractive-looking café with a saxophone on its sign: New Orleans Café. It certainly merited investigation so they went inside. They were pleased to see that everything looked clean and inviting with a warm friendly atmosphere. Jazz music played softly in the background.

While they were enjoying a pleasant breakfast, which included chocolate in the form of light crispy croissants, a Nepalese gentleman approached them. He introduced himself as Ram, the editor and publisher of the Nepali magazine, *The Quarterly Development Review*. He explained that his magazine covered many different aspects of politics, environmental issues and current affairs but also included a section on the opinions of tourists. He asked Ian if he could interview Rachael because he was eager to find out why she and her father were in Nepal; he had a feeling that their purpose was different from that of the average visitor, who only concentrated on trekking. Ian asked Rachael if this was okay and when she agreed, she was questioned comprehensively. Ram was amazed when he heard the details of all their plans and about the many explorations that Rachael had already done. He clearly admired her earnest desire to learn all she could about Nepalese culture, faith and lifestyle, which, he remarked, was most unusual for a girl of twelve years old. He thought she was wonderful and a good representative of her school and young English people in general.

Unbeaten!

'I guess that your dad has always been a good mentor,' he said, to which Rachael nodded enthusiastically.

Ram thanked them profusely and told them that he would include his interview with Rachael in his next quarterly magazine. He added that he too was a Rotarian but a member of one of the other Rotary Clubs in Kathmandu.

'Cool!' was Rachael's response.

Ian and Rachael then wandered around the shops mainly browsing but also looking for small presents they thought relatives and friends at home would really appreciate. They found a copy of *The Ascent of Rum Doodle* – an unusual, humorous book about climbing a mythical mountain. The Rum Doodle Restaurant, a favourite of Rachael's and mine, which sadly had closed, was named after this book so Rachael wisely decided that it would be exactly the right present for me. How right she was! It is sitting on my bookshelf at this moment and is well thumbed as I often read excerpts from it which make me chuckle.

After buying some maps of the region around Everest Base Camp, they slowly wended their way back to the Pumpernickel Café. Ian was ready for a drink and Rachael was attracted by the speed of their WiFi but also by the quality of their famous chocolate cake! When Ian saw the massive piece she was given, he doubted that even Rachael could manage to eat all that. Unsurprisingly, he was wrong again! With her usual enthusiasm she tackled its many layers valiantly and demolished the lot.

'Wow, Dad!' she exclaimed flourishing her fork. 'That was a huge slice but I didn't let it beat me, did I?'

'No, you didn't!' Ian responded smiling indulgently.

Back in their bedroom, Rachael spent a long while patiently preparing a PowerPoint presentation of all her experiences to date in Nepal. She had promised to do this for her school but she also hoped to use it when she visited Kathmandu Metro Rotary Club and spoke to them. She concentrated very hard and, with much thoughtful discussion and help from Ian, she put together a really splendid presentation. However before she could save it, suddenly and disastrously, the Internet crashed. All her efforts were in vain! She was very upset but incredibly philosophical.

'Well I guess, Dad, this is what often happens in Nepal. The Internet and software are just not reliable! I feel sorry for poor Khushi trying to do work for school. She must get very frustrated. I will try again tomorrow but if it crashes again, that's it!'

Ian was so proud of her attitude: his young daughter had really embraced and understood the problems inherent in a Third World country and dealt with them maturely.

DAY 16 – OCTOBER 22ND

Before she had climbed into her bed fairly early the previous evening, Rachael had reminded Ian that the next day they were going to see the school and village at Suntakhan. Santosh, past-president of Kathmandu Metro Rotary Club was picking them up at 6 a.m. hence the need for an early night.

Rachael was visiting Suntakhan as the Young Ambassador for Bakewell Rotary Club, my Rotary Club in Derbyshire, England.

After my trek in 2005 to Everest Base Camp, I had met Santosh who was then President of Kathmandu Metro Rotary Club. He told me about the work that his club did to help people less fortunate than themselves. One huge project was 'adopting' the poor remote village of Suntakhan in the Himalayan foothills and endeavouring to improve its environment, farming, housing, water supply and education facilities: the whole package. He had explained that one of the greatest problems was that because the villagers had never received any support, they had become apathetic and lost all hope. They desperately wanted a better life and education for their children but did not know how to move forward.

Because I was a member of Bakewell's International Committee, I encouraged our club to work with Kathmandu Metro to help the people of Suntakhan. For over ten years we have worked together and the results have been unbelievable. We have put in a clean, safe water system and upgraded the subsistence farming to a level where the villagers are providing people in Kathmandu with organic vegetables from their surplus harvests thus earning an income. We have educated them in effective animal and poultry husbandry and improved the educational facilities in the school beyond all recognition. Where children once sat on bare concrete floors in windowless classrooms, they now have desks and benches made by the village carpenters and glass in the windows. They have a comprehensive library with books in Nepali and English, a science block and equipment and a computer room with Internet access for all the computers. The children are proudly dressed in beautiful bright school uniforms made by the village seamstresses. This sewing project illustrates how both our clubs worked together: teaching the villagers how to help themselves thus gaining self-respect. Bakewell Rotary Club supplied the material for the uniforms; Kathmandu provided the sewing machines and the village ladies made them. Now those same sewing machines are also used to make a variety of clothes, which are sold in Kathmandu market: a good source of income and, perhaps more importantly, pride.

Together we have improved all the housing and, with other Rotary Clubs, extended the school buildings and toilet facilities. Most significantly, all the villagers are now proactive and full of hope. I have always felt a warm, vibrant and positive atmosphere throughout the community whenever I have visited Suntakhan. They have a Village Committee led by the headmaster of the school and this committee works directly with Kathmandu Metro members. We all work together and have built up a wonderful relationship of trust and mutual respect. Although the villagers can only contribute a small amount of money, they contribute immensely to all projects by providing willing and sustained hard labour and a wide variety of skills: it is a true partnership. In approximately ten years, by working together, Bakewell and Kathmandu Metro Rotary Clubs have improved the lifestyle of Suntakhan to such an extent that we were considering 'adopting' a different village that needed our help. This spirit of co-operation, commitment and sheer love of humanity shows what can be achieved by good-hearted people of different nationalities working together: politicians of all countries please take note!

However in 2015 Nepal suffered two devastating earthquakes with many aftershocks. The school and the extension at Suntakhan were damaged along with the water pipes and reservoir, and lots of the houses suffered severe damage too. As soon as they could, members of Kathmandu Metro went to the village to assess what help was needed. Santosh told me that although many village houses had been wrecked and villagers had lost facilities and possessions, there was still an amazing positive spirit throughout the community. This was perfectly summed up by the school's headmaster who said, 'We have built things up before and we will do it again; we are not going to let an earthquake defeat us!'

Of course, many Rotary clubs, including Bakewell donated money to help with the rebuilding.

When I told the president and members of my Bakewell Rotary Club, that my 'granddaughter', Rachael, was planning to visit Suntakhan with her dad, Ian and Santosh, they nominated her as our Young Ambassador in Nepal, gave her our Rotary banner, asked her to take photographs of the rebuilding in Suntakhan and assess how the scholars and villagers were recovering from the effects of the earthquakes. This was a huge responsibility and honour for a twelve-year-old. Rachael was justifiably a very proud young lady.

Ian had set his alarm for 5 a.m. because they wanted to be down in reception ready for Santosh at 5.45 a.m. Unfortunately as soon as she woke up, Ian could see that Rachael's face was quite flushed. Anxiously he asked her if she was feeling poorly and she confirmed that she had felt hot and cold in the night.

'I feel as though I have a bit of 'flu but I'll be okay when I've had a drink of water. Don't worry Dad.'

Ian knew that the visit to Suntakhan would be quite arduous so he told Rachael he thought he should ring Santosh and postpone the visit.

'No! Please don't do that Dad,' Rachael begged. 'I'll be okay, really I will. I so want to go to Suntakhan and see the school and village. I want to fulfil my duty as the Young Ambassador for Bakewell Rotary Club. Please don't postpone our visit. Please, I feel much better already!'

Indeed she was looking much brighter and her forehead was cooler so Ian reluctantly agreed that they would carry on. He knew that if Rachael were poorly at any time during their visit, Santosh would bring them back to the hotel immediately. They dressed and packed quickly; an easy task as they had left most of their things with Pari and C.P. Ian asked at reception if they could put their rucksacks in the store room to collect just after lunch.

'No problem, Sir!' he was told. All Nepalese seem very obliging.

Santosh arrived promptly at 6 a.m. in his new car and greeted them warmly – Rachael especially whom he had not met before. They all set off through the unusually quiet and almost deserted streets of Kathmandu. In another hour or so they would be noisy and bustling with traffic, people and animals. As they left the city, the road became more uneven and winding. Ian noted that Rachael was far from her normal vivacious self. He explained to Santosh that Rachael wasn't feeling too well that morning; Santosh immediately said that he would change the plans he had made for them. Because Santosh knew of Rachael's love of trekking, he had planned to park a distance from Suntakhan and take them on a scenic walk of about ten miles in the foothills surrounding the village before they visited the school. He suggested that instead he should find somewhere to park his car as near to the village as possible so that they would only have a short walk of about two miles. Had Santosh known Rachael wasn't very well, he would have picked them up in a 4x4 so they could have driven right up to the village and left the car in the school playground. (As I know only too well the last few miles of the 'road' to Suntakhan consist of a dirt track full of holes and rocky outcrops; certainly not accessible in an ordinary car.)

Rachael seemed to be a lot better once she was out in the fresh air and looked eagerly around her. The surrounding fields were full of different crops as well as the small gardens next to the little village houses. Some of these still showed evidence of earthquake damage but many had been repaired. As they neared Suntakhan, Santosh pointed out the area high above the village beyond the houses where the spring was located that they had used to provide clean, fresh water for the entire village. He told Rachael and Ian how all the Rotarians had helped the villagers to build a wall around the spring to prevent contamination by animals and had helped to lay the new water pipes down the hillside.

'It was absolutely freezing that November,' he said. 'We all worked very hard just to keep warm!'

He went on to confirm that although some of the pipes had been damaged in the earthquake, they had all been repaired so that there were new standpipes in the village streets and outside each house.

'You can put that in your report, Rachael,' he said. 'It is wonderful now that everyone has safe water to drink, especially the babies, children and old people. Now there is very little sickness in the village and we have to thank Rotary Clubs like your grandma's that helped us fund this project, maintain it and sent donations to help with the repairs after the earthquake.'

By now they had reached the school and were greeted enthusiastically by the head teacher. The playground and courtyard in front of the school were being used by the local volleyball team as a practice ground. They were very voluble and enthusiastic and many seemed really skilled.

'Unfortunately there are no pupils in school today,' the head teacher explained, 'because they are all celebrating the Festival of Tihar or Deepawali with their families.'

It would seem that this particular five-day Hindu Festival of Lights is almost an extension of Dashain as it not only shows reverence for humans and gods but also celebrates the relationship of humans with animals, especially dogs, cows and crows. As at Dashain, dogs have garlands of flowers (often marigolds) put around their necks and the crows and other birds feast from bowls of special sweets placed on rooftops. The dates of all Nepalese festivals seem to be somewhat fluid so this festival can extend and merge with the most important Festival of Lights: Diwali. The observation that in Nepal every other structure is a holy shrine and every other day is a festival is somewhat of an exaggeration but it's not far off the truth!

Rachael listened very carefully to the head teacher's explanation and remarked quietly to Ian that she would rather like to attend school in Nepal because then she would have far more holidays! As always, Ian just smiled. The head then took them on a tour of the whole school and the extension showing them the well-furnished classrooms, the huge, new, well-stocked library, the science lab and the computer room. A new addition on the ground floor of the main school was a nursery for the young children of the village; this made it easier for their mothers to work. This old main part of the school had been repainted in its former pinkish-orange colour but the new extension was the brilliant blue so popular with the Nepalese. The head pointed out where all the repairs had been done and said how grateful he, the villagers and their children were for the massive help they had received from Rotarians and other volunteers to rebuild and make urgent repairs.

'Thankfully, because of all the support we had, we were able to re-open the school a few weeks after the disaster. It became a haven for our children,' he explained with a charming smile.

Ian and Rachael thanked him enthusiastically and Rachael promised that when she came back to Nepal, she would come up to the school again and would love to spend some time with the pupils in their classrooms. She told him how she had spent a day at Khushi's school.

'You will be most welcome!' the head assured her, 'so I hope we will see you next year, Rachael.'

Rachael beamed with delight and put her hands together saying 'Namaste' and bowing very politely.

Now it was the turn of Santosh to take them on a tour of Suntakhan village so Rachael could take photos of the repaired houses and new cottages under construction. The building work here was well advanced. The villagers waved affectionately to them and when Santosh explained who they were, everyone expressed their joy and gratitude. It was good to see their happy and positive attitudes. A little further up the hillside, Ian and Rachael could see the wreckage of the once extensive poultry houses; there was just one small shed still in use. Santosh explained that immediately after the earthquakes, all the men from Suntakhan and surrounding villages, whom Kathmandu Metro experts had educated in effective poultry husbandry, had returned to their homes to repair and rebuild their own houses and facilities. Understandably they had not yet returned.

Most of the poultry that Bakewell Rotary had funded were scattered all around: truly free-range hens but Santosh was sure that soon their small poultry industry would be up and running again, as well as it had before the earthquakes.

'Education is never lost, Rachael,' he said. 'The farmers now have the knowledge and expertise needed to carry on. I think that when all the poultry is rounded up they will have sufficient to start again and we will help them.'

As they continued on their tour, Santosh pointed out how all the gardens and fields were full of many varieties of healthy-looking produce, and cows and calves were grazing anywhere they could. When Rachael and Ian looked carefully, they were amazed to see how many of those escapee hens they could spot – in fact it became quite a competition! Just below the school, the beds of organic vegetables were thriving again and some men were busy repairing the greenhouses. Clearly all the people of Suntakhan had risen to the challenge of rebuilding their village and their community and had achieved an amazing amount in less than sixteen months after the devastating earthquakes. Santosh, Ian and Rachael were full of admiration.

They set off to walk back to Santosh's car and reached it in no time at all, possibly because the track was slightly downhill. Santosh drove them back to the Hotel Shakti and waved them goodbye.

'I'm looking forward to our next Rotary meeting, Rachael and Ian, when you both will be there. All our members are eager to meet the twelve-year-old Young Ambassador of Bakewell Rotary Club and hear her talk. Good Luck!'

Before Ian and Rachael went out into the hotel garden to relax and enjoy a well-earned cooling drink, Ian phoned Gobinda to ask him to take them back to Pari's house as soon as he could. So it was no surprise that he arrived with his taxi within ten minutes. Ian rescued their rucksacks and thankfully they were soon speeding on their way home.

Pari welcomed them warmly and promptly suggested that Rachael went to bed because she was looking very tired. Later Rachael wrote in her diary, *'I can't believe that I went to sleep in Khushi's bed at 3 p.m. in the afternoon! It was good though because when I woke up, I felt a lot better.'*

Luckily this was true because after they had all eaten, Khushi asked Rachael if she would like to go swimming. Rachael readily agreed after giving Ian a pleading look. Ian was a little reluctant to let her go but Rachael really did seem to be better. Her skin was cool and she was bright-eyed and seemingly bursting with energy. His daughter was certainly resilient so he agreed suggesting she didn't stay in the water too long. Pari explained that she would take them because only ladies and girls were allowed in the swimming pool together. This was obviously a Nepalese custom and part of their cultural heritage, notions that Rachael thoroughly understood. While they were away, Ian spent the time chatting to Ubick, showing him their photos and telling him all about Suntakhan. When Ian mentioned the volleyball, Ubick's face lit up. He confessed that he loved playing that sport and proudly announced that he played for a very good team. Ian congratulated him warmly.

When Pari and the girls returned, their faces were glowing. After Pari had made them hot drinks, Rachael and Khushi watched some DVDs in Khushi's room before they all went to bed. Just before she fell asleep, Rachael turned towards Ian sleepily:

'You know Dad that swimming pool was great but it was absolutely freezing. It was colder than the lakes in Iceland but I loved it!'

Ian reflected on all Rachael's marvellous experiences and wondered if there was another twelve-year-old girl in the world who had the knowledge to compare authentically the temperature of lakes in Iceland with a Nepalese swimming pool. Rachael could because she had swum in both!

DAY 17 – OCTOBER 23RD

As soon as Khushi had gone to school, Rachael began to rewrite the PowerPoint presentation (that annoyingly had crashed at the Hotel Shakti) for her school and Kathmandu Metro Rotary Club. Again she worked very diligently because she wanted to use it as a basis for her talk that evening. Unfortunately when she was about halfway through arranging the photos and the text, the whole presentation was lost again when the electricity and Internet connection went down.

'Well, that is that, Dad! Who needs a presentation? I am sure I can remember everything I want to say off the top of my head – I'll just wing it!' Rachael exclaimed. 'You will help me if I get stuck, won't you Dad?' she added.

'Of course, I will, darling,' Ian reassured her.

He felt very pleased that, once again, Rachael had accepted the situation with good humour.

Gobinda picked Ian and Rachael up just before 6 p.m. as arranged and drove them across Kathmandu City to where the Rotary meeting was being held.

Kathmandu Metro met in the upper conference room of an insurance company owned by one of the members. Santosh met them and introduced them to all of the members and visitors. There were far more people than Ian and Rachael had expected. Besides around twenty Kathmandu Metro Rotarians, there were twelve young Rotoract Members, who had come especially to listen to Rachael, and fourteen French Rotarians who were visiting the club. Most of the French Rotarians spoke very little English so one of the Kathmandu members translated Rachael's words so they could understand.

Potentially this was a very stressful situation for an adult, let alone a twelve-year-old but Rachael took it all in her stride: she was completely unfazed! With an enchanting smile, she spoke clearly and enthusiastically. Everyone in that room soon realised just how much she loved being in Nepal. Ian was astonished and very proud of her. She told her audience briefly about all the adventures she had undertaken with her dad, Ian and explained how this longer visit to Nepal was very different. She had been given permission from her school to extend her half-term holidays so she could learn all she could about the lifestyle, customs, faiths and education in Nepal. By visiting children's homes and orphanages, she would also learn how vulnerable children are cared for. Rachael held out her hands expressively and, looking around her entranced audience, smiled and ended with these words:

'I really enjoyed all my trekking in your beautiful mountains but this time I just wanted to learn more about the people of Nepal because you are all so kind, happy and loving – even Nepalese who have very few possessions. I have made some fantastic friends here – thank you all. Namaste.'

She put her hands together and bowed. The applause she received was long and loud: she had won everyone over!

Ian had tears of love and pride in his eyes as he took lots of photos of her amazing achievement. Then Rachael gave our Bakewell Rotary Club banner to Santosh and he presented her with the banner of Kathmandu Metro Rotary Club. The President, Binod Kumar Gautam, thanked her formally on behalf of his members and visitors. Of course lots of people wanted to ask her informal questions but she coped with all these admirably. She was a very popular young lady and it was clear she thoroughly enjoyed being the centre of attention.

Eventually they all drifted out onto the rooftop terrace where a splendid buffet and drinks had been laid out. Both Ian and Rachael circulated among all the members and visitors and chatted happily. Rachael spent some time talking with a lovely young lady called Neha who was half-German, half-Nepali and had an engaging Canadian accent! They compared schools and homework and discussed the recent earthquakes. Neha told Rachael how lucky she and her best friend had been. Apparently they were celebrating her friend's birthday when the first earthquake began. The house they were in began shaking and bricks started falling but they were able to rush outside. Thankfully most of the house remained standing so they were very grateful to be spared. Neha invited Rachael and Ian for dinner at her house and gave Rachael her address and phone number. Rachael thanked her warmly and

promised that when she returned to Nepal next year to trek to Everest Base Camp with her dad, she would get in touch with Neha and take up her invitation.

When the meeting and meal ended, Ian and Rachael thanked their hosts and Santosh put gold, silken kata scarves (which celebrate friendship and respect) around their necks before he bid them goodbye and a safe journey. Lovely Gobinda, as promised, had been waiting patiently in his taxi all the time Ian and Rachael had been at the Rotary meeting and drove them back to Pari's. When they entered her house, they were surprised to see that she had visitors: her mum and Pari's best friend. They were delighted to meet Rachael and clearly were fascinated by her story. They particularly wanted to know why such a young girl from the UK wanted to learn all she could about Nepali people. Both Rachael and Ian told them how much they loved Nepal and how Rachael didn't just want to trek in the Himalaya but wanted to learn about what is was like to live and be educated in their

lovely country. Although Pari's mum and her friend did not speak English, Pari and Khushi translated all that Rachael and Ian said. There were lots of smiles and everyone had a very pleasant evening. Rachael remarked to her dad later that she had loved talking with Pari's mum and her friend just as much as she had enjoyed the successful meeting with the Rotarians because 'they are ordinary lovely Nepali ladies, the kind of people I really wanted to meet and have as my friends.'

DAY 18 – OCTOBER 24TH

Just after breakfast, Gobinda arrived to drive Ian and Rachael to the Hotel Nepalaya where Ian had booked a twin-bedded room for one evening. They intended to return to Pari's in a few days' time so together they could all celebrate Diwali, the most important Festival of Light. However, because Ian knew that Rachael desperately wanted to revisit PA Nepal's children's homes with Indira, they needed to be in central Thamel for a while. Also in Kathmandu, he planned to book a very special surprise for Rachael.

It was actually Rachael who had chosen the Nepalaya. She had searched the Internet for hotels in Thamel and when she saw the Hotel Nepalaya had been awarded Hotel of the Year in 2015, she investigated further. She told Ian that the foyer, rooms, bathrooms, roof terrace and restaurant looked fabulous so he had taken her advice and booked immediately. As they approached the hotel through the narrow, less-than-salubrious back streets of Thamel, both Ian and Rachael began to question their choice. The price of their accommodation had seemed to be extremely cheap for all the facilities being offered. The appearance of the outside of the hotel did nothing to allay their fears, however it was for only one night so they could 'tough it out'. Somewhat reluctantly, they went inside.

To say that they were both gobsmacked is the understatement of the year: the huge foyer was fabulous! Gold gleamed everywhere and the floor was made of marvellous slabs of marble. Intricately carved pillars of rustic brick divided up the huge space and there were pots of beautiful flowers and ferns along the walls and in every nook and cranny. There was even an

More cake!

ornate ornamental pool with a bubbling fountain creating a calm, musical atmosphere. Up the middle of the foyer was a wide deep-red carpet that led to the stairs and reception desk. When Rachael and Ian walked up this luxurious carpet to book in, they felt like a pair of celebrities.

They were handed their key and directed up to the fourth floor. They gazed in amazement at their large twin-bedded room: it was wonderful. The beds were both a small double size with immaculate bedding and colourful cushions and throws. There was a fridge and well-stocked mini-bar, a tea and coffee machine, a big coffee table, desk and chairs as well as a lovely wooden double wardrobe and a set of drawers. The en suite was sparkling clean with a power shower, Western-style toilet, a large shining mirror and beautiful washbasin. Rachael was delighted to find that the WiFi connection was reasonably good and she quickly searched in the drawers and found a hairdryer, extra towels and throws. They could have been in a five-star hotel, the standard was so high! Obviously the Hotel Nepalaya had thoroughly earned the accolade of being Hotel of the Year in 2015 despite rooms being only £16.98 per night!

Once they had freshened up they decided to check out the roof terrace and restaurant. It was really picturesque with fairy lights, multi-coloured plants and trellises full of shady green vines and creepers. As the hotel was six storeys high, there was a wonderful view to the north: the snow-capped mountains of the fabulous Himalaya. However as they had shopping to do, they could not linger. So they went downstairs and out into the crowded, noisy streets of their beloved Kathmandu.

Their first stop was the Pumpernickel Café for some essential drinks and snacks. I bet you can guess what Rachael had – yes, a huge piece of their famous chocolate cake! (She pointed out to Ian that it was just an experiment: she had to compare this piece of chocolate cake with the one she had eaten there previously to make sure that the standard was being maintained … clever girl!)

Refuelled, they wandered around the shops slowly, enjoying the vibrant life, energy and magic of the crowded, noisy, dusty and, at times, smelly streets that are uniquely Kathmandu. You either love it or hate it: and we love it! It speaks to your soul so you are drawn back again and again. They spent so much time just chilling out that, when they were near to the New Orleans Café, they decided they needed a proper meal. While they were waiting for their order to be cooked and served, Rachael asked Ian if she could go to a nearby shop by herself where they had seen some very attractive woven throws. They were very light and colourful – ideal as presents so she wanted to negotiate a price herself.

'Please, Dad, I want to do this myself. I am very good at bargaining!'

As Ian could see the shop from where he was sitting, he readily agreed. He knew that Rachael had the confidence and knowledge to negotiate so he realised he must give her the opportunity. It wasn't long before she returned with a fantastic variety of throws – ten in total – with beautiful tassels. Each one was woven with contrasting but compatible vibrant colours and was soft and light but incredibly warm.

She had negotiated an amazingly low price for all ten.[2]

While they were eating their meal, Rachael brought up the subject of Everest Base Camp.

'You know, Dad, the first time we came to Nepal and I said that I wanted to trek to Everest Base Camp, you told me that I would have to wait until I was a teenager. Do you remember?'

Ian remembered very well!

'Yes, darling,' he answered, knowing full well what was coming next.

'Well, Dad, I am a teenager next year so that means I can go to Everest Base Camp, doesn't it?'

When Ian didn't respond immediately, she adopted a very innocent look.

'I know just how early you have to book to make sure that you can do the EBC trek on the dates you want so we really should book with Pradip's Mountain Monarch Adventures Company before we go home, shouldn't we, Dad? Then when we go back to Pari's, C.P. will be there – we can tell him the dates so that he can lead us. I really, really want to do that trek with C.P. and you, of course!'

I have said previously how well Rachael can negotiate with understanding, knowledge and logic; poor Ian really didn't have a chance!

'We'll talk about it later, Rachael,' he promised and added that they would have to ask her mum's permission and sensitively encourage her to agree.

'Leave it to me, please,' he said, 'I'll sort it out.'

When they were back in their room in the Hotel Nepalaya, Ian said he was going to stretch out on his bed and relax for a while. Rachael began playing games on her iPad and relaxed on her bed too. It was so quiet and the bed was really comfortable that Ian soon fell fast asleep. When he awoke some time later, he was alarmed to find Rachael was not in the room. He guessed that she had gone downstairs to the foyer because the WiFi reception there was better and she had probably not wanted to disturb him when he had fallen asleep.

He hurried downstairs and, sure enough, he found Rachael on FaceTime, having an argument with her mum. She had been so full of joy and elation that she would (probably) be fulfilling her dream to trek to Everest Base Camp next year, she had decided she simply had to tell her mum just how excited she was. Her mum had not been impressed to have this information thrust at her as a fait accompli and had immediately reacted by saying she would not allow Rachael to go. Rachael had replied heatedly that she had made lots of promises to return the next year and that she was determined to go to EBC with her dad, C.P. and Mountain Monarch Adventures. Ian knew that he needed to intervene and told Rachael that this was not the place or time for such a conversation. He told her to apologise to her mum; that at this moment both of them simply needed to agree to disagree. And so the conversation with her mum ended reasonably amicably but Rachael clearly was very upset. She felt her dream was slipping away: she had so been looking forward to the superb challenge of reaching Everest Base Camp with her dad and her lovely 'older brother' – C.P. Eventually she settled down in her bed and watched a DVD on the impressive television but was obviously really subdued.

Quite a while later that evening, her mum sent an email to Ian explaining that she had revised her decision. She said that she had done some research on the Internet and had consulted people who had actually done that trek and realised that children far younger then Rachael had successfully reached Base Camp. She had also looked up the Mountain Monarch Company and had been impressed by their record, their care and professionalism and, of course, she knew of C.P. and what a competent leader he was. She accepted that Rachael was a very fit and capable walker and had the necessary knowledge and skills. Besides, the following year was not such an important school year but for the two years after that, Rachael would have to concentrate on achieving good results in her high school examinations. She gave her permission because she knew Rachael would be safe and the following year would be the ideal time to go.

Ian immediately told Rachael what her mum had said: she shouted with joy and delight.

---

2 Rachael gave me a lovely, blue, purple and red one as a present and at the moment it is stretched across the bottom of my bed.

'I'm going to Everest Base Camp next year! That is just fab!'

Her face just glowed with eager anticipation and ecstasy.

'I can't wait!'

When, at last, she settled down for the night, Ian looked at her and wasn't at all surprised that she had gone to sleep with a grin of pure contentment on her youthful face. He made up his mind that the very next day, he would book that Everest Base Camp trek with Pradip and Mountain Monarch. What a lucky dad he was, to be able to fulfil another of his brave daughter's dreams and give her more memories to treasure forever. He was a very happy and proud man.

An empty EBC – Rachael's dream destination.

DAY 19 – OCTOBER 25TH

Before Rachael woke up, Ian researched hotels in Thamel on the Internet because it was his turn to choose the next one. He selected the Kathmandu Grand Hotel, which looked very impressive considering the price of a twin-bedded room was only £27. He did not want to wake Rachael up by ringing immediately so, because there were lots of rooms available in nearby hotels, he decided they would go to the Kathmandu Grand directly after breakfast and book in person.

As was their custom, they went to the Pumpernickel Café after they had packed their rucksacks and left them in reception at the Hotel Nepalaya. They relaxed and, as they ate, chatted about the Everest Base Camp trek

and what they had planned for later that day. Rachael could hardly wait to go back to PA Nepal and see Indira and those gorgeous babies. Then they picked up their rucksacks, Ian paid the bill and they made their way to the Kathmandu Grand Hotel on the main street. The Hotel was indeed grand with wide majestic marble steps leading up to the entrance and a really attractive façade. The section of the steps used by guests was covered in red carpet while on either side there were endless tubs of brilliant orange marigolds, more than Ian and Rachael had ever seen in a group display before. To add to their delight, a security guard dressed in a Nepalese Gurkha uniform complete with his traditional inwardly curving Kukri knife, saluted them as they went through the doorway.

'Wow Dad!' exclaimed Rachael, 'What a fab choice you've made – this is really cool!'

Ian crossed his fingers as he approached the reception desk and asked if a twin-bedded room was still available. He was in luck: there were several so he booked in for two nights. The smartly dressed reception clerk asked Ian if he and Rachael would like the large twin-bedded room on the top floor. He explained that it had two comfortable double beds, lots of furniture and all the necessary facilities as well as a wonderful view. Both of our intrepid travellers readily agreed and were not disappointed when they walked into their room. Although it was only one room, it was massive – more like a penthouse suite. The quality of the beds, linen and furniture was extremely high and just like their previous hotel, there was a fridge and mini-bar, a large TV and DVD player and a roomy well equipped bathroom with large fluffy towels and bathroom slippers. Everything was immaculate; they were both amazed at the range of wonderful amenities for so little cost.

After unpacking, they decided to explore the hotel before walking to PA Nepal. First they went out onto the roof terrace, which was enhanced by twinkling lights, beautiful flowers and ferns and decorative trellis-work. But the main attraction was the fabulous, panoramic view: they could see all over Kathmandu city; the surrounding verdant hills and, beyond these, to the majestic high Himalaya. The scene was absolutely breathtaking.

Downstairs was equally impressive: there were lots of seating areas with comfortable-looking settees and easy chairs, coffee tables, several bars and a beautiful dining room. The lounge area had a fantastic mural showing the main buildings of interest in the city including a superb depiction of the huge Boudnath Stupa. All the staff wore uniforms of long-sleeved white shirts, black trousers and black bow ties: they looked very neat and efficient and more importantly, were really friendly, helpful and polite. Ian had chosen well.

The smiling security guard saluted them again as they left the Kathmandu Grand Hotel which made them giggle. The weather was still quite warm but had been a little cloudy for the last few days. It didn't take them long to reach The Firefly Children's Home where they were greeted enthusiastically by Indira. Rachael immediately asked if she could go and play with Bha and Mir so Indira directed her up to the nursery. She found that both babies were asleep but Bha soon woke up when she realised that Rachael was cuddling her. She put her arms around Rachael's neck and squealed so loudly with joy that Mir woke up too. Rachael sat cross-legged on the floor, initially with one child at each side but naturally they crawled all over her, each one eager to sit on her knee. They chuckled and laughed when Rachael tickled them and as before, were fascinated by her phone. The babies, who constantly pressed the camera button, took some very funny photos! When Rachael sang to them, they joined in humming musically and seemed to understand what she said. They were completely happy and relaxed with her. Small children instinctively seem to know the people who love them; those who have that special way of showing tender care and devotion. Hugs, kisses and smiles are a universal language.

Ian spent some time in the office with Indira and her team and learned about her future plans and ambitions. Of course, these concentrated on caring for vulnerable children, prisoners and their families but also involved ways of encouraging people all over the world to help with her life's work.

While he was in the office, Ian rang Pradip at Mountain Monarch headquarters and booked the trek to Everest Base Camp for Rachael and himself the following year: in October 2017. He asked if it was possible for C.P. to be their leader. Pradip was overjoyed! I'm sure that you remember that when he gave Rachael that signed book about Everest, he had written, 'Another destination for you Rachael. Sure you can do it!' He realised long ago just how passionately Rachael wanted to trek to EBC, especially as Grandma Joyce had already been there. Pradip knew that she was more than capable of achieving her dream. He thanked Ian for the booking and promised that he would reserve places for them on the October EBC group trek, assuring them that C.P. would be one of the leaders. Ian thanked Pradip profusely – he was thrilled; a group trek was exactly what he wanted Rachael to experience: to spend time trekking with people of different nationalities, cultures and presumably different levels of fitness and skill.

He went upstairs to tell Rachael what he had done and she was so ecstatic that she bounced up and down with joy just as she had done when she was much younger. Bha and Mir realised that Rachael was extremely happy and excited so they clapped and gurgled with happiness. Indira and her team congratulated Rachael; they said she was a very lucky young lady and, of course, wished her every success.

'I know that next October I shall be at Everest Base Camp with my wonderful dad and C.P. but when I get back, I really, really want to come back here and see you all again. I promise that I'll come. I have had the best time here!' Rachael avowed, her eyes shining with affection.

This statement delighted Ian as much as the joy and gratitude Rachael had shown when he told her about booking the EBC trek. It showed her commitment and

The author at Everest Base Camp with two hunks! October 2005.

devotion to helping vulnerable children in the future in some way – perhaps in a Third World country like Nepal.

Before they left, Indira asked if they would like to accompany her the next day when she visited one of the prisons. Rachael nodded eagerly so Ian agreed. It was something that he had wanted to do for some time but had been unsure whether or not Rachael would cope. When he took into consideration just how much she had matured on this trip and the eagerness and dedication she had shown, he was sure that she was really up for it. It would be another challenge for her but a very different one and a valuable learning experience.

DAY 20 – OCTOBER 26TH

When they woke up, the sun was shining and the sky was a beautiful cerulean blue with not a cloud in sight. These were exactly the conditions that Ian had been waiting for; you will shortly find out why.

Mid-morning, Ian and Rachael were picked up by Indira in the local taxi that she always uses. The driver is her friend and an ardent supporter of all her work. Indira was sitting in the front with Bha and Mir on her knee so Rachael and Ian sat on the back seat. However as soon as Bha saw Rachael, she struggled to climb into the back of the taxi so she could sit on Rachael's knee. Rachael was delighted and hugged Bha making sure that she was secure and comfortable. Then they picked up a man called Toby; despite being quite squashed in the back, it was fun. Toby was Dutch but spoke excellent English. He was working for the Dutch Penal System, studying the prison organisation and conditions in Nepal and comparing them with systems in his homeland. He told Ian and Rachael that this was the first time he had visited a prison with Indira. He was really inspired by her work, very interested in all her penal reforms and wanted to learn more about PA Nepal. They all had a lot in common and chatted amicably.

Before Indira began to initiate her reforms, prisoners had no advocates and no rights. No one seemed to care about them or their families, including the children. When women were sent to prison, their children became street children – virtual orphans. In Nepal most men, especially the poor, have to work very long hours and are not expected to care for children. It is not part of their culture, and consequently most men are not aware how to do it.

Subsequently there was no one responsible for the children's welfare: they were simply abandoned and all family bonds were broken. Because of Indira's dedicated work, more and more prison reforms have taken place and the conditions in prison and within the prisoners' families have improved immensely.

In female prisons, there are now excellent schools for the children within the prison itself so they are no longer separated from their mothers. The mothers cook

This is why PA Nepal exists.

all their children's meals: breakfast, dinner and tea, and they all eat together, thus maintaining strong family bonds. In the men's prisons, there have been improvements in conditions too. But sadly, because there are no special facilities like hospitals and homes for the mentally handicapped, many of the male prisoners who had committed crimes did so because they were suffering from mental health issues. Male prisoners are still not allowed to see their children while they are in prison.

Later, on her www.rachaelexplore.com website, Rachael wrote, *'PA Nepal offers support programmes and prison welfare visits, housing for rescued children and aid for families across Nepal … I was really inspired by the work they do.'*

About halfway through their hour's drive to the prison, Indira asked the taxi driver to stop at the market so she could buy boxes of apples and bananas for Rachael to give to the prisoners. As you may imagine, when these were loaded into the taxi, conditions were even more cramped! Indira emphasised to Ian, Toby and Rachael that although the men's prison they were about to visit looked intimidating, she begged them not judge it on first sight as the conditions inside would amaze them. She was right to warn them because their first glimpse of the prison was of high walls topped by razor wire and in a tower there was a guard in combat uniform with a machine gun. (The gun was actually hidden below the palisade of the tower but Ian was told that all the prisoners were aware of its position.)

Understandably Toby, Ian and Rachael were a little apprehensive as they approached the prison. Indira was welcomed warmly by the unarmed guards at the gates, which they unlocked so that Indira and her party could enter. No passes or identification documents were necessary as the guards obviously knew Indira really well and were accustomed to her bringing visitors and gifts. Then the group was conducted by uniformed guards through several gates into a courtyard about the size of a tennis court, where they found all the prisoners sitting on the floor in a relaxed way. There were about seventy male prisoners of various ages who had been given the option of meeting Indira and her guests. Then, amazingly, the guards went away, leaving Indira, Toby, Ian, twelve-year-old Rachael and two babies alone with the prisoners. Ian's eyes were like a hawk's as he scrutinised all the prisoners diligently but Indira was completely unperturbed as amazingly was Rachael! Ian was astonished to see Bha and Mir toddling about among the men, smiling and happy, just as if they were among friends. He looked questioningly at Indira who smiled and mouthed, 'Honestly, it's okay!'

Indira drew them closer to the sitting prisoners and introduced them all and asked the prisoners how old they thought Rachael was. They all responded with suggestions that she was between seventeen and twenty and were astonished when Indira told them that she was only twelve! She went on to tell them about all the things Rachael had done and the men smiled happily and gazed at Rachael with complete admiration. As a caring and loving dad, naturally Ian was still rather concerned about his precious daughter's safety; after all, there were no guards! He voiced his concerns to Toby who told Ian to look at the prisoners' feet. Ian's keen eyes soon spotted that most prisoners were barefoot or wearing flip-flops or Crocs

A box is the best toy!

but some had heavy boots on. Toby explained that the prisoners with the boots were the 'senior' prisoners and were responsible for maintaining order, for which they earned privileges. In effect the prisoners policed themselves and Toby was here to study how this system worked and if it could be adopted in the Netherlands.

Indira then showed the prisoners the boxes of fruit that Rachael was about to give them. All the prisoners lined up in an orderly queue organised by the 'senior' prisoners and gratefully thanked Rachael with a cheerful 'Namaste' as she handed them an apple or a banana. Then most of the prisoners sat down again but some produced instruments and started to play the loveliest Nepalese music. Bha and Mir clapped their hands and began to dance joyfully. Some prisoners danced with them and were clearly enchanted by those beautiful babies – quite a few had tears in their eyes. Indira's objective was to remind the men of their own children and to encourage them to think ahead and plan for family life after they had left prison. In this way she hoped to maintain their family bonds. The whole atmosphere was not in the least threatening: it was warm, friendly and relaxed. Ian was amazed. To the great amusement of the prisoners, Bha, tired out by her enthusiastic dancing, sat down in the discarded fruit box!

Rachael's words sum up the situation perfectly:

'Today I did something I thought that I would never do. Me, Dad, Indira Ranamagar, Toby and two little one-year-olds, Bha and Mir all visited an adult male prison. We met all the dads who are locked up and missing their own children, which is sad cause many of these men have mental health problems. It was lovely to see how they liked meeting the babies and playing with them.'

After about an hour, a guard came to say that the prisoners needed to go back to their duties and the governor of the prison would like to see Indira and her visitors. When the men had drifted back inside in an orderly fashion, Ian asked the guard what facilities the men had to overcome the boredom of being in restricted circumstances.

'I'll show you,' said the guard.

As he led them towards the governor's office, he pointed out the music room, well-stocked library, TV room, sports room, and the room used as an adult classroom with many high-grade educational activities.

'We also have medical facilities too,' he added with a smile.

The governor welcomed them in a friendly manner and offered them tea. This is an honourable gesture so they felt obliged to accept. Ian was dreading this because the tea offered to visitors in Nepal is strong and extremely sweet as it is nearly always sweetened with condensed milk and has a blob of yak butter floating on the top. I can confirm that it is disgusting! (Rachael has her own method of dealing with this: she just smiles, gives Ian a wide-eyed look and when no one is looking, surreptitiously switches her full cup for her dad's empty one. Poor Ian always has two cups to drink but manfully manages both!)

After tea, Ian and Toby had lots of questions they wanted to ask about the systems operating in the prison. The governor was very polite and obliging because he clearly admired Indira and realised that her friends were genuinely interested and supportive and were there to learn. At Ian's request he gave them more details about the way the prison was run using the policy of prisoners policing them-selves, which seemed to be very successful. The governor confirmed this; guards were not necessary. The prisoners slept in dormitories of around ten beds, not in cells. In each dormitory, one 'senior' inmate, (the one with boots), was responsible for maintaining order and discipline. In addition, he acted as a kind of mentor and any prisoner could talk to him about problems or concerns they had. He would listen and then follow up these concerns so each prisoner knew they had a link with the management of the prison and would not be ignored. In addition to the boots, if these 'seniors' did their job efficiently, they were rewarded with the equivalent of five rupees (five pence) per day, which, at the end of the week, would buy them an extra cup of tea. More importantly, they could earn up to a year's remission on a ten-year sentence. All the 'seniors' seemed to be very proud of their privileged position and were respected among their fellow prisoners. When a 'senior' was released, there was always keen competition to fill his place. The governor went on to explain that although many of the prisoners had committed crimes because of mental health problems and as yet there were no special facilities for them, beyond medication, they seemed to benefit from living in a supportive, caring community. Providing specialist care was an ongoing project but he emphasised that, thanks to reformers like Indira, they had made immense progress.

Ian then asked if any of the prisoners had ever escaped and was told that in twenty years, there had never been a single attempt. In fact the Governor confirmed that all the guards were unarmed except the guard in the tower whose gun had never

Indira Ranamagar.

been fired. He added with a smile, 'I'm not sure that the gun even works now. It is ages since it was tested!'

Ian, Rachael and Toby were astonished but full of admiration. On the way back to the hotel in the taxi, they discussed all they had experienced and were totally won over. As Indira pointed out, they had been as safe in that prison as they would have been walking down the streets in Kathmandu or any other city in the world – probably much safer. Toby and Ian earnestly believed that such a mutual trusting and caring system would be hard to introduce in both of their countries, where long-established penal systems are based on punishment and incarceration with no real understanding or empathy between the criminals and the prison officers whose job it is to guard them.

Ian reflected in wonder that a poor Third World country had taught them so much. He realised with awe that the gentle, caring and peaceful nature of the Nepalese, their sheer humanity had influenced and would continue to influence the development and progress in the organisations of all their institutions. All they had ever needed was the energy, dedication and direction of people like Indira to show them the way. He had seen for himself that the standard of education was now higher in Nepal, including the prison schools, than in the UK and that, even in incarceration, their gentle, caring and protecting nature shone through. In that prison, despite lack of specialist treatment, prisoners with mental health problems were cared for by the officials of the prison system and by the prisoners themselves. This was a real demonstration of Care in the Community. We all have much to learn. Ian genuinely felt that in all his years of experience in caring for and protecting the most vulnerable in society, particularly children, he had never been so inspired.

He realised, with gratitude, just how much valuable understanding Rachael would have gained throughout this visit: an experience that could direct and influence her future life and career.

Ian and Rachael thanked Indira sincerely and arranged to go back to The Firefly Children's Home the next day so that, with Toby's help, they could download the photos Ian had taken on his camera (mobile phones were not allowed in the prison). Then the taxi driver dropped them off at the Kathmandu Grand Hotel.

After a quick shower, Ian said he was just popping out to do some shopping; he wouldn't be long.

'It's okay, Dad,' said Rachael, 'I've lots to do. I must fill my diary in as I've so much to say and I'm going to look up nearby hotels and choose one for us because it is my turn. Can I book it, please?'

'Yes, of course you can,' replied Ian. 'I trust you to make a good choice.'

And with that he went quickly downstairs.

A surprise ticket to fly over Everest.

Actually he wasn't strictly going shopping, as you will see. Just round the corner from the hotel, about three minutes away, was the office of the agency with whom he had booked their Chitwan Safari Trip. He knew the office stayed open until 9 p.m. He had been waiting for a period of clear weather so that he could book a mountain flight over the Himalaya for Rachael. He wanted to give her the opportunity of seeing Everest in all her majestic beauty before she returned next year to trek to Base Camp. He was advised that the very best and safest airline for this adventure was Simrik Airlines so he booked two seats on one of their planes. He put the tickets in his back pocket and made his way back to the hotel.

As soon as he entered their room, Rachael eagerly told him that she had booked the Tibet Guest House for their last night in Thamel.

'It looked super on my iPad, Dad,' she explained.

Ian was thrilled because that was the one hotel he had always wanted to stay in so he congratulated her for her selection. His face took on a serious countenance:

'Come on, Rachael, you need to shower and go to bed early.'

Immediately he got the usual loud protestations that she was not tired and it wasn't fair. Then she looked at Ian's smug face.

'What's going on? Why must I go to bed early, Dad? You are being tricky again!'

'This is why!' Ian replied and like a magician, he produced the tickets for the flight over the Himalaya – just like that – and dropped the tickets in her lap. She read one slowly then gasped.

'Wow! Wow!' she shouted, incandescent with joy, 'I am going to see Everest and all the other mountains. You are the very best dad in the world. Thank you! Thank you! I am so happy!'

'You have earned that treat, darling,' replied Ian, 'and that is why you need to go to bed early because as you can see, the flight is at 7.30 a.m. We have to be at Tribhuvan Airport an hour before that so the company car is picking us up around six o'clock.'

There were no more protests. Rachael gave Ian a hug and dashed into the shower. A few minutes later she snuggled down in her bed and, turning to Ian, she smiled.

'Tomorrow is going to be so cool. I am such a lucky girl to have a dad like you. I do so love you!'

DAY 21 – OCTOBER 27TH

Rachael was awake even before Ian's 5 a.m. alarm went off – she was just so excited. She quickly glanced out of the window to check on the weather: the sky was clear and it promised to be a gorgeous day. She bounded out of bed and proceeded to shake Ian awake.

'Dad, Dad! It's going to be a fantastic day. Look outside: the sky is cloudless!'

They dressed quickly, packed and were downstairs in the foyer well before 6 a.m.

Ian went to the reception desk, which was manned twenty-four hours a day and asked to pay their bill. He had a wry smile on his face because he knew what was going to happen. Even though the Kathmandu Grand was a really high-class hotel, Ian expected the same response as always when he produced his debit card. He was right.

'Sorry sir,' said the reception clerk regretfully, 'our card machine has broken down so you need to pay cash, please.'

Surprise, surprise! Every card machine in every hotel, shop and café in the whole of Kathmandu seems to suffer from the very same disease: it is called 'a culture of cash'!

'Oh, come on!' protested Ian, thoroughly enjoying this expected exchange. 'This is a superb hotel – I'm sure you can get your card machine to operate and we are waiting to be picked up.'

'I'm really sorry, sir. I have tried but it is truly broken,' was the sorrowful answer. The clerk added that there was a cash machine nearby. Ian had predicted this would happen so he had drawn out the necessary amount on his way back from booking their Everest flight; however he had been unable to resist teasing the reception clerk. With a resigned look, Ian handed over the cash and asked if it was possible to leave his and Rachael's rucksacks in reception to be collected later that day.

'Of course, sir!' was the quick reply. 'Your rucksacks will be perfectly safe. We are always eager to help all our guests.'

'Really?' Ian responded with a sardonic smile. (Except enabling payment by credit, he thought but did not say, though his eyebrows were raised knowingly.)

This interplay had taken some time so it was fortunate that the agency's company car did not arrive until almost 6.30 a.m. They climbed in quickly and were outside Tribhuvan Airport within twenty minutes. Miraculously, as they went inside, they spotted a very familiar, smiling face: that of C.P. He was returning from a trek with his MMA group. They greeted one another enthusiastically and as C.P. ushered his group towards the luggage reclaiming area, Rachael called out to him:

'See you sometime tomorrow, C.P. Please give my love to Khushi and Pari. I'm going on my Everest flight now!'

'Good luck!' was C.P.'s earnest reply.

Unfortunately, within a few minutes of arrival, Ian and Rachael were told that their Everest flight would be delayed three hours until 10.30 a.m. Although the sky was clear in Kathmandu, apparently at Lukla, there was thick mist. Lukla is the airport to which Everest Base Camp trekkers are flown and it has a tiny and extremely difficult landing strip. It is surrounded by mountains and the approach can be hazardous, as I know very well. In mist and strong cross-winds it is completely inaccessible; delays are inevitable. Only STOL (short take-off and landing) aircraft can be used and these were blocking the runway at Tribhuvan so no other flights could take off until the mist at Lukla had cleared. Ian and Rachael did not mind at all: strangely they enjoy waiting in airports! They just bought some drinks and snacks and studied the route that their aircraft would take over the high Himalaya.

Eventually, around 10 a.m. they were told to collect their boarding passes and were taken to their aircraft. It was a small fixed-wing plane with a pilot and co-pilot and had just single window seats with a narrow aisle between them. Ian directed Rachael to a left-hand-side seat near the back of the plane and sat directly across from her. He knew that from this position, she would be on the side nearest the mountains.

They took off and headed westwards towards those magnificent snow-capped peaks. The first huge mountain that came into view was the majestic bulk of Dhaulagiri with its sheer spectacular face rearing over the wide-bottomed Kali Gandaki Valley, guarded on the east by the fabulous Annapurnas: one fantastic peak after another, divided by the dark blue depths of passes and hidden valleys. Actually between Dhaulagiri and Annapurna 1, the Kali Gandaki Valley is deeper than the Grand Canyon in the USA. Everyone in the aircraft was utterly spell-bound; the views were truly breathtaking and completely panoramic.

Next were the rugged peaks of the Ganesh and Langtang Himal and, as they flew eastwards towards the Everest range, the pristine-white peak of Cho Oyu at the head of the Gokyo Valley dominated the scene. As with many of the Himalayan mountains, the southern ramparts of Cho Oyu are in Nepal and the northern in Tibet. They form a spectacular and at times impenetrable barrier. As they flew ever nearer to Everest, the highest mountain in the world at 8,848m, Rachael spotted the large settlement of Namche Bazaar. She pointed it out eagerly to Ian because she knew that next year, when they did their Everest Base Camp trek, Namche would be the second place they would stay after landing at Lukla. (She had studied the maps of the Everest region and researched the EBC itinerary very well.) Then they were over Everest herself: shining like bluish-white glass as she reflected the beautiful sunshine and the intense blue sky. She glowed just as if she was illuminated from within. Her immense bulk was enhanced by her satellite mountains, Nuptse and Lhotse, which guarded her flanks. The co-pilot left his seat and invited a delighted Rachael to sit in the cockpit so she could take photos. She gasped in awe and joy and vowed that, one day, she would climb right to the summit. Ian looked at her face as she returned to her seat, her eyes shining like stars.

Everest was formerly just called Peak XV but later was renamed Everest after Sir George Everest, the British Surveyor General of India. Everest seems a fitting name for the highest mountain in the world as it appears 'to go on forever', although, apparently the Everest family pronounced their surname 'Eve-rest'. The Nepali name for the mountain is Sagarmatha which means 'Peak of Heaven' and the Tibetan name is Chomolungma which means 'Goddess Mother of the World.'

Mount Everest as taken by Rachael from the co-pilot's seat.

The infamous Khumbu Ice Fall.

From Everest, they flew over the smaller peak of Ama Dablam at 6,812m – one of my favourite peaks because to me it is a classic Matterhorn shape: a slim spectacular spire which dominates the village of Dingboche nestling in the snowy valley far below it. Beyond Ama Dablam were the last two mountains to the east: the beautiful peak of Makalu and spectacular Kanchenjunga, which at 8,586m is the third highest mountain in the world and like K2 (the second highest), is notoriously difficult to climb. The plane then turned round and made its way back along the whole length of the wonderful Himalayan range so that the passengers could see all the mountains from a different angle. However, knowing that Rachael would love to be looking directly at those magnificent peaks again, Ian switched places with her so the Himalaya were just the other side of her window as on their outward flight.

All too soon they landed back at Tribhuvan Airport and were driven back to the Kathmandu Grand Hotel. Rachael was unusually quiet so that Ian asked her what was wrong.

'Absolutely nothing, Dad. That flight was awesome!' she said. 'It's just that the mountains were so stunning, I can't find the words to describe them or how I feel – it was the most exciting thing I have ever done!'

Ian knew just how she felt because he felt exactly the same. It had been an out-of-this-world experience.

Before they went to collect their rucksacks from the Kathmandu Grand Hotel, Ian and Rachael decided they should go to The Firefly Children's Home so that Toby could upload the photos of their inspiring prison visit from Ian's camera. When they arrived, they were pleased to see that Toby was already there, as well as Indira.

BE AWARE !!!

Any sexual activities with the children is a **CRIME** in Nepal

If.....................Jail upto 16 years

E OF CHILDREN

GOVERNMENT OF NEPAL
MINISTRY OF WOMEN, CHILDREN &
SOCIAL WELFARE

It did not take long to upload all the photos and Toby in particular was thrilled because they were excellent. Toby thanked Ian and told him that some of the photos would be included in the report he was compiling for the Dutch Penal Organisation. Before Rachael and Ian left, Indira gave Rachael a hug and told them both they would be welcome to return any time.

'Of course, we'll be back, Indira,' Rachael confirmed enthusiastically. 'I have had the best time ever with you, Bha and Mir. When Dad and I have finished our EBC trek next year, I am definitely coming back here. It will be great to see just how much Bha and Mir have grown by then. I wonder if they will remember me.'

With a beaming smile, Indira assured her that those little girls loved her so much, she was certain they would remember Rachael for a very long time.

Ian and Rachael went to retrieve their rucksacks from the hotel and walked to the Tibet Guest House, only five minutes away, situated at the junction between the Thamel and Chetrapati districts. It had an eye-catching reddish-pink frontage with the name Tibet Guest House emblazoned across and down a huge central panel. Ian was eager to find out what the interior was like; he had heard so much about this hotel – a recognised favourite of trekkers for many years. In many ways it was

A balmy evening at the Tibet Guest House.

similar to their previous hotel, but as it was established before tourism in Kathmandu began to be popular, it was much more traditional and looked a little old-fashioned although still very attractive and scrupulously clean. Heavy ornate carvings decorated the pillars, covings and ceilings, some of them multicoloured and very intricate. Huge old-fashioned bladed fans whirred continuously and everywhere there were ornaments and a huge variety of ferns and flowers in beautifully carved tubs. There were lots of imaginative murals of animals for which Nepal is famous including a huge 3D one in the courtyard which depicted a tiger, an elephant with a monkey on its back and a very strange creature that looked half lion and half snow leopard.

Initially there was a problem when they tried to take up the reservation Rachael had made through a travel website. The puzzled-looking reception clerk checked the bookings and confirmed apologetically that they had no reservation under the name of Moseley and anyway, at the Tibet Guest House, they did not deal with the company in question! This was blatantly untrue as the hotel was advertised and rated by the website. However when Ian said they would go elsewhere, the clerk offered them an upgraded twin-bedded room for the same price if they paid cash. (The old cash-culture story!) Ian could not be bothered to argue so soon they were established in a large room with twin double beds and all the usual facilities.

After having a short rest and much-needed showers, Ian and Rachael made their way up to the roof terrace over which dozens of prayer flags fluttered in the breeze, creating a special feeling of peace and goodwill. Even though it was late October, it was a beautiful warm balmy evening so they decided to relax in the comfortable armchairs, have a drink and absorb all the craziness and atmosphere of this fabulous city. The views were completely panoramic: the distant mountains and foothills were just dark shadows on the horizon while the lights of the city surrounded them and the noise of the traffic, people and animals drifted up from the streets below. The spell of Kathmandu had captured them both and kept them enthralled. They felt utterly relaxed and happy. As they gazed upwards, delicate skeins of clouds drifted across the silvery face of the moon as the sky gradually darkened. A myriad of stars shone brilliantly, casting their ethereal light earthwards; the pretty twinkling fairy lights on the terrace were no match for their natural glory. What a wonderful, enchanting place to spend their last night in that magical city.

Later, as Rachael sank into her comfortable bed, she sighed with pure contentment. It had been an awesome day: one she would never ever forget, and tomorrow they were going back to the home of C.P. Pari and Khushi for several days to celebrate the Festival of Diwali.

DIWALI WITH THEIR SECOND FAMILY – OCTOBER 28TH–30TH

Gobinda and his trusty taxi arrived around 10 a.m. to take Ian and Rachael to C.P.'s home so they could all be together for this important family celebration in Nepal. They felt really sad to be saying a fond farewell to Gobinda because he had always been so friendly and cheerful and had helped them enormously. He too seemed subdued and rather emotional; he was obviously going to miss his English friends. Ian assured him that when he and Rachael came back next year to do the EBC trek, they would most certainly use his taxi again. Ian confirmed that he still had the card with all Gobinda's contact details and said that he would recommend him to all his friends. Gobinda beamed happily at this and wished Rachael and Ian a safe journey home.

When they arrived, C.P. rushed out enthusiastically to greet them and led them inside his home. As soon as they entered they realised that Pari and Khushi were very busy cleaning the house from top to bottom. To an outsider this would seem unnecessary as proud Pari kept their long-awaited home immaculate. However both Rachael and Ian understood that this was part of the traditional preparations for Diwali: everyone cleaned, renovated and decorated their homes for this, the most important holy Hindu festival of the year. Apart from helping to move and carry things, there was little for them to do, however Rachael, as always, was completely up for it. Eagerly, she threw herself wholeheartedly into helping wherever she could.

Diwali: the Holy Hindu Festival of Lights celebrates the triumph of light over darkness, good over evil, justice over injustice and intelligence over ignorance. During the whole five days of the festival, devotees burn innumerable Diwali lights and worship their gods with frequent ritual pujas or long time-honoured prayers said and chanted either at communal shrines or private ones. In Nepal, the main goddess worshipped is Lakshmi – the wife of the powerful Lord Vishnu. She is the goddess of wealth and prosperity, light, beauty and fertility. Another goddess revered at this time is gentle and wise Saraswati: the goddess of knowledge, learning and music. Offerings are also made to Ganesh – the elephant god of ethical beginnings and remover of obstacles for true believers. Other gods and goddesses are worshipped in different regions and countries throughout the Hindu world according to their specific Diwali customs.

At Diwali, everyone dresses in their very best clothes, many of which have been bought especially for the occasion. Nepali ladies look amazing in their beautiful brightly coloured saris embellished with intricate embroidery in gold and silver. They have gorgeous henna patterns on their arms and wear lots of multi-coloured bangles. Their carefully applied make-up enhances their facial features especially their lovely dark eyes, which are outlined with kohl. They wear the traditional red tika marks on their foreheads, as do the men. The Nepali men look very splendid and proud in their best suits and all wear the traditional headgear – beautifully patterned hats that resemble the Moroccan fez.

The ladies of the house prepare a huge variety of dishes: rice, dry fruits and special sweets called 'mithai' for family, friends, neighbours and visitors. The bowls and plates are replenished regularly and are never allowed to be empty throughout the festival.

Children are told ancient traditional stories especially the long and inspiring legend of Lord Rama and his wife Sita. Helped by the monkey god, Hanuman, they returned in triumph after many years of peril, wandering in the wilderness. Eventually Lord Rama defeated and utterly destroyed the evil devil, Ravana and was reunited with his beloved wife, Sita. Thousands of Diwali lights or 'diyas' were used to light their path from Ceylon (Sri Lanka) back home to Nepal, hence the importance and significance of keeping Diwali lights burning night and day. They are placed inside and outside homes on steps, windowsills, terraces and rooftops, which are also festooned with fairy lights. Where there is water, Diwali lights are floated on the surface to represent the illuminating influence of the holy mother of rivers: the Ganges. The whole of the Kathmandu Valley is a huge bowl of glowing patches of luminescence. To the south, the city and the night sky are lit up by fire-works exploding in brilliant sparkling multi-coloured patterns like an enormous galaxy of stars. While to the north, in the foothills of the Himalaya, the myriad of Diwali lights twinkle and glitter like a billion fireflies. Above all though, Diwali is the time when loving families come together and are united sharing a holy enlight-ening experience that has a deep devout significance for all of them.

As soon as everything was absolutely spotless to the total satisfaction of Pari and C.P. the first task for Khushi and Rachael was to complete a Rangoli design on the marble floor of the inner sheltered entrance of the house. These traditional intricate decorations are done by women and are believed to bring good luck to the house-hold and to all who visit during Diwali. They incorporate beautiful geometric designs with symbols and flowers and are very brightly coloured. Generally, natural materials are used like powdered rice and flour augmented by brick dust and sand. To these are added brilliant colours like vermilion (sindoor) and turmeric and the mixture put into little pots. Pari showed the girls how to do the design and then left them to finish it. Of course Khushi had seen her mum do Rangoli patterns before but this was the first time one had been done in their very own house. She felt very honoured and so did Rachael. They worked together very diligently and carefully while Pari went into the kitchen to begin her cooking. She had lots to do. When they had finished, they went to help Pari make the special sweets for all their family, friends and visitors and – just like children all over the world – they had to sample some!

Their next task was to put up all the multi-coloured fairy lights. It took ages and Ian's help was needed to secure the higher ones. Everyone held their breath when C.P. plugged them in: they worked! Fantastic! When Pari lit the flickering Diwali lights and placed them all around the house, inside and outside, their home became a magical place of light and warmth. She even floated some lights in their little candleholders on tubs of water to represent the holy river Ganges – the sacred river of all Hindus.

Eventually when Pari had finished all the cooking, she and Khushi showered then went to dress in their finest clothes. Rachael helped Khushi with her gorgeous sari, hair arrangement and accessories and then with her make-up. When they emerged from Khushi's bedroom, Ian and C.P. clapped in admiration: Khushi looked very lovely. She smiled shyly but they could see she was really pleased. C.P. too looked resplendent in his crisp white shirt, newly acquired suit and multi-coloured hat. Before Pari reappeared, C.P. explained that he had to go and perform his puja with his male friends at the holy shrine in his local temple: this was all part of the rituals of Diwali. So when Pari walked into the lounge dressed in all her finery, there was only Khushi, Rachael and Ian to see her. They all gasped with wonder and disbelief: Pari looked absolutely wonderful – like a Bollywood star! Ian told her that he thought she looked really beautiful and both Rachael and Khushi readily agreed. Pari beamed with happiness; they had made her day.

'Do you know, truly I feel beautiful, thank you all!' she whispered.

This was an amazing speech for Pari who is the most gentle and modest of ladies. Then she and Khushi went upstairs onto the roof terrace where C.P. had built their home shrine to carry out their pujas while Ian and Rachael chatted and watched TV.

Over the next couple of days, there were numerous visits from neighbours and friends as well as family members. Each person was greeted warmly, hugged and plied with delicious food. Everyone admired the beautiful Rangoli pattern done by Khushi and Rachael. She and Ian were universally welcomed and accepted as part of the family. Pari was overjoyed when her mother arrived with her friend, and when Ubick came back to see Rachael and Ian, they truly felt that their second family was complete.

Although the little house was often full of noisy, chattering people and there were many ritual traditions and pujas to be carried out, the whole celebratory time

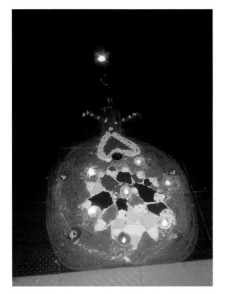

Rangoli by Khushi and Rachael.

C.P.'s house with Diwali lights.

was an unbelievably relaxing one. Everyone seemed genuinely happy and appreciative and supportive of each other. When Pari, her mum and friends went into the kitchen and sat on the floor to make decorative woven mats to place under the Diwali lights, Rachael and Khushi spent time in Khushi's room and did 'girly things' like plaiting hair, selecting jewellery and watching DVDs. Ian, C.P. and Ubick watched kabaddi together on TV and celebrated with a few drinks. Kabaddi is a contact game played on a court with seven members on each team. It is rather like a skilful game of tag where one runner invades the opposition's half of the court, tagging as many of that team as he can while avoiding being caught. Once Ian understood the rules, he became quite addicted.

Each evening, they would all drift outside to admire the fabulous displays of fireworks illuminating the starlit sky, marvel at the different patterns and jump at the loud explosive noises. C.P. told Ian that whenever he looked back at their little house, he could hardly believe he had managed to build a home for Pari and Khushi. He had worked so hard but building his own house had always been a dream: one that he had now fulfilled. Ian told him that he should be very proud of his achievements and that he had a wonderful family: Pari and Khushi were lovely, lovely people.

'But you and Rachael are part of our family too,' C.P. told him happily. 'This is your home so please come back and stay with us again. You are always very welcome.'

Ian had tears in his eyes as he said, 'Thank you C.P. and thank you for sharing Diwali with us. It has been a great privilege. One we will always remember.'

In her journal, Rachael summed up the Diwali festival very well:

'Diwali is like Christmas, New Year, Bonfire Night and Fireworks and the Fourth of July all rolled into one with mountains and mountains of delicious food! It is fab to be part of all this. We are so lucky!'

When Ian was in bed that night, he reflected on the whole occasion. Although he had done very little to help with the preparations for Diwali or indeed taken part in the Hindu celebrations, nevertheless he had somehow sensed that something very spiritual was happening. He was sure that Rachael had felt this too. Neither of them was particularly religious, but the all-pervading atmosphere of love and care, empathy and serenity – the sheer love of humanity – had raised the festival of Diwali above that of a celebration. They had been cherished and made part of a wider family and that was a totally inspiring, illuminating and magical experience.

DAY 25 – OCTOBER 31ST – GOING HOME

Rachael and Ian were up very early on the last morning of October as the taxi taking them to the airport would be waiting at 5 a.m. Their taxi driver was C.P.'s next-door-neighbour. As they emerged from their bedroom, they discovered that all their lovely Nepalese family, Khushi, Pari and C.P. were waiting for them in the lounge to wish them both good luck and a safe journey. There were many hugs, kisses and a few tears, especially from Pari. She had obviously enjoyed the company of Ian and Rachael so much that she was going to feel rather lonely when they had gone. Rachael gave her an extra hug and Ian reminded her that she still had some Diwali customs to celebrate with the rest of her family.

'Anyway, Pari, we will be back next year, won't we Rachael?' he emphasised.

'Of course we will because we are going to Everest Base Camp with C.P.' Rachael affirmed. 'And I'll contact you all the time Khushi, on FaceTime and by email, I promise!'

Ian thanked them sincerely for sharing their home and especially the Festival of Diwali with Rachael and himself.

'It really has been an honour and a privilege,' he said fervently.

C.P. loaded the luggage into the taxi and with lots of waving and shouts of 'Namaste', Ian and Rachael sped towards Tribhuvan Airport.

When they arrived, they were amazed to find the airport was shut and a large crowd was gathering outside. Some very puzzled would-be passengers were knocking loudly on the closed entrance doors trying to discover why they could not get inside. Eventually an airport official appeared and informed everyone that as it was Diwali, the entire airport was closed until 7.30 a.m. There were no other members of staff and no aircraft had landed or taken off during the night. As more passengers arrived, there were lots of questions being asked but few were answered satisfactorily. Quite a few of the people were Nepalese flying to Delhi but some of the long-haul passengers were concerned about arriving in time for their onward flights from Delhi. Totally bewildered, they were animatedly discussing times of departure flights with each other. The confusion increased when they realised the pilots and crew of the local aircraft, who were supposed to be flying them to Delhi, were among the crowd. They could not get into the airport either! The planes were sitting on the runways with no aircrew. The whole situation was complete chaos but then, this was Nepal and it was the most important Hindu festival of the whole year.

Ian and Rachael just smiled and thought, 'Get over it! This is Nepal!' They understood completely. They just sat down on their luggage and waited patiently as they had done so many times before. Nepali time is 'fluid' especially during festivals when worship, prayers and time spent with loving families is paramount. It is sad that many visitors to Nepal never truly appreciate this; they miss so much when they cannot tune into what is truly important to these gentle, caring people. Timetables are far less important than people and their faith. In the end, most of the travellers just threw their hands in the air and resigned themselves to waiting and waiting … and waiting. There was a spirit of camaraderie with people telling stories of their adventures and laughing and joking.

Finally the entrance doors opened and everyone cheered. The airport staff hurried to their posts and the aircrew joined their planes. Soon passengers were being checked in and allocated seats. As always, Rachael sat next to the window with Ian beside her. When they flew near to the Himalaya, Rachael waved at those fabulous mountains.

'I'm going home now but next year I'll be back with my dad and, if you let us, we are going to trek to Everest Base Camp. I promise! So see you next year!'

She genuinely understood that climbing and trekking in those majestic peaks was a privilege and the mountains had to be respected.

Fortunately because of the delay at Tribhuvan Airport, Nepal, Ian and Rachael did not have such a long stopover at Delhi Airport. By the time they had walked across the enormous complex to the correct transfer desk, it was almost time to board their Jet Airways plane to Heathrow, London. They settled down in their comfortable seats for the ten-hour flight. As I have said before, Ian and Rachael thoroughly enjoy flying even on long-haul trips, whereas for me the flights to Delhi and back just have to be endured. Ian relaxed and watched films while Rachael played on her iPad. It wasn't long, however, before they were both fast asleep; they had got up very early so they were both exhausted.

Ian woke up about half an hour before they were due to land at Heathrow. Rachael was still in the land of dreams with a lovely smile on her face. I'm sure that readers, like me, will be able to guess what she was dreaming about … yes, trekking to Everest Base Camp with C.P. and her beloved dad. 2017 was going to be the adventure of a lifetime.

I cannot think of a better way to end these stories about my brave and inspiring 'granddaughter', Rachael, than to quote from Ian's journal, written shortly after they returned home from their last trip to Nepal: a wonderful adventure and learning experience for both of them.

'On the plane journey home, Rachael woke up just before we landed at Heathrow, London. Sleepily she asked that time-honoured question familiar to all parents on a journey with their children: "Are we nearly there, Dad?"

When I said that we were almost home, Rachael responded with, "Well I am sad that our adventure is ending but I am the happiest I have ever been in my life. Thank you, Dad!" Then she turned to face me and I could see that her eyes shone like stars as she added, "Just think how I am going to feel next year when we are standing at Everest Base Camp together! I shall be over the moon and on top of the world! Wow!"

Her words made me cry but I still had a huge smile on my face.'

THE END

See you next year, Nepal. x
PHOTO BY: Ian Griffiths.

AND FINALLY...

Look what I couldn't fit in the book!

ABOVE: Belgium 2007. TOP RIGHT: Chessington 2010.
RIGHT: Blackpool 2009. BELOW: With Dad 2008.

TOP LEFT: Graduation 2010. LEFT: Florida 2016.
ABOVE: Edinburgh 2009. BELOW: Disneyland, Paris 2010.

ABOVE: High School 2015. TOP RIGHT: Rachael Explore 2014.
RIGHT: Ullswater 2012. BELOW: Photo shoot 2012.

All this fun and great school grades achieved too.
What a wonderful childhood!
W☺W
X

TOP LEFT: Halloween 2011. LEFT: Ullswater Show 2011.
ABOVE: Manchester 2012. BELOW: Derbyshire 2013.

ABOUT THE AUTHOR – JOYCE BUXTON

I am a Derbyshire 'girl' – now happily retired to the Peak District. I became a Rotarian many years ago and I am now a member of The Rotary Club of Bakewell, where I serve on Youth and International Committees and so I am privileged to be able to help people locally, nationally and internationally. Working with The Rotary Club of Kathmandu Metro, we support a village in the Himalayan foothills and orphanages in Nepal as well as participating in numerous worldwide projects like those in villages and schools in the Gambia.

A few years ago, I was awarded a Paul Harris Fellowship; the dedication reads:

'In appreciation of tangible and significant assistance given for the furtherance of better understanding and friendly relations among peoples of the world.'

It is an honour of which I am very proud.

I am also International Ambassador of F.I.N.C.H. – Friends International Network of Children's Homes, founded by my friend, and Rachael's dad, Ian Moseley. It is a network of like-minded people who care for vulnerable children all over the world.

I am an ex-nurse and a retired teacher and have walked most of my life, completing many of the long distance walks in the UK, including The Pennine Way, The West Highland Way, Hadrian's Wall and, like Rachael, three memorable Coast to Coast crossings: my absolute favourite walk in the UK. In addition, I have successfully undertaken many hard treks in Nepal including the Everest Circuit and Everest Base Camp, the Annapurna Circuit and Annapurna Base Camp, twice – the last time at the age of seventy-eight. I really love that spectacular country and its gentle, caring people. So, as you can see, we are all part of a walking 'family'.

Throughout this book I have relied heavily upon Ian's diary notes, his remarkable memory and endless long phone conversations with that very patient man. Thank you my dear friend! Rachael's journals, written and amusingly illustrated by her over these wonderful adventurous years, have been invaluable too. So thank you, Rachael!

In addition, I would like to express my gratitude to everyone who has contributed to the completion of this book: Mr. Pattinson for granting Rachael additional time away from school. This enabled her to gain invaluable knowledge and cultural experience on her Nepal 3 odyssey.

Fran and the team at Macs Adventures for generously sponsoring and arranging Rachael's trips to Scotland and Iceland.

Catherine Moseley, who provided inspiration for the lovely cover design.

Jon at Vertebrate Publishing for all his help and advice.

Susie, my incredibly patient and understanding editor.

Nathan, my designer, for his inspiring layout.

Chandra Prakash Rai (C.P. to his friends) and the wonderful team at Mountain Monarch Adventures for all their support in organising the treks in Nepal and the Himalaya.

I sincerely hope that you enjoyed reading the book as much as I enjoyed writing it. Happy walking and exploring!

Joyce Buxton – July 2017

RACHAEL

A REMARKABLE CHILD EXPLORER